T0336537

# Analysis of the Development of Beijing in China

Beijing Academy of Social Sciences

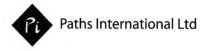 Paths International Ltd

 社会科学文献出版社
SOCIAL SCIENCES ACADEMIC PRESS(CHINA)

# Contents

Analysis and Prediction of Beijing's Economy from 2016 to 2017 ............................ 5

    1. Domestic and international conditions for economic development of Beijing ... 5

    2. Review and analysis on economic situations of Beijing in 2016 ..................... 7

    3. Analysis on decisive elements for endogenous economic growth of Beijing ... 14

    4. Analysis of supply-side structural reform in Beijing ...................................... 21

    5. Issues need solving during economic growth of Beijing ................................ 27

    6. Overall judgement and prediction of economic development of Beijing in 2017
.............................................................................................................................. 32

Thoughts on Construction of Beijing as National Center for Science and Technology
Innovation .............................................................................................................. 37

    1.Strategic Value of Building Beijing into National Center for Science and
Technology Innovation ........................................................................................... 37

    2. Analysis on the in-depth problems existing in Beijing's building of the National
Center for Science and Technology Innovation ..................................................... 41

    3.Thoughts on Beijing's Building National Center for Science and Technology
Innovation .............................................................................................................. 44

Current Situations, Major Tasks and Implementation Paths of Beijing Supply Side
Structural Reform ................................................................................................... 53

    1. Situations and urgency of Beijing's pushing forward the supply-side structural
reform ..................................................................................................................... 54

    2.Main tasks to promote supply-side structural reform in Beijing ..................... 67

    3.Main approaches for Beijing to promote supply-side structural reform ........... 77

Promote Social Fairness and Increase Residents' Sense of Gain ........................... 85

    1. Analysis on Current Social Development ...................................................... 86

    2.The main problems facing social development .............................................. 92

    3. Proposals to promote sound social development .......................................... 102

New Progress, Problems and Prospects of Beijing Social Governance in 2016 ....... 115

    1. Overview of Beijing's Social Governance in 2016 ........................................ 116

    2. Some Problems to Be Solved in Beijing Social Governance ......................... 127

    3. Proposals to Enhance Beijing's Social Governance Capacity ....................... 130

The "Dual Structure" of Basic Public Service for Floating Population Health in
Beijing and Its Solution - Taking maternal and child health for example ................ 135

1. Public health services for migrants ............................................................... 136

2. Health care for migrant women and children ................................................ 138

3. Discussion and Policy Suggestions.............................................................. 143

Innovation and Development of Geriatric Education and Community Geriatric Education in Beijing ............................................................................................ 151

1. Geriatric education and community geriatric education ................................ 151

2. Analysis of the Current Situation of Geriatric Education ............................ 152

3. Main Problems and Causes of Geriatric Education in Beijing ..................... 156

4. Solutions and Countermeasures ................................................................... 158

Beijing Strengthens the Construction of National Culture Center with the Aim of Becoming World Famous Cultural City............................................................ 164

1. Blueprint new development pattern of national cultural center and make a good start at the opening year .................................................................................... 164

2. Current situations and trends of Beijing's cultural development in 2016....... 171

3.A Comparative Analysis of Beijing's Urban Competitiveness and Cultural Power in 2016 among China's Cities................................................................. 189

4.Problems and Suggestions ........................................................................... 200

Beijing Tourism Report under the Framework of "Global Tourism" ...................... 209

1. Policy Changes for Tourism Development ................................................... 209

2. Tourism market development of Beijing in 2016 .......................................... 213

3. 2016 Beijing tourism development characteristics ....................................... 222

4. Beijing tourism development trends and suggestions.................................... 229

Historical and Cultural City Protection of Beijing in 2016 ................................... 231

1. The basic protection of Beijing's historical and cultural cities...................... 232

2. Annual priorities.......................................................................................... 236

3. Constraints of Beijing historical and cultural city protection ...................... 243

4. Protection methods, countermeasures and suggestions ................................ 246

Investigation Report on Productive Protection of Beijing Intangible Cultural Heritage---Taking the four non-heritage conservation demonstration bases in Beijing for example ............................................................................................................ 249

1. The effectiveness of the "model base" for productive protection................... 249

2. The main problems in the production protection .......................................... 257

3. Countermeasures and Suggestions.................................................................259

Quantity to Quality Transformation of Beijing's Public Service ...............................263
1. Overall comments .................................................................................263
2. Science and education have been developing steadily, and the structural reforms on the supply side still need improving.................................................267
3. Targeted alleviation of poverty increased social security benefits..................273
4. The capacity of urban operation support has risen and the level of infrastructure intelligence needs to be improved.............................................277
5. The public security situation is generally favorable and the number of cybercrime cases and accidents is still relatively large.....................................279
6. Significant achievements have been made in air pollution control and a long way to go in ecological civilization construction ...............................................284

Comprehensive Evaluation of Public Service Performance of Sixteen Districts in Beijing........................................................................................................289
1.Comprehensive Evaluation Index System for Public Service Performance....289
2. The source and processing of comprehensive evaluation of public service performance ................................................................................................291
3. The weights of comprehensive public service performance evaluation indicators...................................................................................................303
4. Score and evaluation of public service performance ......................................305
5. Greater efforts have been made to construct Beijing's urban sub-centers of public service .................................................................................................312

Problems and Countermeasures in the Construction of Beijing Government Service Centers ...........................................................................................................315
1. The significance of building a government service center ...........................315
2. Features of Beijing Municipal Government Service Center..........................317
3. Problems in the government service center of Beijing...................................323
4. Suggestions on the Construction of Beijing Municipal Government Service Center.........................................................................................................324

# Analysis and Prediction of Beijing's Economy from 2016 to 2017

Project Group on Economic Analysis and Prediction[1]

## Abstract

The year 2016 sees a slower reduction in the growth of Chinese economy and an increase in growth equality while the global economy is keeping a continuous low-speed growth. Under such circumstance, Beijing's economy lifts up steadily, "soft landing" taking preliminary shape. Econometric model inspection observes that long-term economic growth is driven by input for research and development (R&D), especially more participation of R&D staff and free and open environment of learning, rather than factors of production including capital and labor. Moreover, it is found that expenditure expansion by government on infrastructure and public services make obvious Pareto improvements towards economic growth. To boost economy, Beijing has to tackle with the following issues: low capacity of economic intensive development, accelerated inner differentiation of the tertiary industry and relatively backward industrial aggregation and high end promotion, rocketing house prices along with increasing risks in real estate market, as well as slight rising of employment pressure. It is likely that the economic growth rate of Beijing will exceed 6.5% in 2017, living up to the expectation of stable growth.

Keywords: Learning by Doing, endogenous growth, R&D input, supply-side structural reform

1. Domestic and international conditions for economic development of Beijing

Under the background of economic globalization, Beijing's economy heavily relies on both domestic and international economic conditions, a clear understanding of which, therefore, is a precondition to figure out the current economic situations of Beijing.

1.1 Low-speed increase of global economy expected to speed up slightly in 2017

According to statistics from the United Nations, the world economy expanded by just

---

[1] Tang Yong, Ph. D in Economics, Assistant Researcher at the Research Institute of Economics, Beijing Academy of Social Sciences. Research areas include Macroeconomics and economic growth theories. Yang Song, Associate Researcher, Deputy Head of the Research Institute of Economics, Beijing Academy of Social Sciences. Research areas include urbanization and economics, public governance

2.2% in 2016, the slowest rate of growth since the global financial crisis of 2008. In comparison, the IMF is relatively positive. The latest IMF's World Economic Outlook predicts a growth rate of 3.1% of world economy in 2016 with a minor decline compared to that of 2015 (3.2%). Specifically speaking, new economies and developing countries grow at 4.2%,0.2 percentage point higher over that of 2015; developed economies see an average increase of 1.6%, 0.5 percentage point lower than that in 2015. UN's World Economic Situation and Prospects (WESP) 2017 states that the world economy is projected to grow by 2.7% in 2017, being better but not much than that of 2016.

The world economy shows a low speed of growth in general and distinct differentiation among nations and regions. According to the IMF, US economy expanded by 1.6% in 2016, lower than generally anticipated 2.2% in market, and is expected to recover slowly in 2017. The EU continued to glide with an increase of only 1.7% in 2016 and is projected to fall to 1.5% in 2017. Japan's economy was still stuck in the period of slow growth with a 0.5% of growth rate. India becomes the fastest-growing economy worldwide by 7.6% in 2016. Russia still suffered 0.8% negative growth but is expected to resume positive in 2017 as its economic downturn slows down.

Under the circumstance of low-speed economic growth, the increment of inflation, investment, interest rate, and international trade remains low while that of debt and currency supply relatively high. In terms of price index, the inflation rate of developed economies was 0.3% in 2015, the lowest since the global financial crisis, among which that of the US remained around 2% and less than 1% in the EU and Japan, and that of emerging economies and developing countries kept low and stable. As to capital circulation, investment in emerging economies started to regain in the latter half of 2015. Successive net outflow from China due to exchange rate becomes mild compared to that in the latter half of 2015. Judging from monetary policy and financial market, the asset price of the US reached at a elevated level since the financial crisis, that in UK beginning to recover after Brexit and other developed economies rising to a relatively high level. Stocks and asset price in emerging economies creep up in a moderate way. That, after all, is a corollary of the governments' persistent implementation of easy monetary policies, which, however, may comes to an end with interest rate raising by the Federal Reserve in the morning of March 3rd, 2017.

1.2 China's economy growth reduction slows and quality rises

China's GDP growth rate was 6.7% in 2016, 0.2 percentage point lower than that in 2015. However, the decline in economic growth slows down, showing a trend to stabilize. Specifically speaking, the total fixed investments was 60.6 trillion yuan, with year-on-year growth of 7.9%; The total volume of retail sales of consumer goods was 33.2 trillion yuan, with year-on-year growth of 10.4%; and net exports in international trade was 2252.3 billion yuan, with year-on-year decline of 330.8 billion yuan. It can be observed that China's economy realized an increase of 6.7% by replying upon domestic demand while exterior demand is declining, and consumption needs grow faster than fixed investments, showing intensified promoting function of domestic consumption needs.

In 2016, China's economic growth quality rises. Service industry is playing a more important role. The value-added of tertiary industry in 2016 took up 51.6% of GDP, with an increase of 1.4 percentage point compared to that in 2015. Regional integration proceeds faster. Cooperation and exchanges becomes increasingly frequent in regions such as the Belt and Road, Beijing-Tianjin-Hebei Region, Yangtze River Economic Zone, the Pearl River Delta Economic Zone, Ha-Da-Qi Economic Zone, Metropolitan Interlocking Region of Taiyuan, Yellow River Delta, Wanjiang Economic Area, Hercynian Economic Zone, Nanchang-Jiujiang Industrial Economic Corridor, Beibu Gulf Economic Zone, Chang-Zhu-Tan Urban Agglomeration, Wuhan Urban Circle, and Central Plain Economic Zone.

Meanwhile, some crucial problems in economic development of China undermine the foundation for the stabilization of economic growth. Private investments grow slowly, which mirrors the deficiency in the confidence of social capital in economic prospect. Total factor productivity contributes little to economic growth, calling for step-up technological advances. Continued easy monetary policy leads to asset bubble expansion, in real estate market in particular, posing serious threats to real economy.

2. Review and analysis on economic situations of Beijing in 2016

In the background of gradually recovery of global economy, eased downturn in national economy, and deepened supply side structural reform, Beijing's economy keeps a steady operation with a preliminary soft landing.

2.1 Economic growth keeps moderately steady and soft landing takes form

In 2016, the GDP of Beijing in the whole year and in its entire region reached 24.8993 trillion yuan with a growth of 6.7% from 2015. The growth rate kept moderately steady. In terms of GDP growth rate, the year 2010 was a turning point (with a GDP growth rate of 10.3%), since when Beijing's economic growth has consecutively declined in the following six years. Nevertheless, the downturn slows down and recent years witnessed that the economic soft landing take a preliminary shape. Comparing Beijing to the whole nation, Beijing's economic growth rate has been similar to the national GDP for three consecutive years (Graph 1).

As to the growth rate of each quarter in 2016, Beijing's GDP in the first quarter increased by 6.9% compared to the same period in 2015. And its economic growth rate was 6.7% for the second, third and fourth quarter (Graph 2). The situation where GDP growth rate remained the same for three consecutive quarters occurred to Beijing as well in 2013, followed by an unexpected downturn in 2014. Although we cannot tell whether Beijing's economic growth will continue to decrease in 2017, it is unlikely in light of the trend in recent years. However, it is not absolutely impossible since the economy of the U.S. entered into a rate-interest cycle. Therefore, Beijing should stay positive and alert at the same time.

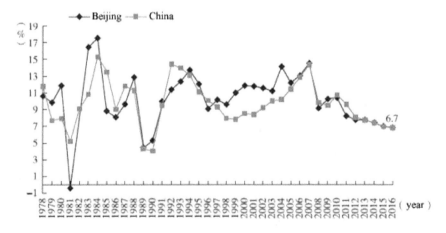

Graph 1 GDP Growth Rate of Beijing and whole China from 1978 to 2016

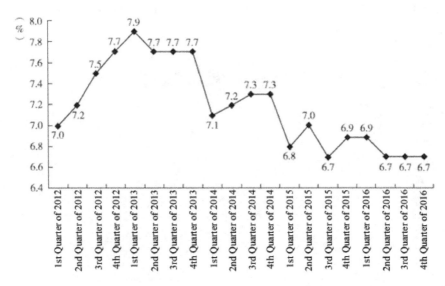

Graph 2 Accumulated Beijing GDP Growth Rate from 1<sup>st</sup> Quarter of 2012 to the 4<sup>th</sup> Quarter of 2016

2.2 The growth rate of investment remains low and rebounds in the year end

In 2016, the social fixed asset investment in Beijing was 8.4617 trillion yuan, increasing by 5.9% compared to the same time period in 2015. Its growth rate rose by 0.2 percentage point compared to that in 2015, however still falling to record lows. Specifically, investment in infrastructure grew fastest, making 2.3995 trillion yuan with a year-on-year increase of 10.3% and becoming the main driving force of the growth in fixed asset investment. However, most infrastructure investors were governments and private investment were found descending to 2.766 trillion yuan in 2016 by 5.6% compared to that in the same time period of 2015. The decrease is because of the highly expanded base by a fast growth (25.8%) in private investment in 2015 on the one hand, while it shows the concerns of private investors towards the uncertainty that lies in the economic future.

As to the fixed asset investment in each month, the growth speed showed a trend of starting high, falling down later, and rebounding slightly in the year end. To be specific, the growth rate of investment, being 6.7%, reached the top of the year from January to March, suffered a shock decline continuously to 5.8%, touching the bottom of the valley, and rebounding in the following two months (Graph 3). As one of the key links in the troika of national economy, a steady low growth rate in investment

9

demands is crucial to keep a smooth and stable growth of economy through the whole year.

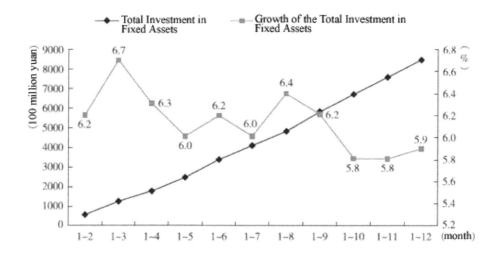

Graph 3 Monthly Beijing Social Fixed Asset Investment and Accumulated Growth Rate in 2016

2.3 Consumption growth continuously declines and on-line consumption rockets

In 2016, the whole year market consumption was 19.9262 trillion yuan with a year-on-year growth of 8.1%, of which service-based consumption was 8.9211 trillion yuan with an increase of 10.1%. The fast growth in service-based consumption suits well the big GDP proportion of Beijing's tertiary industry.

The year 2016 witnessed 11.0051 trillion yuan of total retail sales of consumer goods, rising by 6.5% compared to the same period in 2015. In the long term, the consumption growth climbed up to the peak of 21.1% during the global financial crisis in 2008 and slided down afterwards to the lowest ever since 1978 in 2016 (Graph 4).

Graph 4 Beijing Total Retail Sales of Consumer Goods and Growth Rate from 1979 to 2016

In 2016, the retail sales of the above-norm wholesale and retail enterprises reached 7.9875 trillion yuan, with a year-on-year increase of 6.6%. The on-line retail sales were 2.049 trillion yuan, rising by 20% compared with the year earlier. It took up 25.7% of the whole retail sales of goods, increasing by 6.7 percentage point from the year earlier, showing a trend that the on-line consumption is squeezing the space of off-line one. In terms of categories of goods, sales of those related to sports and entertainment grew fastest by 21.1% on a year-on-year basis. It mirrors the increasing attention that residents pay to sports and leisure activities and the general lifting of living standard and life quality of Beijing's citizens ever since Beijing entered into the post-industrial era.

2.4 Some of emerging industries grow faster, taking bigger proportion in GDP

In 2016, the strategic emerging industries in Beijing showed a year-on-year increase of added value by 3.8% and 2.7 percentage point higher than 2015 in terms of grow rate. The added value of modern manufacturing industries enhanced by 11.9% compared to the same time last year and its grow rate was 5.6 percentage point higher than that in 2015. The avenue of agricultural viewing gardens in Beijing reached 2.8 billion yuan, increasing by 6.3% and growth rate being 0.7 percentage point higher than that in 2015. The avenue of folk tourism reached 1.44 billion yuan, increasing by 11.7%.

Among the emerging industries, the added value of cultural creative industries reached 357.05 billion yuan in 2016, taking up 14.3% of the regional GDP of Beijing, 0.5 percentage point higher than 2015. The added value of information industry was 379.76 billion yuan, taking up 15.3% of regional GDP, 0.3 percentage point higher than 2015, and high-tech industry 564.67 billion with its regional GDP proportion increasing by 0.2 percentage point than 2015.

2.5 Price index decrease slightly while housing prices continuing grow

In 2016, the CPI of local residents in Beijing was 101.4%, declining by 0.4 percentage point than 2015, while PPI of Beijing was 98.1%, 2.1 percentage point higher than 2015, indicating squeezed profit margins as a price grow was found in raw materials from upstream firms but not for downstream ones. It shows that traditional manufacturing industry of Beijing is still suffering from excess capacity and therefore badly in need of supply-side structural reform.

From the perspective of CPI trend of Beijing, it can be noticed that its CPI reached a phasic culmination in 2008 (105.1%) and then, because of the global financial crisis, fell to a phasic low (98.5%), and later rose along with the economy as both the central and local governments launched a series of proactive fiscal policy and monetary policy to spur the economy. However, since Beijing's economy entered into the "new norms" in 2012, economic growth fell from a high point, causing CPI to slide to a low of 101.4% in 2016, nevertheless still a little bit higher than 2009 (Graph 5).

Contrast to CPI, price index of new apartments and houses in Beijing dramatically increased (Graph 6). The chain index in Graph 6 shows that the new round of housing price rise (chain index larger than 100%) started from March 2015 and continued till the end of 2016, increasing month by month. In December 2016, the price of newly built houses rose to a phasic peak of 27.8% compared to the rise in same month last year. The upward tendency slowed from then.

2.6 Income steadily grows while consumption expenditure down in growth

In 2016 the per capita disposable income (PCDI) of Beijing residents was 52530 yuan, up by 8.4% year-to-year.

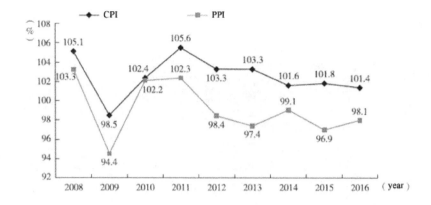

Graph 5 Beijing CPI and PPI from 2008 to 2016 (last year=100)

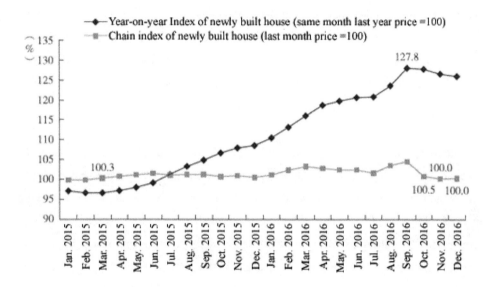

Graph 6 Monthly House Sales Price since 2015

The PCDI of urban residents was 57275 yuan, year-on-year up by 8.4% (Graph 7) and 0.5 percentage point lower than 2015 in terms of growth rate. The PCDI of rural residents was 22310 yuan, year-on-year increase by 8.5% and 0.5 percentage point lower than 2015 regarding increase rate. Fitting the overall economic situations, the residents' income keeps growing steadily in general.

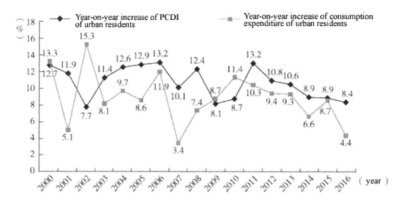

Graph 7 Income and Expenditure Growth of Beijing Urban Residents from 2000 to 2016

From Graph 7, it can be noticed that the average consumption expenditure of Beijing urban residents went down fast from 8.7% in 2015 to 4.4% in 2016, becoming a sub-low since 2000. It demonstrates that people are worried about the uncertainty of economic outlook, resulting in the fall of marginal propensity to consume (MPC) which is unfavorable to future economic growth.

Generally speaking, Beijing's economy has kept a proper and steady growth under the background of low inflation in 2016. Especially in the latter half of the year, the glide of economic growth rate was controlled and the rate kept around 6.7%, making possible for a "soft landing". The steady growth of Beijing's economy owe to government's continuous enlarged investment in infrastructure and projects related to people's livelihood, as well as the government's efforts in pushing forward the supply-side structural reform. This achievement was hard-won, although obstacles such as high sales price of houses, sluggish private investment, fast downturn of consumption growth remains and needs more attention.

3. Analysis on decisive elements for endogenous economic growth of Beijing

As widely acknowledged by theories of modern endogenous economic growth, the marginal returns of capital and labor will decrease to zero in the long run, while the growth of total factor productivity (mainly determined by technological advances) is the key to long-term economic increase. Therefore, the research on "new growth theories" in recent decades is a process of making endogenous all kinds of elements that influence technological progress such education, learning by doing, human capital, financial innovation, systems, and culture. However, the applications of these theories are always confusing. According to endogenous growth theories, per capita output growth in the long term only depends on the growth rate of all factor productivity. But from the data and calculation, Beijing's all factor productivity has been relatively low[1]. How was it possible to support the nearly 10% of economic growth with such a low growth rate of all factor productivity? Bewildered by this question, the project team makes an analysis on the driving factors for long-term economic growth of Beijing from two aspects, namely economic growth theories and the real growth increase of the city.

3.1 Theoretical model stressing on government investment

The theoretical viewpoint of investment driving economy mainly derives from three famous models. The very first attention to the role of investment is the IS-LM Model by Keynes, being made up of investment, consumption and net export. In the time of severe economic recession when overall demands is far low than total supply at the level of full employment, government investment will increase demands to reach the level of economic growth at full employment through multiplier effect. At the same time, the increase in investment demands will not drag up interest rates because of the "liquidity trap" during the recession period. This model and its viewpoint helped to some extent the U.S. to get out of its economic crisis. However, when applying the model, other nations always forget about the important assumption that the economy has to be in a serious recession. The expansionary monetary policy suggested by the model can only solve recession problem in the short term. As for long-term economic growth, answers lie in the growth theories.

The second model paying attention to investment is the Harrod - Domar Model which was created early as well. The model presupposes that the ratio of capital to output remains unchanged in a long term, so the growth rate of investment and that of output should be in a fixed proportion in order to realize long-term and balanced growth. The model has so big a flaw even Domar himself admitted that the so called "long-term and balanced growth" is hard to come true. Nevertheless, because of its emphasis on the role of investment, it has been widely adopted among developing countries. Economist could easily work out the volume of investment needed for economic growth with the assistance of this model and then get the "investment gap" by

---

[1] Please refer to the calculation of Beijing economic growth rate factors in the general report in *Report on Economic Development of Beijing (2013-2014)*.

subtracting savings. The policy implication from this model is that economy could embark on a steady path of growth once the investment gap is filled up. With the guidance of this model and upholding humanitarian spirit, some western developed countries offered aids and loans to developing countries to solve the investment gap of the latter, but unfortunately getting little improvement in terms of steady economic growth.

The third model advocating investment is the "Learning by Doing" Model put forward successively by Arrow, Romer and Lucas. This report mainly presents the model raised by Romer in 1986. Romer's model presupposes that there are N manufacturers in a economy, each of them accumulating knowledge via learning by doing during individual investment and the increase of the volume of knowledge as public goods poses a spillover effect. In other words, as the stock of knowledge rises, each producer in a economy will benefit from it. Thus as for the production function, the total factor productivity $A$ is the function of total social capital $A$, making exogenous variable $A$ in the the Solow Model endogenous. Specifically speaking, according to the Solow Model, the production function of a producer $I$ in the economy is:

$$Y_i = F(K_i, A_i L_i) = F(K_i, KL_i).$$

Supposing that the production function is a homogeneous concave function as to each element, the production function of output per capita becomes:

$$y_i = Y_i / L_i = f(k_i, K),$$

among which $k_i = K_i / L_i$ is per capita capital stock and $K$ is total social capital stock, and at the same time

$$K = \sum_{i=1}^{N} k_i$$

Supposing that all manufacturers in an economy are of same size and production function, the commonly used cobby-douglas production function will presents the following:

$$y = f(k, K) = A \, k^\alpha K^{1-\alpha}$$
$$\text{of which } K = Nk, \ 0 < \alpha < 1.$$

If the utility function of consumers has unchanged substitution elasticity, that is

$$U(c) = \frac{c^{1-\sigma} - 1}{1 - \sigma}$$, of which $c$ is per captia consumption, $6$ is alternate

16

substitution elasticity, and $0 < 6 < 1$, the maximation of alternate utility of representative residents with unlimited life can be presented as the following:

$$max \int_0^\infty U(c) \ e^{-\rho t} dt, U(c) = \frac{c^{1-\sigma} - 1}{1 - \sigma}$$

$$s. t \ \dot{k} = A k^\alpha K^{1-\alpha} - c$$

By solving the optimization issue, we can get the equilibrium rate of growth:

$$g = (A\alpha \ N^{1-\alpha} - \rho)/\sigma$$

and the optimized rate of growth if

$$g^* = (A \ N^{1-\alpha} - \rho)/\sigma$$

The conclusion from Romer Model presents the following policy meanings. First of all, as people can learn while doing, the investment of materials and capital will produce a kind of by-product, namely knowledge, this, because of its spillover effect, prevents in return the revenue of capital investment from diminishing. Secondly, in a well-developed free market economy, the equilibrium rate of growth of the economy is lower than the social optimal growth rate ($g<g^*$), for which reason government sectors bring about Pareto improvement of investment on public services, or in other words, government investment has a long-term growth effect.

3.2 The raise of assumption

Based on Romer's "Learning by Doing" Model, empirical tests could be carried forward on the following assumptions.

Assumption 1: capital stock plays a positive role in economic growth.

Capital stock is a basic element of the production function. Economists and especially governments, always have a preference towards investment. Fixed capital investment is omnipresent in both growth theories and policies of government intervention in economy. Researches and empirical studies regarding this assumption can be found in not a few literatures, although a specified test on the assumption is indispensible.

Assumption 2: Labor growth has a positive impact on economic growth.

As one of the traditional production elements, labor force has always been extremely essential to theories about economic growth. Most growth theories believe that per capita economic growth rate has no relevance with the quantity of labor force. However, it still needs testing to see if there is relevance between overall economic growth rate with the growth of labor force.

Assumption 3: The quantity of patents has a positive effect on economic growth.

A large number of theories about economic growth hold that total factor productivity is a decisive element of economic growth. The main presentation of total factor productivity is technological progress, which are usually measured by quntity of patents. The number of patents in Beijing is rocketing, while the total factor productivity calculated via growth elements is low. The strong contrast calls for test on the assumption.

The three assumptions above are all based on traditional theories of economic growth. The next three assumptions derive from the conclusions and policy significance from Romer's learning by Doing Model.

Assumption 4: Free and open environment of acquiring knowledge has a positive impact on economic growth.

According to Romer, when an enterprise increases fixed capital investment, it will hire workers to carry out production activities, during which workers gain knowledge and experiences and thus improve their technical skills and productivity. In this case, a free and open environment for learning is essential, not only for knowledge accumulation and improvement of productivity, but as well for making the best out of the Learning by Doing Model.

Assumption 5: R & D investment has a positive impact on economic growth

Based on the concept of learning by doing, companies' investment on research and development during operation and production directly decide their labor productivity. At the same time, the R&D results will be spread over to the whole society via spillover effect, preventing benefit of capital elements from declining and making possible long-term economic growth. Therefore, tests on this assumption are indispensible.

Assumption 6: Government's expenditure has a positive impact on economic growth.

According to the conclusion of Romer's model, the equilibrium growth rate in free market economy is lower than optimal growth rate. The expenditure of government, on public services especially, will be of strong externality, diminishing costs of elements, of systems, and trades and boosting economic growth to reach the optimal growth rate.

3.3 Choice of variables and data processing

Generally speaking, all variables in econometric models can be divided into four categories: dependent variable, independent variables, and control variable, and dummy variable. This paper addresses only the first three variables. As the variables are economic growth rate, the paper chooses the commonly used GDP, or as in Beijing's case regional GDP.

Independent variables are those used to check or test the mentioned assumptions. Capital stock, which strictly speaking shall be calculated via some professional approaches, is often taken place by fixed capital investment during empirical tests. As to labor force, the quantity of employees by year end is usually used in tests. The quantity of patents is conventionally represented by numbers of patents being granted. It is hard to quantify free and open learning environment, so close substitution by some instrumental variables is preferred and the numbers of book types are chosen in this paper. The reasons are on the one hand workers improve their knowledge and skills by publishing and reading books, and on the other hand the publication of books extends the influence of the spillover effect of knowledge. Research and Development are measured by either R&D personnel FTE or R&D internal expenditure, being decided according to test situations. Government expenditure is measured by local government expenditure.

When it comes to control variables, four variables namely paid-in value of FDI, floor space under construction, RMB savings of Chinese-funded financial institutions, and foreign exchange earnings from tourism are chosen to respectively control the influence of the FDI, real estate, deposit rate, and tourism income on Beijing's economy.

As we are going to observe how the increase of the variables affect GDP growth, the first step at the start of empirical tests is to process the raw data to get its form of growth rate. The growth rate $g$ of a variable $x$ can be approximately presented in the following form: ……. Accordingly, the current study takes the natural logarithm of each variable, followed by difference processing. The data acquired then is the form of growth rate. The symbols of variables and explanations are as in Table 1.

Table 1 Symbol and Explanations of Variables

| Types | Symbols | Names | unit | Range of samples |
|---|---|---|---|---|
| Dependent Variables | GDP | Gross Domestic Production | 100 million RMB | 1978-2015 |
| Independent Variables | INV | Fixed investment | 100 million RMB | 1978-2015 |
| | LAB | Labors | | 1978-2015 |
| | PAT | Patents | 10000 persons | 1986-2015 |
| | PUB | Publications | Pieces | 1978-2015 |
| | RDP | R&D Personnel FTE | Pieces | 1996-2015 |
| | RDE | R&D internal expenditure | Man-year | 1996-2015 |
| | FIS | Local fiscal expenditure | 10000 RMB 100 million RMB | 1978-2015 |
| Control Variables | FDI | Paid-in value of FDI | 10000 USD | 1987-2015 |
| | SPA | Floor space under construction | 10000 m² | 1978-2015 |
| | SAV | Savings of Chinese-funded financial institutions | 100 million RMB | 1978-2015 |
| | TRA | Tourism income | 100 million RMB | 1978-2015 |

The econometric model is set up based on the above assumptions and explanations of variables:

$X_i$ represents variables. $\beta_i$ represents regression coefficient of the variables. $T_j$ is control variables and $\gamma_j$ is the regression coefficient of the control variables. $\varepsilon$ represents random error and meets:

$$E(\varepsilon \mid X_i) = 0, E(\varepsilon \mid T_j) = 0, Cov(\varepsilon, X_i) = 0, Cov(\varepsilon, T_j) = 0$$

3.4 Test results analysis

As the variables are a time series, their stationary shall be tested before analysis. After processing of natural logarithm and of difference, Dickey-Fuller test shall be added and the test results are shown as Table 2.

If the time series of all variables reject the possibility of unit root, the variables can be taken as stationary and dummy regression will therefore be avoided when doing regression analysis.

Table 2 Unit Root Test Results of Variables

| Variables | p Value | Test Results |
| --- | --- | --- |
| D (LNGDP) | 0.0104 | Stationary under 5% |
| D (LNINV) | 0.0008 | Stationary under 1% |
| D (LNLAB) | 0.0541 | Stationary under 10% |
| D (LNPAT) | 0.0010 | Stationary under 1% |
| D (LNPUB) | 0.0117 | Stationary under 5% |
| D (LNRDP) | 0.0004 | Stationary under 1% |
| D (LNRDE) | 0.0000 | Stationary under 1% |
| D (LNFIS) | 0.0033 | Stationary under 1% |
| D (LNFDI) | 0.0000 | Stationary under 1% |
| D (LNSPA) | 0.0022 | Stationary under 1% |
| D (LNSAV) | 0.0028 | Stationary under 1% |
| D (LNTRA) | 0.0000 | Stationary under 1% |

## 3.5 Conclusions and policy meanings

From the above test results, it's not hard to conclude the following viewpoints. Firstly, traditional production factors, namely capital and labor, are affected by marginal income so they cannot drive economic growth in the long run. Secondly, patents in Beijing, although increase in number, cannot be transformed into productivity in time, so they cannot be a driving force for long-term economic growth of Beijing. Thirdly, physical capital investment remarkably improves technical level and enlarges knowledge stock through learning by doing, during which R&D investment, in particular more participation of R&D staff in the open and free environment of learning, is the key to long-term economic growth. Fourthly, the expanded expenditure of government on infrastructure and public service has distinct Pareto improvements towards long-term economic growth.

## 4. Analysis of supply-side structural reform in Beijing

The nature of supply-side structural reform is the reform and innovation of relevant key links and areas in order to exercise the role of market mechanism on the allocation of production elements, to improve effective supply of the real economy including strategic emerging industries, high-precession manufacturing, modern service industries, cultural creative industries, modern agriculture, and state-owned enterprises, to reduce low-end supply, to eliminate ineffective supply, enlarge mid-to-high supply, and to advance quality and efficiency. The reform should be in strict accordance with central government's overall principle, namely "cut overcapacity, de-stock, de-leverage, reduce costs, and improve weak links", based on features of economic development stage of Beijing and the work focus of dispersing non-capital functions, and aimed at solving accumulated problems and contradictions during economic growth of the city. Beijing is faced with both the problems besetting the whole country, and real situations, essential tasks and special contradictions of local economy. It requires that Beijing should pursue a steady growth of its economy by not only touching upon issues of the quantity, speed and size of growth, but as well dealing with deep-seated problems including growth quality, efficiency and structural imbalance.

## 4.1 Cutting overcapacity

Generally, there isn't overcapacity in heavy and chemical industries like cement, electrolytic aluminum, coal, and iron and steel in Beijing. However, the city is now concentrating on cutting off low-end processing and manufacturing industries, labor-incentive industries, and low-end service industries at the terminal link of circulation. During the "11$^{th}$ Five-Year Plan" and "12$^{th}$ Five-Year Plan", Beijing actively adjusted industrial structure, closed a batch of traditional industries and eradicated excess capacity. During the "12$^{th}$ Five-Year", Beijing made great efforts to withdraw coal capacity strategy. In 2016, Beijing resolved 1.6 million tons of coal capacity in 2016 with only 6 million tons left and it was estimated that coal mines will be completed closed by 2020. Shougang Group started to move out of Beijing since 2005 and its operation of smelting and hot rolling was stopped in Beijing by the end of 2010, leaving only part of crude steel capacity. The "12$^{th}$ Five Year" also witnessed the general adjustment and withdrawal of twelve industries of heavy pollution, including those producing tiles, lime, stones, bituminous waterproof sheet material, building ceramic, furniture, coating, printing and dyeing, as well as foundry, forging and electroplating industries. In 2014 and 2015, Beijing successive announced *New Added Ban and Limits List of Industries*, excursing strict entrance limit to "three-high" (high contamination, high energy consumption, and high water deprivation) and low-end manufacturers. At present, over-capacity in Beijing mainly refers to common low-end manufacturing industry, labor-intensive industry, and commercial trading markets with many terminal links of circulation. Low-end manufacturing industries include those focusing on waste recycle, automobile repair, food processing, and preliminary processing of raw materials and locate mainly in areas of urban-country fringe, warrens, villages in the city, and relocated villages. Labor-intensive industries consist of garment making, food processing, toys manufacturing, and furniture production, distributing mainly in clothing markets and outskirt villages, and around wholesale markets. Those industries don't fit the functions and directions of industrial development while they assume large amount of resources and energy, falling into the category of low-end capacity. There are over 2000 low-end commodity transaction markets, largely gathering in central urban areas, traffic hubs, and urban-country fringe. Most of those markets are stalls with inadequate facilities, low-end, extensive and wholesale operation, and main customers from outside Beijing, exceeding local demands of the city and becoming overcapacity.

3.6 Destocking

The inventory of commodity houses in Beijing is around 200 thousand square meters (including those to be built and to be put in market), which is not too much for a extra-large city like Beijing. In this case, Beijing destocks while striking against jacking up housing price by hoarding, price hike, and disguised price increase. At the same time, Beijing deals with structural contradictions in real estate market, circles more land to build indemnificatory apartments and puts more in the market, and prevents the price of commodity houses from continuously rising. According to statistics by Centaline Property, commodity houses in stock in Beijing has been pushing down and reached 68949 by March 7, 2017, less than 70 thousand for the first time since ever since May 10, 2014. The pure commodity houses in stock, deleting indemnificatory housing, are only 62 thousand. Medium and small sized commodity houses even become short in supply. Large proportion of stock goes to districts of Chaoyang, Daxing, Tongzhou, Changping, Shunyi, and Fangshan.[1] Public announced statistics from Beijing Municipal Statistics Bureau show that the total floor space under construction and completed of housing in Beijing was respectively 216.777 million square meters and 49.675 million square meters in 2014 and 200.091 million square meters and 41.702 million square meters in 2015, down by 7.7% and 16.1% year-on-year. The total floor space under construction and completed of

---

[1]  Retrieved from Sina Real Estate, http://new.offices.com.

indemnificatory housing in Beijing was 43.68 million and 12.016 million square meters in 2014, and 38.705 million and 8.818 million square meters in 2015, down by 11.4% and 26.6% year-on-year. From these figures also demonstrate low pressure in terms of commodity house stock in Beijing. The problem is that the house price in Beijing rose too far and fast. Demands towards commodity houses in Beijing kept going up along with house price from 2015 to 2016. Statistics show that the sale price of newly built houses in Beijing (including commodity and indemnificatory ones) increased by 12.9%, 16%, 18.3%, 19.5%, 20.3%, 20.7%, 23.5%, 27.8%, 27.5%, 26.4%, 25.9% and 24.7% year-on-year from February, 2016 to January, 2017, and that of second-hand houses was up by 27.7%, 35.1%, 37.2%, 34.5%, 33.4%, 32.2%, 34.8%, and 40.5%, 40.4%, 38.7%, 36.7% and 34.6% year-on-year during the same period.[1] To prevent the fast rising of house price, Beijing should apply multiple methods at the same time, including demands management, price control, inventory release, and policy adjustment and control. To be specific, Beijing should highlight the nature of housing, that is for living rather than for speculation, take the housing system that focuses on both purchasing and leasing as the guiding principle, adjust housing structure and land supply policies from the supply side, enlarge indemnificatory apartments supply, give more efforts to reconstructing shanty towns, and more proportion of commodity houses of medium and low price and size, advocate rational assumption, meet reasonable demands for housing, insist on curbing demands for speculation, and combating against real estate speculation.

4.3 De-leveraging

The debt ratio of Beijing government is lower than the national average and debt risk is still controllable and not threatening, so Beijing should make the best of its capital advantages, bring government's role in normalizing borrowing to its full play, and make a good use of debt capital. By the end of 2015, Beijing government had a debt of 668.9 billion yuan, down year-on-year 8.81% with a debt ratio of 83.3% that is a little bit under the average 84.4% nationwide. Some general debt accounted for 149.5 billion yuan, taking up 22.4% while specific debt was 519.4 billion yuan, taking up 77.6%. Approved by the State Council of China, Beijing issued and paid back on its own 117.8 billion yuan in 2015, including 17.2 billion yuan of new securities and 100.6 billion yuan of replaceable securities, for use of coordinated development of

---

[1] Retrieved from Beijing Statistics, http://www.bjstats.gov.cn.

Beijing, Tianjin and Hebei Province, urban road construction, agriculture, forests, and water. Verified by the Ministry of Finance, there was 52.2 billion yuan of new government debt including 49.2 billion yuan of general debt and 3 billion yuan of specific debt for Beijing local government in 2016. Generally speaking, the government debt of Beijing is risk-controllable and within range of safety, being below the precaution line by the Ministry of Finance. From the perspective of directions of the debt capital goes, Beijing's government debt is mainly for people's livelihood, such as rail transportation, sub-center construction of the city, new airport, dispersion of non-capital functions, and reconstruction of shanty towns, and most of the corresponding assets are real assets of high-quality. As to repayment capacity, the general public budget revenue of Beijing reached 472.39 billion yuan in 2016, plus revenue from returns and subsidies by the central government, resulting in total revenue of 670.03 billion yuan[1] and showing a strong repayment capacity. For Beijing, the first step it should take at present is to, according to the requirements of *Suggestions on the Implementation of Strengthening Government Debt Management by People's Government of Beijing Municipality*, digest existing debt, properly control debt size, control and dissolve government debt risk, resolve and prevent fiscal and financial risks, and establish pre-warning system for debt risk. Secondly, Beijing should set up a standardized financing mechanism for local government to borrow money and give it to full and positive play. At the same time, Beijing should take the advantageous opportunity when current interest rates are relatively low and the state is advancing debt replacement and invest more on construction of sub-centers, rail transportation, and infrastructure so as to provide strong support to city construction and development.

## 4.4 Lowering costs

When it comes to cost reduction, the main task of Beijing is to lower costs in relation to institutional transaction through streamlining government functions and administration, delegating powers while improving regulation, and optimizing government services. At the same time, Beijing should improve business environment, and decrease labor cost, taxes, financial cost, energy and land consumption, and logistic cost in social enterprises by deepening reforms and applying the policy of "replacing business tax with value-added tax". In accordance with the unified

---

[1] Beijing Municipal Bureau of Finance. *Report on Implementation of Financial Budget in 2015 and Budget Draft for 2016 of Beijing*. Retrieved from http://www.mof.gov.cn.

deployment of the central government, Beijing should clear out and standardize all kinds of enterprise-related charges and funds, cancel or lower administrative fees, implement all aspects of the policy of "replacing business tax with valued-added tax" and the preferential policies of R&D costs deduction and venture capital, and encourage innovation and entrepreneurship by giving more financial support and creating new debt financing tools for technology-based firms. Under the circumstance of coordinated development of Beijing, Tianjin, and Hebei Province, Beijing should explore and apply diversified approaches to further help eliminate regional and policy barriers, to realize integrated clearance system of the region with lower costs, to improve green channels for in-coming fresh agricultural products to Beijing to reduce logistic costs, and to fasten the integration of traffic management of the region and build a modern traffic network of connectivity in order to lower transportation costs. When it comes to the dispersion of non-capital functions, extra-attention should be paid to lowering the dispersion cost for enterprises and administrative units, making the best use of the "capital for dispersion, ordering and improvement", and the exertion of the guiding role and service-oriented functions of policy funds.

4.5 Weak links improvement

As to improve weak links, the main task of Beijing is to address the weak points in resources supply, ecological environment, public transportation, and public services. The contradiction among population, resources and environment is one of the key elements constraining economic growth of Beijing. Beijing heavily replies on external energies. As an extra consumer of energy and resources, Beijing will use 260 million kilowatt of electricity, 30 million cubic meters of natural gas, 50 thousand tons of coals and coke, and 10 million cubic meters of water.[1] Per capita hold of resources (land, water, forests, etc.) is relatively low. In the case where the population is close to the "ceiling", bottleneck constraints of resources become a prominent shortage. Beijing and its suburban areas are suffering from fragile ecological environment with frequent occurrence of fog and haze, severer air pollution at the turn of winter to spring, and heavy pollution in some rivers. There are 5.71 million motor vehicles in the whole city. The congestion index is controlled at around 5.7 (light jam) in 2016 and 2017, although the general congestion changed little while the congestion index are rocketing to over 9 in specific sections and at specific time periods. Public

---

[1] "Beijing: Lowest GDP Energy Consumption Nationwide", *China Reform Report*, April 29th, 2015.

services grow unevenly. Resources like high-quality education, health care services, cultural services, and social insurance distribute mainly in kernel areas. Large gaps are found between urban and country areas, city center and sub-centers, core function districts and developing and ecological conservation areas. High-quality public services, in particular, appear far from enough to satisfy demands. To improve these shortages calls for deepened reforms and the influence of both market and government. The government should focus on institutional and policy supply, improve public services, open the market broader, enhance efficiency of public sectors, give full play to the decisive role of market mechanism in resource allocation, help to achieve proper allocation of resources, and boost efficiency of resource usage and public service supply.

5. Issues need solving during economic growth of Beijing

5.1 Intensive economic development capacity needs improving

In reference to the objectives of building a moderately well-off society in an all-round way, Beijing is still weak in terms of balanced, coordinated, and continuous development and the contradiction among population, resources, and environment appears to be the most significant problem. By the third quarter of 2016, both the amount and speed of increase in permanent population of Beijing kept going down while the population gross went up. The total amount, intensity, and increase of energy consumption in Beijing lowered while the total size was expanding. Water usage was mounting and low utilization of collective and industrial land still existed. Air quality was in badly need of improvement and special measures such as shutting down factories and production curtailment might be used to achieve the clean air plan and phased goals of the 13th Five-Year Plan. Those problems during economic development mirror the generally extensive way of economic growth in Beijing. Specifically speaking, the extensive mode of development can be concluded from large gaps between Beijing and developed cities worldwide in terms of the indexes of unit energy consumption, per capita output, average land production, and development intensity, relatively low degree of economic intensiveness, and low intensive development capacity. The root ways to solve the problems are advancing supply-side structural reform, improve ways and means of factor supply, change growth pattern that purely depends on factor input, and stress on the key role of innovation as a driving force in economic growth while improving efficiency of factor input.

5.2 Accelerating internal differentiation of tertiary industry and relatively low progress in industrial aggregation and optimization

The dispersion of non-capital functions and adjustment of industrial structure proceed simultaneously. The adjustment of various industries and differentiation of industries speed up. Traditional industries become slow in growth. In 2016, the added value of lodging and catering industries, leasing and commercial service industries, wholesale and retail industries increased by 0.9%, 1.6% and 2% year-on-year, ranking the last three among all industries. That of information transmission, software and information technology services, scientific research and technological services, and financial industries grew by 11.3%, 10.2%, and 9.3% year-on-year, ranking top three among all industries.

In 2016, the cultural creative industries the whole year round produced an added value of 357.05 billion yuan, up by 12.3% year-on-year and taking up 14.3% of local GDP. High-tech industries realized an added value of 564.67 billion yuan, up by 9.1% year-on-year and taking up 22.7% of local GDP and information industry 379.76 billion yuan by 10.1% and 15.3% of local GDP. These three industries grew relatively faster than others and their added values took almost half of the local GDP, from which we can conclude that the city's industrial structure has been further optimized, high-end and aggregated industries took shape however with slow progress.

First of all, the proportion of high-grade, precision and advanced industries is low, taking only about 8% in the whole city. Affected by technological progress and other factors, the high-grade and precision enterprises change and update frequently with large output fluctuation and weak continuity and stability.

Secondly, high-end industrial function zone is faced with issues like relocation, upgrading towards high grade and precision, and enhancing radiating capacity. Generally speaking, the high-end industrial function area in Beijing is focused on manufacturing industries, which expand fast, use relatively more land resources, assume much energy and resources, and thus need upgrading and transforming to a high-end pattern. In this case, the function area should pay more attention on research and development than on manufacturing to lengthen the chain of high-tech manufacturing industry and to increase added value of the products. It should depends more on independent development and innovation than on capital and technology import as before, so as to make an essential transformation from "made in Beijing" to "create in Beijing". It should enrich itself into an integration of industry and urban city, realizing a coordinated progress in both industrial development and city functions and becoming a inhabitable and industry-friendly modern urban space.

Thirdly, service industries may become slow in growth. In 2016, the tertiary industry in Beijing was 80.3% of regional GDP. Beijing took the lead in forming an economic growth pattern based on service industry. However, the growth of the financial industry and business circulation industry may slow down. Affected by interest rate liberation and marketization of exchange rate, traditional financial industry, represented by banking industry, is suffered from a huge pressure of transformation, profit basis is challenged, the growth of financial industry will continue to slow down, and growth rate of added value may fall under 10%. Under the background of dispersion and adjustment, business circulation in Beijing remains low growth.

5.3 Housing price rising too fast, adding risks to real estate market

From 2010 to 2016, the investment gross in real estate each year has kept around 353.67 billion yuan with an average yearly growth of 9.24%, taking up over half of total fixed investment. Both the annual average gross and growth rate of investment in real estate are higher than those in infrastructure during corresponding period. Investment in office buildings and dwellings grew fast. As for dwellings, annual investment gross was 178.79 billion yuan, up by 15.3% and office buildings 56.79 billion yuan by 25.9% (Table 4). Investment in real estate, dwellings in particular, has kept a relatively high speed of growth, playing a crucial role in stabilizing housing price and meeting basic demands of residents. However, the over rising of housing price in Beijing is worth noticing as it increases the risks of the real estate market.

Table 4 Investment in Real Estate in Beijing from 2010 to 2016

Unit: billion yuan, %

| Year / Investment | 2010 | 2011 | 2012 | 2013 | 2014 | 2015 | 2016 | Average |
|---|---|---|---|---|---|---|---|---|
| Investment gross | 290.1 | 303.6 | 315.3 | 348.34 | 391.1 | 422.6 | 404.5 | 353.67 |

| | | | | | | | | |
|---|---|---|---|---|---|---|---|---|
| Year-on-year growth | 1 24.1 | 3 10.1 | 4 3.9 | 10.5 | 3 12.3 | 3 8.1 | 4 -4.3 | 9.24 |
| Investment in dwellings | 150.9 | 177.83 | 162.8 | 172.45 | 196.2 | 196.27 | 195.09 | 178.79 |
| Year-on-year growth | 66.4 | 21.7 | -8.5 | 5.9 | 13.8 | 8.1 | -0.6 | 15.3 |
| Investment in office buildings | 15.91 | 36.38 | 38.48 | 61.17 | 75.02 | 90.66 | 69.9 | 56.79 |
| Year-on-year growth | 55.4 | 40.4 | 5.8 | 59.0 | 22.6 | 20.8 | -22.9 | 25.9 |
| Investment in business, non-public houses and others | 33.63 | 29.67 | 27.59 | 114.71 | 119.91 | 135.7 | 139.55 | 85.82 |
| Year-on-year growth | 67.5 | -11.8 | -7.0 | 0.6 | 4.5 | 13.2 | 2.8 | 9.97 |

Source: Beijing Municipal Commission of Housing and Urban-Rural Development

From 2010 to 2016, the annual average sales of commodity houses in Beijing was 16.593 million square meters with a growth of -18.9% year-on-year. Annual average sales of dwelling houses was 11.922 million square meters, up by -6.3% year-on-year, that of office buildings being 2.551 million square meters with an year-on-year increase of 17.1% and that of commercial, non-public and other houses reaching 1.74 million square meters up by 7% year-on-year (Table 5).

Table 5 Sales in Real Estate Market in Beijing from 2010 to 2016

Unit: million square meters, %

| Year / Sales | 2010 | 2011 | 2012 | 2013 | 2014 | 2015 | 2016 | Average |
|---|---|---|---|---|---|---|---|---|
| Sales of whole commodity houses | 16.395 | 14.4 | 19.437 | 19.031 | 14.59 | 15.547 | 16.751 | 16.593 |
| Year-on-year growth | -30.6 | -12.2 | 35.0 | -2.1 | -23.3 | 6.6 | 7.7 | -18.9 |
| Sales of dwellings | 12.014 | 10.35 | 14.834 | 13.637 | 11.413 | 11.273 | 9.935 | 11.922 |
| Year-on-year growth | -36.1 | -13.9 | 43.3 | -8.1 | -16.3 | -1.2 | -11.9 | -6.3 |
| Sales of office | 2.081 | 2.114 | 2.535 | 3.179 | 1.368 | 2.43 | 4.154 | 2.551 |

| | | | | | | | | |
|---|---|---|---|---|---|---|---|---|
| buildings Year-on-year growth | -18.6 | 1.6 | 19.9 | 25.4 | -57.0 | 77.6 | 70.9 | 17.1 |
| Sales of business, non-public houses and others | 1.421 | 1.087 | 1.14 | 2.215 | 1.809 | 1.844 | 2.662 | 1.74 |
| Year-on-year growth | -9.5 | -23.5 | 4.9 | 7.1 | -18.3 | 1.9 | 44.4 | 7.0 |

Source: Beijing Municipal Commission of Housing and Urban-Rural Development

As the increase of both the investment in real estate and floor space sold slow down, housing price in Beijing shows an upward trend recently. According to the market information provided by China Real Estate Association, housing price in Beijing has risen for 17 consecutive months. The average housing price has increased from 37221 yuan per square meter in October, 2015 to 60738 yuan per square meter in February, 2017, up by 63.18%.[1] From February, 2016 to January, 2017, housing price in Beijing has grew continuously on year-on-year basis with low chain base growth rate but fast growth of the comparison base. The extreme high price is a result of reasons of various aspects. In terms of economic rule, the reason is the imbalance of supply and demand and failure of supply to meet the overwhelming demands. There are several specific factors. First of all, restricted by Beijing's supply policy and ability of land resources, supply of state-owned land in market decreased year by year. Statistics show that the trading area of state-owned land in market in Beijing was respectively 2118.64, 1245.05, 896.89, and 477.29 hectares from 2013 to 2016[2], trading volume coming down year after year and enlarging gap between supply and demand. Secondly, the floor space under construction of dwelling houses show a descending tendency, being 61.76, 71.681, 75.104, 74.069, 69.997, 63.146, and 59.276 million square meters from 2010 to 2016, up by 11.2%, 16.1%, 4.8%, -1.4%, -5.5%, -9.8%, and -6.1% year-on-year. Taking deeper consideration, the over rising of housing price results from increase of floating population, uncertain strictness of policies for house purchasing, relatively easy credit environment, illegal flow of capital into real estate market instead of real economy, and real estate speculation.

The excessively quick rising of housing price brings along the following risks. Firstly,

---

[1] China Investment Consulting, "17 Months' Consecutive Rise of Housing Price in Beijing, Growth by 63.18% ". Retrieved from http://www.ocn.com.cn.
[2] Source: Beijing Municipal Commission of Planning and Land and Resources Management

bubble for real estate market and financial risks become bigger. Secondly, the lose of capital for real economy leads to its slow development. Thirdly, burdens caused by house purchasing on common people become heavier and social anxiety worsens, undermining sustainable, harmonious and stable development of the city.

5.4 Employment pressure mounts

As non-capital functions are being dispersed and the adjustment of new and old industrial patterns fastens, differentiation will still exist in employment in industry and service industry. Replacement of industries and conflict related to aggregate employment will become prominent. Structural contradictions still remain and the total employment pressure will go up to some extent. Taking the influence of dispersion of non-capital functions and of other factors into consideration and based on the estimated economic growth rate of 6.4% in 2017 and average elasticity employment index of 0.35 in recent years, it is expected that the employed population will reach 12.39 million in 2017. The tertiary industry will become the main employer. With the industrial adjustment in wholesale and retailing, leasing business, and storage logistics, employ pressure has slightly increased.

6. Overall judgment and prediction of economic development of Beijing in 2017

6.1 Overall judgment of economic development in 2017

6.1.1 The objective environment of Beijing's economic development and trace of economic growth are basically the same as the whole country. Under the background of the national economy turning from high-speed growth to medium-high speed growth and from resources investment based to innovation driven, the motive mechanism that supports economic growth had a fundamental change. Same as the whole country, Beijing has entered a crucial phrase in its supply-side structural reform, transformation of economic growth pattern, adjustment of economic structure, reform and improvement of supply system. From economic trend in 2016, a soft landing appeared to first occur to Beijing's economy, although economic downturn could continue for a while due to inertia and pressure remains big. Particularly when 2017 starts, the policy judgment of "dispersion of non-capital functions is supply-side structural reform" marks the beginning of the most crucial stage of the dispersion task, when adjustment of industries that don't meet the capital functions will be fastened, and the speed, strength, and range of dispersion will be unprecedented. From the indexes of internal demands, growth impetus, and quality and benefit of Beijing's economy, it is necessary to further reform and optimizes the economic structure. As no pains no gains, proper lowering of economic growth will earn more space and time for economic transition, adjusting growth rate, and higher-quality growth. To clean out overcapacity, reduce low-end supply, eliminate invalid supply, and expand medium and high end supply aims at boosting quality and efficacy of economic growth of the capital city.

6.1.2 Comprehensively deepened reform gives momentum to Beijing's economy

As reforms in key fields make steady progress in 2017, deepened reform in an all-round way will be furthered, development vitality of economy released, and driving force of economic growth strengthened. Firstly, supply-side structural reform, opening-up pilots of service industries, reform of state-owned enterprises and other measures are in favor of giving full play to Beijing's advantageous resources and optimizing industrial structure. The implementation of policies like "replacing business tax with value-added tax" and streamlining government functions and administration and delegating powers to lower levels will set free the development vitality of enterprises. Secondly, new motives are coming into being. As stable progress has been made in building coordinated innovation community among Beijing, Tianjin and Hebei Province, and comprehensive innovative reform in Beijing, the advantages of technological innovation of the city will be uplifted and continue to usher economic development. Thirdly, nonstop stress will be exerted on construction of key areas and projects such as the sub-centers, the International Horticultural Exposition, and the new airport, which will promote greatly the bearing capacity of capital functions and advance steady growth of economy. Fourthly, as the institutional reform of scientific research management, the energy of motion in scientific and technological innovation will be effectively discharged. The General Office of CPC Central Committee and the General Office of the State Council of China issued *Several Suggestions on Policies to Further Improve the Management of Central Financial Funds for Scientific Research Projects* in July, 2016. On September 1$^{st}$ of the same year, Beijing municipal party committee and municipal government issued *Policies and Measures of Beijing on Further Improving the Management of Scientific Research Projects and Funds*. The two documents indicate a series of approaches to "free + spur" researchers. Encouraged by these policies, researchers will be more positively engaged in their scientific projects and the energy of motion for scientific and technological innovation will be discharged effectively.

## 6.2 Predictions for main economic indexes of Beijing in 2017

### 6.2.1 Slight slow in economic growth

Influenced by economic situations, Beijing will be faced with pressure from economic downturn in 2017, and it will take more efforts to disperse non-capital functions to give room for economic transition. Adjustment of industrial structure will be strengthened. Fasten the clearance of common manufacturing industries and low-end capacity. It will takes a long term for structural transition of high-precision and high-grade industries. Therefore, economic growth will slows down in 2017 and continue to keep an "L" type of development trend. It is estimated that GDP growth of Beijing for the whole year of 2017 will be around 6.4%.

### 6.2.2 Steady growth in increase rate of investment

In 2017, Beijing will fasten the construction of sub-centers, new capital airport, urban rail transit, and International Horticultural Exposition (IHE) and IHE village. Venue of Winter Olympics and supporting facilities come into operation and infrastructure investment will enlarge but industrial investment growth will slow down. Government investment mainly goes to infrastructure and people's livelihood projects and investment in indemnificatory houses will continue to grow steadily. Affected by downturn of real economy and dispersion operation, demands for enterprise investment continue to abate while private investment will keep growing at a relatively fast speed with the stimulation of favorable policies like PPP model. Taking the method of component analysis, based on trend judgment of growth rate of industry, infrastructure, and real estate investment in the investment structure of fixed capital, and referring to growth rate indexes such as industrial investment (6.8%), infrastructure investment (10.3%), and real estate investment (-4.3%) in 2016, it is expected that growth rate of fixed investment will reach 6.5% in 2017, slighting going upwards than last year.

### 6.2.3 Slight fastened increase in consumption demand

Generally, the demand for market consumption levels off with that in 2016. Catering, wholesale, and retailing industries remain low due to the influence of objective environment. The willingness of consumption of residents are low. Consumption hotspots need exploring. New economy and new commercial activities like Internet economy, sharing economy and tourism economy are expected to become future hotspots of consumption. Consumption in services and cultural and leisure activities will maintain fast increase. As Beijing start to set limits to vehicles of outdated emission standards, the policy will hopefully drives up the automobile consumption in 2017. Therefore, total volume of retail sales of consumer goods in 2017 is expected to increase by 6.6% year-on-year, little bit higher than that of 2016.

6.2.4 Slight uplift in inflation

As the price reform on resource products, the differentiation policy towards prices of water, electricity, gas and heating in non-residential areas make progress and the dispersion and adjustment of logistics industry, prices of part of resource products, agricultural products such as fresh food and vegetables, and articles for daily use are likely to rise. The advancing of regulation and control of population and the lessening of working-age adults will push up the market transaction costs of labor and the lift of the minimum wage standard will increase labor cost of enterprise. Nevertheless, the still low price of international raw oil and staple commodities and the slowing down of economic growth will curb the price rising to some extent. According to the predication method of CPI components, referring to the fact that food price was up by 3.3% in 2016 and year-on-year index of consumption price kept rising from June 2016 to February 2017, and based on the trend, it is expected that the consumer price will be up by 1.8% year-on-year in 2017 and the inflation increases slightly compared with 2016.The predictions results of the main economic indexes in Beijing in 2017 are shown as Table 6.

Table 6 Beijing Main Economic Indexes Prediction in 2017

Unit:%

| Index Name | 2016 (Real value) | 2017 (predicted value) |
|---|---|---|
| Growth rate of regional GDP | 6.7 | 6.4 |
| Growth rate of first industry added values | -8.8 | -8.0 |
| Growth rate of second industry added values | 5.6 | 5.5 |

| | | |
|---|---|---|
| Growth rate of tertiary industry added values | 7.1 | 6.9 |
| Growth rate of fixed investment | 5.9 | 6.5 |
| Growth rate of retail sales of consumer goods | 6.5 | 6.5 |
| CPI year-on-year growth | 1.4 | 1.8 |

# Thoughts on Construction of Beijing as National Center for Science and Technology Innovation

## Zhao Hong[1]

Abstract: In February, 2014 when Chinese President Xi Jinping inspected the performance of Beijing municipal government, he gave the city a new role as the "National Center for Science and Technology Innovation". Beijing is featured as being abundant in technological innovation resources and it has obvious advantages to facilitate the construction of the National Center for Science and Technology Innovation. However, there still exist many prominent problems and weak links in aspects of technological innovation and reform, use of technological resources, management service system, and innovative cultural concepts. In days ahead, it is necessary for Beijing to pinpoint the deeply rooted contradiction and problems, stress on scientific and technological reform, create new service philosophy, and clear out mechanism and institutional barriers in the progress of innovation and development, so as to create favorable conditions for the construction of National Center for Science and Technology Innovation.

Keywords: National Center for Science and Technology Innovation, innovation and reform, innovation-driven, technological innovation

## 1. Strategic Value of Building Beijing into National Center for Science and Technology Innovation

Innovation is the first driving force for development. Further pursuing innovation-driven development and forming the important source for national innovation system and original creation are the strategic choices and fundamental impetus to live up to the strategic focuses of Beijing, advance the coordinated development of Beijing, Tianjin and Hebei Province, and back up the cause of innovation-oriented country.

### 1.1 National Center for Science and Technology Innovation as a mission to implement national strategy of innovation-driven development and lead the country to enter for

---
[1] Zhao Hong, Ph.D in Economics, Researcher, Deputy Director of Beijing Academy of Social Sciences. Research areas include economics, specifically, regional economy and industrial economy.

global innovation contest. The new-round competition in technological innovation around the globe becomes increasingly fierce, each country strengthening innovation one after another to contend with the commanding height of innovation competition. Nowadays, the new round of scientific and technological reform and industrial transformation are ready to launch. Developed economies like the U.S., Europe and Japan are putting more emphasis on innovative development and drawing up related strategies to seek for and fortify the advantageous position in global innovative competition so as to seize the commanding height of science and technology competition in the future and master international voices. For instance, the United States released the U.S. National Innovation Strategy (2015), launched the National Innovation Network for Manufacturing Industries, planned to build 45 manufacturing innovation centers in 10 years and prioritized the development of nine major areas such as advanced manufacturing, precision medical, brain planning, advanced vehicles and space exploration. The EU has formulated "Horizon 2020" strategy and focused on fields of information and communication technology, nanotechnology, advanced manufacturing, robotics, biotechnology and space technology and is committed to become the most internationally competitive national consortium. Japan proposed the "Comprehensive Strategy for Science and Technology Innovation 2014 - a Bridge to Create a Future for Innovation" and focused on promoting technological development in the three major cross-cutting fields of information and communication technologies, nanotechnology and environmental technologies, making it a source of growth in Japan's industrial competitiveness. Our country has become the second largest economy in the world, but its position in the global competition in technological innovation needs to be improved urgently. In 2010, China's GDP exceeded Japan, becoming the second largest economy in the world. However, there is still a big gap between China's capability of independent innovation and the world advanced level. Core technologies in key areas are not yet fundamentally free from dependence on foreign sources. For example, in the field of new generation of information technology, the phenomenon of "lack of core and base" is relatively common. About 80% of China's chips rely on imports, of which the import rate of high-end chips exceeds 90%. Our country lacks the mold steel needed to produce the "ball" on the ballpoint pen. Although it produces 38 billion pieces of ballpoint pens each year that accounts for 90% of the global supply, 90% of the "ball" needs to be imported from Japan, Germany and other countries. In the field of aerospace, the engines of China's high-performance aircraft rely heavily on imports, mostly foreign-funded and joint-venture brands. Our country must take the road of innovation-driven development to overcome the "middle income trap". China's per capita GDP jumped from 930 U.S. dollars in 2000 to 8,016 U.S. dollars in 2015. According to World Bank standards, China is now in a middle-high income stage, climbing across the "middle-income trap". International experience tells that only a handful of economies in the world successfully moved from a low income level to a high income level after World War II, while many countries have long been stuck in a "middle income trap". According to the report of the World Bank, there were 101 middle-income countries or regions in the world in 1960. Only 13 countries or regions such as Japan, South Korea and Singapore became high-income economies by 2008, accounting for 12.9%. Up to 87.1% of countries have not successfully crossed the "middle income trap". The reason is that the economic restructuring in these countries was unsuccessful, the innovation-driven development model was not formed, and the economy was slow or even stagnating.

1.2 National Center for Science and Technology Innovation to promote the construction of the Beijing-Tianjin-Hebei collaborative innovation community and support the innovation-oriented construction of a world-class urban agglomeration. The evolution from a single innovation city to an innovation city cluster centered on a central city is an important trend of world-class science and technology innovation centers. Through the diffusion and spillover of knowledge and technology in the region, the San Francisco Bay Area promotes the optimal allocation of innovative resources among cities and forms an innovative city group centering the Silicon Valley that includes the San Francisco Peninsula, North Bay, South Bay and East Bay. The metropolitan area of Tokyo, through the spillover of core cities such as Miyoshi-ku (Chiyoda-ku, Minato-ku and Chuo ward), has led to the innovation and development in such areas as seven Fukutoshin, three outer Shinsei and 22 business nuclear cities. Beijing should not rely solely on itself to build a national technological innovation center. It needs the joint efforts of the Beijing-Tianjin-Hebei region so as to promote the optimal allocation of talent, capital, technology and other innovative resources within the region, fully release radiation of the effectiveness of the Center to the surrounding areas, advance the integration of the innovation chain, industrial chain, capital chain and policy chain in Beijing, Tianjin and Hebei Province, and create a trans-regional innovation network to enhance the region's overall innovation capability and innovation-driven development capability and build an innovative urban agglomeration. It is a fundamental way to promote the coordinated development of Beijing, Tianjin and Hebei that the capital should play a leading role in promoting innovation and building a coordinated innovation community in Beijing, Tianjin and Hebei Province. There is a big gap between Beijing, Tianjin and Hebei in terms of development stage, public service level and social security level, leading to difficulties in docking industries in the periphery of Beijing and "missile spillover" in Beijing's development effectiveness. Many industrial transfers directly to the Yangtze River Delta region, bypassing Tianjin-Hebei region. From the experience of international metropolitan agglomeration, the key to narrowing the gap between Beijing, Tianjin and Hebei and realizing coordinated regional development is to give full play to the leading role of Beijing as a National Center for Science and Technology Innovation. Through regional synergistic innovation, the internal industrial gradient in Beijing-Tianjin-Hebei region should be optimized and the capacity of Tianjin and Hebei upgraded to undertake Beijing industry. At the same time, the increasingly prominent environmental problems in Beijing, Tianjin and Hebei in recent years have shaped the mechanism of forcing the development of the three places. It is now a must for them to take the path of innovation-driven development, replace the outward development mode of dependence on factors and scale expansion with an inward one focusing on the release of innovative and entrepreneurial effectiveness and innovation-driven development, promote industrial restructuring and upgrading, effectively reduce resource and energy consumption and improve the regional ecological environment.

1.2 The construction of a national center for science and technology innovation is of strategic importance to Beijing in building a "high-grade, precision and advanced" economic structure and accelerating the economic transfer of energy. At present, the new situations such as economic development entering a new normal, accelerated resolution of non-capital functions, and governing the "big city disease" have set new requirements for the capital's economic development. On the one hand, it is necessary to implement the strategic positioning of the capital city, speed up efforts to ease the non-capital functions, optimize and enhance the core functions of the capital, and strive to achieve "decency." On the other hand, we must take the initiative to adapt to the new normal of economic development, promote the economic structure from incremental expansion to the adjustment of stocks and taking both optimal and incremental measures to promote the in-depth adjustment of the three internal industrial structures and accelerate the formation of a "sophisticated" economic structure, continuously improve the quality and efficiency of economic development. Building a national center for science and technology innovation and enhancing its capability of innovative development will help Beijing take the lead in building a "sophisticated" economic structure, create an innovation-led development model, speed up the conversion of economic development momentum, achieve higher quality sustainable development and provide strong support for building first-class harmony of livable city.

2. Analysis on the in-depth problems existing in Beijing's building of the National Center for Science and Technology Innovation

2.1 The coordination and comprehensiveness of science and technology reform are still inadequate and there is still a gap with the requirements of a systematic innovation and entrepreneurship ecosystem, which will affect the release of scientific and technological innovation. At present, the scientific and technological reform has moved toward coordinated reforms in various fields beyond. In recent years, Beijing's scientific and technological reforms have been confined to the fields of science and technology. The reform in the social fields accompanying them has been relatively slow and cannot meet the needs of technological innovation and development. For example, the reforms of the household registration system related to the introduction of talents from other provinces and cities, the immigration control of expatriates, the mechanism for the transfer of foreign high-level talents and industry professionals from work permit to permanent residence has been slow, hindering the introduction of talents with innovative ideas. Personal income tax policy design does not match the incentive policies to encourage personnel of innovation and scientific research. The incentive policy of personal income tax deferred equity, aiming at encourage personnel by conversion of technological achievements into shares, is still not perfect in high-tech enterprises and SMEs. In other words, the policies haven't shown enough support and encouragement towards those engaged in scientific research. The bottleneck of the research funding management reform has not yet been broken through. Till now, the scientific research funding mechanism regards wages and allowances as the only way to compensate researchers for their intellectual contributions. The wage standard is not determined according to the laws of the market but refers to salary standards of civil servants. The "compensation for intellectual contribution" is excluded from expenditure range of scientific research projects.

In the meantime, the government departments at all levels have not coordinated with each other on the work of scientific and technological innovation, and they haven't made concerted effort in the implementation of policies but offset each other, resulting in greater constraints on the release of scientific and technological achievements. For example, the science and technology sector's talent introduction policy requires that departments of education, human resources and social security, and public security cooperate with each other, or science and technology park plans formulated by science and technology departments need coordination with development and reform, land and planning departments. However, lack of effective co-ordination mechanism has caused many planning and policy decisions on science and technology to be difficult to play its due role.

2.2 The integration of innovative resources in the capital is confronted with institutional obstacles and it is difficult to form a competitive and differentiated cluster of innovative industries

The decentralization of innovative resources is not conducive to the differentiated development of parks and the formation of innovative industrial clusters. In terms of innovation elements, the innovative resources from enterprises, research institutes and higher education institutions, as well as the central enterprises and local governments have not been used integrated and the long-term cooperation mechanisms based on innovation chain and industry chain have not been established. In this way, we cannot concentrate superior resources, nor form a joint force conducive to promoting scientific and technological innovation. From the carrier of innovative space, Zhongguancun National Innovation Demonstration Zone is the main battlefield of Beijing's construction of the national center for science and technology innovation center, playing a leading role in the city's innovative development. However, as an administrative body, the Zhongguancun Administrative Committee is the lack of effective management of all sub-parks. As the sub-parks in their own park land, talent, capital and other resources to use more power, the Zhongguancun Administrative Committee in the park planning, industrial layout and other aspects of policies on the park development and industrial agglomeration of the guiding role is not strong , Leading to a more serious homogeneity competition tendencies in all sub-districts. Since the sub-parks master great powers in land use, personnel, capital and other resources in their own terrories, the role of Zhongguancun Administrative Committee to guide the development of the park and promote industrial agglomeration through policies regarding planning and industrial distribution, etc. is not strong, leading to serious homogeneity competition tendency among sub-parks.

At the same time, it is difficult to establish an ecosystem to promote industrial development due to the insufficient industrial connection between high and new technology enterprises in sub-parks and the difficulty in obtaining supporting public services. For example, the establishment of industrial clusters around the life sciences makes specialized public testing laboratory platform possible to achieve resource sharing of clustered enterprise in parks. In addition, due to the large number of parks and uneven development of parks, using the same brand of "Zhongguancun" will affect the brand and the shaping of the sub-brands, which makes the market less penetrative and less attractive to resources.

2.3 The management and service system that fits the development of the new economy has not yet been established, being beset with identification difficulty, lack of effective supervision and inadequate service and other problems.

While bringing new markets, new rules, new concepts and new environments, the new economy also poses new challenges to the government's service management. Insufficient sensitivity, inclusiveness and control over new economic forms such as shared economy and Internet economy may lead to mistakes in identifying and judging the new economy. For example, Ma Yun was in hope of getting the support from Beijing or Shanghai when he located Alibaba headquarter but its headquarter finally settled in Hangzhou. The two metropolises missed the chance of holding the largest e-commerce headquarters of China because of lack of awareness towards the development trend of e-commerce. The new economy tends to have an impact on the old one. New formats, represented by inclusive financial services such as P2P and Yu'E Bao, and transport services like "Didi Taxi" and based on Internet technologies, have created new business models, improved market allocation efficiency, and replaced outdated market rules. However, such new formats represented by the shared economy have also encountered unprecedented challenges in terms of market access and market supervision. For example, certain policies issued against internet-based taxi for example "Didi Taxi" have shown that the government lacks adequate inclusiveness and effective protection of the new economy.

2.4 Fail to establish a culture concept and value system that fit innovation and entrepreneurship

At present, there is still a lack of sufficient innovative ideas, values and culture to support the development of science and technology innovation in Beijing, resulting in lack of persistence and profit orientation. Many entrepreneurs in Beijing do not seem to have found the spiritual source of innovation and entrepreneurship. Compared with Silicon Valley in the United States, we can see that entrepreneurs there mostly have strong curiosity and exploration spirit, driven by a force to innovate and start their own businesses. The sense of achievements and pride when they succeed has also become their incentives, followed by economic interests. The entrepreneurs in Zhongguancun are showing the opposite characteristics. First, most of them copy the money-making model. Take the "Unicorn" enterprises in Zhongguancun as an example, most of these companies are concentrated in Internet industry of relatively low entry, imitating each other and chasing only short-term economic interests. Second, many entrepreneurs cannot totally understanding the value of innovation and have no patience towards it. From the government level, excessive pursuit of GDP growth and short-term local fiscal revenue increase, as well as emphasis on short-term economic benefits, also have a negative impact on the formation of cultural concepts and values that are suitable for innovation and entrepreneurship.

3. Thoughts on Beijing's Building National Center for Science and Technology Innovation

3.1 Deepen innovation and reform and improve the innovation and entrepreneurship ecosystem

At present, the "Systemetic and Comprehensive Innovation Reform Pilot Program for Beijing-Tianjin-Hebei Region" has been approved by the State Council. This is a mission that the country has given to the three cities and province, as well as a great opportunity for Beijing to deepen its reform. However, this plan only points out the direction for regional reforms. The real reform practice comes from the grassroots level and therefore it requires innovation, creativity and exploration of the grass-roots. Judging from Beijing's current situation, Beijing's innovation and development are confronted with many institutional constraints. Relevant specific and common problems are intertwined. The traditional methods of administrative management are difficult to meet the requirements of modern innovation and entrepreneurship. The innovation system and policy supply still cannot fit the demands of enterprises. Therefore, we should pay attention to realize a systematic, integrated and coordinated reform. Through the "one package" top-level design and full, systematic and comprehensive reform, Beijing should maximize the innovation vitality of science and technology personnel and improve as much as possible the momentum of technological innovation and release the most potential of regional innovation and development. In the near future, Beijing will deepen innovation and reform and make breakthroughs in the following three areas.

Firstly, the reform is centered on "people", namely how to gather together the talents and to inspire human vitality during reform. For example, it is necessary to actively explore the possibility of allowing permanent residence of qualified foreign nationals or giving them a residence permit for a certain period of time, allowing foreign students to start innovative and entrepreneurial activities after graduating from higher education institutions in our country. Establish and perfect a market-oriented talent evaluation and incentive mechanism, set up an evaluation system for science and technology personnel oriented by capability, performance and contribution, and carry out classification and evaluation of researchers engaged in different innovative activities. The establishment of intellectual compensation mechanism for scientific research personnel improves labor costs, indirect funding management of research projects, arrange reasonably performance expenditure of indirect expenses based on work performance of scientific research personnel.

Second, we will revolve around "enterprises" to inspire the vitality of various innovative entities such as high-tech enterprises, R & D institutes of central enterprises, university research institutes and non-public organizations, reduce their burden, decompress them and loose their constraints. For example, we can give full scope to the decisive role of market in allocating innovative resources, break the monopoly and market segregation of industries that restrict innovation, and eliminate barriers to market access for the development of new technologies, products and business models. We will deepen the reform of the commercial system and relax the registration conditions for activities of innovation and entrepreneurship to facilitate them. We should implement preferential tax policies for innovative activities to promote innovation and entrepreneurship through the fiscal policies.

The third is to reform around the "environment", to be specific, to build an ecological system that is most conducive to innovation and entrepreneurship. For instance, we should break everything that is detrimental to innovation and entrepreneurship, clean up and repeal all outdated policies and regulations that hinder innovation and development; accelerate the construction of innovative service platform, vigorously develop all kinds of scientific and technological service agencies such as pilot research, testing and examination, and technology trading, and actively build a platform for professional and technical innovation for small and medium-sized enterprises; improve the scientific and technological financial service system covering the whole process of innovation chain and guide social capital to jointly establish sub-funds such as angel fund, venture capital fund, industrial fund and M & A fund to increase the supply of venture capital; create a strong culture of innovation and entrepreneurship, give full play to the culture to lead the way forward, unite the efforts, and encourage innovation and entrepreneurship.

3.2 Intensify the integration of resources and achieve major breakthroughs in innovation in key areas

In recent years, Beijing has continuously improved its innovative capabilities and a group of original achievements with international influence have emerged, leaping from "follower" to "runner" and "leader" in terms of global innovation. For example, in the field of mobile communications, China was a follower in the era of 2G and 3G. In the 4G era, the TD-LTE standard led by Datang Telecom and other organs has become one of the two major 4G standards in the world and has achieved its goal of running side by side with the world. In the era of 5G, Beijing Institute of Information and Communication Research of China, Datang Mobile and others are actively participating in and leading the development of 5G international standards, and at the same time, they have made important achievements in the research and development of 5G key technologies. However, compared with internationally renowned innovative regions, Beijing's ability to integrate innovative resources is not enough, its original capability of innovation being weak and disruptive results few in number. For example, in the field of biomedicine, the proportion of generic drugs in China reaches more than 90%. Among the high-end medical devices currently in use in China, 90% of the ultrasound devices, magnetic resonance devices, electrocardiographs, 85% of the test instruments, and 80% of surveillance cameras are foreign sources. In the field of new materials, taking special steel as an example, China's crude steel output ranks first in the world, but the proportion of special steel output is only about 5%, far below the world average of 15% to 20%. Many special categories of high quality steel relies on import. In the future, we should base ourselves on serving the overall national innovation and strengthening the integration and gathering of high-end innovative resources so as to achieve a number of major technological breakthroughs in the field of advanced science and technology and common key technologies and seize the global high ground. First, strengthen the cooperation between the central and local governments to achieve comprehensive layout of original innovation in key areas. We will give our full support to the implementation of the National Science Center, the National Laboratory, major national science and technology projects, major science and technology infrastructure and major scientific programs in Beijing. We should concentrate on implementing large-scale scientific projects such as brain science, quantum computing and quantum communication, and nanoscience, leading the study of key scientific issues in frontier domains, and strengthen the support on information science, basic materials, bio-medicine and human health, agricultural biological genetics, environmental systems and control, energy and other areas, and strive to obtain a number of original innovation results of international influence.

Second, Beijing should promote fine and differentiated innovation and development in all districts of the capital and to optimize the layout of scientific and technological innovation. The six districts of Beijing focus on promoting basic science, innovative development of strategic cutting-edge high-tech and high-end service industries; the plains outside the six districts focus on accelerating the transformation of scientific and technological achievements, promoting the innovative development of productive service industry, strategic emerging industries and high-end manufacturing industry;

mountainous areas focus on the innovative development of low-carbon and high-end industries such as tourism and leisurement and green energy. At the same time, it is necessary to accelerate the construction of "Three Cities" of Zhongguancun Science City, Future Science and Technology City and Huairou Science City to form a more powerful pole of innovative growth.

3.3 Focus on key areas and cultivate a number of globally competitive industrial clusters

The development of strategic emerging industries has become a key strategy for the major countries in the world to seize the commanding height of the new round of economic and technological development. In recent years, Beijing has made good achievements in the development of strategic emerging industries and has continuously enhanced the support and leading role of the capital's economic and social development. For example, the added value of Beijing's strategic emerging industries in 2014 increased by 17.9% over the previous year, which was 11.7% higher than the city's average industrial output above designated size and contributed 62.7% to the city's above-scale industrial growth. However, due to the lack of key technologies and the imperfect innovation eco-system, the overall size of Beijing's strategic emerging industries is small and the effect of industrial clusters is not obvious. The impetus to the capital's economic and social development needs to be improved. In the future, we must focus on key areas and cultivate a number of globally competitive industrial clusters.

First, vigorously develop the strategic emerging industries. Vigorously develop strategic emerging industries such as electronic information, bio-medicine, new energy, new materials, smart manufacturing, aerospace, new energy vehicles, and rail transit, make key breakthroughs in a number of worldly advanced key common technologies and core bottleneck technologies such as high-performance computing, grapheme materials, and intelligent robots, form a series of competitive international standards, cultivate a group of innovative leading enterprises with international competitiveness, and build a batch of innovative industrial clusters with technology dominance.

The second is to speed up the cultivation of the new economy and the form of superior industries. We should speed up the growth of new products, new services, new industries, new formats and new models with a view to enhancing the sensitivity, inclusiveness and control of new economic forms such as shared economy and the Internet economy. We will speed up the development of a batch of leading enterprises and accelerate the formation of superior industries in new economic situations.

3.4 Promote collaborative innovation of Beijing-Tianjin-Hebei region and stimulate innovation and development in the region

The Beijing-Tianjin-Hebei Collaborative Development Plan clearly states that it is necessary to promote the formation of the Beijing-Tianjin-Hebei Collaborative Innovation Community, establish and improve a regional collaborative innovation system and work together to create a strategic high-tech development zone that will lead the whole country and radiate the surrounding areas. At present, there are still many obstacles in the co-innovation and development of the region. For example, the innovative elements such as the three localities are hard to move freely and the cooperation and innovation are scattered. The industrialization of inter-regional innovations faces the problems of policy docking and benefit-sharing. In the future, to promote coordinated innovation in Beijing, Tianjin and Hebei, we should focus on the following three aspects.

First, focus on key areas to create a number of co-construction and innovation cooperation platforms. For example, based on Zhongguancun, Hebei and Tianjin are formed into distinctive butt-ups. According to the concept of industrial clusters, pilot projects are selected in key areas to focus on the industries and form competitive advantages and brand advantages. By building the Beijing-Tianjin-Hebei Science and Technology Parks chain, Beijing, Tianjin and Hebei industrial chain, innovation chain, capital chain and service chain formation. Give full play to the radiation leading role of science and technology resources in the capital, push forward concentrated dispersion to surrounding areas of scientific and technological innovation links such as conversion of scientific results and incubation to create a number of innovative "micro-centers". For example, based on the development of high-tech industries and strategic emerging industries in Baodi District, efforts have been made to promote the industrialization of science and technology in Zhongguancun in Baodi and create a new metropolis where high-tech results are transformed.

The second is to create innovative ecological environment in Zhongguancun and to strengthen resource sharing and policy docking. Actively promote the open sharing of scientific and technological innovation resources and achievements of the three places, promote the orderly flow of elements of innovation and entrepreneurship, and guide Beijing's resources for innovation and entrepreneurship to extend services to Hebei and Tianjin. For example, Zhongguancun's Peking University Entrepreneurship Training Camp, 36 Krypton, Maker's Headquarters, YOU + International Youth Community and other innovative incubators have signed contracts in Tianjin and Hebei, bringing fresh entrepreneurial ideas, quality entrepreneurial services and rich venture capital to help convergence entrepreneurial projects. We will promote the sharing of key cooperation areas by piloting policies and priorities in Zhongguancun, and further clarifying the specific pilot projects such as "1 + 6" and "New Article 4" so as to promote them to the key cooperation areas of Beijing-Tianjin-Hebei.

The third is to speed up making up for the two aspects of "shortcomings" in surrounding areas of Beijing and increase the attractiveness of innovative elements. On the one hand, it is necessary to strengthen the construction of hardware, accelerate the construction of a regional transportation system with the suburban railway as the core, build a large-capacity, fast, one-stop, and low-cost suburban railway and form a 1-hour commuter circle to enhance the   carrying capacity of traffic in the region. On the other hand, it is necessary to strengthen the building of software, for instance, pushing forward the distribution of quality public service resources and narrowing the gap in public services in the region. At the national level, efforts should be made to solve the bottleneck constraints in the household registration system, entrance examination system and social security system, and to eliminate invisible barriers in the development of public service in Tianjin and Hebei Province. At the same time, it is necessary to intensify the investment in public service resources in Hebei and Tianjin and to promote the balanced and integrated development of public service in Beijing, Tianjin and Hebei. For Beijing, it is necessary to further accelerate the dispersal of public service resources such as education and medical services to Tianjin and Hebei and lift the overall level of public service in the region through the establishment of branches of prestigious schools or institutions.

3.5 Implement two-way open innovation, building a hub for global innovation network.

Advancing independent innovation at a higher starting point by making full use of international and domestic innovation resources is an important path for implementing innovation-driven development strategy and building a national center for science and technology innovation. In the past, Beijing's science and technology innovation paid much attention to the introduction, digestion and absorption of foreign technologies. Input-type inward-looking innovation played an important role in enhancing the capability of independent innovation and promoting the economic and social development of the whole city. In the context of globalization, Beijing should grasp the new characteristics of the times, promote a bidirectional opening-up and innovation, make active use of global innovative resources, build a global innovation network, enhance the strategic level of independent innovation and enhance its initiative and voice in international technological competition.

On the one hand, it is necessary to continue to create an international business environment, promote innovative service concepts, and set up service standards in line with international ones and further increase the introduction of international high-quality and high-end innovative resources. For example, relying on platforms for the introduction of overseas high-level talents, such as the "Thousand Talents Program" and "Hai Ju Project" in Beijing, Beijing should introduce a group of scientists and innovative talents who master the key technologies and lead the development of emerging disciplines.

On the other hand, Beijing must speed up "going global", make use of global innovation resources to build a global innovation network, and encourage competent enterprises to set up innovative carriers such as overseas R & D centers and support powerful cultural ideas. Enterprises in industrial design headquarters should set up branches overseas and use their advantages in international advanced technology and personnel to enhance their innovative capabilities. For example, Lenovo has set up R & D centers in Beijing and Raleigh of the United States, aiming at building a "global innovation triangle" with Japan's Daiwa Institute of Research. Encourage Beijing's science and technology leading enterprises to actively participate in the "Belt and Road" initiative and actively explore the international market. At the same time,

Beijing should play a leading role of science and technology enterprises, relying on major strategic projects and jointly promoting the "going global" of small and medium-sized science and technology enterprises, increase the overall competitiveness of innovation chain and industrial chain.

References:

World Bank, State Council Development Research Center. *China in 2030*, China Financial and Economic Publishing House, 2013.

Liu, Xiaojun. Beijing: from Follower to the Leader of Mobile Communication Technology. *Technology Daily,* July 17, 2016.

"State-owned Steel Industry in China: Low proportion of special steel in crude steel and low proportion of high-end special steel in special steel", *Zhuochuang Information*, Oct 21, 2015.

Beijing Municipal Bureau of Statistics. *Statistical Communique of Beijing on the 2014 National Economic and Social Development, 2015.*

# Current Situations, Major Tasks and Implementation Paths of Beijing Supply Side Structural Reform

## Yang Song[1]

## Abstract

Beijing faces many outstanding contradictions and problems in its economic development such as the lack of innovation and competitiveness in the supply side, the constraints of supply of factors, the imbalance in the supply of public goods and public services, the lack of supply in the mid-to-high-end industries and the supply shortage in the high-end manufacturing industries. It is an important task for Beijing to disperse non-capital functions during its cause of pushing forward the structural reform of the supply side at present. It mainly focuses on functions dispersion, scale control, layout improvement, lowering costs and making up shortcoming. Beijing should tackle first with easing non-capital functions, speeding up the structural adjustment and expanding the mid-to-high-end supply during supply-side structural reform. We must put the enhancement of scientific and technological innovation capability first in the supply-side structural reforms, give full play to the functions of the national center for science and technology innovation to further stimulate supply-side innovation vitality. Beijing also should consider the improvement of the supply structure system and enhancement of competitiveness as the core content of supply-side structural reforms, and enhance the adaptability and flexibility of supply structure to demand changes. Connotative intensive development promoted by red-line constraints and enhancing intensive resource utilization should be taken as important goals of supply-side structural reform in order to reduce supply costs and improve the efficiency of supply efficiency. We should bring together the global high-end elements, enhance global resource allocation and gather capacity to make up for shortcomings and strengthen weak links.

Keywords: supply-side structural reform, function dispersion, size control, layout optimization, cost reduction, making up for shortcomings

---

[1] Yang Song, Associate Researcher, Deputy Head of the Research Institute of Economics, Beijing Academy of Social Sciences. Research areas include urbanization and economics, public governance

The supply-side structural reform is an important judgment and decision making made by the party Central Committee with General Secretary Xi Jinping as the core by focusing on the domestic and international economic development environment and the status quo and development trend of China's economy. It is a major strategic plan to adapt and lead the new normal of economic development in China, deepen reform in an all-round way and promote China's steady economic growth, as well as a major innovation and development in Marxist political economy. Supply-side structural reforms have provided important guiding ideology and development direction for Beijing to ease non-capital functions, manage the "big city disease" and promote the capital's economic restructuring and development. In the case of Beijing, the solution to non-capitalist functions is an important task for Beijing to promote structural reform on the supply side.

1. Situations and urgency of Beijing's pushing forward the supply-side structural reform

Since 2016, Beijing Municipal Party Committee and Municipal Government have been firmly implementing the spirit of the speech made by President Xi Jinping during his inspection tour to Beijing on February 26, 2014, the "Outline for Beijing-Tianjin-Hebei Collaborative Development" and the central government's major strategy on supply-side structural reform, promoting supply-side structural reform as the main line, and issuing a series of policies with clearly defined work arrangements. On July 24, Beijing municipal government promulgated the *Measures on Promoting Supply-Side Structural Reform to Further Non-Governmental Investment Work*. On July 28, the *Measures on Promoting Supply-Side Structural Reform and Accelerating the Building of a World-Class Harmonious Capital* was issued. On December 25, the 12th Plenary Session of the 11th Municipal Party Committee put forward the principle of "aiming at quality and efficiency improvement and based on the advancement of supply-side structural reforms, speeding up function dispersion, methods change, environmental governance, shortcomings making-up, coordination promotion, and achieving steady growth, accelerated reform, structural adjustment, beneficiary to people's livelihood, and risk prevention".[1] After a lapse of three years, from February 23 to February 24, 2017, President Xi Jinping visited Beijing again and delivered an important speech on

---

[1] "Make steady progress while firmly grasp the main line of supply-side structural reform", *Beijing Daily*, Dec 5, 2016.

Beijing's urban planning and preparation for the Winter Olympics. On the 26th, the Standing Committee of the Beijing Municipal Party Committee held an enlarged meeting centering around the question of "what kind of capital to build and how", calling for comprehensive and accurate understanding and implementation of such major requirements as the city's overall planning and orderly defusing Beijing's non-capital functions. Judging from the situation of Beijing's economic development, it is an arduous task for the economy to change from an element-driven growth model to an innovation-driven one and to eliminate backward production capacity and optimize structure. Economic development is faced with many outstanding contradictions and problems such as the lack of innovation and competitiveness in the supply side, the constraints of supply of factors, the unbalanced supply of public goods and public services, the lack of supply in the mid-to-high-end industries and the supply shortage in the high-end manufacturing industries.

1.1 Economic growth is facing a fundamental shift from an element-driven growth model to an innovation-driven one. The power conversion of economic growth requires supply-side structural reforms be given top priority.

The process and rate of economic growth of Beijing is basically the same with the national economic growth pathway. From 1999 to 2010, Beijing maintained its high-speed double-digit economic growth rate with an average annual increase of 11.4% during the 11th Five-year Plan period. Since 2011, Beijing's economic growth has slowed down. During the "12th Five-Year Plan" period, the city's GDP grew by an average of 7.5% annually. In 2016, Beijing achieved a GDP of 2489.930 billion yuan, an increase of 6.7% over the same period of the previous year, and the growth rate continued to decline, with the growth rate decreasing by 0.2% (Graph 1).

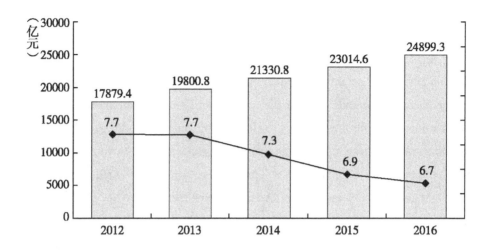

Graph 1 Beijing GDP and Growth Rate from 2012 to 2016

Resources: Statistical Communiqué of Beijing Municipality on the 2016 National Economic and Social Development

There's a trend of slowdown in Beijing's economic growth, reflecting the changes in the underlying growth momentum mechanism. It is difficult to fundamentally solve the impetus of sustained economic growth by relying solely on capital input and demand stimulation. Beijing Economic Development Report has comparatively analyzed the contribution rate of total factor (TFP) to economic growth between Beijing and other countries or regions. The results show that the contribution rate of Beijing is only 13% while that of capital accumulation is as high as 76%. The contribution of capital stock growth to economic growth exceeds the sum of contribution of labor and total factor productivity, becoming the decisive factor for Beijing's long-term economic growth.[1] However, this mode of growth based solely on the input of capital elements is unsustainable, leading to a lack of innovative driving forces for economic growth. Therefore, Beijing's economic growth and development mode must shift from demand orientation to supply-side structural reform in a timely manner, from epitaxial growth to connotation-based development and from a capital-element-driven pattern to an innovation-driven one. To carry out   supply-side reform, Beijing must resolutely implement the overall requirements of the "three

---

[1] Yang Song (ed.), Beijing Economic Development Report (2013 ~ 2014), Social Sciences Literature Publishing House, 2014, pp. 16-17.

routes, one catch-one-one plan" of the central government. It is faced with basically the same problems as in other provinces and regions across the country. However, the basic conditions, key areas and tasks of Beijing's supply-side structural reform due to the phased characteristics of Beijing's economic development are different from others. The industrial structure of the three industries, namely primary industry, secondary industry and tertiary industry, is optimized fast. The ratio of the three industries are developed from 0.9: 23.6: 75.5 in 2010 to 0.5: 19.2: 80.3 in 2016, showing that Beijing's industrial structure evolves towards high-end, service-oriented and integrated composition so as to bed for the supply side structural reform. When it comes to the key areas and key tasks of the supply-side structural reform, Beijing gives top priority to the disfusion of non-capital functions. The key tasks of supply-side reform are to reduce supply at the low end, eliminate ineffective supply and expand supply at the middle and high ends, improve public services, improve shortages in resources and environment.

1.2 The task of resolving non-capitalist functions is still very arduous, and it is necessary to further push forward stock adjustment, elimination of backward production capacity and structural optimization

In 2016, Beijing made every effort to ease non-capitals functions. The city shut down 335 general manufacturing and polluting enterprises and dispersed 117 various types of commodity markets. With strict implementation of the new list of banned and limited industries, a total of 16,400 registration applications have been rejected and the resident population continued to decrease in both growth and increment.[1] However, the task of defusing non-capitalist functions is still very heavy. First, so far only about 1/4 of the over 2,000 professional markets to be diffused has been done. These markets cover industrial fields of building materials and stones, small commodities, clothing, lights, furniture and home improvement, toy junk, luggage, antique coins, auto parts, and aquaculture, with an employment of millions of people. In 2017, the city plans to ease and relocation 120 professional markets and 38 logistics centers. Second, the clean-up and rectification of general manufacturing industry, warrens, underground space, group-oriented leasing for waste recycling and low-end manufacturing is still underway. At present, the urban areas are trying their best to eliminate the low-end processing and manufacturing industries by combining

---

[1] Cai Qi, 2017 Government Work Report. Capital Window. Retrieved from http://beijing.gov.cn, January 14, 2017

the governance of "wall breaking and wall-through hole making", illegal rental houses and "six small stores", and the city plans to demolish over 40 million square meters of illegal construction area in 2017 (Main urban area see Table 1). Third, the relocation of education, medical care and other public service institutions just started and substantive progress hasn't been realized. Fourth, the relocation of municipal administrative institutions and the central general administrative institutions has not yet begun. By the end of 2017, the "four sets of teams" of Beijing municipal government will be the first to be relocated to the sub-center of Tongzhou district, which will drive a batch of municipal administrative units to move to the sub-center. Fifth, the long-term mechanism to ease non-capitalist functions has not yet been fully consolidated. How to consolidate and mitigate the effectiveness of the work and prevent the re-occurrence and repetition are issues that need to be considered and dealt with in the future. Sixth, it is necessary to further strengthen the top-level design and policy support to ease non-capital functions. The dispersion of non-capital functions should start from supply-side structural reform. We need to integrate the alleviation of non-capital functions into the supply-side structural reform in close connection with the requirements of overall urban planning, industrial restructuring, urban spatial planning and sophisticated industries layout so as to make a favorable top-level design. We need to step up efforts in administrative law enforcement, administrative guidance, policy advocacy and mobilization of the masses, and make a clear overall requirements, work procedures and time nodes to orderly and effectively promote the work. Moreover, interest adjustment among different aspects and parties, policy convergence, policy coordination, relief and supporting services are needed as well.

Table 1 Dismantled illegal construction and eliminated backward production capacity

| Urban Areas | Illegal Construction | Key Spots of Regulation and Improvement | Backward Production Capacity Eliminated |
|---|---|---|---|
| Dongcheng District | 100,000 m² | Guijie Street area, Luogu Lane, Yonganmenwai area, etc; Vegetable | Relocate low-end wholesale markets |
| Xicheng | 120,000 m² | Shichahai, Finance Street, etc.; 30 | Relocate low-end |
| Chaoyang | 7.5 million m² | Guangqu Road, Chang'an Street, | Relocate low-end |

| Haidian District | 4 million m² | Yuquanshan Mount area, Babaoshan area, Yongding River, etc. | Relocate low-end electronic |
|---|---|---|---|
| Fengtai District | Over 1 million m² | Wholesale markets like Dahongmen market, warehouses, yards for leasing, shanty towns transformation and relocation | Relocate low-end wholesale markets and logistics |
| Shijingshan | 3.95 million m² | Warrens, leased underground space | Eliminate raw iron |
| Tongzhou | 3.95 million m² | Governance of "wall breaking and | Governance of |
| Huairou District | 350,000 m² | Governance of "wall breaking and wall-through hole making", surrounding environment of | Eliminate low-end manufacturing production capacity |
| Mentougou District | 710,000 m² | Governance of "wall breaking and wall-through hole making", shanty towns transformation and relocation | Clear up and eliminate scattered, disordered, and polutting enterprises |
| Shunyi | 4 million m² | Governance of illegal construction | Clear up and |

Source: http: //www. beijing.gov.cn/.

1.2 Inadequate vitality and competitiveness of supply side, far behind world-class cities

Compared with other major cities in the world, Beijing still lag behind in terms of innovation vitality and competitiveness of the supply side. When it comes to the urban GDP, per capita GDP, average land output, the number of multinational headquarters and other indicators in recent years, there is a big gap between Beijing and cities like New York, London, Tokyo and Paris (see Table 1), and the GDP energy consumption per unit area is higher than major metropolises in the globe (see Figure 2). The *International Urban Development Report (2017)* by Shanghai Academy of Social Sciences ranked the world's top 40 cities in the world in terms of "overall upgradeability". London, Tokyo, Paris and New York ranked the top 4 in the world and Beijing the 21st. In terms of individual indicators, Beijing ranks the 8th in "economic upgrading capability", the 12th in "cultural upgrading capability", the 40th in "ecological upgrading capability" and the 20th in "governance upgrading ability", and the "space upgrade capability in the 35th column, and the first only in "social upgrading ability".[1] The labor productivity in various industries in Beijing was significantly lower than that in Tokyo. Specifically speaking, the labor productivity of Tokyo's primary industry is 32 times that of Beijing's, secondary industry three times, and tertiary industry four times. In the rankings of domestic cities' competitiveness, although Beijing is at the forefront, its economic growth mainly depends on the aggregation of factors while innovation contributes little to economic growth. According to a study conducted by Capital University of Economics and Business, "radiation and cohesion" are the major factors that affect Beijing's comprehensive development. However, "creativity" of the city hasn't been given full play.[2]

Table 2 Comparison of Supply Efficiency and Competitiveness between Beijing and International Metropolises (2015)

| Cities / Indicators | Beijing | New York | Tokyo | London | Paris |
|---|---|---|---|---|---|
| GDP (billion USD) | 369.50 | 900.68 | 947.27 | 518.78 | 735.06 |
| Per capita GDP (USD) | 17100 | 10,5000 | 70,000 | 60,000 | 59,000 |
| Share of country's GDP (%) | 3.34 | 8. 8 | 17. 8 | 18. 1 | 30.3 |
| Everage land output (million USD/km$^2$) | 23 | 1,142 | 433 | 329 | 60 |
| Multinational corporations HQs | | | | | |
| In manufacturing industry | 26 | 111 | 326 | 96 | 96 |
| In financial industry | 46 | 141 | 181 | 91 | 46 |
| In software service | 1 | 26 | 36 | 6 | 6 |
| In high-tech industry | 11 | 36 | 81 | 46 | 21 |
| Regional HQs | 537 | 1339 | 530 | 1550 | 1415 |

Source: http: //www. imf.org/external/datamapper, http: //www.shijiejingji.net.

---

[1] Tu Qiyu (ed.). International Urban Development Report (2017). Social Sciences Literature Publishing House, 2017, pp. 63 - 66.
[2] Wen Kui, Zhu Erjuan(eds). Beijing-Tianjin-Hebei Development Report (2016). Social Sciences Academic Press, 2016, pp. 201-202.

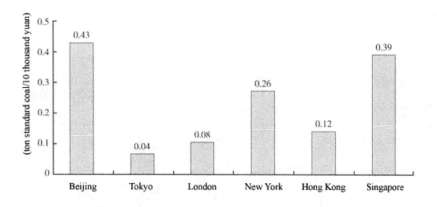

Figure 2 Regional GDP Energy Consumption per Unit Area of Beijing and Major
Cities in the World (2015)

Source: Based on *Beijing Statistical Yearbook* and other relevant data

1.4 Highlighted contradiction among population, resources and environment and
many constraints to the supply of factors

Beijing's economic development is faced with the grim situation of the contradiction
among population, resources and environment and the shortage of supply of factors.
The total population of Beijing is close to the "ceiling" of urban environmental
capacity. The city's total population, population density in its urban areas and in its
downtown areas far exceeds that of cities in other countries (Table 3). The population
density in downtown Beijing is the highest in the world. The closer to the core area,
the higher the population density is. According to the survey by Beijing Municipal
Bureau of Statistics in 2015, the population density in the urban core area of Beijing is
2.9 times, 22 times and 109.9 times that of urban function expansion area, new urban
development area and ecological conservation area respectively. Beijing is beset with
a serious shortage of water resources. The per capita availability of water resources is
much lower than that of the world's cities, and the level of water resources
exploitation and utilization is much higher than that of other cities in the world (Table
4). Coupled with heavy polluting weather and frequent haze, Beijing's bearing
capacity of resources and environment peaks near the "ceiling".

Table 3 Comparison of population size and population density between Beijing and the world cities (2016)

| Cities / Indicators | Beijing | New York | Paris | London | Tokyo |
|---|---|---|---|---|---|
| Total population (million) | 21.729 | 8.008 | 3.39 | 2.764 | 8.95 |
| City area (km$^2$) | 1350 | 785.55 | 890 | 319 | 621.98 |
| Population density in | 23953 | 7815 | 10565 | 10036 | 14389 |
| Population density in city | 16095 | 10194 | 3801 | 4542 | 6017 |

Note: "Total population" of Beijing refers to resident population. For sake of comparison, the "city area" only calculate completed city areas. The "city area" and "total population" of Tokyo calculate the areas and population of the 23 districts in central Tokyo.
Source: Ni Youpei, "A Comparative Study of the World's Big City Construction Indicators" (*Beijing Planning and Construction*, 2007, No.1) and public data by survey team of Beijing Bureau of Statistics in 2015.

Table 4 Water Supply Capacity Comparison between Beijing and Cities in the World (2015)

| Cities / Indicators | Beijing | New York | Paris | London | Tokyo |
|---|---|---|---|---|---|
| Annual rainfall (mm) | 585 | 1200 | 642 | 611 | 1533 |
| Per capita available water | 123 | 323 | 490 | 257 | 398 |
| Per capita water | 161 | 185 | 122.6 | 127 | 122 |
| Development and utilization of water resources (%) | 112 | 15.8 | 25.04 | 49.4 | 31.6 |
| Sewage treatment rate (%) | City area: 98 Whole city: 90 | 100 | 100 | 100 | 100 |

Sources: Yang Shengli et al., "Comparative Study on Water Resources Development Indicators in World Cities and Beijing" (*Beijing Water Resources*, 2011, No.4) and Beijing Statistical Communique on National Economic and Social Development in

2016.

The prominent contradictions in the population, resources and environment and short supply of factors have become bottlenecks in Beijing's supply expansion and have forced the supply-side reform to step up. It is necessary to fundamentally change the mode of economic growth at the expense of the environment and make efforts to make up for the supply of resources and the construction of the ecological environment.

1.5 The supply of public goods and public services is not balanced, and high-end quality services are under-supplied

The main problems in the supply of public services in Beijing are the unbalanced supply of public services and the large differences in the level of development between urban and rural areas, among urban functional core areas and new urban development areas and ecological conservation areas. The research shows that in addition to the balanced service level of basic education, the level of development of public services such as social security, health care, culture and sports in the urban functional core area is significantly higher than that in the new urban development areas and ecological conservation areas (see Figure 3). Quality educational resources, cultural resources and high-end medical services and facilities are mainly concentrated in Dongcheng, Xicheng, Chaoyang, Haidian and other central districts. Second, the development of public services in urban sub-centers lags behind. Tongzhou District, as a sub-center and a bridgehead for the coordinated development of Beijing, Tianjin and Hebei, is equipped with outdated infrastructure and relatively low public services like basic education, medical care, culture, sports and social security. In 2015, there were 4.85 community service agencies per thousand people in Tongzhou District, only higher than Changping District and Daxing District in the new urban development area and ecological conservation area, ranking 11th in the city, 2.44 physicians per thousand people, 2.45 nurses per thousand people, ranking last.[1] Third, the supply of high-quality services is not enough, for example, in basic education, medical care, leisure centers, retirement care, public culture and other services. Supply far falls short of demand, resulting in less access to a good school or a good retirement home.

---

[1] Source: "Beijing Public Service Development Report" research group, Beijing Municipal Bureau of Social Sciences.

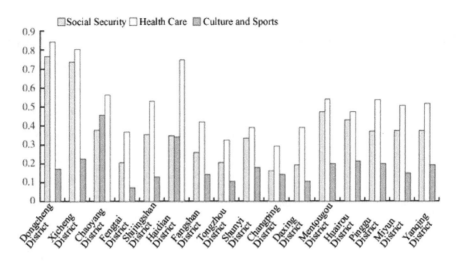

Figure 3 Comprehensive Evaluations of Public Services of Social Security, Health Care, Culture and Sports in Beijing in 2015

Source: Data from "Beijing Public Service Development Report" research group, Beijing Municipal Bureau of Social Sciences.

1.6 Sophisticated industrial structure has not yet formed; high-end manufacturing supply capacity needs to be further improved

In 2015, Beijing released *"Made in China 2025"Action Outline of Beijing,* specifying the general requirements and key industries, etc. for building a sophisticated industrial structure. However, the construction is still facing enormous challenges and pressures, such as low high-end manufacturing Industry share and inadequate supply capacity (Table 5). There are three main reasons leading to the problem. First is the slow conversion of industrial development momentum mechanism. The construction of industrial and technological innovation system with enterprises as the mainstay objectively requires a long process. Second, the transformation and upgrading of stock-based manufacturing industry are faced with multiple difficulties such as industrial choices, direction choices, technical choices and policy choices. The sophisticated industries continue to evolve, technological advances are accelerated, and the economic benefits are highly volatile, which leads to certain uncertainties and risks in the choice making of highly sophisticated industries. Third, the mechanism of safeguard and coordination of industrial transfer and relocation is not yet perfect, and industrial coordination policies are not matching, nor perfect. In particular, in order to increase the motivation for the transfer of enterprises and attractiveness of the enterprise-receiving places, it is necessary to carry out reforms and institutional design to support industrial policies under the overall framework of coordinated development of Beijing, Tianjin and Hebei and in line with the division of labor and positioning of industries in the three places.

Table 5 Development Status and Key Tasks of Beijing's Sophisticated Industrial Structure

| Sophisticated Industries | Situations and Problems | Key tasks |
|---|---|---|
| Fields choosing | Complete range of industries while not prominent sophisticated industries; transformation and upgrading of low-end manufacturing industry faces the dilemma of policy choices | Focus on the development of producer services (strategic emerging industries such as finance, information and technology services (new-generation information technology, biology, energy conservation and environmental protection), cultural creative industries, and living-oriented service industries |
| Development focuses | Low share of high-end manufacturing products; imperfect development of the industrial value chain | Focus on the development of high-end industry sectors and key industrial clusters; do a fine mid-level link and enhance reform in mid-level manufacturing |
| Space layout | The spatial layout is not balanced, concentrating mainly in Haidian District and central | Focus on the construction of the two zones (the zone of innovation and |

| | urban areas; sophisticated and non-capital industrial functions are interwoven with each other; stock adjustment and incremental control need to be arranged rationally in terms of space | development in the north and south centered on the demonstration zone of Zhongguancun); and form the industrial layout of "4 + N" in the vast space of Beijing-Tianjin-Hebei region |
|---|---|---|
| Coordinated policies | The homogeneity and isomorphism of the industries in Beijing, Tianjin and Hebei are serious. The coordinated development of industries needs to be strengthened. The management mode of "building, managing and sharing" is not perfect | Promote industrial cooperation between Beijing, Tianjin and Hebei and co-construction of Beijing-Hebei Parks; improve relevant policies on Beijing's industrial transfer to promote enterprises to transfer initiatively and to enhance the enthusiasm of industry receivers |
| High-end industry zones | The positioning of high-end industry zones needs further refinement;The "Six High & Four New" function areas have low power of industrial gathering and influence | Enhance the gathering ability and influence of high-end industry zones and build the high-end industry zones into the main development areas of sophisticated industries |
| Low-end industry relocation | Large pressure on technology and resources during restructuring and upgrading of general manufacturers; relatively slow transformation and upgrading process | To further refine the directory of relocation for general manufacturing enterprises and production links in high-end manufacturing enterprises; Clear transfer timing and |

| | | layout requirements; improve safeguard mechanism |
| --- | --- | --- |

## 2. Main tasks to promote supply-side structural reform in Beijing

According to the general requirements of "implementing supply-side structural reform and accelerating the building of a world-class harmonious and livable capital" issued by the CPC Beijing Municipal Party Committee and the municipal government, the main tasks of Beijing's structural reform on the supply side is to maintain the five major concepts of innovation, coordination, greenness, opening up, and mutual sharing, to center on five key missions of "cut overcapacity, de-stock, de-leverage, reduce costs, and improve weak link", to be in close connection with the five working focuses of "dispersing functions, changing modes, improving environment, making up for shortcomings, and promoting coordination", to emphasize "elimination", "governance", and "improvement" to ease industrial burdens, make up for shortages, and achieve comprehensive innovation, to make special efforts to address institutional problems that constrains economic and social development, to realize economic development with higher quality, more efficiency, more fairness and stronger sustainability. The author believes that the main tasks should be focused on the following five aspects.

### 2.1 Dispersing functions

Defragmenting the non-capital function is actually a supply-side structural reform. On January 15, 2017, Cai Qi emphasized in his government work report at the Beijing Municipal People's Congress, "At present and for a period in the future, we should work closely around the coordinated development strategy of Beijing, Tianjin and Hebei focusing on the solution of non-capital functions. The dispersion of non-capital functions is actually the supply-side structural reform. Indeed, it requires the structural adjustment and mode changes, clearing up the cage for new birds, the upgrade of the quality of urban development, the improvement of living environment, the alleviation of contradiction between population and resources and environment, and well performance of the duties of the city as China's capital."[1] Deep down, to ease non-capital functions is to reduce inefficient and low-end supply. It is a matter of

---

[1] Cai Qi, "Dispersing non-capital functions is actually supply-side structural reform", *Beijing Daily.* January 15, 2017.

"de-", namely "cut capacity, de-stocks, and de-leverage". Further enhance the supply capacity that serves capital's core functions and fortify the strategic positioning of the "four centers" of the city by relocating non-capital functions. Therefore, dispersing function is an important measure and approach to fundamentally optimize and improve the supply structure, as well as a main task of Beijing to deepen its structural reform on the supply side.

First, we must improve the long-term incentive mechanism to speed up inventory ease and strictly implement incremental control. In February 2017 when President Xi Jinping inspected Beijing, he emphasized that "to disperse non-capital functions is the key for Beijing's city planning and construction. In this regard, we should further unify our thinking, focus on moving out and settling down, study and formulate supporting policies to form an effective incentive and guidance mechanism."[1] It is necessary to speed up the dispersion of key agencies, industries, and enterprises including "general industries (especially low-end manufacturing industries), regional specialized markets, some education and medical services, some social public services, and some administrative services", so as to achieve remarkable results in the upgrading of the city's regional wholesale markets and industrial format and the moving out of a group of medical and educational institutions by 2020. At the same time, strictly enforce the newly added catalog of banned and restricted industries and promote the implementation of more stringent access standards for environment and resources so that the increment of non-capital functions could be strictly and effectively controlled.

The second is to "cut capacity", resolutely resolving overcapacity and reducing ineffective supply. The "capacity cutting" work mainly focuses on industries with overcapacity and "three highs" such as steel and coal. Currently, Shougang Group still retains about 10 million tons of pig iron and crude steel production capacity, which calls for further resolution of the excessive steel capacity and promotion of the transformation and upgrading of its old industrial zones. In the context of strict control and governance of air pollution, the city is still facing 6 million tons of coal production capacity to exit and the goal of full closure of coal mines by 2020.

---

[1] "Xi Jinping inspects Beijing: do a good job in city planning and construction and in preparation of the Winter Olympic Games". Retrieved from http://www.china.com.cn.

Third, we must "de-leverage" to strengthen regulation and control of and to promote supply and demand balance in the real estate market. In terms of "deleveraging", Beijing's main task is not to face the debt risk of local governments in comparison with other provinces and cities but the leverage risk in real estate. According to the local government debt data released by provinces, autonomous regions and municipalities in 2015, the debt ratio of Guizhou, Liaoning, Inner Mongolia and Yunnan provinces exceeded 100% warning line. In 2015, the balance of local government debts in Beijing reached 668.9 billion yuan, down by 8.81% year on year and its debt ratio was 83.3%, slightly below the national average of 84.4%. Among them, the general debt was 149.5 billion yuan, accounting for 22.4% and the special debt was 519.4 billion yuan, accounting for 77.6%. In 2016, the Ministry of Finance approved Beijing its new government debt of 520.2 billion yuan (of which general debt was 49.2 billion yuan and special debt 3 billion yuan). Looking at the overall level of debt, the local government debt in Beijing is within controllable and safe range. From the perspective of the structure of the debt funds, the debts of the Beijing local government are mainly in livelihood-related areas such as rail transit, the construction of city sub-centers, the new capital airport, dispersion of non-capital functions, and transformation of shantytowns. The corresponding assets are mainly substantive assets. Therefore, the main task of Beijing's "deleveraging" should be to resolve real estate risks and high leverage rate. In the case of prominent contradiction between supply and demand, the price of commercial housing in Beijing has been at a high level for a long time. The real estate bubble is more serious. High leverage has increased the speculative property of real estate and the real estate market risk. It is necessary to resolutely stick to the positioning of "the house is used for housing rather than for speculation" put forward at the Central Economic Work Conference and the living attributes of houses and apartments. We should comprehensively use such means as finance, land, taxation, investment and legislation to curb speculative activities and maintain stable housing price and resume the living attribute of houses. Moreover, a housing system focusing on both purchasing and leasing should be established, the government should play its role in providing basic housing support, and the market should take the lead to meet people's multiple demands for housing so as to promote supply and demand balance in the real estate market.

2.2 Scale control

Controlling the scale mainly refers to controlling the scale of Beijing's urban development and the total population size so as to overcome the blind expansion of the city and promote "smart growth", to prevent population explosion, traffic congestion, and environmental pollution, and to fundamentally cure the "big city disease". Cities are likely to form economies of scale. However, polarization of resource gathering may lead to diseconomies of scale and significantly enhanced negative externalities. Agglomeration effects lead to urban expansion and proliferation effect to urban fission, which is the basic law of "expansion - fission" of city size. Therefore, the size of a city does not expand indefinitely and it must be properly controlled in the case of diseconomies of scale. The blind expansion of Beijing and the rapid growth of population are fundamentally caused by the disorder of supply, the expansion of demand and the imbalance between supply and demand. Controlling the scale means "resolving the contradiction between the supply side and the demand side from the source"[1], ensuring effective supply, restraining excessive and unreasonable demand, and balancing the supply and demand in the process of development.

First, we must control the excessive growth of population, and optimize and adjust the population structure. The regulation of population includes two tasks. First, we must coordinate the population size and distribution, that is, to achieve "Beijing's permanent population is controlled within 23 million by 2020 and permanent residents in its six urban districts reduce by 15% compared with 2014", controlling total population while realizing a balanced distribution of population. Secondly, we must coordinate the size and structure of population. While controlling population size, we should constantly optimize and adjust population structure so as to adapt to and meet the demands of special talents like high-tech professionals in line with the strategic positioning of Beijing as "four centers".

The second is to rationally control the scale of urban development, delineate the rigid boundary of urban growth, and prevent blind expansion and savage growth of cities. The new urban development plan being edited will shift from "incremental planning" to "reduction planning", demarcating the boundaries of urban growth and the red line of ecological protection in the whole city, dividing the urban space into the ecological

---

[1] Zhao Hong. "Advancing path and effect of Beijing supply-side structural reform", *Beijing Daily*. 26 September 2016.

protection zone and concentrated construction area and limited construction area, and implementing differentiated control policies. Bottom line is emphasized in the ecological protection zone; border of construction is strictly governed in the concentrated construction area; and "reducing construction land and increasing green land" is to be realized in the limited construction area.

2.3 Layout optimization

To optimize layout mainly refers to the rational arrangement of various resources, elements and industries in the city within the scope of space and region through optimized planning. In the process of urban construction, management and operation, urban planning plays an important role of leading and rigid control. That is, planning comes first. Therefore, urban planning is essentially a kind of supply management. Optimize the layout, in essence, is to optimize planning and supply, to achieve scientific planning, to better meet the needs during city construction, management, production and living. In February 2017 when President Xi Jinping inspected Beijing, he pointed out that "What kind of capital to build and how to build the capital are the questions Beijing should consider during its city planning. At the same time, Beijing should grasp the strategic positioning, spatial layout, and elemental configuration, stick to urban-rural integration and implement 'unification of multiple standards'. Form a blueprint for planning and make efforts to enhance the core functions of the capital so as to ensure that the service support capability is in line with the city's strategic positioning, that the population, resources and environment is coordinated with the city's strategic positioning, and that urban layout is in accordance with the city's strategic positioning, and to strive towards the goal of becoming a world-class harmonious and livable city."[1] As for Beijing, the optimization of layout mainly refers to the optimization of urban spatial layout, structural layout of industries, and the layout of urban sub-centers, as well as the construction of a world-class urban cluster with the capital as its core.

First is to optimize the layout of urban space in Beijing to achieve compact, efficient and green development. Beijing used to set up an urban space layout of "two axes - two belts - multiple centers". With the implementation of Beijing-Tianjin-Hebei coordinated development strategy and the further ease of non-capital functions, the

---

[1] "Deliver, study and implement the important speech by General Secretary of Xi Jinping during inspection in Beijing", *Beijing Daily*. February 26, 2017.

structure and layout of space in the city have also been changed and optimized. Generally, the city aims at "compact, intensive and green" development, with coordination among Beijing, Tianjin and Hebei Province and in line with the layout of "one core, one sub-center, two axes, multiple centers and micro-centers", shaping an urban space pattern of clear functions, combination of center and sub-centers, reasonable division of labor, and distinctive characteristics. "One core" refers to the central area of the city. Its spatial layout mainly focuses on the functional orientation of "political and cultural center" that embodies the combination of high end with modernity, and integrates history and culture with modern civilization. "One sub-center" refers to the urban sub-center; "Two axes" refer to the extension of Chang'an Avenue and the central axis; "Multi-centers" mean new urban areas represented by Shunyi, Yizhuang, Daxing, Changping, Fangshan, Huairou, Miyun, Yanqing, Mentougou; "Micro-centers" refer to key towns around metros and emerging small towns. At the same time, it is necessary to greatly expand green and ecological space in the city, reduce production space, and appropriately increase the proportion of residential land and supporting land. We should also implement the green extension projects to form an urban green landscape of "green and colorful all year round". Through the implementation of projects "first green belt circles city parks, second green belt circles countryside parks, and capital-centered wetland park ring" to build green and ecological leisure circle and put green development into urban space layout. Second is to optimize the structure and layout of industries in Beijing and strive to form a sophisticated industrial structure. Under the background that the tertiary industry accounts for more than 80% of GDP, the focus of industrial restructuring in Beijing is to continue to push forward the transformation of the industrial structure toward high-end, service-oriented and agglomeration, strive to promote the development of modern high-end manufacturing and strategic emerging industries, advance the transformation and upgrading of the stock manufacturing industry, strengthen the reserve of highly sophisticated projects, cultivate new industry formats, and spur integration and service-oriented development of industries.

Third is to make high positioning of the sub-center. The construction of Beijing's sub-center is an important decision of the Party Central Committee. Beijing should uphold the planning and construction of the sub-center in accordance with the world vision, international standards, Chinese characteristics and high positioning and with the spirit of creating history and pursuing art, and build the sub-center into a demonstration area for world-class harmonious and livable community, for new urbanization, and for coordinated development of Beijing-Tianjin-Hebei region. The development of Beijing's sub-center will be in accordance with the layout of "one belt, one axis and many groups"[1], aiming at the eco-city layout with intertwined blue and green colors, freshness and brightness, water and city integration, and intensive development of multiple groups. "One belt" refers to the formation of a blue and green ecological civilization zone with the framework of the Grand Canal; "One Axis" means to form an axis of innovation and development along the Sixth Ring Road; "groups" means to form livelihood sharing group by relying on networks of water, green plants and roads.

Fourth, we must establish and improve a world-class city group with the capital as the core. The development of Beijing should be planned from the large perspective of Beijing, Tianjin and Hebei Province as a region, and examined from the large scale coordinated development of the region. It also requires efforts to construct and perfect a world-class urban cluster with the capital city as the core, to achieve functional complementation and regional linkage among the three places, and to form a network space development pattern with traffic arteries and ecological corridor as links.

## 2.4 Costs reduction

Cost reduction is a systematic and long-term work that refers to reducing the comprehensive cost of business operations, including those for institutional transaction, labor, taxation, financing and financial affairs, production factors, and logistics and so on. Cost reduction is to clean up all kinds of non-compliant and unreasonable policy measures, remove barriers to business innovation and entrepreneurship, reduce the overall cost of social enterprises and form new advantages of economic growth and development in Beijing from the perspective of system supply and through optimized policy design.

First is to reduce institutional transaction costs. Publicize the list of government powers and responsibilities, comprehensively clean up and regulate policies and measures about fees and charges related to enterprises, order all types of

---

[1] "Mayor of Beijing: City Sub-center should be a metropolitan area without urban diseases", *Beijing News*. March 7, 2017.

enterprises-related charging and funds, and cancel or reduce some administrative fees. Continue in delegating powers while improving regulation, and optimizing government services. Continue to streamline a number of items require administrative examination and approval, a number of items need vocational qualification identification and a number of pre-and post-approval matters during industrial and commercial registration, and put an end to non-administrative licensing examination and approval. We will deepen and improve pilot reform of the investment examination and approval system, improve the online regulatory approval platform for investment projects and improve service efficiency. Deepen and improve pilot for reform of investment examination and approval system, perfect online regulatory approval platform for investment projects and increase service efficiency.

The second is to reduce corporate financing costs, financial costs and tax costs. We will step up efforts to increase financial support, strengthen the construction of the national center for science and technology innovation in Zhongguancun, vigorously develop the angel investment and venture capital, enhance the share transfer system for MSEs, regional equity markets of Beijing, and the quotation and service system for private placement products in institutions, and push forward innovation of debt and financing tools for tech-corporations. Pilot banks for investment in loans should be set up to improve the investment and financing mechanisms for small and medium-sized and micro enterprises, to reduce financing and financial costs. The police of "replacing business tax with value-added tax" should be fully implemented, as well as favorable taxation policies such as R&D costs deduction and venture capital.

Third, reduce labor costs. The minimum guaranteed wage of employees has been increasing steadily. The expenditure on social insurance for employees has been gradually increased. The labor cost has risen rapidly, resulting in the continuous increase in labor costs. Affected by the slowdown in economic growth in recent years, although the minimum wage benchmark in Beijing in 2016 remained at 9%, down compared with 12% in 2014 and 10.5% in 2015, the minimum wage growth in 2016 Off-line was 4%, up by 0.5% from 3.5% in the previous year. In the coming "13th Five-Year Plan" period, the minimum wage in Beijing will keep increasing. Therefore, we should keep the income growth in line with the improvement of the enterprise's labor productivity, establish a reasonable income growth mechanism, and improve the minimum wage guarantee system that suits the level of economic development. It is the principle to uphold to both protect the legitimate rights and interests of workers and to ensure that rising income levels while reducing labor costs.

Fourth, reduce the cost of production factors such as resources and logistics costs. Beijing's overall energy costs, raw materials, land and other factors of production are on an upward trend. Reducing the cost of production factors aims at improving the utilization efficiency of energy, raw materials, land and other factors of production, reducing energy consumption per unit of GDP and improving land use effectiveness. We should rationalize the pricing mechanism for resource products, continue to improve the mechanism of resources' price being mainly determined by market, increase resource allocation efficiency and reduce the cost of production factors. In 2016, the total cost of social logistics in China accounted for 14.8% of GDP while that of Beijing was nearly 12%, its proportion of GDP being slightly below the national average. In the current context of dispersion of non-capital functions, transformation of some large-scale commercial logistics facilities, coupled with urban traffic limits, logistics costs in Beijing are facing upward pressure. Therefore, it is crucial to strengthen scientific and technological innovation in logistics, to achieve quality instead of scale, to upgrade low-end logistics to high-end, to shift from high consumption to low carbon and environmentally friendly, to achieve organizational innovation in logistics, and to reduce logistics service costs.

2.5 Make up for shortcomings

Make up for shortcomings is essentially to supplement and improve the supply. It is necessary to adhere to the people-centered development thinking and focus on current major tasks of implementing the strategic positioning of the capital city, dispersion of non-capital functions, the governance of "urban diseases" and the construction of sub-centers. Starting from dealing with most concerned and urgent issues among the people, we should launch a series of tactics and measures from the supply side to solve the key problems such as ecological environment and traffic congestion, raise the overall governance level, enhance development of public services, and facilitate a convenient, comfortable and better city life.

First, we must strengthen the ecological environment governance. Serious air pollution like frequent occurrence of smog and continuously high PM2.5 and the contradiction among population, resources and environment are prominent, constraining the development of the city. Therefore, we must take more efforts in governing air pollution, speeding up the reduction of pollution caused by using coals, and basically realizing coal free in the six urban districts and plain areas such as Tongzhou District, Daxing District, and Fangshan District. Motor vehicle pollution should be strictly controlled. Beijing's sixth phase of motor vehicle fuel standards should be implemented. More stringent traffic control measures on high-standard emission vehicles should be posed. Beijing should make resolution to reduce production pollution, through differential energy prices and sewage charges, and enhance the comprehensive disposal of rubbish, and establish rubbish classification and a system of rubbish collection, transferring and disposal that covers full area of the city.

The second is to speed up control on traffic congestion, a prominent manifestation of "urban disease" in Beijing as well as an issue that raises great concern of the entire society. More importantly, it is another shortcoming that restricts the development of the capital and a chronic illness that hinders the city life from becoming more convenient, comfortable and wonderful. Thus we should develop the urban rail transit system, encrypted rail transit network cable, optimize road network, connect the micro-circulated roads in the six urban districts, integrate and upgrade the intelligent traffic management system, enhance the operation efficiency of urban roads, and effectively solve the difficulties of the masses of people in traveling.

Third, we must improve the city's comprehensive management. In accordance with the requirements of the Central City Work Conference in December 2015, we will perfect the urban governance system and improve the governance capacity, build a comprehensive governance system and mechanism that is in line with the role of mega city of the capital and make every effort to solve such prominent problems as "urban disease." To this end, management of the city should be "as fine and detailed as embroidery"[1].

---

[1] General Secretary Xi in the Two Sessions: urban management should be as fine as embroidery. Retrieved from http://china.cnr.cn. 9 March 5, 2017.

3. Main approaches for Beijing to promote supply-side structural reform

Beijing's supply-side structural reform must meet the overall requirements of the capital city's functional and strategic positioning. Based on the phased characteristics of Beijing's economic development, the overall requirements of defusing non-capital functions and the characteristics of industrial structure and by defining focuses and grasping the main objectives, directions, key areas and core elements of the supply-side structural reform, precise measures are taken and implemented steadily so as to deepen the reform.

3.1 Take defusing non-capital functions, speeding up structural adjustment and expanding middle and high-end supply as the main direction of supply-side structural reform

The structural reform on the supply side must first pinpoint the major contradictions during and the main direction of the reform. At present, it should lay emphasis on defusing function, adjustment of structure and expansion of middle and high-end supply.

Accelerate non-capital functions dispersal. Deconstructing the non-capitalist functions is an important task and main direction of Beijing's supply-side structural reform. In accordance with the strategic positioning of the "four centers" of the capital, non-capital functions should be systematically defused from the urban centers. By doing so, we will make reasonable adjustments to urban spatial structure, industrial structure, elemental structure and population distribution so as to reduce the supply of low-end and eliminate ineffective supply, fundamentally solve the complicated problems exposed in the process of urban development in Beijing, and promote the fundamental transformation of Beijing's economic development mode. Undoubtedly, to ease non-capital functions is the focus of Beijing's supply-side reform at present.

Continue to expand high-end supply. Firstly, we must upgrade the supply of medium and high-end public services, adhere to the principle of paying equal attention to both producer services and livelihood services by guiding the producer services to the specialized, branding and the high-end extension of the value chain and promoting life services to be fine, high-quality, customer-oriented, multi-level and diversified, and create "a quarter of an hour community service circle" to meet the ever-increasing needs of the people towards public service and enhance their sense of happiness and acquisition. Second, it is necessary to expand the supply of high-end manufacturing industries, implement the *Beijing's Action Plan for "Made in China 2025"* as well as the "3458" Action Plan, break through shortcomings bottlenecks in industries, focus on cutting-edge innovative products and technologies, facilitate the transformation from "Made in Beijing " to "Create in Beijing", promote docking and inter-regional integration and high-end development of industries. The third is to focus on the platform economy, sharing economy, cloud computing, big data and Internet of things. We should actively cultivate new technologies, new services, new models and new formats based on "Internet +" and "big data" to expand supply. We will support the moderate and standardized development of sharing bicycles, internet-bound taxis, and logistics and express delivery which are based on Internet technologies and actively develop new economic formats such as mobile payment, online services and internet finance.

3.2 Give the promotion of capability in scientific and technological innovation during supply-side structural reform, give full play to the function as the national center for science and technology innovation, and implement innovation-driven actions to further stimulate the supply-side innovation vitality

Science and technology are primary productive forces. It is necessary to give play to the advantages of science and technology of Beijing, put the promotion of scientific and technological innovation in the first place in the supply-side structural reform, and always firmly grasps the kinetic energy of scientific and technological innovation, stick to innovation-driven orientation, and stimulates innovative vitality.

Strive to build a science and technology innovation center with global influence. Define functional positioning and requirements for the National Center for Science and Technology Innovation and make the best use of scientific and technological and personnel advantages, and make efforts to enhance the original innovation ability. Therefore, it is necessary to intensify the leading role of Zhongguancun Demonstration Zone in terms of innovation and further tap the existing policy potentials of "1 + 6" and "New 4 Articles" so as to take the lead in building the Zone into a technological innovation base with global influence.

Focus on improving the enterprise-based technology innovation system. The emphasis of technological innovation is in enterprises. We should actively build a business-led collaborative innovation system, strengthen the dominant position of enterprises in innovation, optimize the environment for business growth, attract enterprises to increase investment in technological innovation, and reduce costs for business innovation and entrepreneurship.

Establish major technology projects, especially some major projects that suits Beijing, reflects directions of scientific and technological innovation and represents scientific and technological forefront from both technical supply and demands. Focus on key scientific fields such as new materials, biomedicine and human health, earth system and environment. Pay special attention to emerging industries of strategic significance such as new-generation information technology, biology, energy conservation and environmental protection, and new energy vehicles, so as to select from them a group of key and leading technological projects.

3.3 To improve the supply structure and enhance competitiveness as the core content of supply-side structural reform and enhance the supply structure's adaptability and flexibility to changes in demand

Constantly improve and perfect the supply structure system and enhance the competitiveness of the supply structure are the core contents of Beijing's supply-side structural reforms. Specifically, it is necessary to strengthen the system of supply, improve the supply of elements, perfect the supply system, give play to the initiative on the supply side and the initiative of policy supply, and enhance the adaptability and flexibility of the supply structure to changes in demand.

Strengthen institutional supply. In the supply structure and system, the institutional supply is at the core. Supply-side structural reform is essentially an innovation-based reform of institutional supply. In recent decades, the process of China's economic reform has been essentially a supply-side structural reform process. The "Chinese miracle" created by economic growth is essentially a "supply-side effect"[1] and system effect. Through deepening the reform of the system, strengthening the supply of the system, correcting the distortion of the distribution of resources, removing the bottleneck of system constraints and supply restraint, and releasing the vitality of the micro-main body, Beijing must deepen the reform of "running the service" and vigorously promote the simplification of key areas Decentralization, institutional innovation in key areas such as investment and financing system, construction of science and technology innovation center, reform of state-owned enterprises and industrial coordination of Beijing, Tianjin and Hebei.

Improve the supply of elements. From the perspective of Beijing's economic structure, overcapacity mainly concentrates in areas of high energy consumption, high pollution and low-end industries. The insufficiency of supply mainly lies in the weak supply of middle and high-end, unbalanced supply of public services and the failure of social security housing construction to meet the demand. This supply structure reflects the serious distortion of resource allocation. To eliminate this distortion, we must deepen the marketization reform of labor, land, capital and other factors of production, rationally allocate production factors and resources and allocate resources to industries and fields with high marginal efficiency through market mechanisms. At the same time, through the supply side of the supply of elements to curb unreasonable demand, especially the abnormal development of the real estate market, appropriately increase the supply of affordable housing to curb the rapid growth of housing prices, and resolutely curb real estate speculative demand.

Improve the supply system. We should actively develop the supply of multi-agents, give play to the role of the market mechanism, stimulate the enthusiasm of various market players, encourage non-governmental capital to participate in the city's infrastructure construction, public service supply and environmental governance, and strive to provide education, health care, affordable housing, health care, Other areas such as the formation of a new supply.

3.4 Redline Constraints to Promote Intensive Development and Promote Resource Intensification Making Use of the Important Objectives of Structural Reform of Water

---

[1] Fang Min & Hu Tao. "Political Economy of Supply-Side Structural Reform", *Shandong Social Sciences*, 2016, No.6.

Supply Side to Reduce Supply Costs and Improve Supply Efficiency

Beijing's economic development needs to take the path of intensive development and strengthen the hard constraints. It is necessary to implement "double control" of the total amount and intensity of the use of resources and energy, and reduce the inefficient utilization and use of resources and energy. We should increase the level of resource and energy utilization and supply efficiency as an important goal of supply-side structural reforms.

Strengthen the population "ceiling", ecological red lines and urban development boundaries "hard constraints." Beijing must unswervingly follow the path of intensive development. Mayor Cai Qi pointed out that the "population ceiling" 4 means that the resident population in Beijing should be controlled within 23 million by 2020. The ecological red line means that the area of ecological red line area will reach 75% by 2030 from 73% today. Urban development boundary is to adhere to the development of urban and rural areas to reduce the development of urban and rural construction land for the current status of 2921 square kilometers, reduced to 2800 square kilometers in 2020 less than 2,700 square kilometers by 2030[1]. The "hard constraint" between the red line and urban development boundary is to force the supply side to define the boundary, bottom line, red line and warning line of urban development.

Strictly implement the total amount of water and intensity of "double control." Beijing is an extremely resource-poor city. In 2016, the per capita available water resources in Beijing was 123 cubic meters, while that of water resources development and utilization reached 112%, indicating that Beijing has overused and exploited its water resources. Therefore, Beijing should implement the most stringent water resources management system, refine the control of water resources development and utilization, limit the "three red lines" of water use efficiency control and water functional areas, and reduce the water consumption per unit GDP.

Strictly implement the total energy consumption and consumption intensity "double control." Beijing is an energy-hungry mega-city with a serious lack of energy self-sufficiency and high dependence on foreign countries. Natural gas, oil products and electricity rely mainly on external inputs. In recent years, Beijing's total energy

---

[1] "Cai Qi First Debut in Beijing Open Day during Two Sessions, Responding to Capital Construction Outlook" Retrieved from http://wepaper.jinghua.cn.

consumption and its intensity upward trend have been brought under control. However, the situation is still very serious. Therefore, it is necessary to strictly control the energy consumption cap, strengthen the target responsibility assessment, strengthen the real-time monitoring and intelligent control of energy consumption of key energy consuming units and industries, and reduce the energy consumption per unit GDP.

3.5 Put together the world's high-end elements, enhance the ability of global resource allocation as an important way to supply-side structural reforms to make up for shortages and weak links

From the formation process of international cities, they generally follow the five development paths of "location path, political path, economic path, cultural path and environmental path". ![1] As a national capital and a world city with Chinese characteristics, Beijing should further implement the functional orientation of Beijing International Exchange Center and give full play to its path advantages in location, politics, economy and culture. With the implementation of the "four services" and "the Belt and Road Initiatives" National strategy and opening up to the outside world, we should take the initiative to integrate into the process of economic globalization and "bring in" through "going global" to bring together the global high-end elements and make efforts to enhance our own ability to allocate resources globally.

Improve global high-end resource allocation and aggregation capabilities. To be a world-class, harmonious and livable city, Beijing must gather the world's most advanced elements and enhance its ability to allocate and gather resources around the world. First, we must enhance international activities and the gathering capacity of international organizations and strive to build Beijing into an ideal place for major international events, an international first-class convention center, an international tourist destination, and a headquarters or regional headquarters of major international organizations. We will promote the gathering of high-end international trade, culture, science and technology by hosting major international conferences, the Winter Olympics and horticultural expositions. The second is to enhance the ability of international high-end talents to gather, provide more convenient conditions for foreigners to leave and enter the country, reside in Beijing, work and children's

---

[1]  Li Liping. "Theory and Practice of International Cities - The Forming Mechanism, Development Model and Forming Path of International Cities", Group Co., Ltd., 2016.

education, and strengthen the introduction and gathering of high-end international talents by further simplifying visas and establishing a green card for personnel.

Make up short supply and weak links. Beijing supply-side short-board mainly focused on insufficient innovation and vitality, unbalanced development of high-quality public services, inadequate protection of resources and energy supply, high levels of energy resources such as urban hydropower and oil and gas, and insufficient sewage garbage disposal capacity. First, we should make up for the lack of innovation vitality of the short board, vigorously implement the innovation-driven strategy, give full play to the advantages of scientific and technological innovation in Zhongguancun, through the "one area of 16 parks" to promote innovation and development in the city. Second, we must make up for the shortfall in social welfare and solve the problem of uneven development in the provision of quality public services. We will make overall plans for the development of public services in urban and rural areas and promote the balanced, balanced and coordinated development of public services in urban and rural areas as well as between urban and rural areas, urban sub-centers and suburban areas, and vigorously develop public services such as high-quality medical care, education and pension. In the era of moderate cross-aging population in Beijing, we must pay special attention to pension short-board, and actively develop the "medical-health-integration" model to effectively alleviate the structural conflicts such as the uneven distribution of pension institutions, lack of care and nursing care . We will encourage social capital to enter the non-basic public service areas, promote innovation in service industries and cross-border integration, expand effective supply and strive to solve people's livelihood problems such as "difficulties in finding people's homes, difficulty in seeing a doctor, and endowment insurance for the aged." Third, we must make up for shortcomings of municipal utilities, vigorously improve the urban sewage and garbage disposal capacity. Beijing faces the risk pressure of lack of garbage siege and sewage treatment capacity. It is necessary to vigorously promote the marketization reform of municipal utilities, popularize and apply the PPP model, and encourage social capital both at home and abroad to enter the public service of municipal services. Fourth, we must make efforts to make up for the city's weak links. Strengthen hydropower, oil and gas and other resources, energy scheduling, reserves and security capabilities to enhance emergency warning and management capabilities to ensure the safe operation of super-large cities in the capital.

References:

Zhao Hong. "Advancing path and effect of Beijing supply-side structural reform", *Beijing Daily*, September 26, 2016.

Ju Jinju. "The Main Contradictions and Supply-Side Structural Reforms in the New Normal of Economic Development", *Journal of Political Economy*, Volume 7, Issue 2, 2016.

Wei Lu & Wang Xiaoyan. "Thoughts and Suggestions on Promoting Supply-Side Structural Reform in Shanghai", Shanghai Economic Research, No.8, 2016.

Li Liping. "Theory and Practice of International Cities - The Forming Mechanism, Development Model and Forming Path of International Cities", Group Co., Ltd., 2016.

Tu Qiyu(eds), International Urban Development Report (2017), Social Sciences Academic Press, 2017.

Wen Kui & Zhu Erjuan (ed). "Beijing-Tianjin-Hebei Development Report (2016)", Social Sciences Press, 2016.

Ni Youpei. "Study on the World's Big Cities", "Beijing Planning and Construction". 2007, No.1.

Yang Shengli, Wu Wenyong, Hao Zhongyong, "Water Development Indicators of World Cities and Beijing Comparative Study ",*Beijing Water Resources*, 2011, No.4.

Beijing Municipal Bureau of Statistics. *Beijing Statistical Communique on National Economic and Social Development in 2016.*

# Promote Social Fairness and Increase Residents' Sense of Gain

## Li Weidong[1]

## Abstract

In 2016, the social development in Beijing was in a good state. However, there are still some problems. For example, the rapid rise in housing prices has led to more serious problems of people's livelihood, traffic congestion, poor social satisfaction with motor vehicle number shaking policies, large income gap between urban and rural areas, Unfair distribution of outstanding issues, the pressure of employment requirements still exist; early arrival of an aging society, the quality of social life of the elderly groups urgently need to be improved; foreign migrants should pay attention to the form of family relocation, social services need to be improved; community governance complex contradictions, Pattern to be formed. Through the analysis of the above issues, this report proposes: appropriately increase residents' income, strengthen the planning and construction of affordable housing; vigorously promote green travel to ensure fair distribution of resources; promote rural industrial upgrading, strive to narrow the gap between urban and rural areas; promote technological innovation and industrial upgrading, improve the level of employment; adhere to the classification of governance, key governance and local governance, improve the level of community governance; according to the law to organize social services, improve service level of society; emphasis on community education of the elderly, improve the quality of life of the elderly, correctly handle the floating population The current situation of family mobility, improve their sense of city access.

Keywords: Beijing, people's livelihood, social development, social fairness

In 2016, Beijing enjoyed steady social development, slowed population growth and considerable achievements in various fields of social construction. The social public service system was further improved and the governance level improved. The social work system was consolidated and its vitality for social development was enhanced. The social security beneficiaries expanded and the level of protection was gradually

---

[1] Li Weidong,Associate Researcher,Research Institute of Sociology, Beijing Academy of Social Sciences. Research areas include community governance and social policies.

raised. The labor system and service mechanism were advanced.

At the same time, there are still many problems that deserve our attention: rapid housing prices, resulting in the problem of people's livelihood is still grim; traffic congestion is still an important social issue, social satisfaction towards motor vehicle blind selection is not high; the income gap between urban and rural areas is still very The pressure of large and new employment needs still exists. With the advent of an aging society, the quality of social life of the elderly needs to be improved urgently. The absolute number of migrants is still huge. The form of family relocation is worthy of attention. The demand for social services still needs to be improved; Community governance complex contradictions, multi-party governance pattern has yet to be formed.

From the perspectives of people's livelihood, community governance and services of disadvantaged groups, this report provides a preliminary review of the social development in Beijing over the past year and puts forward relevant suggestions.

1. Analysis on Current Social Development

1.1 Social economy developed steadily, and the population growth slowed down

Statistics show that in 2016, the economic growth in Beijing was stable with a GDP of 23014.6 billion yuan, a per capita capital of 106,497 yuan and a value of 17,099 U.S. dollars (see Figure 1). Compared with the "12th Five-Year Plan" period, the pace of economic development in Beijing has slowed down but still maintained a relatively high level of growth. Moreover, with the relocation of non-capital core functions and the gradual improvement of urban functional space allocation, the quality of economic growth will be enhanced.

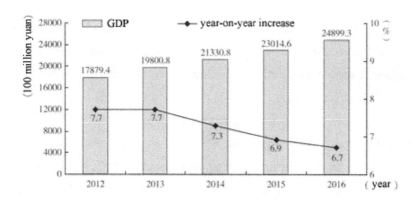

Figure 1 Regional GDP and Growth Rate (2012-2016)

Resources: Beijing Municipal Bureau of Statistics

In 2016, the resident population in Beijing slowed down and made initial achievements in alleviating the core functions of the non-capital city. With the transfer of non-capitals, "taking the lead in management" achieved some success. The growth rate of population slowed down year by year. For the first time in 2016, it achieved single-digit growth (see Figure 2), laying a solid foundation to ease the pressure on capital resources and the environment.

1.2 The public service system has been further improved and the level of social governance has been continuously raised.

Community service system continues to improve. The city's urban community basically achieves management and service space standards. In 2016, 106 newly built "one-minute community service circles" in Beijing totaled 1,342 and the community coverage reached 84%. Beijing Municipal Commission of Social Work continued to promote the "Top Ten Coverage Projects" for community service and continuously enriched its services and facilities. The city built 1,700 commercial and convenience outlets and 550 new business outlets. Social Work Committee also deeply carry out social psychological services into the community, into the grass-roots activities, organized 278 psychology activities of public service activities, community psychology service station standardization pilot project, the establishment of 32 community psychology service station .

Community governance continues to improve. In 2016, Beijing completed 161 Pilot

Self-Service Management Projects in Old Residential Areas. The number of registered community volunteers in the city reached 1.6 million. The integration of urban and rural community service management has been continuously promoted. 117 new village-level social service pilot projects have been set up and pilot projects of "1 + 3" governance has been carried out. Under the unified leadership of a large party organization, villager organizations, community organizations and economic organizations have been jointly negotiating Co-governance, and further enhance the social governance level of urban-rural integration. Among them, Pinggu District, "four members to promote the development of the four post to contribute" activities to enhance service management of the old district; Tongzhou District Loumen culture building to strengthen, Yanqing District, actively create theme parks such as the World Park and the Winter Olympics community, achieving good social effect.

The level of social services is constantly improving. In 2016, the basic public service system in Beijing was further improved. More than 400 billion yuan was invested in people's livelihood in the city, and 28 important livelihood practical projects of the municipal government were fully implemented. Relevant departments in Beijing have made efforts to increase the employment income of urban and rural residents by setting up social welfare employment organizations in 179 townships to help them find jobs in urban and rural areas with difficulty; steadily increasing the level of social security; introducing the integration plan for urban and rural residents' health insurance; establishing 53 nursing home care centers and 150 community care service centers.

1.3 The social work system has been consolidated and its vitality for social development has been constantly enhanced.

Beijing's "hub-type" social work system has become more complete. In 2016, Beijing Municipality newly identified 15 municipal-level "hub-type" social organizations, bringing the total number to 51 and covering 90% of the social organizations in service management. 231 district-level "hinge-type" social organizations, 467 Home, the basic formation of a three-tier system framework

Social organization registration service management further strengthened. The civil affairs department in Beijing canceled the application for preparation for registration of social organizations, canceled the examination and approval of affiliates and representative bodies of the Foundation, and reformed the system of verifying the qualifications of social organizations. The system of registration of social organizations promoted "one card for three certificates and one card for one card" simplify social work procedures, the establishment of municipal social organization development service center. The city's industry associates Chamber of Commerce and administrative departments to work in an orderly manner.

Social organizations foster support to further increase. Beijing's social construction sector invested 67.7 million yuan in municipal-level social construction funds and 20 million yuan in public welfare departments in Beijing's civil affairs departments, purchasing a total of 611 social service organizations. Beijing Federation of Trade Unions, Beijing Disabled Persons Federation, Beijing Municipal Bureau of Science and Technology, Beijing Municipal General Sports Association and other municipal "hub-type" social organizations and most of the district have arranged special funds to purchase social organization services. Beijing Association of Science and Technology to actively promote science and technology community to undertake government transfer functions, a total of 58 sciences and technology community to undertake 158 government transfers and related tasks. The network of social organization services (hatching) has been further improved. Beijing Social Organizing Incubator Center held a total of 146 business training sessions of various types with a total of over 6000 training sessions. The Communist Youth League Beijing Municipal Committee, Beijing Women's Federation and Beijing Human Resources Service Industry Association Municipal "hub-type" social organizations set up a service (hatching) platform, 16 districts have set up their own service (incubation) platform, 81 streets set up the corresponding platform. Use the municipal social construction special funds to purchase social organization management positions 360. Beijing Municipal Commission of Social Work organized social organization governance innovation and ability to enhance senior seminars, training social organizations.

The vitality of social organizations further stimulates. Beijing Municipal Committee of Social Work carries out social organizations, "public welfare line" series of activities, a total of 3048 15,000 events throughout the year, serving more than one million residents.

1.4 The social security system has been further improved and the level of protection has been gradually raised.

The coverage of various social insurance has been expanded. According to statistics from the Bureau of Statistics, the number of basic old-age care workers, basic medical care, unemployment, work-related injuries and maternity insurance that participated in the urban workforce at the end of 2016 was 14,591,000, 1,517,600, 1117.5 thousand, 1060.2 thousand and 9.81 million respectively People, an increase of 348,000, 419,000, 35.2 million, 401,000 and 390,000 respectively over the previous year. At the end of 2016, the number of urban and rural residents participating in endowment insurance was 2.157 million. The number of people participating in the basic medical insurance for urban residents was 1.192 million. The number of people participating in the new rural cooperative medical care was 2.191 million.

The coverage of social assistance is higher, and the construction of service institutions is steadily promoted. According to the Bureau of Statistics, in 2016, the number of people enjoying the minimum living allowance for urban residents in the city was 82,000 and the number of people enjoying the minimum living guarantee for rural residents was 47,000. By the end of 2016, there were 641 adoptive units of various types with 140,000 beds and 80,000 people of various kinds. A total of 11,907 community service agencies have been set up, including 198 community service centers.

Social security standards have also been raised. Compared with 2015, the minimum standard of unemployment insurance, the minimum living standard for urban residents and the minimum wage for employees have been raised (Table 1).

Table 1 Social Security Related Standard of Treatment

Unit:yuan/month

| Indicators | 2016 | 2015 |
|---|---|---|
| Minimum standard for unemployment insurance | 1212 | 1122 |
| Urban residents minimum living standards | 800 | 710 |
| Minimum wage | 1890 | 1720 |

1.5 Further coordinate labor relations and constantly push forward institutional and institutional development.

The laws and regulations for coordinating labor relations have been constantly improved, providing a powerful institutional support for building harmonious labor relations. On November 27, 2015, the 23rd meeting of the Standing Committee of the 14th Beijing Municipal People's Congress passed the "Beijing Municipality, Implementing the Measures of the People's Republic of China on Trade Union Law," and since January 1, 2016 Execution. The amendment has perfected the legal provisions on collective bargaining and democratic management. Increase the "one party to put forward the consultation request, the other party shall not refuse or delay for any reason" obligations; require not sign the collective contract of enterprises should be in accordance with the local regional, industrial collective contract standards; clear the employer refused or To delay the legal responsibility of equal consultation; To break the ownership restriction of the enterprise's democratic management, propose to establish and perfect the democratic management system based on the workers' congress regardless of ownership form, and identify its legal status for the first time.

Labor contracts, collective bargaining and the continuous strengthening of the six-party linkage provide a mechanism guarantee for the prompt and effective resolution of labor relations conflicts. According to the statistics of the Beijing Federation of Trade Unions, as of the end of September 2016, the signing rate of employees' labor contracts reached 96.3% and that of urban workers reached 94.8%. 13,442 collective contracts were signed among the enterprises under regular management, Covering 64,810 enterprises and covering 2677,382 employees, the collective contract construction rate was 90.9%; 12,127 contracts for collective wages were signed, covering 61749 enterprises, covering 21,14869 workers, and the establishment rate of collective contracts for wages was 86.7%; There are 80,636 units established the system of employee representative system, the establishment rate of 86.41%, covering 3.6 million workers; 80,814 units established a factory system, the establishment rate of 86.59%, covering 3.63 million workers; 1630 established the system of employee directors , 1708 established a system of employee supervisors.

2. The main problems facing social development

The current situation of social development is in good shape, but there are still some social contradictions and problems that need to be explored and solved. These problems are mainly manifested in the following aspects: high house prices; the problem of urban traffic travel is still grim, the social security of blind selection policy is not high; the urban-rural gap of residents' income needs to be gradually overcome; the pressure of new employment needs to be alleviated; Deep research and crack; social organizations still face many problems; the quality of life and social services such as the elderly, the floating population and other social vulnerable groups also need to be gradually raised.

2.1 Rapid growth in housing prices, and low satisfaction in motor vehicle blind selection rule

The basic problems facing the basic needs of the people are the aspects of housing, housing prices have increased by a large margin, the success rate of motor vehicles has not been high, and people's satisfaction has been low.

2.1.1 Rapid growth in housing prices, people's livelihood greater pressure

In 2016, the rapid growth of house prices in Beijing showed a strong growth trend both in the year-on-year and the week-end.

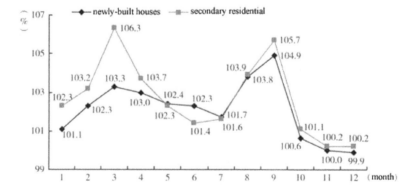

Figure 2 MoM residential and secondary residential sales price index in 2016

Source: Beijing Bureau of Statistics

92

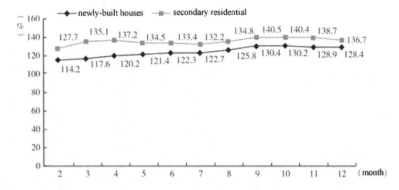

Figure 3 2016 Beijing new commercial residential and second-hand residential sales price growth index

Source: Beijing Bureau of Statistics

As can be seen in Figure 2, except for the price of newly built houses which remained relatively stable in December, Beijing's housing prices maintained a year-on-year growth, with two peaks in March and September in particular. The year-on-year growth figure in Figure 4 shows that as of December 2016, the prices of newly-built houses in Beijing have increased by one-third, the prices of second-hand houses have also increased by nearly 30%, and the changes in housing prices within a year have been immense. It is also reasonable to cause some social shock and panic.

2.1.2 The idea of green travel still needs to be tested by practice. The social satisfaction of motor vehicle blind selection policy is not high

Traffic has always been one of the "big city diseases" that have plagued Beijing. To alleviate urban traffic pressure, Beijing has set a transit priority strategy for public transport and controlled the growth of private motor vehicles (Figure 4). In recent years, as bicycle travel has become a new fashion city, rental bicycles quickly covered the streets and became the new urban landscape of Beijing. It not only facilitated the daily traffic but also popularized the environmental protection concept of green travel. The effect is looking forward to. In the near future, considerable management problems have been exposed: the failure to regulate the use efficiency of vehicles caused by vehicles, the traffic order caused by indiscriminate disruptions and the man-made damage caused by improper use of vehicles.

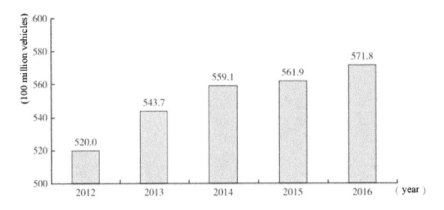

Figure 4 2012 ~ 2016 vehicle ownership

Source: Beijing Bureau of Statistics

Bus priority strategy to alleviate traffic congestion in Beijing contributed a great deal. However, controlling the ownership of cars with motor vehicle plate blind selection policy has also caused some dissatisfaction in society. Beijing Municipal Government issued the "Interim Provisions on the Regulation of the Number of Passenger Cars in Beijing" at the end of 2010, which stipulates that the purchase of passenger cars by resident and institutional organizations in Beijing requires an application and the unified acquisition of passenger cars by means of a rocker number in order to realize the number of passenger cars Reasonable and orderly growth to ease traffic congestion. However, although the current purchase restriction policy restrains the growth of motor vehicles too fast and alleviates traffic congestion, it also causes the public to be unable to meet the demands of car purchase in time. People are not satisfied with the current motor vehicle plate blind selection policy. Since the implementation of the motor vehicle plate blind selection policy in 2011, the number of passenger cars has been declining, but the number of applicants has been continuously expanding. The success rate of success in the index has continued to drop. In 2016, the success rate dropped to about 0.5%, resulting in the widespread waiting time for motor vehicle plate blind selection applicants Too long, "a long time can not shake" widespread, triggering the interests of small-passenger motor vehicle plate blind selection applicants on the low evaluation of the policy. Relevant surveys show that in the motor vehicle plate blind selection applicants, 70.8% of the respondents evaluated the policy as "very dissatisfied" and "not very satisfied", with 29.2% "very satisfied" "more satisfied" and "normal".

2.2 The income gap between urban and rural areas is still large, and employment is still under considerable pressure

2.2.1 The overall income growth is stable, but the gap between urban and rural areas is still huge

According to the Beijing Municipal Bureau of Statistics data, in 2016 the city's per capita disposable income reached 52,530 yuan, an increase of 8.4% over 2015; after deducting the price factor, the actual growth of 6.9%. According to the permanent residence, per capita disposable income of urban residents 57275 yuan, an increase of 8.4%; rural residents per capita disposable income 22,310 yuan, an increase of 8.5%. After deducting the price factor, the actual growth rate of urban and rural residents income was 6.9% and 7.0% respectively. In recent years, the income growth rate of rural residents in Beijing has been slightly higher than that of urban residents. Although the gap is small, it has maintained a good trend after all (see Figure 5). The problem lies in the absolute income gap between urban and rural areas: the income of urban residents is equivalent to more than twice that of rural residents. With the current income gap, it is not only impossible to shorten the distance between urban and rural residents in the short run, but also because of the large base gap Further expand the actual income gap.

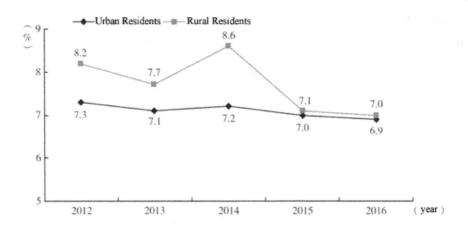

Figure 5 Real growth of per capita disposable income of urban and rural residents from 2012 to 2016

Source: Beijing Bureau of Statistics.

The gap between urban and rural areas is also reflected in consumer spending. According to the Beijing Municipal Bureau of Statistics data, in 2016 the city's per capita consumption expenditure reached 35416 yuan, an increase of 4.8% over the previous year. On a constant basis, the per capita consumption expenditure of urban residents reached 38,256 yuan, an increase of 4.4%. Per capita consumption expenditure of rural residents reached 17,329 yuan, an increase of 9.6%. The per capita consumption level of rural residents is less than half of urban residents, and the gap between the two is obvious.

2.2.2 Employment increased steadily and employment pressure remained strong

The pressure of employment in Beijing in 2016 remains high. The "Statistical Communique on the 2016 National Economic and Social Development in Beijing Municipality" shows that the number of new jobs in 2016 has been steadily increasing compared with the "12th Five-Year Plan" period (see Figure 6), but the number of new jobs still constitutes a big employment pressure . The number of new jobs in urban areas reached 428,000, an increase of 0.2 million over the previous year. Under the premise of a slowdown in the growth rate of permanent residents, the newly employed population still maintained growth. As a result, the employment demand remained high. Another data also verify the above judgment: Beijing Bureau of Statistics data show that by the end of 2016, the registered urban unemployment rate was 1.41%, an increase of 0.02 percentage points over the previous year. Despite the small change in the unemployment rate, the structural pressure of employment persists, taking into account the fact that the overall population growth has slowed down.

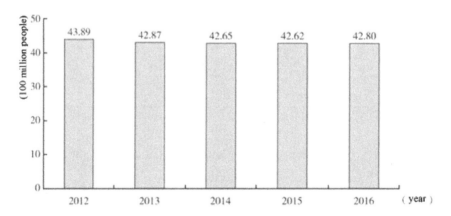

Figure 6 Urban Employment (2012 - 2016)

Source: Beijing Bureau of Statistics

96

2.3 There are many problems in grass-roots social governance and the social organizations need to improve their methods of purchasing services

2.3.1 Social governance at the grassroots level exist relatively serious problems, social cognition, participation and mobilization being inadequate.

The grass-roots social governance is the basis of urban governance, but the survey shows that the current community governance has a certain gap with the actual needs of the grass-roots people in governance, in terms of resident awareness, social mobilization and participation, and organization of activities.

First of all, residents do not know enough about urban community governance. The construction of urban communities and self-government of residents should be consciously carried out by residents under the direct guidance of various departments at higher levels and directly under the guidance of community party committees and community residents committees. However, the survey shows how residents 'opinions on the neighborhood committees are based on the relationship between the community affairs supervisory bodies and community party organizations and community residents committees, the relationship between the people's government and its agencies and the grass-roots community residents committees, the meetings of community residents committees, owners' committees and community representatives There is a certain degree of cognitive bias with the power of the property company. In the process of further promoting the construction of urban communities and residents' self-government, the concept of community residents should be changed step by step, and ideological concepts should be prepared for the further promotion of community governance.

Second, residents' lack of initiative in participating in community governance is insufficient. Urban community construction and residents 'autonomy are directly related to the improvement of residents' welfare level. Concerns are the precondition of participation. However, residents 'attention to major community issues such as participation in community residents' meetings, resident representative meetings, members of community party branches, residents The enthusiasm of members of the committee, members participating in the resident forums, democratic forums and other activities to reflect the problems in the construction of the community to the government departments remains to be further strengthened.

Finally, the basic conditions for residents to participate in the construction of urban communities and residents' autonomy need to be further improved. As an important condition for promoting the participation of residents in the community, the number of government departments holding hearings on community-based construction in communities, the number of community resident forums and democratic forums, and the annual reports of residents 'committees to resident meetings or residents' representatives meetings The number of times, all need to be further increased.

2.3.2 Rapid development of purchasing services for social organizations and deep-seated problems in development Beijing has also made long-term exploration to meet people's livelihood needs by purchasing services from social organizations and has achieved some success. However, there are still some shortcomings. Currently, there are mainly four types of problems in social service purchase by social organizations.

The first is the scope of government services to be extended. At present, the service projects undertaken by social organizations are mainly community convenience services, social work services and social psychological services. The functions of government transfer undertaken by the social organizations are not wide-ranging and are not conducive to the growth of social organizations and the transformation of government functions to some extent.

Second is the urgent need to improve the capacity of social organizations. Social organizations have insufficient social capacity to serve their own needs, such as limited number, small scale, lack of independent resources and social environmental factors, such as government's lack of support for the growth of social organizations and lack of sympathy for the growth of social organizations.

Once again, the government purchase service management needs to be strengthened. The current management problems are mainly scattered management, civil affairs departments, mass organizations, social construction departments have their own purchase services, is not conducive to the centralized use of project resources, and the lack of integration between different departments to consider the project, affecting the efficiency of resource use. In the specific management methods also need to be innovative. Projects to declare the way the industrial budget, the total amount of funds, service details have a clear budget requirements, often lead to the lack of flexibility in the implementation of the project is really unable to meet the real needs of society.

Finally, there is a need to improve the government procurement service regulatory evaluation mechanism. The current project evaluation focuses on the number of service visits, the time, the number of attention activities, these indicators unified quantification, reducing the difficulty of inspection, but the distance from the actual implementation of the project inspection is still some distance.

2.4 The total number of vulnerable groups is huge, and the quality of social life deserves attention

2.4.1 Aging society is approaching; the community education of the elderly population is outstanding

This report has long been concerned with the issue of aging. There have been special discussions on home-based care and medical care. The focus of this year is on education for the elderly. At this stage, the problems facing the development of Beijing's elderly education are mainly reflected in the following aspects.

The first is cognitive bias, management fragmentation. The construction of a lifelong learning society complements the development of the elderly education in an aging society, both indispensable. Although the development of the Internet makes intelligent living possible, the general public's understanding of the concept of old age education is still relatively traditional and conservative. At the same time, we also see that although Beijing has pointed out the ways and means for the development of education for the aged from the aspect of policy design, in the specific operation process, the management system of education for the elderly has the problem of fragmentation, that is, the administration is still not clear , Some by the Aging Committee, veteran cadres or civil affairs department management, some by the education sector management. This also led to the management of the block division, long management, unclear powers and responsibilities

Followed by monotonous education content is the implementation of a single body.

From the perspective of the content of education for the elderly, the setting mainly focuses on the interesting edge as the leisure education, information and science and technology with the dominant needs of the elderly such as calligraphy, chorus, English, computer and square dance. There are very few activities on knowledge education involving the hidden needs of the elderly such as medicine and health. From the perspective of teaching methods, although organizations such as Beijing Radio and Television University already have the experience of distance education for the elderly population, the implementation of education activities for the elderly is relatively simple due to the relatively slow adoption of new birth by the elderly. From the perspective of faculty, the full-time teachers in traditional senile universities recruit more from the society, while the faculty resources in towns and communities are mostly composed of community residents and young volunteers. As a whole, there is still a lack of a team of senior teachers for senior education, which is not conducive to the long-term systematic development of senior education.

Finally, the resources for education for the elderly are less than demand and the distribution is not balanced. Elderly schools operated by social organizations are under-resourced, with some well-equipped older university degrees generally tense and older schools run by some civil society organizations struggling. The elderly education institutions in Beijing, run by social forces, account for a large proportion, and the difficulty of capital investment are a major bottleneck in the development of education for the aged. The distribution of geriatric education resources in urban and rural areas in Beijing is also unevenly distributed, which is manifested in the backward development of geriatric education in rural communities in terms of faculty, funding and educational facilities. It is imperative to promote the development of geriatric education through urban elite resources.

2.4.2 Migrant families increase family mobility, living environment needs to gradually create and perfect.

The family-based migration of migrants is becoming more prevalent, and their aspiration to live in inflows is also growing. However, it is not easy for migrant families to live in big cities.

First, there is a conflict between settlement capacity and willingness to settle.

Restricted by the economic capacity, the floating population mainly lives in rented houses. High rent and the huge demand market cause group rent, transformation of underground space, and illegal construction of old bungalows. A considerable part of the families live in poor quality. Although the housing leasing market has been rectified many times, the phenomenon of various group rent rebounds is also great. This not only brings difficulties to urban management but also reduces the living quality of renters. Leasing on the market housing quality is low, welfare rent or purchase but by qualification or housing restrictions cannot solve the actual needs of the floating population application policy to be eligible for a new housing breakthrough. Due to the restriction of the household registration system, mobile families can apply for public rental housing in affordable housing without the qualification of low-rent housing and affordable housing. The purchase of commercial housing requires proof of social security and tax payment for five consecutive years in Beijing, while the high housing prices make family does not have the purchasing power.

Second, informal employment leads to inadequate protection. The large number of informal employment also affects the social security and social welfare of migrants. Migrant population mostly concentrates on the secondary labor market. Informal employment is large. The weakness in the job market makes social insurance coverage for migrants lower. Coupled with the urban-rural dualistic system of social security system and the overall planning of decentralization and floating population Of the social security system has many problems, which brings a lot of inconvenience to the floating family members in seeking medical care and pension.

Finally, there are institutional constraints on the education of children of migrant workers. For migrant families, there are also many policy constraints on children's school attendance. In 2015, Beijing Municipality released the Opinions of Beijing Municipal Commission of Education on Compulsory Education 2015, and non-Beijing children in Beijing asked for "five cards", that is, employment certificates in Beijing, certificates of residence in Beijing, residence booklets, In Beijing, temporary residence permit issued by the local township government issued a certificate of non-custodial conditions, all districts and counties to develop rules on this basis, the need for additional proof. Moreover, due to the scarcity of public education resources, the poor working conditions of migrant children, the difficulties of children learning, the difficulty of entering schools, and the high transfer rate, it is a common problem for migrant families.

3. Proposals to promote sound social development

In view of the above analysis of the current social issues, this report proposes: appropriately increase the income of residents and increase the planning and construction of affordable housing; vigorously promote green travel and ensure the fair distribution of resources; actively promote the upgrading of rural industries and gradually reduce urban and rural areas Gaps in technology innovation and industrial upgrading as a motive force to improve employment level; Focusing on classification, key management and local governance, improving the accuracy and efficiency of community governance; organizing social organizations to purchase services in accordance with the law and ensuring service quality; Community education as the starting point to improve the quality of life of the elderly; a correct understanding of the floating population of the family flow of the status quo, improve their sense of city access.

3.1 Improve livelihood services such as basic livelihood and improve social satisfaction

3.1.1 Increase residents' income appropriately and strengthen the construction of affordable housing.

Given the current price level of housing in Beijing, ordinary people want to live in peace and pressure is great. Since 2010, Beijing has taken a series of measures to stabilize housing prices. The main policy measure is purchase restriction. Increasing the threshold of the purchase of speculators to control the real estate speculators, of course, have some effect, increasing the level of down payment also try to avoid the financial risks of the housing market, stable prices cannot be said that there is no contribution, but soaring house prices in 2016, how much such measures The effect on price control is not satisfactory. The impact of high prices on the lives of ordinary citizens is obvious. According to the existing house prices and income levels, ordinary white-collar workers struggle to buy a house in Beijing all their life. High housing prices will certainly play a role in squeezing the population and will have some effect on controlling the population growth. However, due to the fact that quite large floating population does not target the ownership of housing in Beijing, the effect will be rather limited. For the general public, how to meet the housing needs is a very serious problem.

First of all, appropriately raise labor income to suit current housing prices. We should appropriately increase the income of laborers, especially those who eat "financial meals", such as government agencies and scientific research personnel in public institutions, in order to adapt to the current housing price level. At present, most young people, especially the young college teachers, research institutions and grassroots government workers recently settled in Beijing, generally have lower wage levels and are under a lot of pressure to live in high prices. People in this part of the population are generally better educated and have a Beijing *hukou*. They are theoretically "Beijingers", but they cannot rely on their own income to find shelter for themselves in Beijing's housing market. Beijing's fiscal revenue has maintained a relatively high level of growth for a long period of time and depends on the existing fiscal capacity to appropriately increase the government's wage earners' income and increase their economic capacity so as to adapt to economic and social changes and help them cope with life challenges.

Second, increase the supply of affordable housing and increase social benefits. Under the existing housing price level, we should explore the housing market classification management measures to meet the housing needs of different groups. The existing housing market in Beijing is dominated by commercial housing supply, while the proportion of government-guaranteed housing accounts for a small proportion. In order to stabilize the general livelihood of the people, apart from increasing house price interventions and controlling the vicious rise, more active measures should be taken to meet the housing needs of the general public and increase the supply of affordable housing. In combination with the residence permit system, we should explore ways to increase the coverage of floating population applications Housing opportunities.

Finally, scientific planning and protection of housing communities, to avoid social sleaze a single city. In the protection of housing planning and construction process, should avoid the Tiantongyuan, Huilongguan, such as the general volume, single-living community building. Due to their over-unified functions, such communities often form slumbers of big clumps, putting severe pressure on traffic and traffic in areas and creating new social problems. In the planning phase of affordable housing, we must also consider the social matching of different income groups and age groups in order to avoid over-concentration of homogeneous groups. In the long run, a large number of homogenous people live in concentrated habitats with less social diversity and a single social ecology, which is not conducive to the exchange and interaction among different social groups. In the long run, social unhappiness is likely to occur, the social vitality of communities is reduced, and social governance and social stability in the region are affected.

3.1.2 Promote green travel and ensure fair distribution of resources

First, encourage green trips and increase urban affinity. Green travel is the city's future direction, in recent years to solve the problem of congestion, green travel by the government and civil unanimously agree. In terms of policies, it is feasible to create a green trip by strengthening public transport and rail transport. The rise of rental bicycles in technology has become a more concrete embodiment of the concept of green travel. Since 2016, with the popularization of mobile internet technology, convenient travel tools such as sharing cycling and riding bicycles have become the new urban landscape. Green travel has become a solid social practice from concept and has been unanimously sought after by different groups.

Second, promote civilized travel, enhance the city's image. To cope with the ever-present problem of rental bicycle management, the use of parked bicycles and the management of parked bicycles should be strengthened, and the credit records of users of rental bicycles should be rated through technical means to avoid the uncivilized phenomena of indiscriminate chaos, unauthorized locking, malicious vandalism, Advocate green travel, civilized travel.

Finally, explore and improve the rules of motor vehicle plate blind selection to promote more fair and reasonable allocation and use of resources. At present, the policy of shaking number of motor vehicles effectively controls the growth of the number of motor vehicles, and has a certain contribution to alleviating traffic pressure and improving air quality. However, the urban family's desire to spend must also be considered. With the improvement of living standards, the car has become a general consumer goods for many families to meet the needs of new lifestyles such as leisure travel. The survey shows that congestion caused by motor vehicles is mainly concentrated in the urban center and outskirts of the city, and the surrounding areas of the city basically do not have such problems. In this sense, what should be limited for a typical home motor vehicle is its use in the downtown area rather than the purchase. In the control of the use, it should focus on entering the city center of the vehicle, this goal can be achieved through appropriate policies and measures, such as the collection of congestion in the city center and so on. For suburban counties with little traffic pressure, under the premise of total control, they can consider appropriately increasing the equipment for purchasing automobile indicators and meeting the wishes of the local people without sacrificing traffic in urban areas. At the same time, in order to ensure the fair distribution of resources and explore family-based methods for the allocation of purchasing indicators to meet the needs of more families for car consumption.

3.2 Gradually narrow the gap between urban and rural areas and strive for the harmonious development of urban and rural areas.

3.2.1 Promote rural industrial upgrading and narrow the gap between urban and rural areas

First of all, a correct understanding of the existing urban-rural development gap. The process of urbanization is a process of continuous upgrading of industries, continuous development of secondary and tertiary industries, and gradual replacement of primary industries that mainly focus on agriculture. Resident income in rural areas of Beijing is lower than that of urban residents for a long time, which is not only the result of competition and distribution among industries but also some historical and social reasons. In terms of income differences among industries, it is normal social phenomenon that there is a certain income gap between different industries. Tokyo, Japan, engaged in agriculture, the income of residents is also the lowest, but with other industries and the income did not reach such a high Beijing level of differentiation only.

Second, we should actively explore industrial upgrading in rural areas and achieve leapfrog development. In the process of high-speed urbanization, rural development lags behind the city is an unavoidable historical and social facts. As a sunset industry, agriculture cannot rely on its own profits to bring about overturning changes in rural areas. In order to increase the incomes of residents in agricultural areas, it is necessary to actively explore industrial upgrading. At present, the outskirts of Beijing have the ecological conservation as their main function, and there is no possibility of large-scale development of the secondary industry. Exploring the high-end leisure services that serve urban residents is a possible option. Using the relatively superior natural resources in the outer suburbs, through the planned and high-level creative development, a relatively high-end supply of leisure products can be formed, which not only meets the requirements of holidays and entertainment for urban residents, but also increases the incomes of residents in rural areas without destroying In the case of natural ecology, it is expected to achieve the best development effect of a win-win situation between urban and rural areas.

Finally, increase the government's public investment in rural areas, vigorously improve the infrastructure and create a sound investment environment. The urban-rural development gap in Beijing is not only the natural process of long-term economic and social development but also the result of a long-term policy choice. The urban-rural gradient development strategy implemented in the pre-urbanization phase has led to the concentration of resources and urban agglomeration, which is the historical reason that the current urban-rural development gap cannot be avoided. At present, the rural areas are lagging behind the public facilities and services in urban areas, both in terms of meeting the needs of local people and adapting to the development of the high-end leisure industry. The closing of this gap requires that the urban government, taking the overall consideration. The form of public investment is completed. The government should vigorously increase investment in rural public facilities, improve living standards and quality in rural areas, and create basic conditions for developing attractive leisure industries.

3.2.2 Actively innovate employment opportunities to ensure urban stability and vitality

With the non-capitalist functions of relocation, low-end wholesale market remediation, facing the street "opening a hole" small business governance, Beijing's low-end employment market space is gradually compressed, urban service industry also usher in opportunities for upgrading. How to allocate newly-employed population to all walks of life in the city depends on the market's own ability to regulate and also brings challenges to urban industrial planning. Beijing's urban orientation is no longer the center of economic development goals, science and technology innovation is the future development of the main areas of growth. In the future, Beijing's industrial upgrading, social development and technological innovation will still bring about considerable employment opportunities.

First of all, promote the development of industries such as information, finance and convention and exhibition and increase new employment opportunities. In the exhibition industry, financial industry and information industry that meet Beijing's long-term development planning and urban orientation, they all have very good potential for job creation. There is still plenty of room for development in these fields. Compared with recognized world cities such as Tokyo, Beijing There is still plenty of room for employment in related fields in the city, which is expected to attract a certain number of employed people.

Second, adapt to the emerging needs of the community, and actively guide employment. Social development brings new occupational needs. With the advent of an aging society and the increasing proportion of second child births, there will be more employment needs in the pension service and child service industries. People in these industries will gradually become the new darling of the professional market.

Finally, encourage technological innovation and create new jobs. Technological upgrading brings new jobs. Relying on the development of mobile Internet, a number of new jobs have been created, such as courier staff, express car drivers, etc., to provide certain jobs.

In these fields, talents need to be trained and reserved to meet the needs of employment. From a national point of view, skilled skilled workers cannot meet the needs of the manufacturing industry. Similarly, in the big cities like Beijing, high-end service personnel also have vast employment opportunities. Beijing should make good use of its rich resources in education and training to provide its talent pool to high-end service industries.

3.3 Improve the quality of community governance, and strengthen the cultivation of social service providers and the supply of resources

3.3.1 Improve the accuracy and efficiency of community governance, and create a consensus for co-governance

First, the classification of governance to improve governance targeting. Systemic governance of community issues is the ultimate goal, but the current choice should be categorized governance. Community issues have a common, common side, which is the basis of our understanding of community governance issues, but in a certain stage of historical development, different types of communities face specific problems will be different. Classification has some advantages. First, the classification of governance can effectively improve the governance effect of resource investment. Due to the limited level of the overall economic development in society, there is a certain limit to the amount of community governance resources put into operation in any area. The priorities of different types of communities in the same historical period are different. Community governance is ultimately to meet the needs of community residents, the resources to the most urgent needs of the community will achieve the best social effect. Second, the classification of governance can be the right medicine, enhance the pertinence of governance. Third, the classification of governance can improve the validity of the policy. The universal policies covering all kinds of communities tend to pay more attention to commonality and neglect the individuality of different communities, so as to obscure the goals. Classification of governance policies can improve the accuracy of the policy.

Second, focus on governance and improve resource efficiency. The community is made up of different people. The concern about people's needs is the purpose of governance and an important means of governance. Focusing on the needs of the major groups in the community, it is possible to do more with less, to promote the overall community through governance by key groups. Expatriates, the elderly and the handicapped population are those who rely more on public governance. Whether their needs will be satisfied or not will determine the ultimate success or failure of community governance. Their satisfaction will determine the ultimate community satisfaction. We can see that for the key population of "short board" for governance in order to improve the community's overall level of governance satisfaction. The key social groups have a good governance social effect, which is conducive to arousing the enthusiasm of community participation and striving for social support. The needs of the key groups such as the elderly and the disabled are all involved in the fundamental interests of the community residents, especially the elderly. Almost all families are involved. The governance of these groups is easy to mobilize residents' awareness of participation and create a social atmosphere of common governance.

Finally, local governance increases the participation and accuracy of community governance. Locals know best about local needs. In advocating state governance, the effective actions and participation of local governance forces can correct the choice of governance tools and improve the governance accuracy. Local governance is also easy to form a long-term mechanism. The participation of local people can effectively form the atmosphere of supervision. It can not only maintain the goal of governance but also facilitate social mobilization, renew participation and maintain long-term governance. Local governance can also form a good social atmosphere. The core of social governance lies in the common governance and the negotiation of common governance. Only locals participate in community governance, the setting of governance goals, the management of resources, the supervision of the governance process all have a credible guarantee and can participate in social participation Atmosphere to improve social integration efforts to promote social solidarity, improve social cohesion and promote the formation of the consultation and governance.

3.3.2 Organize social organizations according to law to purchase services and ensure the quality of grass-roots social services

First of all, change the government function, expand social service space. The transformation of government functions is a long-term process. The improvement over the years is a positive one. However, compared with current social needs, the problem of excessive government administration remains severe. First, the boundary between government services and the self-serving boundary of social organizations should be gradually clarified from the law. In particular, in the field of community life that has close relations with the people's lives, we should try to limit the entry of government executive orders and encourage community mass self-government Organizations and community social service organizations to grow and assume corresponding social service functions. Second, we can try to introduce grassroots service lists and gradually draw the line between power and responsibility of the government and society in grassroots affairs so as to increase the basis and operability of grassroots social self-service. Thirdly, based on the principle that resources should be leveled at the grassroots level, grassroots social organizations should try their best to collect the wishes of the masses, put forward their service needs, complete demonstration and organize their implementation. The government appears mainly as a sponsor and supervisor to avoid direct service.

Second, change the way of thinking, and effectively cultivate the growth of social organizations. Beijing has made great efforts to support the growth of social organizations and has made remarkable achievements. In particular, it has taken the lead in building a hub-oriented social organization and has explored a unique experience in social organization and management. However, according to the quantity and quality of social organizations and the effect of participation in social governance, there is still a great shortage. The existing hub-based organizational structure should be utilized to gradually straighten out the management of grass-roots social organizations and gradually lower the registration threshold so as to effectively promote the sound development of science and technology, public charities and urban and rural community service social organizations that serve the people's livelihood. In the meantime, we must constantly explore new forms of social organizations and, in the spirit of service public welfare, give more policies and resources to emerging social organizations such as social enterprises and cultivate the power of social self-service.

Third, improve project operation, and gradually expand the service area. Use "Internet +" and other new technology platforms to explore the exchange of social services between different departments to buy services, communication, and gradually promote information sharing. At the same time in the management services, relying on the social organization service platform to achieve social organization information, project information, project management processes, social organizations and other needs of online operations, reduce management and communication costs. In addition to taking full-time purchase and substituting premiums and other means, it is also possible to explore more flexible ways such as partial subsidies and differential purchase, to expand social benefits of existing resources and promote social service forces Self-growth.

Finally, strict supervision and management, and strengthen performance evaluation. In project management assessment, in addition to adherence to management measures such as process management and internal management, it is necessary to increase the assessment and supervision power of third parties, enhance the status of professional assessment, and guide social services to grow in the direction of specialization. In particular, the performance appraisal should pay more attention to the effect of serving the society and gradually change the performance appraisal relying only on the static quantitative indicators such as the number of times of activities and the participation of the population, gradually realize the dynamic management through the evaluation of the project service stakeholders, and effectively improve the service items Social influence and reputation.

3.4 Give full attention to the social needs of the disadvantaged groups and improve the general happiness of society
3.4.1 Community education as the starting point to improve the quality of life of the elderly
In order to improve the quality of life for the elderly, community education should be used as a platform to actively integrate relevant resources for gerontological education, promote exchanges among the elderly and meet the needs of learning new knowledge and developing new interests. "Live to Old, Learn Old", the idea of lifelong education has existed in our country. In the knowledge-based economy, the renewal cycle of knowledge is shortened. For the elderly to adapt to the development of the society, apart from receiving the education of the professional knowledge of the elder schools, they need to carry out secondary development and secondary training through community and social organizations.

First of all, at the content level, we should continue to enrich the contents and forms of elder education in the community and explore a new mode of combining education and education. Such training should involve many aspects such as interpersonal communication, intergenerational coordination, the application of social networking tools, codes of conduct and social morals. At the level of implementation of specific organizations, basic education, higher education, vocational education and adult education should be co-ordinated with the concept of lifelong education and a platform for mutual coordination and mutual exchange of various kinds of education should be set up. To establish a platform for exchange and interaction of elderly human resources outside the system and between schools and communities to create fair educational opportunities and conditions for senior citizens and mobilize their enthusiasm for self-management, self-improvement and active learning.

Second, in the implementation of education, relying on the self-organization of the elderly to achieve benign interaction within the group. The specific practice of self-organization of the elderly also depends on the community to provide the necessary human, material and financial support. By providing venues and financial support, the community assists older people to establish grass-roots community organizations and carries out regular activities to further promote their participation in the discussion of community public affairs and the conversion of functions to the organizations of mutual benefit. For example, on the basis of the interest groups, the elderly can learn to plan a reasonable retirement life, ensure personal and property safety, learn consumer finance, deal with pain and death, and at the same time, establish a mutual aid group for the elderly on the basis of this Older seniors provide possible service and support to elderly people in need of care, and promote the self-organization of senior citizens from functional change to mutual benefit.

Finally, in the implementation of the main body, by professional social organizations involved in the community, provide professional education and training. Such training not only provides the elderly themselves with special seminars that meet the needs of the elderly, but also provides community workers with the fields of nursing care, psychological counseling, social work, nutrition and health care.

3.4.2 Correctly understand the current situation of migrant families and improve the sense of urban acquisition of non-permanent residents

Subject to factors such as regional imbalances in social and economic development, Beijing is currently in a period of population influx and the phenomenon of floating population will persist. Cities can take corresponding measures to adjust and control the size of the inflows, but they cannot control the influx of people in the short term. On the basis of the above understanding, on the one hand, we should guide the population flow through measures such as industrial policy adjustment. On the other hand, we must also recognize that the population flow is a normal social phenomenon and actively improve the management and service of non-resident residents who have been working in Beijing for a long time, to protect its due development benefits and benefits.

First of all, promote institutional reform and improve the service level of migrant workers. In 2016, the "Opinions of Beijing Municipal People's Government on Further Promoting the Reform of the Household Registration System" put forward the policies of establishing a unified urban and rural household registration system and residence permit system by steadily moving households as they move along and integrating points, and steadily advancing the overall population of urban basic public services cover. This provides settled opportunities and choices for permanent residents capable of stable employment and livelihood in Beijing. For a still larger group of floating population that does not meet the requirements for settling the points, it is necessary to establish and improve the service management system and social security system for migrant workers through a residence permit system to promote the equalization of basic public services. However, due to the characteristics of floating population groups, the implementation of residence permit system needs a process. In this process, it is necessary to give full play to the role of multiple subjects in society, especially the role of community and social organizations. While doing well in service work, promote social integration.

Second, standardize the job market and protect the working welfare of migrants. Urge enterprises to standardize their employment and strengthen the supervision over employment contracts of enterprises so as to ensure the corresponding social security and welfare rights of floating population. At the same time, it also plays a role of population quantity management through the regulation of the employment market.

Finally, take the Beijing-Tianjin-Hebei one as an opportunity to guide the orderly flow of mobile families. Family flow decision-making is a family-autonomous rational choice behavior, when the mobile income is greater than the cost when it may choose to move. Family flow generally has a strong desire to stay. Relevant surveys also found that the relevant deconstruction policies formulated by Beijing have little effect on the settlement intentions of migrants. Therefore, in the process of the integration of

Beijing, Tianjin and Hebei, in addition to the overall industrial transfer and transportation and other hardware facilities, it also needs supporting policies in employment income, social services and social welfare so as to increase the support for migrant families in the Jin-Ji region Attraction, to guide the flow of families in an orderly manner to move outside Beijing. Strive to ease Beijing's population, optimize the demographic structure, and make mobile home quality of life from greater impact, so as to achieve a win-win government and mobile families.

# New Progress, Problems and Prospects of Beijing Social Governance in 2016

## Zhang Su[1]

## Abstract

In 2016, Beijing further refined the level of social governance and further consolidated the effect of comprehensive social security. The mechanism for resolving social conflicts and safeguarding fairness and justice further achieved results. The important role of the rule of law in social governance has become even more prominent. At the same time, there are still some deficiencies in the construction of a mechanism for pluralistic solutions to social conflicts, the establishment of a mechanism for assessing the risks to social stability and the establishment of a social security prevention and control system. To this end, Beijing should further improve the mechanism of pluralistic solutions to social conflicts, resolve key issues in the work of assessing social stability risks, and further improve the construction of social security prevention and control system.

Keywords: Social governance, social order, social contradictions, social stability and the rule of law

2016 is an extraordinary year. "Beijing's" Social Management Plan for the Thirteenth Five-year Plan "was formally promulgated by the Beijing Municipal Party Committee and Municipal Government and described a blueprint for the social governance of the capital in the next five years. In the "13th Five-Year Plan" period, Beijing will comprehensively strengthen social construction, deepen the reform of social system and accelerate social governance innovation. This is an inevitable requirement for thoroughly implementing the overall arrangement of the "five in one" and the strategic layout of "four comprehensives" and the "five major development concepts," and is the proper meaning of accelerating the modernization of the state governing system and governing capability. It is a principle that is further implemented General Secretary Xi Jinping made important speeches and made an important directive to work in Beijing. Speeding up the Beijing non-capital functions, accelerating the

---

[1] Zhang Su, Deputy Director of Capital Institute of Public Security Comprehensive Administration,Beijing Academy of Social Sciences    Associate Researcher, Ph. D in laws, and research areas include criminal law and criminology.

coordinated development of Beijing, Tianjin and Hebei, taking the lead in building a well-off society in an all-round way and accelerating the building of a world-class harmonious and livable capital. In this context, we need to sum up experiences, sort out problems and look to the future.

1. Overview of Beijing's Social Governance in 2016

In 2016, the various tasks of social governance in Beijing are constantly being refurbished and have been greatly developed, which is shown in the following aspects.

1.1 The degree of refinement of social governance has been further enhanced

Strengthening system governance and speeding up the refinement of social services and urban management are one of the key tasks of the innovative social governance mode proposed in the Opinions on Deepening the Social Governance Reform in Beijing. The development in this area in 2016 is mainly reflected in the following aspects.

1.1.1 Urban service management grid has been further promoted

In 2016, in accordance with the relevant requirements of "Opinions on Strengthening the Gridding System of Urban Service Management in Beijing", all districts and districts, based on the actual conditions, took the streets and villages as the basic framework, implemented the areas, units and grids and improved gridding Management, through the electronic map annotation, the implementation of specific events to the film, tracking in place, the implementation of people. For instance, a) strengthen the supervision of public security by science and technology, realize high coverage in the monitoring area by means of scientific and technological means such as camera and remote terminal system, realize remote mobile office, and find problems in the first time. Command and dispatch for the first time and reasonable disposal for the first time; b) Improve the municipal 12345 non-emergency rescue mechanism; c) improve the real-time command and dispatch system; and d) improve the integrated assessment of business negotiations, improve the command center to undertake video surveillance, grid team construction and non-emergency relief to reflect the incident collection, aggregation, distribution, supervision, Analysis, research and other functions.

1.1.2 The refinement of urban service management has been further improved

Beijing will involve all aspects of urban operation and management of fine management, covering the city operation management and social services issues, users include government function units, towns, streets, village committees, neighborhood committees and promote the refinement of urban management With service. To promote the development and application of gridded mobile APP, grid members can upload information at any time through the mobile client. Depth of people organizations to mobilize various types of public order prevention and control power, security and stability tasks implemented to the grid, the power allocation to the grid, the problem is solved in the grid, and further improve the network of social service management pattern. In January 2016, Sun Xinjun, director of the Beijing Municipal Municipal Commission on City Appearance, was invited to attend the seminar on "City Culinary Management". He emphasized that modern cities need both modern management methods and modern management strategies. In 2016, the meticulous management mainly aims to support science and technology, and enhance the development of big data, Internet of Things, gridding, two-dimensional code, satellite Technology and other scientific and technological means in the city management contribution rate.

1.1.3 Wisdom community construction made new progress

Currently, the number of smart communities in Beijing has reached 1,672 and the grading system of smart communities has been further improved. At present, there are 224 five-star smart communities, 215 four-star smart communities, 814 three-star smart communities, and three-star and The smart community accounts for 75% of the total number of smart communities. According to Beijing's "Social Management Plan for the Thirteenth Five-year Plan" in 2016, Beijing will improve its community public service system and implement the "Top Ten Coverage Projects" such as community employment, social security, retirement assistance and health care and family planning, By 2020, Beijing will build a "one-quarter-hour community service circle" to achieve full coverage of self-service management in old communities. "The quarter of a circle of community service circles" refers to the residents starting from home, walk no more than 15 minutes, you can enjoy community services, including the convenience store to buy breakfast, beauty salons, grocery shopping, living expenses collected most of the payment Daily needs. In the meantime, the wage of community workers will be adjusted dynamically according to the standard of not less than the average social wage in Beijing in the previous year. In 2016, the task of building 100 "one-quarter-minute community service circles" in Beijing has been basically completed. The total number has reached 1,336, covering 83% of urban communities.

1.1.4 The judicial management of the process of refined management steady progress

In 2016, the procuratorial organs in Beijing thoroughly implemented the Opinions on the Implementation of the Pilot Reform of Judicial Responsibility System in Beijing's People's Procuratorate, improved the system of procuratorial supervision and control, established a procuratorial management and supervision mechanism that meets the requirements of the judicial responsibility system, and refined the judicial handling of cases management. The procuratorial organs in Beijing have promulgated the Opinions on Perfecting the Procuratorial Work Management and Supervision, focusing on enhancing the standardization of prosecutors and their responsible handling teams in enforcing laws and judicial interpretations, procuratorial work practices, procuratorial work discipline, and fulfilling job responsibilities . According to the factors such as the nature of the case, the amount involved the consequences of the case, the social impact and the source of the case, the Attorney General divides the cases handled by the hospital into cases that need to be reported for examination and approval and cases that can be decided by the prosecutor class. Among them, the prosecutors decided to implement the case by rotation distribution, to be submitted to the approval of the case decided by the Attorney General assigned to prosecutors in handling the source of the case to be restricted, to strengthen the handling of case management refinement, to explore a new mechanism of internal oversight Approach to the quality of cases as the core, strengthening the case management and supervision, effectively raising the standardization of judicial and judicial credibility.

1.2 The effect of comprehensive management of social order has been further consolidated

1.2.1 The construction of social order prevention and control system steadily progressed

In 2016, the Company thoroughly implemented the spirit of "Opinions on Strengthening the Construction of Public Security Prevention and Control System in a Three-dimensional Society" and steadily pushed forward the building of a social security prevention and control system. A) Taking the three levels of Comprehensive

Treatment Center as a platform, establish coordinated social order prevention and control system. Relying on the advantages of comprehensive management system and taking Comprehensive Center as a platform, the coordination and guidance system for prevention and control of public order at the three levels of towns, townships (neighborhoods) and villages (communities) will be established to conduct an overall analysis of the situation of social order and investigation and resolution of conflicts and disputes, Rectification and social patrol prevention and control work to form a synergy between departments and from top to bottom and improve coordination and guidance efficiency of social order prevention and control so as to build the first line of defense for safeguarding the stability of grassroots units. B) Both science and technology prevention and control network and social prevention and control network should pay equal attention to the coverage of social security prevention and control network. Built to cover the city and township government intelligent image sharing exchange platform. Rely on the image of the network, in urban areas intersection, bridges, squares, stations and other key parts of the new high-definition monitoring. Completion of residential high-definition monitoring system construction, residential area to complete the original monitoring system repair and integration.

1.2.2 Beijing, Tianjin and Hebei police coordinated the initial formation of the pattern
In January 2016, the public security organs in Beijing, Tianjin and Hebei signed the framework agreement on the coordinated development of Beijing-Tianjin-Hebei Police. Based on the idea of "coordinated development, joint construction and sharing, joint prevention and control and integrated operation" The "eight integrated" police coordinated development pattern, including joint logistics command system, intelligence information system. Formed a "Beijing Cheng seven districts and counties defense system" and "Jingdong eight districts criminal investigation cooperation" and other police cooperation circle. In the police cooperation, police agencies in Beijing, Tianjin and Hebei insisted on sharing information on resources and intensified the joint operation of command and liaison to gradually establish a police mechanism integrating information, command and operations and developed the integrated regional policing cooperation Command and information platform and set up the Beijing-Tianjin-Hebei Regional Police Cooperation Office to realize the direct point-to-point communication among the headquarters of Beijing, Tianjin, Hebei and 14 public security organs.

1.2.3 Deepening the integration of prevention and control, the people's sense of security has been further enhanced

During the period of April 21, 2016 to the end of August, Beijing Police cracked up more than 250,000 various kinds of criminal cases and sentenced more than 12,000 people to criminal detention during the "Peace and Security Campaign in Spring and Summer 2016". The city's criminal categories, obstructing the social order type of police intelligence fell 13. 6% and 18.3%, respectively. During the operation, Beijing police eradicated more than 90 criminal gangs and dropped 6 gangs and 16 pseudo-base stations and black radio dens. According to statistics, among the eight types of criminal cases that have seriously endangered public safety, such as intentional homicide, arson and robbery in the "Peace and Security Campaign in Spring and Summer 2016", a total of more than 1,900 cases have been solved by the public security organs in the city of Beijing, with a detection rate of 74.3% The highest level since 2000. Among them, the number of cases of "robbery and robbery" detection increased by 12.9% over the same period of last year, and the number of cases of using network telecommunications frauds decreased by 36% in terms of the previous month. In response to the public's strong prostitution, gambling, black car, bicycle piracy, hospital traffickers and other chronic illnesses, the Municipal Public Security Bureau and the city traffic, urban management and other departments to carry out joint law enforcement operations, breaking the yellow and gambling criminal syndicates over 1,800, Investigate and deal with about 550 hospital traffickers, more than 6,500 illegal "day trips" and banned more than 1,300 tourists. In the meantime, the number of burglary cases in the city dropped 8.5% from a year earlier, and the number of penalties for various types of traffic violations increased by 24% over the same period of last year. Give full play to the advantages of regional policing cooperation. Central Beijing Public Security Checkpoint investigated a total of 9.3 million vehicles in Beijing and arrested about 1,500 criminal suspects, and the people's security awareness improved significantly.

1.2.4 The joint management of public safety hazards between urban and rural areas has achieved tangible results

The problem of public safety hidden dangers in the junction of urban and rural areas has always been the short board of urban management, which has seriously affected the process of urban-rural integration and the capital's modernization in the whole city. In 2016, Beijing Municipality established the general headquarters of the comprehensive renovation work in the key urban-rural junction areas and coordinated the comprehensive management of the urban-rural junction areas in an effort to increase regulation in many aspects. In view of the outstanding problems and serious hidden dangers in key areas such as the urban-rural junction in the aspects of building structure, fire safety, public order and production and operation order, the special rectification work sub-headquarters respectively take the lead in organizing illegal construction, public order, fire safety, Safety violations, illegal operations, environmental pollution, food and drug safety, illegal rental housing eight aspects of special rectification, establish and improve the normalization grassroots joint law enforcement mechanism, focus on law enforcement, and achieved remarkable results. Take Daxing District as an example, there are 10 key districts with hanging-offs at the municipal level and 11 districts at the junction of urban and rural areas in this district. 84 villages are demolished in the junction of urban and rural areas, over 12 million square meters of illegal construction is demolished, 13 million square meters Meters, demolition of industrial compound, logistics compound 65, clearance of more than 7,000 low-end enterprises, the floating population reduced 330,000, afforestation a total of 10 square kilometers, the interface between urban and rural areas changed a lot.

1.3 The mechanism for resolving social conflicts and safeguarding fairness and justice has achieved fruitful results

1.3.1 Judicial system reform has made substantial progress

Beijing Municipality is the third pilot area for judicial reform determined by the Central Government. Beijing No. 2 Intermediate People's Court (hereinafter referred to as "No. 2 Intermediate People's Court"), as the first batch of judges in Beijing to implement the appointment, set up a professional trial team and fully implement judicial responsibilities In 2016, the Judicial Reform was launched. The first batch of judges to be selected within the control of 29.3% of the judges is 152. The number of judges assigned to the judiciary will be strictly limited to the judicial bodies and positions directly exercising jurisdiction, not directly No judicial post shall be set up for the exercise of judicial power or any department that has no connection with the case handling function. Improve the system of performance and protection of judges, non-statutory procedures, not due to statutory reasons for the judge to make a transfer, dismissal or removal, demotion and other treatment decisions. And set up a mechanism for quitting the post of judge posts that "can and can not be competent". It will try to implement an exit mechanism for posts that do not meet the job requirements in terms of political performance, knowledge, experience, performance and discipline. Under the premise of the adjustment of jurisdiction, changes in the number of cases, and the reform of the registration system, a comprehensive statistics on the situation of the trial courts and judicial personnel in the past five years has led to the formation of "big data" and its analysis. As a result, Court has a small account, each judge has details. " Based on this, through independent research and development of "Judicial Workload Verification System", according to the judge's quota, trial workload, the trend of case growth and other variables, the formation of judge posts, personnel classification management to form a basic calculation report for the reform After the staffing and workload assessment laid the foundation. The Second Intermediate People's Court formulated 25 complementary reform measures, such as the Detailed Rules for the Implementation of the Pilot Reform of Judicial System Reform, and provided institutional guarantees for improving the quality of judges, the quality of trials, and the credibility of the judiciary.

1.3.2 Multivariate dispute resolution mechanism was innovated

The Beijing court system actively implemented the spirit of the "Opinions on Improving the Mechanism of Pluralism in Conflicts and Disputes" issued by the Central Government and gave full play to the mechanism of pluralistic resolution of conflicts and disputes in accordance with the requirements of "prevention and control of risks, service development, solving problems and filling in shortages" In the lead, promote and safeguard the role of service economic and social development, promote the mechanism of multivariate dispute resolution mechanism innovation. In March 2016, the city's trial authorities gave full play to the role of people's mediation power and conducted pilot pretrial procedures in pre-trial mediation in Shunyi, Xicheng, Fengtai, Changping and Fangshan District 5 courts. Select civil disputes such as inheritance of marriage and family, property heating, compensation for damages caused by traffic accidents, sale and purchase of loans under RMB100,000 and other five kinds of mediation disputes suitable for mediation. The people's mediators stationed in the people's court shall mediate before filing the case and the full-time mediation judge is responsible for the entire guidance , The quality of people's mediation work to pass. First, the establishment of "seven mediation room" mode. For example, after the Fengtai District's "7th Conciliation Room" was put on the market in March 2016, it gradually docked with litigation activities such as filing a case registration, filing a case with speedy proceeding, judicial confirmation and other litigation activities. According to "2 days entrusted, mediation within 7 days, within 30 days Complete the mediation, "the basic requirements, to explore" 1 + N "7th conciliation room brand cluster construction mode, creating a distinctive new model of people's mediation. The second is to speed up the work mechanism innovation. Although the mediation fails, but the facts of the case clearly, the legal rights and obligations of the clear and controversial, by the court quickly judge, improve the efficiency of the trial. At present, the trial work mechanism reform has been opened in the city. Third, set up a multi-mediation development association. Gradual establishment of commissioned mediation mechanism, that is, after the filing, the scheduled period of time before the hearing, will involve Internet disputes, insurance contract disputes, securities and futures disputes, pawn disputes, medical disputes, real estate disputes, the subject of a larger trading And loan disputes entrusted to the promotion of mediation, or entrusted to the promotion of member units to mediate. The Promotion Association shall be responsible for the statistics, assessment, supervision and regulation of the activities of the mediation organizations and shall investigate the violations committed by the mediation organizations in the mediation commission through clues fed back by the courts.

1.3.3 Resolve the contradiction between letters and visits work continues to introduce new ideas

In 2016, the "Work Plan for Letters and Calls of Letters and Visits from Beijing during the 13th Five-Year Plan" was promulgated. Each district revolved around the relevant requirements and explored the mode of resolving the contradictions of innovative letters and visits. Among them, Changping District launched three measures. First, the implementation of a single method of work, according to the "petition petition single" content, in accordance with the order to visit the masses, carry out registration, resolution, reporting, filing, and promote conflicts resolved in time. Second, the implementation of "5 +2" contradictory dispute resolution mode. "5" refers to visit, visit, visit, interview and return visit, "2" refers to the "talk room" and "legal aid workstations." All villages and communities in the Changping area have set up a "chatting room," where village cadres and "three old and one young" (veteran party members, veteran cadres, senior patriarchs and university graduate village assistants) shift their shifts. In the district social conflicts mediation center set up migrant workers legal aid workstations, arrange for full-time lawyers for migrant workers to provide free legal aid. Third, we should establish a "two mechanisms and one center" and open channels of appeal and expression. The "two mechanisms" refer to the people's proposal of soliciting mechanisms and agencies, guiding and organizing the masses to safeguard their rights according to law. "One Center" refers to the key functional area petition reception center. Focusing on the outstanding letters and visits in the construction of key functional areas, the center directly set up reception centers for letters and visits in the frontline headquarters and properly coordinated the demands of the masses, effectively preventing mass incidents and extra-level visits. Daxing District, highlighting the two separate, deepen the petition reform. First, focus on strengthening the separation of petitions. In the context of "deepening the reform of the system of letters and visits and speeding up the construction of letters and visits under the rule of law," we focused on co-integrating the work of letters and visits into the track of rule of law, strictly implemented the system of separation of petitions and visits, innovated and implemented the principle of "six no-receptions" and patiently counseled , And actively led the law-related matters involved in arbitration into arbitration and litigation procedures and properly resolved them in accordance with the law, effectively bringing non-petitions into the correct channel of solution from the source and reducing the cost of administrative operation. The second is to strengthen the separation under the net. According to the unified requirements of "making online petitions the main channel for mass petitions," making full use of the outstanding features and advantages such as the ease of service and rapid processing of the Internet, we should actively educate and guide the masses to reflect problems, express their demands and safeguard their rights and interests through online channels. Since 2016, people receiving letters through the Internet have accounted for 63% of the total number of people's letters and visits.

1.4 The position of the rule of law is even more prominent in social governance
1.4.1 The disposal of the economic-related crimes involving the people according to law has been clearly checked in the criminal situation

Stakeholders involved in economic crimes have more than 100 victims in each case, which has a long duration and bad influence. The complaints and over-level visits that occur from time to time have occurred. Stakeholder-type economic crimes have become a major factor that has seriously affected the social stability in the capital at present . With the ups and downs in the stock market and the pursuit of high-interest wealth management products, the cases of illegal financing of borrowed wealth products gradually become more and more concentrated. In particular, various types of investment companies, private lending mushroomed rapidly growing, of which, investment banking and high interest lending there is a great risk hidden dangers, which led to the large-scale economic crime involving stakeholders, a direct damage to the property interests of the masses, the impact Social harmony and stability. In 2016, the Beijing Municipal Public Security Bureau Economic Investigation Corps led the special work "Fighting Stakeholders in Economic Crimes" and took the initiative to attack the stakeholder-type economic crimes, maintaining the momentum of high-pressure deterrence. In order to fully display the achievements of the Beijing police in cracking down on economic crimes, on May 15, 2016, Beijing Municipal Public Security Bureau organized and organized the "Seventh Propaganda Day on Combating and Preventing Economic Crimes". At the same time, the 16 districts of the city also focused their efforts on publicity by exposing the common Economic crimes to improve the people's awareness of prevention and prevention capabilities and promote the joint participation of all sectors of society to combat economic crimes.

1.4.2 By preventing Internet financial risks in accordance with the law, the financial security and stability of the capital has been further enhanced

In 2016, with the economic downturn, the capital chain was affected or even broken. The hidden illegal fundraising activities gradually exposed and potential financial risks were hidden, which would also directly lead to an increase in the crime rate of illegal fund-raising. As of the first half of 2016, Beijing issued 117 new cases of illegal fund-raising, involving a total amount of 7.214 billion yuan, involving 7718 people. The first five districts with the largest number of new illegal fundraising cases in Beijing are: Chaoyang District, Dongcheng District, Xicheng District, Fengtai District and Haidian District. In order to prevent Internet financial risks, the Notice of the General Office of Beijing Municipal People's Government on Printing and

Distributing the Implementation Plan for Special Remediation of Internet Financial Risks in Beijing was issued in October 2016. Clearly proposed to carry out special rectification action, focusing on P2P net loan, equity crowd-funding business, Internet insurance, asset management through the Internet and cross-border engaged in financial services, third-party payment services, Internet financial advertising and information services in six areas Carry out. Seven measures were taken for comprehensive improvement through strict man-in-hand management, enhancement of fund monitoring, establishment of a prize reporting system, rectification of unfair competition, increasing technical support, strengthening risk education and giving full play to the role of industry in self-regulation.

1.4.3 The legal construction of social stability risk assessment has been further strengthened

In the first half of 2016, Beijing held a working conference on major issues concerning social stability and risk assessment of decision-making. It is clear that at present and in the coming period, Beijing will focus on non-capitalist functions, governance of urban and rural junction areas, economic and financial security, social security, environmental protection and social public opinion And other areas involving the interests of the masses to strengthen risk assessment. At the same time, it is necessary to gradually introduce and establish a third-party assessment system, actively study and promote the legal construction of risk assessment work, and enhance the scientific and standardized assessment. Various districts have begun to explore in these areas. Taking Daxing District as an example, the district has gradually incorporated social stability risk assessment into the institutional track. First, establish a third-party assessment mechanism. Through the introduction of "foreign aid", Daxing District launched a third-party assessment of 30 new projects including Beijing New Airport Project and the construction of the South Campus of Peking University Hospital. Relying on the Beijing University of Chemical Education Daxing Social Construction Research Center and other institutions, the establishment of Daxing District Wing Tai risk assessment service center on the biomedical base East supporting garbage transfer station construction, Guanyin Temple Street River Community renovation project 15 projects to carry out third-party assessment . The second is to include assessment into the decision-making process. The district has formulated the Opinions on Incorporating the Risk Assessment of Major Social

Security Measures into the Decision-making Process of the Standing Committee of the District Committee and the District Government, and amended the Interim Measures of the Daxing District Government on Major Administrative Decisions. The Daxing District Government's decision on major administrative decisions Opinions "and other documents, the risk assessment as the district and town party committees and government major administrative decisions must be institutionalized. Third, establish a mechanism to evaluate embedded documents. In order to enhance the pertinence and continuity of the evaluation system, Daxing District has formulated the Opinions on Implementing the Risk Assessment Embedded Document System and perfected the Daxing District Administrative Regulatory Documents Review and Preparation Procedure, requiring all units to formulate policies and guidelines , Project management and special action documents, the main responsibilities of risk assessment and procedural requirements shall be embedded in the general, main text or supplementary provisions of the document and submitted to the relevant department for the record within 15 days from the date of issuance of the document. Fourth, establish a classification and evaluation mechanism. Fifth, establish a review and filing review mechanism.

2. Some Problems to Be Solved in Beijing Social Governance
2.1 The construction of a pluralistic system of resolving social conflicts is still not perfect.
First, the role of the organization is not enough. The district set up by the District Political and Law Commission, the District Bureau of Justice, District Law Office and other members of the District Comprehensive Social Security Commission contradictions diversified solution group and the special group office set up in the Bureau of Justice, however, the Bureau of Justice as a government function Departments, subject to their own functional orientation and the limits of their work rights, have no advantage in organizing, coordinating and promoting relevant work. As we all know, the work of diversifying social conflicts involves various government departments as well as courts and procuratorates. To a certain extent, the courts and procuratorates have more scope and scope than the work of the Bureau of Justice in the work of diversifying social conflicts. Regardless of other departments, the Judicial Bureau should organize and coordinate the courts to carry out relevant work There are some difficulties, which led to the Bureau of Justice in the organization and

coordination of member units do not work hard. Second, the town-level contradictions and disputes diversified mechanism to implement not in place. For the time being, the majority of conflicts and disputes in Beijing are concentrated in the town streets, and mediation organizations in the town streets are required to focus their efforts on resolving them. As the system is not perfect, there is no work flow to standardize the duties and responsibilities of various departments in the mediation of contradictions and disputes. When a dispute arises, there are phenomena in which the leading department is not clear and all departments act independently. More often in practice, the pattern of overall linkage between township and judicial branches has not yet taken shape. The original intention of integrating resources and giving full play to the advantages of various functional departments has not been fully realized. Third, mediating the workforce building is not perfect. At present, the mediation staff has a high proportion of part-time jobs and can not guarantee time and energy during the peak hours of mediation. In addition to the tedious work carried out at the grassroots level, mediation is only one of dozens of jobs. jobs. At the same time, "temporary" mediation teams not only have varying levels of capacity but also frequent mobilization and lack of stability. Some mediation staff members are part-time, no preparation, and some employers without financial security, making the mediation team exceptionally unstable. Fourth, the role played by the industry mediation organizations is not obvious. Although people's mediation committees have also been set up in the areas of tourism, consumption and medical care, most of them do not have full-time mediators. They are far more likely to play a role in organizing the promotion of coordination than in forms.

2.2 The problems of social stability risk assessment need to be solved urgently
Time-consuming, will affect the progress of the project, and some think that social stability risk assessment work is only a procedural work, do not do without affecting the decision-making. Therefore, they did not carry out the assessment seriously or re-evaluated the theory first, and evaluated the formalization of the virtualization. In another example, the implementation of the assessment items is not in place, should be assessed on the evaluation of issues not up to standard, there are still significant gaps in the work. Some departments and grassroots units that bear key projects do not report any risk assessment projects; some project evaluation work is not standardized and does not work completely according to procedures. In another example, the

third-party assessment is not high participation rate, the public participation is not smooth, risk factors are not comprehensive, preventive measures are not implemented, the risk rating unscientific, non-standard, not rigorous, the use of assessment results ineffective.

2.3 There still exist shortcomings in the construction of social order prevention and control system.

First, imperfect legislation in the construction of public order prevention and control system. So far, there is not a national law on the establishment of a three-dimensional public security prevention and control system, and Beijing does not have any local laws and regulations. Second, the level of science and technology in building a social order prevention and control system needs to be improved. This is manifested in the low level of informationization, insufficient "linking" and "sharing" of departments, and the serious phenomenon of "isolated islands of information", which cannot achieve interconnection and interoperability, and has yet to be completed. Video surveillance system HD digital transformation slow, there are information barriers between regions and departments, video networking is not complete, resource sharing is not comprehensive. New technologies such as big data, internet of things, cloud computing, and satellite positioning, smart sensing and geographic information systems are not widely used. Digitalization, networking and intelligence of public safety need to be further improved. Third, the mobilization of social forces needs to be further strengthened. The concept of broad social mobilization, active participation of the masses and common prevention and control of risks urgently needs to be strengthened. Resources such as enterprises and public institutions, social organizations at all levels and trade associations need to be further integrated. Fourth, there is still a big gap between the effectiveness of strike prevention and the expectations of the people. With the rapid development of modern science and technology, the criminalization of science and technology has become increasingly prominent. In this context, the building of a social order prevention and control system needs innovation and must be operated within the framework of the rule of law. How to deal with the lag between reform and innovation and the establishment of a legal system? The contradiction between the requirements of how to deal with precision prevention and precision strike and the contradiction between the relative backwardness of air defense, material defense and technical defense means has become an important task in the construction of social order prevention and control system.

3. Proposals to Enhance Beijing's Social Governance Capacity

3.1 Improve the system of pluralistic solutions to social conflicts

First, adjust the organization settings. According to the relevant circular issued by the General Office of the CPC Beijing Municipal Committee and the Beijing Municipal People's Government, the organizations for the comprehensive management at all levels should give play to the role of good organization and coordination and promote the linkage and co-ordination of all kinds of resolving means. According to the requirements of the relevant documents, in order to give full play to the coordinating and coordinating role of CSRC at various levels in resolving various social conflicts and coordinating with other tasks of the CSRC, special offices for resolving conflicts and disputes may be set at all levels of comprehensive management Commission. At all levels, the judicial administrative organs mainly undertake people's mediation work, co-operate with other departments and units and supervise mediation and judicial mediation and administrative mediation, so as to overcome the inconsistency of authority and responsibility and coordination of organization and administration when judicial and administrative organs undertake office duties Not enough wait for a series of questions.

The second is to strengthen the grassroots contradictions and disputes multi-platform solution. a) Strengthen the construction of a multi-purpose platform for resolving contradictions and disputes at the two levels of town and town. Set up a leading group to resolve conflicts and disputes in towns and townships in a pluralistic manner. According to various contradictions and disputes, they should solve their work functions and positions. Zhenjiang Social Security Comprehensive Management Center, as an integrated organization and coordination department, together with other relevant departments, undertakes investigation and early warning of contradictions and disputes in the town streets, , Supervise the examination of the responsibility to coordinate the parties to participate in the work of contradictions and disputes pluralism. B) Strengthen the construction of information platform. Relying on the town comprehensive treatment center and grid office platform, to strengthen contradictions and resolve the construction of information technology, to achieve resource sharing, improve information dissemination, information communication, information search channels to promote community knowledge and public opinion on the Internet, conflicts and disputes online solution, positive energy online Gather together. C) Strengthen the construction of mediation team. Selection of full-time mediators, comprehensively enhance the mediator's level and ability. D) Establish and improve the expert library. Engage experts in the field of mediation from relevant fields to participate in the work of resolving conflicts and disputes in a pluralistic way. Third, further standardize the construction of industrial mediation organizations. Formulate and improve assessment measures to ensure that all kinds of mediation system is sound and work in an orderly manner. Coordinate relevant departments to strengthen the protection of professional and professional mediation organizations in terms of personnel, office work and funds, give full play to the professional advantages of departments, industries and organizations, and solve various contradictions at a lower cost and with higher efficiency dispute.

3.2 Solve the key issues of social stability risk assessment work

Highlight the focus of risk assessment. At present and for a period in the future, the work of social stability risk assessment should focus on the following aspects. First, strengthen the risk assessment of Beijing's non-capital functions. The Beijing non-capital function and major decision-making social stability risk assessment work with the deployment, with the promotion. Focusing on such key tasks as industrial upgrading and transfer, population size control and compensation for land requisition, demolition and relocation, we must assess the risk of social stability as a necessary procedure before making major policy decisions and before making major project decisions.

Second, strengthen the risk assessment of urban-rural joint management. At present, the floating population in the urban-rural junction area in Beijing still has a large population, prominent population inversion problem, large stock of illegal construction and excessive concentration of low-end industries, resulting in a large number of potential safety problems. We should target some key tasks such as dismantling illegally, loosening the floating population and cleaning up the illegal production and operation of small and medium-sized enterprises, so as to accurately assess the existing risk points, formulate risk prevention and mitigation measures and ensure the smooth progress of governance.

Third, strengthen risk assessment in the financial sector. At present, the economic cases involving stakeholders, especially those involving illegal fund-raising, have become extremely frequent. Since the environment for raising illegal fund-raising is hard to be improved in the short term, the number of cases involving economic-related cases is expected to increase further in a certain period of time. In response to the introduction of financial policy measures and the financial companies, platforms and projects that have exponential problems, we must step up monitoring and early warning, assess risks, take risks ahead of time and make preparation for prevention.

Fourth, we should step up risk assessment on major issues concerning people's livelihood. Some major policies promulgated in areas such as prevention and control of environmental pollution, traffic and congestion control, education, medical treatment and safety production and some major projects that are often implemented involve major public and public rights and interests and involve a wide range of issues that can easily lead to social stability. These major issues must be included in the scope of social stability risk assessment, so that they should be appraised and promptly discovered, effectively resolved social conflicts of interest, to maximize the understanding and support of the masses, efforts to instability before the implementation of policy initiatives Risk to a minimum.

Fifth, strengthen the risk assessment of public opinion. Today, when the media is highly developed, major policy initiatives and major and sudden sensitive cases are raised. All this will cause great concern from the media and from all sectors of society. This requires that prior to the decision-making, we must take public opinion as an important risk factor to be considered, the social public opinion reaction, the negative public opinion may lead to a full assessment and understanding, meticulous public opinion to deal with the work plan. We must take the initiative to plan and organize publicity and reporting. We are good at using the new media such as the Internet, Weibo and WeChat to enhance the dissemination power and influence, effectively guide social public opinions and unite social consensus, and create a good public opinion atmosphere for all work.

3.3 Improve Capital Public Security Prevention and Control System

First, improve the social security prevention and control of the rule of law security system. The system of laws, regulations and systems for the prevention and control of public order in public security should be speeded up, the Regulations on the Comprehensive Management of Public Security amended and the Regulations on the Comprehensive Management of Public Security in Beijing Municipality revised and perfected, and the Law on Prevention and Control of Public Security should be enacted. In terms of special laws and regulations, laws, regulations and local laws and regulations on network management, population control, conflict resolution, anti-terrorism and anti-terrorism and hazardous materials control should be formulated and improved to clarify the main responsibilities and obligations and ensure the establishment of a social security prevention and control system Law can be followed, the rules to follow.

Second, establish and improve the social security prevention and control technology platform. First, build a fine management system led by science and technology. We will build a vertically integrated, horizontally integrated and safe and reliable information platform to comprehensively collect and input all kinds of basic information such as population, housing, places and organizations. The second is to build a set of services, management in one of the one-stop platform. Adhere to the peace construction as the key point, grid management as the foundation, information technology as the support, institutionalization as the guarantee, standardization as the guide, optimize the integration of resources, personnel integration, business integration, and strengthen the system to promote Standard operation. Third, we should build a big data information center that covers all aspects of the overall situation. For key industries and the management of dangerous goods, the Bank strengthened the risk management by supplementing and improving the video surveillance system and using the "Cloud Computing" "Internet of Things" and "Face Recognition" Wi-Fi fences.

Third, enhance the level of social participation in building a three-dimensional public order prevention and control system. Actively set up various platforms for social participation and provide protection for the society to participate in accordance with the law. First, improve the social participation system. Legislation makes the existence and activities of social organizations law-based. Social actors should be clearly defined in the main body position, functions and functions, ways of participation, rights and obligations in the construction of social order prevention and control system. Give full play to the advantages of social organizations, guide them to participate in social governance, actively undertake social affairs entrusted by the government, and provide social services in accordance with the law. Second, strive for the best effect of social participation. By strengthening the cultivation, guidance and management of social organizations, we have mobilized and led social forces such as economic organizations, social organizations and mass self-governing organizations in the prevention and control of public order in economic and social fields.

References:

Gong Weibin: "Research on Social Governance in China", Social Sciences Academic Press, 2014.

Jiang Bixin: "National Governance Modernization and Social Governance", China Legal Publishing House, 2011

Zhang Linjiang: "Social Governance twelve", Social Sciences Literature Publishing House, 2015.

Feng Shizheng: "Social Governance and Political Order in Contemporary China," Renmin University of China Press, 2013.

Li Peilin: "Social Reform and Social Governance", Social Sciences Academic Press, 2014.

# The "Dual Structure" of Basic Public Service for Floating Population Health in Beijing and Its Solution - Taking maternal and child health for example

## Liu Yang[1]

## Abstract

The health and well-being of migrants are often important shortcomings in health services in developed cities and regions. Through the data and material analysis of maternal and child health field, it is found that there is a clear "dual structure" of basic public health services for migrants in Beijing compared with the household population and other provinces and municipalities, that is, for the purpose of people's health, daily service management As a way of community health service has not been fundamentally strengthened, and to public health and epidemic prevention and social security as a motivation, exercise focused on the implementation of the "intensive immunization" as an increasingly important mode of curing. This dual structure is clearly incompatible with the future vision of building a healthy China, such as providing health and health services for the entire life cycle of the people and other future health and well-being visions of Beijing. From the strategic perspective of transforming the basic mode of work, Change working thinking, change the dimensions of resource allocation and examination and incentive system, and strengthen community-based public health services to break the "dual structure."

Keywords: Floating population, basic public services, maternal and child health care, dual structure, leading region of goodness

The "Shanghai Declaration" promulgated by the Ninth World Health Promotion Congress emphasizes "a healthy life of people of all ages" with a higher degree of specificity and stronger pertinence and rejects the especially popular health promotion in China as equating to health care The erroneous practice and proposed "to reduce the health inequities of all age groups." President Xi Jinping at the National Health and Health Conference speech, also stressed that "we must adhere to the correct health and work guidelines," "Health into all policies," "people to build and share", especially "to provide people with a full life cycle Health and Wellness Services. "

[1] Liu Yang, Assistant Researcher, Research Institute of Sociology, Beijing Academy of Social Sciences

The "Healthy China 2030 Plan" takes the strategy of "building and sharing and universal health" as its strategic theme. The "13th Five-year Plan for Health and Health" of the country also changes the mode of development from "treating disease as the center to taking health as the center" As the "13th Five-Year" period health and health development guidelines. The unhealthy and healthy congress in Beijing also put forward the slogan of "building a region of the nation's benevolent health." It can be foreseen that in the next 5 to 10 years, there will be a big change in the pattern of health care services and health promotion across the whole country and Beijing. The strategic focus of change lies in the abstract dual pattern of getting rid of the traditional "disease treatment + public health" , To a more specific and at the same time more integrated health promotion of "people's life cycle" or "people of all ages". From this perspective, this article gives a brief overview of the situation of maternal and child health in migrants with relatively weak health promotion, and attempts to see through some perspectives Beijing's structural problems in promoting the health of different groups.

1. Public health services for migrants

Beijing's policies on public services for floating population have generally experienced three stages of different nature. Before the "SARS" broke out from the mid-1990s of the 20th century, the government strictly monitored and managed the floating population from the point of view of health and epidemic prevention in strict compliance with the control of migrant population and infectious disease. The "Beijing field personnel from other places in Beijing Health and Anti-epidemic Regulations, "Beijing officials are required to handle" Health Card "and the employer is responsible for conducting regular medical examination, but does not provide services to Beijing-based floating people for their own health. The outbreak of SARS in 2003 contributed to the transformation of Beijing's public health public health policy. On the one hand, in order to cope with the outbreak, it further strengthened the control of floating population and the administration of epidemic prevention, which was different from emphasizing the responsibilities of employment units in the previous stage. This stage highlighted the specificities of the community in terms of floating population registration, accommodation management and physical examination On the other hand, the "returning home for treatment" and "evasion from the disaster" in Beijing at the time also caused a considerable spread of the epidemic in the whole country, exposing the negative impact of migrant workers' lack of medical insurance and infectious disease prevention and control services on public health Influence, thereby promoting the public health services to the floating population from a simple health and epidemic prevention to real public health service changes. At the end of 2004, these provisions and their supporting documents were abolished. In 2006, Beijing issued the Opinions on Strengthening the Public Health and Population Services of Population (hereinafter referred to as "Opinions"), in addition to strengthening disease surveillance of floating population and controlling certain infectious diseases In addition, it provides for free vaccination for migrant children and migrant children, as well as provision of basic medical services to migrants through community health service institutions. As a result, Beijing's public health services for migrants have entered the third phase[1], especially since the launch of the "National Basic Public Health Service Program"[2] in 2009. Driven by the national policy background, the public health services for floating population in Beijing in recent years have been significant progress, the problems are still great. This section first for a brief analysis of the face, the following section and then focus on the details of maternal and child health for a specific discussion.

The current status of basic public services for migrants in Beijing is obviously different from those in other provinces and cities with similar economic and social development levels. The establishment of a health file for residents is the first of eleven major national public health service projects and the basis for other services. The data of 2013 in Beijing, Shanghai and Guangdong provinces show that the three places are mobile.[3] The proportion of communities with health records in population is 30.5%, 28.8% and 43.3% respectively. The overall proportion is not high, especially in the two most developed municipalities in Beijing and Shanghai. The level is very low. As the national project started five years, the achievements made

---

[1] Fu Hongpeng et al .: Background, Changes and Trends of Public Health Management Policies for Floating Population in Beijing, China Health Policy Research, No.3,2008.

[2] Since 2009, the new medical reform started at the national level has included this project in the field of public health. The central government has formulated a detailed list of service items and services and provided financial assistance to provide free vaccinations for urban and rural residents, children and pregnant women Maternal and Elderly Health Management, Health Management of Some Chronic Diseases, Infectious Diseases, and Public Health Emergencies Reporting and Disposal. The subsidies provided by the state have been increasing year by year from 15 yuan per person in 2009 to 45 yuan in 2016. Specific service items are also fine-tuned every year.

[3] The relevant raw data come from the "Dynamic Monitoring Survey of Floating Population" hosted by the State Health Planning Commission, but the data application procedures are very complicated. The authors do not have the application conditions. This article directly uses the published analytical results, so less timely. See Wang Hui and other "Beijing, Shanghai and Guangdong floating population health planning basic public service status", "China Maternal and Child Health" 2016, No.5.

since then are very worthy of review. When it comes to the personal level of migrants, the data are even uglier: only 9.3% of migrant workers living in migrant workers and 8.5% of migrant workers living in migrant workers 17. 1%, better than nothing, and Beijing is only about half of Guangdong (see Table 1).

Table 1 Health Records of Migrants in the Most Developed Provinces and Cities in Eastern China

Unit:%

| Type | Shanghai | Guangzhou | Beijing | Average |
|---|---|---|---|---|
| Proportion of communities that have health records for migrants | 28.8 | 43.3 | 30.5 | 34.2 |
| Migrants personal filing ratio | 8.5 | 17.1 | 9.3 | 11.6 |

Sources: Data from Wang Hui et al., "Basic public service status of health planning for migrants in Beijing, Shanghai and Guangdong".

2. Health care for migrant women and children

2.1 Women's pregnancy test & birth control

Maternal and child health care is the most important component of the current public health services for migrants. In megacities like Beijing, the proportion of floating population is already high, and the age structure is far younger and the fertility rate is higher. According to statistics, in 2010, the live-to-live ratio of migrant and census population in Beijing reached 0.989 ®[1], that is to say, every birth to a child of the hukou population, the floating population is almost born one. Beijing Municipality has included immunization and maternal and child health care among migrant workers in the service area since the "Opinions" in 2006. So what's going on, what's

---

[1] Compilation of the National Maternal and Child Health Surveillance and Annual Report Materials (2010), quoted from Zhang Pei et al. Comparative Analysis of Prenatal Health Care Utilization of Urban Mobility and Census Register, China Maternal and Child Health Care, Vol. 27, No. 9.

going on? The following two sections analyze the data available.

From the data, since 2008, the proportion of mobile pregnant women filing has been hovering at a low level of about 40%, no significant increase in 2008 was 43.3% in 2010 35.5% in 2013 was 39.4%; More than 5 times the proportion of childbirth, in 2008 was 59.5%, since then no significant increase. Both figures have a much larger gap than pregnant women who have local household registration[1].

Recent data of Beijing and the economic development of the same level of brother provinces and cities are as shown in Table 2.

Table 2 2013 maternal health survey data of Beijing, Shanghai and Guangdong

Unit:%

| Region | Proportion of women spending motherhood in flow-in region | registration in flow-in region/ registered | pregnancy tests of over 5 times | child visit one week after birth | child visit 42 days after birth | child visit within one week after birth | Visit rate of one-month child |
|---|---|---|---|---|---|---|---|
| Beijing | 61.3 | 39.4 | — | 42.2 | 42.2 | — | 48.5 |
| Shanghai | 80.5 | 65.9 | — | 81 | 68.4 | 80.3 | 71.2 |
| Guangdong | 77.1 | — | 44.7 | 39.8 | 50.8 | 40.4 | |
| Average of the three cities | 73.3 | — | 66.0 | 54.5 | 56.3 | 54.7 | 57.3 |

From Table 2, it is clear that in addition to more than five birth control tests and other data on maternal health services, Beijing is obviously low, with active services such as establishing booklets and visiting inflows, with Shanghai's bimodal cities as first-tier cities Almost 1 times higher than Beijing.

---

[1] Relevant data from Du Qing and other "urban floating population of maternal prenatal care status and its influencing factors analysis", "China Primary Health Care" 2009 the fourth period; fruit Lina and other "825 cases of mobile pregnant women in Chaoyang District, Beijing Pre-check status and influencing factors analysis "," Chinese Journal of MCH "2012 the second period; Wang Hui and other" Beijing, Shanghai and Guangdong migrant population health public health basic public service status "," Chinese maternal and child health "in 2016, No. 10.

2.2 0 to 6 years old children's health maintenance

0 to 6-year-old children are in a critical period of growth and development, problems often endure lifelong, and particularly vulnerable, dependent, well-regulated, timely health intervention is very important for its growth. Migrant children are disadvantaged relative to hukou children in terms of nursing care, nutrition and health and health knowledge, therefore, in theory, more stringent health regulation is needed. Beijing's work in this area can be divided into two parts, one part is the daily health management ", the other part is vaccination.

2.2.1 Daily health care

From the growth of the health level, migrant children than the registered children have a significant gap. A 2010 study showed that migrant children aged 0-6 years had a 1.2 times higher prevalence of anemia and a 2.1 times[1] higher prevalence of malnutrition than their cousin children. However, the number of migrant children in Beijing who set up a health handbook to obtain a systematic health management ratio is always low. According to the survey data of different districts and counties available in each year, they are still hovering between 35% and 55% No obvious trend of progress (see Table 3).

Table 3 Mobile Children's Health Care Registration Rate in Beijing

Unit:%

| Time of Survey | 2005 | 2006 | 2006 | 2007 | 2009 | 2009 | 2014 |
|---|---|---|---|---|---|---|---|
| Region under survey | Shijingshan | Chaoyang, Daxing | Whole city | Whole city | Fengta i | Xichen g | Miyu n |
| Rate of Filin g | 12.5 | 48 | 53.0 | nearly 50 | 36.39 | 43.5 | 36.8 |

Source: Xiao Danqiong and Wang Xiaoli: "A survey of 152 migrant children health conditions in Shijingshan District of Beijing" and "Maternal and Child Health Care of China" 2009 No. 23; Duan Jianhua: "Health status of migrant children under 5 years old in Chaoyang District and Daxing District of Beijing Investigation, "Chinese Center for Disease Control and Prevention, Master's thesis in 2009; Huang Aiqun et al .:" Status quo of health care of migrant children under 5 years of age in Beijing and Hangzhou "," China Public Health "2/2008; Yan Shujuan, "Analysis of Health Status

---

[1] Zhang Xiaowen: "Xicheng District, Beijing mobile child health care review and status investigation and analysis," "Medical Information", 2001, No.10.

and Demand for Floating Children under 5 in Beijing," "China Children's Health Journal", 2008, No. 5; Wang Qian et al., "Investigation and Analysis of Current Status of Floating Children's Health in Fengtai District of Beijing", "Maternal and Child Health Care of China" Zhang Xiaowen: "Beijing Xicheng District mobile child health care review and status quo", "Medical Information", 2010, No.10; Feng Xiaorong: "floating child health status quo and influencing factors", "everyone Health "2015, No. 14.

In comparison, the rate of registering children has long been over 90%, and relevant surveys also show that 80% to 95% of migrant children's parents think it is necessary for their children to have regular physical examinations. This shows that the government's effective health care for migrant children Supply is far from meeting demand. Floating children are not easy to find and find, parents are not active and so is not the main reason, such as the existence of a large proportion of migrant population in Hangzhou, in 2006 the construction rate reached 69% ©[1]. In addition to the main indicator of the establishment rate, other important indicators also reflect the low level of health care for migrant children. If the survey shows that the two-week prevalence of migrant children is as high as 13.4%, 10 times higher than that of the registered children, Add rate is only 22%[2].

It is noteworthy that, often less than 50% of migrant children handbook construction rate, is still a large extent, children receiving vaccination, the relevant health staff to remind, urge the results of a survey showed that children In the proportion of 65.2% through vaccination and urged community supervise only 26.1%. Why is it that vaccination rates for migrant children are much higher than those who have been hovering at low levels?

2.2.2 Immunization

Data show that in Beijing as early as in 2006 5% of migrant children vaccination rate reached 91.4%[3], and is still rising thereafter, stabilized at 95%[4]. Achievements in this area have been rare compared to other indicators of health management. Of course,

---

[1] Huang Aiqun et al .: "Status quo of mobile child health in Beijing and Hangzhou".
[2] Yan Shujuan: "Mobile child health status and needs analysis."
[3] It refers to polio, hepatitis B, BCG, diphtheria and measles and other five major vaccine. See Huang Aiqun and other "Beijing and Hangzhou mobile child health survey."
[4] Hou Wenjun et al .: "Dali District of Beijing pre-school children vaccination enhanced leak investigation", "Occupation and Health" 2012 the twenty-first period.

parents are very conscious of this. But this vaccination awareness is not natural. We found that while vaccination rates were relatively high and comparable to those of hukou children, the rate of full-time vaccination was low, and some survey data showed that only 29% of migrant children were vaccinated on a timely basis. 51%, while the number of registered children reached 61. 16%[1], this may be more tense working parents of migrant children, nursing conditions than the factors of household children, but not to such a large gap. The difference actually stems from the way of migrating children to achieve immunization.

Since 2000, Beijing Municipality March and April each year, the citywide unified preschool children migrant selective immunization activities. Specifically, the district-level health department is responsible for organizing and mobilizing grass-roots government and village (neighborhood) committees to organize investigation teams to go home-to-home registration of all preschool-aged children one by one on a household basis and issue a "Notice of Vaccination" on the spot. Notify parents to bring children's vaccination certificate and check the replanting according to the agreed date to the designated place. The actual inspection of replanting by the district-level disease prevention center guidance and training, grassroots government Preservation Section[2]. In this "exercise" intensive replanting mode, although the vaccination rate remained at a high level, but failed to timely vaccination ratio is bound to be higher.

The proportion of migrant children participating in routine vaccination and replanting can be roughly deduced from the data of full-time vaccination of pre-diversion children and those of registered children. The proportion of migrant children participating in regular vaccination and replanting is almost 100%, of which about 6 The same proportion of projections, the proportion of full-time vaccination of mobile children 29. 51%, corresponding to the proportion of conventional vaccination should be about 50%, this ratio with the flow of children's health booklet collection rate is relatively close. Taking into account the poor care of migrant children, and the lower proportion of full-time vaccination under routine vaccination, the proportion of routine vaccination may be about 60% -70%, that is to say, at least 20% Species "to

---

[1] Zhou Bing et al .: "Study on Factors Influencing Children's Regular Immunization in Mentougou District, Beijing", "Public Health in the Capital" 2, 2014, No.3.
[2] Hou Wenjun et al: "Daxing District mobile children vaccination survey."

achieve immunization. Obviously, this non-timely and time-varying manner of vaccination, the healthy growth of children is very negative.

3. Discussion and Policy Suggestions

3.1 The "Dual Structure" of Public Health Services for Floating Population in Beijing and Its Policy

Through a brief discussion of the public health services for migrants, we can find that it is inaccurate to simply evaluate Beijing's work in this area. On the one hand, from the perspective of public health services (that is, to establish a healthy population for migrants Archives) and the level of general maternal and child health services, the level of public health services for migrants in Beijing is indeed relatively low, not only much lower than that of the census register population, but also often lower than those in cities and developed areas (such as Shanghai, Hangzhou and even Guangdong). However, on the other hand, the immunization rate of migrant children is quite high, close to the level of registered children, and no significant difference compared with other cities and regions. In other words, there is "duality" in some sense in the public health services for floating population in Beijing. That is, the overall level is relatively low, but a particular job is relatively outstanding. In fact, the duality of work effectiveness is the result of the dualism of working mechanisms: the public service of floating population in a general sense relies on the perfection and effectiveness of community-based health services and institutions, and the immunization coverage of children The relatively outstanding achievements have largely relied on the "mobilization" mechanism or the "sporty" mode that is different from the normal community health service mechanism: the regular intensive re-enrichment every year not only mobilizes the health sector and Institutional personnel, but also need to street, the town government and village, a considerable part of the neighborhood committees to mobilize to get involved and informed.

The following we make a simple tentative discussion of the formation of this binary structure. First look at a high level of dollar. The reason why migrant children's vaccination is so valued is to a large extent related to the health and immunization tradition of Beijing's public health. As mentioned above, prior to 2006, Beijing's migrant population health management service focused on the prevention and treatment of communicable diseases, mainly considering the impact of the health status of the floating population on other social groups rather than the health of the floating population itself. With the improvement of overall social hygiene level, the threat of common infectious diseases to society will gradually decrease, but its foundation is precisely the childhood immunization. Because domicile and migrant children can not be completely isolated, the risk of receiving infection remains high for *hukou* children if immunization is only common among domicile children. In other words, the immunization of migrant children is particularly accomplished and can be seen as a continuation of Beijing's tradition of public health work focusing on the prevention and control of communicable diseases, one aspect of Beijing's special social security requirements as the capital.

Look at the low level of one dollar. Since 2009, the "National Basic Public Health Service Project" has been implemented. The state has formulated detailed norms[1] and has been increasing funding efforts, but why is the progress of basic public services for the health of migrants still so slow? Leaving aside technical issues such as internal oversight, appraisal, rewards and punishments not in place, lack of information disclosure and lack of public monitoring[2], there are two levels of more fundamental issues. First, the source of funding for public health services for migrants. Although Beijing Municipality stated in its Opinions as early as 2006 that basic public health services should be provided to migrants, the source of such funds has not been clearly stipulated.[3] Since the beginning of the state basic public health service project, Per capita subsidy standards have been increasing year by year, but until 2014, the estimated caliber of subsidies in Beijing is generally the registered population, as is the relevant assessment standards, and the floating population is not on the list. This has greatly affected the enthusiasm of local governments and grassroots health institutions in providing basic public health services to the floating population. Until

---

[1] For example, in 2015, "Beijing Basic Public Health Service Catalog" consists of 46 items in 12 major categories, with an average of nearly 100 words in each sub-item and 4000 words in total. The "National Basic Public Health Service Standard (2011 Edition) "space actually reached 74 pages, 43,000 words.
[2] As a project carried out at the national level and heavily funded by the central government, the relevant state departments should conduct regular surveys and assessments and make them available to the public. This is both an accountability for financial investment and an effective measure to effectively urge local governments to actively promote them. However, until now, the project still only uses the traditional system of layers of examination, that is, the provincial examination of cities and counties, the central examination of the provincial level, and the appraisal results and funding allocated to the provincial level is difficult to seriously assess the city and assessment content This includes both fund management and use, as well as "completion of various tasks", with an average force and offsetting each other. See the State Health Planning Commission and other: "on doing a good job of national basic public health service project in 2016 notice" (National Defense grassroots 〔2016〕 27. In fact, the use of funds management should be overseen by the audit department, Health authorities should only be responsible for the completion of assessment and assessment tasks and the effectiveness of the implementation).
[3] Fu Hongpeng et al .: Background, Changes and Trends of Beijing's Public Health Management Policies for Floating Population.

2014, relevant departments of the State issued the Guiding Opinions on Doing Well Health and Family Planning in Migrants before explicitly submitting "Migrant Workers to Community Health and Family Planning Service Objects". In the following year, relevant departments in Beijing issued a document to strengthen the floating population Relevant work was only formally included in the measurement and assessment of the floating population.[1] However, at this time, the basic public health service projects have been carried out for 4 to 5 years. The work mode of ignoring the floating population may have already been cured to a certain extent at the grassroots level.

Second, the allocation of funds, management issues. The current total funding is based on population. There are two ways to actually use the funds. One is the provision of basic public health services under the framework of "two lines of revenue and expenditure" and the other is the provision of services under the service mode of purchase. Under the current mechanism design, both modes have obviously unfavorable factors for improving service quality and equalization. The distribution of funds under the framework of "two lines of revenue and expenditure" is mainly based on the cost-offsetting calculation. This encourages grass-roots health agencies and personnel to provide more services for consumables and to avoid services that mainly consume manpower. Obviously, this is not the case which will be conducive to the development of basic work in public health services. However, under the service mode of purchase, there is a link between performance revenue and business income. That is, primary health care institutions and personnel tend to carry out more charging services such as medical treatment and treatment, not a basic public health service[2].

Inspired by the above analysis, we can more fully classify the public health services for migrants in Beijing and make a clearer picture of their binary structure as shown in Table 4: According to the objectives and mode of work, two Dimension, the service can be divided into four types: one is the general community health public service which takes the population's own health as its goal and the daily service management

---

[1] Beijing Municipal Planning Commission, "on the issuance of" basic public health services plan to implement the equalization of work "notice" (Beijing Wei Guiding Zi [2016] No. 6). Compared to other provinces and cities, it is already quite late for the floating population to be included in the appropriation estimates. For example, Xiamen, Fujian Province, fully extended its subsidy coverage to the permanent population as early as 2011. Of course, Beijing does not do so because of its lack of fiscal capacity. The more important consideration may be that it fears that the quality of public services to migrants will aggravate the urban population.
[2] Zhang Yi: "Talking about the Funds Management of National Basic Public Health Projects - A Case Study of a Certain District in Beijing", "China Economics and Trade" No.8, 2015.

as the main working mode; Second, public health and epidemic prevention and social security as the goal, the daily service management as the main mode of daily routine health and epidemic prevention work (such as condoms free distribution, meat safety and quarantine, etc.); Third, the population itself as the goal of health , The public health service with the mobilization type and exercise type as the main working methods, such as the centralized examination of the occupational health status of the migrant workers; Fourth, the public health and social safety as the goal, to mobilize and concentrate on exercise As the main mode of work, including the major infectious disease outbreak response and mobile immunization of concentrated immunization. Among the four pieces of content, the main content of the second piece does not belong to the generally understood health and hygiene work, and the third piece of content is rarely developed. Therefore, the first and fourth pieces are the major ones, while the fourth Although the outbreak response can focus on the characteristics of this type, it does not happen frequently. Therefore, the remaining truly public health service content of floating population is the dual structure we analyzed above. Obviously, they work against each other both in their work objectives and in their working methods. In practice, they also have some mutual repression effect. If the concentrated vaccination of migrant children can achieve and maintain a relatively high vaccination rate, then public community health services The pressure of development will naturally decrease; the implementation of sports exercise will be kept to a certain level, and the "basic paradigm" of public health services will also be hindered from transforming into a community health public service mode with modern governance (see Table 4).

Table 4 Two-dimensional Classification and Dual Structure of Public Health Services for Floating Population in Beijing

| | | Ways of Work | |
|---|---|---|---|
| | | Daily service and management | Concentrated implementation such as mobilization and sports |
| Work Targets | Centers on the health of people | General public heath care service in communities | Concentrated check regarding occupational health |

| | | Concentrated immunization |
|---|---|---|
| Centers on public epidemic prevention and social security | Daily epidemic prevention | for floating children; Response to major infectious diseases |

## 3.2 Methods and Policy Suggestions on Cracking down the "Dual Structure" and Building a Healthy "Leading Region of Goodness" in China

This duality of public services for floating population clearly falls short of the newly established guidelines on health and sanitation such as "reducing health inequities among people of all ages" and "striving to provide people with life-cycle health and health services" But also runs counter to the goal set by the Beijing Municipal Party Committee in building a healthy and charitable region in China. To achieve the goals put forward by the municipal party committee, it is essential to change this duality.

First of all, we must make a basic adjustment in the thinking of working goals. Public health and social safety are all required in any city or region, as is Beijing's capital. However, the safety at the public health level is indispensable and extremely important. It does not mean that all aspects of health work, especially those related to the floating population, must be directed at this goal. At a higher level, the health of all groups in society, including their full health knowledge and self-protection skills, is instead a more solid foundation for social health and safety. If we do more public health public services from the perspective of our own health rights and interests and the healthy development of floating population while relaxing public epidemic prevention, we will not only meet the value goal of "human beings as our goal," but also provide public Health and safety to achieve such an efficiency goal has laid a solid foundation.

Second, in terms of working methods, we should strategically reinforce community-based public health services based on daily service management. In the past, community health public services for migrants were often simply taken as a task to advance. We must realize that this is not a simple implementation of a work[1], but

---

[1] For example, the "Implementation Plan for Promoting the Equalization of Basic Public Health and Family Planning Services for Floating Population" formulated by the relevant departments of Beijing in 2015 as set out in the preceding paragraph with the task completion time line defined in 2020 will be completely copied in the "Overall Objectives" section At the level of "Guiding Opinions", we can hardly see the high-end positioning of "the region of the nation's benevolent health." In the specific tasks, we have highlighted the immunization of migrant children and migrant workers and set out many specific indicators. However, Only the principle of

the transformation of the dominant public health service mode of operation. It is difficult to achieve such a shift in mode of operation based on the routine issuance of indicators and inspection at various levels. Need to overcome the inertia of thinking, obstacles and habits of habitual constraints, need to be consciously analyzed, a wide range of co-ordination linkage and precision force. Need to change the resource allocation mechanism and work incentives. Combined with the previous article on the basic public health services to promote the effectiveness of the unsatisfactory analysis, here can be made in two aspects of policy recommendations.

First, taking into account the basic public health services for migrants as a short board in the overall project pattern, it may stipulate that the increase of project subsidies for the next period of time will be used to strengthen public health public services for the floating population. This rigid flow of resources to change in order to persecute and guide the transformation of work patterns.

The second is to provide a clear classification of basic public health services assessment. For those services with obvious externalities, which are difficult for the beneficiaries to distinguish accurately, the funds are still matched according to the number of service users. For those services with less externalities such as establishment of health records, visits and health checkups, Funds matching and revenue incentives, apparently so that even without the establishment of the file ratio, the proportion of visitation and other assessment indicators, the popularity of related services will be promptly pushed open, mobile children, migrants do not have to wait each year to "enhance leak detection replant" When you can find out. Through this clear, targeted work motivation, but also effectively guide the transformation of work patterns.

References:
Duan Jianhua: "Status Quo of Health Care for Floating Children under 5 Years Old in Chaoyang District and Daxing District of Beijing," Chinese Center for Disease Control and Prevention Master Degree Thesis, 2009.

---

principle has been established and no binding target has been set. In addition, the former vaccination also emphasizes the exercise of "intensifying leak detection and replanting" every year, and does not stipulate the proportion of routine vaccination. In a word, this document still implements new work along the existing train of thought, and typically embodies the pattern and thinking of "dualized" public health services for floating population as revealed in this article.

Du Qing, et al. Analysis of Prenatal Checkup Status of Migrants in Cities and Influencing Factors, China Primary Health Care 2009, No.4.

Feng Xiaorong: "Current status of migrant children's health care and its influencing factors", "Everyone's Health" 2015, No. 14.

Fu Hongpeng et al .: Background, Changes and Trends of Public Health Management Policies for Floating Population in Beijing, China Health Policy Research, 2008, No.3.

Guo Lina and others: "An analysis of the prenatal status and influencing factors of 825 mobile pregnant women in Chaoyang District, Beijing", "Chinese Journal of MCH" 2012, No.2.

Huang Aiqun et al .: Survey of health care of migrant children under 5 years of age in Beijing and Hangzhou, China Public Health, 2008, No. 3.

Hou Wenjun et al .: Investigation of Strengthened Vaccination and Vaccination of Preschool-age Children's Vaccination in Daxing District of Beijing, Occupation and Health 2012, No. 21.

Wang Hui et al .: "Basic public services for health planning of migrants in Beijing, Shanghai and Guangdong", "Maternal and Child Health Care of China" 2016, No.10.

Wang Qian et al .: "Investigation and Analysis of Current Status of Mobile Children's Health in Fengtai District of Beijing", "Maternal and Child Health Care of China" 2009, No. 24.

Xiao Danqiong, Wang Xiaoli: "Beijing Shijingshan District, 152 cases of migrant children health survey", "Chinese Maternal and Child Health" 2009 the twenty-third period.

Yan Shujuan: "The Status Quo and Demand Analysis of Mobile Children under 5 Years Old in Beijing", "China Children's Health Journal" 2008, No.5.

Zhang Yi: "Talking about the Funds Management of National Basic Public Health Projects - Take a Certain District of Beijing for Example", "China Economy and Trade", 2015, No. 8.

Zhang Pei, et al: Comparative Analysis of Prenatal Health Care Utilization of Urban Mobility and Registered Mothers and Children, Chinese Journal of Maternal and Child Health, Vol.27, No.2, 2012.

Zhang Xiaowen: "Xicheng District, Beijing mobile child health care review and status quo", "Medical Information" 2010, No. 10.

Zhou Bing et al .: "Study on Factors Affecting Children's Regular Immunization in

Mentougou District, Beijing", "Capital Public Health" 2014, No.3.

# Innovation and Development of Geriatric Education and Community Geriatric Education in Beijing

## Li Jinjuan[1]

## Abstract

With the harsh challenges of population aging in Beijing, the subjective needs of the elderly for continuing education and self-improvement are also growing. After more than 30 years of development, the aged education in Beijing has initially formed a pattern of jointly promoting the development of education, civil administration, aging and other sectors. At the same time, there are some problems such as deviation of cognition, fragmentation of management, monotonous education contents, single implementation, insufficient and insufficient educational resources distribution and so on. It should be emphasized that the community as an important social area for the elderly social life, community education for the elderly is also the elderly to improve the quality of life the main path.

Keywords: Aging, Geriatric Education, Community Education, Community Elderly Education

1. Geriatric education and community geriatric education

After World War II, as lifelong education was put forward and expanded as an educational trend of thought, the education of the aged also began to become the focus of scholars in various countries. Chinese scholars have given many definitions of elder education from different perspectives. According to one view, "Elderly education is an education system that focuses on the elderly. It integrates general education, higher education and staff education. It is an integral part of adult education and is the final stage of lifelong education."[2] The viewpoints are interpreted from the sociological dimension that seniors education is part of the service of aging society, that senile education is an effective way to re-socialize the elderly under the background of population aging, Provide support and assistance in life, psychology, social participation and other aspects, and guide older people to

[1] Li Jinjuan, Assistant Researcher, Research Institute of Sociology, Beijing Academy of Social Sciences. Ph. D in Sociology.
[2]

adapt themselves physically and mentally to adapt to the ever-changing social environment. In conclusion, as a theoretical construct, the deepening and further improvement of the theory of education for the elderly depends on the promotion and development of the education of the elderly. The operation of the education for the elderly cannot be separated from the guidance of the theory of education for the elderly in the new era.

Looking at the various forms of the elderly education organization in Beijing, the elderly education in the community is an informal form of education for the elderly compared to the professional older university. Community Geriatric School is a basic and important teaching organization for the development of community geriatric education.[1] Some scholars put forward the concept of community education in the elderly based on the conceptual analysis of both community education and old age education: "Community aged education is carried out within the community and is mainly composed of the elderly and the elderly, aimed at Satisfy their educational needs, guarantee their right to education, enhance their ability to survive and develop, promote their social participation and all-round development, and eventually realize the service activities for the elderly with the elderly and the prospective elderly in harmony with their families, communities and society ".[2]

The author believes that community education for the elderly is a kind of educational organization mainly aimed at the elderly and aimed at improving the quality of life of the elderly. The content covers retirement education, health education, leisure education, knowledge and skills education and life education. As an organic part of community education, educating the elderly groups at the community level, as well as community education targeting migrant groups and young people, rely on community education as guidance and technical support.

2. Analysis of the Current Situation of Geriatric Education

For more than 30 years, the state has targeted the development of education for the elderly from the aspects of law and policy on the rights and interests of its audience, institutional mechanisms for innovation, exploration and development mode, school scale and facilities construction. For example, the "Decision on Strengthening the

---

1

2

Work of Aged People" (Zhong Fa [2000] No. 13); the Outline of the National Medium and Long-Term Education Reform and Development Plan (2010-2020); the 12th Five-Year Plan for China's Aging Development Guofa [2011] No.28) "Outline of the National Medium and Long-term Education Reform and Development Plan (2010-2020)", "National Education Development Thirteenth Five-year Plan" (Jiao Fa [2017] No. 9)

As far as Beijing Municipality is concerned, with the further deepening of the degree of aging and the increasing demand for education for the elderly, the Beijing municipal government has issued a series of policy documents in order to effectively guarantee the full enjoyment of the right of continuing education for seniors. What needs to be emphasized here is that the General Office of the State Council issued the "Plan for the Development of Elderly Education (2016-2020)" in 2016, which elaborates on the development of the education for elders in terms of supply and mechanism innovation. This emphasizes that by 2020, it will basically form a "new pattern of education for the elderly with broad coverage, flexibility and diversity, distinct features and standardized and orderly". Taking this as a backdrop, "Beijing's" Plan for Development of Aging for the Thirteenth Five-Year Plan "pointed out that it is necessary to" rationalize the management system for the development of education for the aged, incorporate the education for the elderly in the lifelong education system for all and realize the systematic development of the education for the elderly ... Encourage the creation of older or older schools to provide learning opportunities for the elderly. "

It can be said that the above policy documents provide policy-level mechanisms for guaranteeing and developing opportunities for the further development of education for the elderly. For now, the development of education for the aged in Beijing has reached a certain scale and there is room for further improvement.

2.1 The four levels of elder education basically formed and the supply of education services became diversified

Since the establishment of Haidian University of the Elderly in Beijing, the first university for the elderly in 1984, the aged education in Beijing has basically established a four-level network of education for the aged in cities, counties, towns and villages, On the scale of the development track, and has accumulated a wealth of practical experience and teaching achievements.

The composition of Beijing senior school is more complicated. In terms of the nature of running a school, it is mainly composed of public-run units, private-run public subsidies, public private-owned units and privately-run units. From the perspective of organizational form of running schools, it generally covers school education, social education, distance education and family education. For the main body of running schools, the author believes that the senior school in Beijing is mainly composed of the following three categories at present: a) organizations and institutions Senile university and Beijing Radio and Television University system. Such elder universities generally have relatively good source of living and teaching resources, fixed places and relatively fixed sources of funding, but they still have to be expanded in terms of the scale of running schools; b) at the municipal level, senior citizens' colleges, towns and neighborhoods Old school. The city-level elder university has a certain scale and faces to the society enrollment with good teaching facilities. The elder schools in the towns and communities are mainly self-organized by the elderly. Such schools are mainly organized by social forces to run schools, lack of funds, the venue is the highlight of the problem; c) pension institutions, the mass media, the Beijing Association of old educators and other institutions of the elderly education activities. As a complement to the above two types of forms, various types of social organizations are involved in the activities of senior education, which is a new type of education for the elderly in recent years. Such educational activities do not rigidly adhere to the traditional old form of child-rearing and have some flexibility. However, the faculty, stability and systematicness still need to be improved.

In short, the diversified structure of education for the aged in Beijing, which is mainly dominated by old-age universities (schools) and community-based schools and complemented by social forces, is currently being established in Beijing.

2.2 Geriatric education is rich in resources, with a limited total amount and small coverage

Since the 18th National Congress of the Communist Party of China, the education for the aged in our country has been developing rapidly and has achieved some success.

According to statistics published in "Statistical Communiqué on Social Service Development in 2015, Ministry of Civil Affairs", as of the end of 2015, there were 53,000 seniors 'schools in our country, 7,328,000 students in school, 371,000 seniors' activity rooms. Although Beijing has more excellent educational resources than other cities because of its advantaged advantages, it is also worth noting that the total amount of geriatric education resources in Beijing is still relatively limited.

As shown in Table 1, as the main positions for seniors to participate in educational activities, the numbers of seniors 'schools and seniors' centers have not changed much in recent years and have not correspondingly increased with the surging population of the elderly. According to a survey on elderly education in Beijing, "the education supply for all kinds of aged schools in Beijing in 2013 only covers 10.7% of the city's census population." According to the 2015 elderly population aged 60 and over in the census register in Beijing 318. According to the data of 10,000, the education supply for the elderly can only cover 7.6% of the elderly population in the household register population, a decrease of 3.1% compared with 2013. Compared with the annual growth of about 150,000 elderly people at this stage, it is obviously not enough to meet the growing education needs of the elderly.

Table 1 Changes of the number of aged people in Beijing's senile schools and their in-school attendance in recent 4 years

| Year / Quantity | 2012 | 2013 | 2014 | 2015 |
|---|---|---|---|---|
| Schools for senior | 2909 | 2514 | 2469 | 2410 |
| Activity rooms for senior | 6465 | 7175 | 6280 | 6756 |
| In-school aged students | 28,4000 | 25,9000 | 24,4000 | 23,7000 |

Source: Beijing public year reports and statistics on civil affairs.

2.3 The center of geriatric education gradually moved down and the grassroots education at the community level was developed

The Outline of the National Medium and Long-Term Education Reform and Development Plan (2010-2020) emphasizes the importance of education for the elderly at a policy level and especially points out that education for the elderly should "gradually extend to the community, towns and streets." Since then, the use of social forces to promote the development of education for the elderly has gradually become the consensus of the government and all sectors of society. The recently issued "13th Five-Year Plan" for National Education Development (Jiao Fa [2017] No. 9) emphasizes that education institutions for the elderly should be well run and a continuous education network covering both urban and rural areas should be formed.

Table 2 Distribution of Senior Citizen Learning Institutions at Street Level (Community) in Beijing's Sixth District Towns

| Name / County-level Districts | Third-age Learning Colleges (branch campus) | Community Senior Learning Schools / Centers | Community Service Centers | Hobby Group ps | Total |
|---|---|---|---|---|---|
| Dongcheng | | 13 | 3 | 2 | 18 |
| Xicheng | 2 | | | | 2 |
| Haidian | 1 | | | | 1 |
| Chaoyang | 4 | 15 | | | 19 |
| Fengtai | 2 | 1 | | | 3 |
| Shijingshan | 2 | | | | 2 |
| Total | 11 | 29 | 3 | 2 | 45 |

Source: Beijing Aging Window, http: // www. Bjageing * gov. Cn / sdyl / main_U / Uswbl / detailOldAgeZdz. Do? Method = detail01dAgeZdz & zdz_ flag = zdz_ lndx.

3. Main Problems and Causes of Geriatric Education in Beijing

3.1 Cognitive bias and management fragmentation

The construction of a lifelong learning society complements the development of the elderly education in an aging society, both indispensable. In the current context of new media, on the one hand, providing the elderly with the right to continuing education requires the help of modern educational equipment and tools; on the other hand, under the existing shortage of educational resources, the expansion of education for the aged Diversified forms become an appropriate choice, that is to say, the implementation of the education for the elderly does not have to be limited to the traditional teaching methods.

However, we found that although the development of the Internet makes possible intelligent living, the public's understanding of the concept of education for the elderly is still relatively traditional and conservative. For example, at the community level, educational activities on older persons are mainly focused on face-to-face groups of self-organization for the elderly, and acceptance of newcomers such as mou classes and online classrooms requires a longer process. At the same time, we also see that although Beijing has pointed out the ways and means for the development of education for the aged from the aspect of policy design, in the specific operation process, the management system of education for the elderly has the problem of fragmentation, that is, the administration is still not clear, Some by the Aging Committee, veteran cadres or civil affairs department management, some by the education sector management. This also led to the management of the block division, long management, unclear powers and responsibilities.

3.2 Monotonous education content and subject

From the perspective of the content of education for the elderly, the setting mainly focuses on the interesting edge as the leisure education, information and science and technology with the dominant needs of the elderly such as calligraphy, chorus, English, computer and square dance. There are very few activities on knowledge education involving the hidden needs of the elderly such as medicine and health. From the perspective of teaching methods, although organizations such as Beijing Radio and Television University already have the experience of distance education for the elderly population, the implementation of education activities for the elderly is relatively simple due to the relatively slow adoption of new birth by the elderly. The main traditional face-to-face teaching, teaching activities and independent experience-based learning, the general lack of a fixed textbook. From the perspective of faculty, most of the full-time teachers in traditional senile universities recruit from the society, while the faculty members in towns and communities are mostly composed of community residents and young volunteers. As a whole, there is still a lack of a professional teaching staff for senior aged education, which is not conducive to the long-term systematic development of senior education. From the perspective of funding guarantee, the current funding for education for the elderly in Beijing is still only at the municipal and district levels. There is no clear policy guarantee for the funding for education for the aged on the streets and at the community level. As a grassroots unit for the management of senior education activities, neighborhood committees face many difficulties in applying for funding and organizing activities. It can be said that most education institutions for the elderly have not included in the educational budget for education, greatly affecting the further development of education for the elderly.

3.3 Geriatric education resources for less than demand and with unbalanced distribution

According to statistics released by China Institute of Gerontology and the China Institute of Gerontology, Renmin University of China in 2016, "China's Aged Society Follow-up Survey" shows that "more than one-third of the elderly have a junior high school education or above; about 1 / 4 The elderly have different degrees of loneliness, etc. " It can be predicted that the total demand of the elderly to adapt to the social environment and enhance life care will also increase.

In the case of Beijing, because of the scarcity of public education resources and the unbalanced development of urban and rural areas, the resources for education for older persons are not evenly distributed in the actual distribution. As a result, the demand for re-education for the elderly cannot be met. The concrete manifestation is: on the one hand, some well-equipped older university graduates are generally tense while older schools run by some civil society organizations are struggling. We can see that Beijing has a large proportion of elderly education institutions run by social forces (as shown in Table 1 above, Beijing has a total of 2410 aged schools of various types at all levels in 2015, of which only 29 are composed of cultural departments There are only 24 old-age universities opened by civil affairs departments and education departments). However, "the difficulty of funding is the major bottleneck in the development of education for the elderly. The social forces have not shown any great enthusiasm." This issue urgently arouses the attention of all sectors of society. On the other hand, the distribution of geriatric education resources in urban and rural areas in Beijing is still unevenly distributed, which is manifested in the backward development of geriatric education in rural communities due to the shortage of teachers, funds and educational facilities. It is imperative to promote the development of geriatric education resources through urban elites.

4. Solutions and Countermeasures

At present, our country has entered the decisive stage of building an overall well-to-do society and 2017 is also an important year for implementing the "13th Five-Year Plan." In the era of knowledge-based economy where the whole people are studying for a lifetime, the individualized education needs of the elderly and diversified learning styles are increasingly becoming an organic component of the daily life of the elderly. Community geriatric education has its unique advantages over other forms of schooling such as elder universities, such as the convenience of location, the enrichment of human resources in the community and the promotion of online and offline activities for the elderly who are able to live in the community. The positioning and realistic development of the "9064" pension service model in Beijing also provides support and certain guarantees for the elderly to obtain services for the old in the familiar communities. Therefore, whether it is for the life individual in the old age or the community orientation development in the sight of modern governance, the elderly education in the community has irreplaceable important functions and significance. At present, we need to develop and innovate the education for the aged from the following aspects.

4.1 Improve recognition, deepen understanding, accurate positioning

First of all, following the law of development in the process of education for the elderly and profoundly grasping the connotation and structure of education for the aged, it provides theoretical guidance for the formation of a comprehensive management system applicable to the development of education for the aged at the present stage. Second, we must scientifically understand the dialectical relationship between the old-age education and the community education and the function and value of the elderly education in the community. Recognizing that geriatric education is an integral part of community education and grasping the richness of geriatric education as a whole, we can get out of misunderstanding and better promote geriatric education and community geriatric education. Thirdly, we should strengthen disciplinary development in gerontology and personnel training in old-age care services to promote interdisciplinary theoretical and policy research on the development of human resources for the elderly and carry out integrated research from the multidisciplinary perspective of demography, sociology, management and economics Geriatric education, especially in community-specific practice provide scientific theoretical guidance. Finally, use the media to create a good social atmosphere. We will step up efforts to publicize the various old-age education guidelines and policies of the country and Beijing and promote the public to form a scientific understanding of old-age education and community-based aged education.

4.2 Strengthen the top-level design and explore the development of diversified patterns of education for the elderly

First of all, the government should encourage social forces to set up elder universities and the government should provide them with some preferential treatment in terms of funds, venues and taxation. They should increase their support and investment in community elders education both in philosophy and practice, and create doors for the elderly At the same time, through various means such as government procurement services and project cooperation, we should attract various social forces to participate in the education for the elderly, promote the linkage between the education for the elderly and related industries, and promote the education and consumption of the elderly in a reasonable manner. Second, the government should actively develop the human resources for the elderly from the perspectives of legislation, policies and management, study and improve relevant systems concerning old age education, and improve the mechanism for inputting funds to give full play to the intelligence superiority of the elderly. Thirdly, led by party committees and governments, they form an elder education management system that interconnects civil affairs, culture and education. Finally, strengthen the construction and optimization of the elder education service personnel team. Through employment policy guidance and personal career development incentives, we encourage more outstanding talents to join the elder education service personnel team to form a teaching and management team with full-time staff as the backbone and combining with part-time staff and volunteers.

4.3 Take community education as a platform to integrate related resources of geriatric education

As a saying goes, "Never too old to learn". The idea of lifelong education has existed in our country. In the knowledge-based economy, the renewal cycle of knowledge is shortened. For the elderly to adapt to the development of the society, apart from receiving the education of the professional knowledge of the elder schools, they need to carry out secondary development and secondary training through community and social organizations.

At the content level, we should continue to enrich the contents and forms of elder education in the community and explore a new mode of combining education and education. Such training should involve many aspects such as interpersonal communication, intergenerational coordination, the application of social networking tools, codes of conduct and social morals. At the level of implementation of specific organizations, we should take the concept of lifelong education as the guideline, and educate different forms of education activities such as basic education, higher education and general education through personal life history and build a bridge of communication and coordination for all kinds of educational activities. For example, we should establish a platform for the exchange and interaction of elderly human resources between schools and communities, so as to create fair educational opportunities and conditions for senior citizens and mobilize their enthusiasm for self-management, self-improvement and active learning. At the audience level, the specific practice of self-organization of the elderly also depends on the community to provide the necessary human, material and financial support. On the one hand, the community provides venues and financial support to assist the elderly to establish grass-roots community organizations, carry out activities on a regular basis, and further promote their participation in community public affairs discussions and the conversion of functions to the organizations of mutual benefit. For example, on the basis of the interest group, the elderly are allowed to learn health care, financial insurance, consumer finance and other knowledge, and promote the elderly to share the achievements of Internet social development. In the meantime, elderly support groups can be set up on the basis of this to help the elderly at lower ages provide possible service and support to elderly people in need of care, and promote the self-organization of seniors from functional conversion to mutual benefit. On the other hand, professional education and training provided by professional community-based organizations is also necessary. Such training not only provides elderly therapies that meet the needs of the elderly themselves, but also provides community workers with professional knowledge in nursing care, psychological counseling, social work and nutrition and health care.

In short, we should not only promote the self-improvement of the elderly under the coordination and support of the community and social organizations, but also build a harmonious and civilized community ecological environment and help the elderly to shift themselves from small families with limited resources to peer groups while enhancing themselves, into the community.

4.4 Learn from foreign advanced experience in community education

As the focus of China's elderly education in the next few years lies in the education of grassroots communities, we mainly introduce some advanced concepts and practical experiences of community education here.

In the Nordic society represented by Denmark, following the spirit of humanism, community education aims to "make every citizen enjoy the right to learn knowledge and develop and achieve the equality of educational opportunities" ®; The main implementing agencies are popular schools, with distinctive features of the popular. In the United States, community colleges are an indispensable organizational element in the development of community education. In the implementation of education, community colleges provide residents with the educational services they need in a flexible and diversified organizational form, such as university transfer education, vocational education, continuing education and other education services. In the management system, the United States implements the "federal-state-local" three-level management system and coordinates with the schools so as to help promote the diversified development of education for the elderly.

It can be seen from the above that the developed countries in developed countries have made a positive reference and inspiration for the effective development of community-based aged education in China in terms of education objectives, educational concepts, education implementation organizations and management systems.

As some scholars have pointed out, the community is the basic unit for building a learning society and has a lot of social resources. ® Community Geriatric Education is not only a basic form of teaching and learning for the elderly, but also an important innovation in the development of the education for the aged. This has become the consensus of the academic community. The "Plan for Education for Elderly Development (2016-2020)" released in 2016 also explicitly states that it is necessary to fully support the development of community education in urban and rural areas through various means to face the grass roots and communities. In short, the education for the elderly in the community can integrate the elderly to promote their participation in public affairs in the community. It can also help the elderly to ease their later life by teaching "what they are taught, what they learn, what they do, what they want to do" The pressure of aging brings great significance to the current social and economic development.

References:

Qiu Feng editor, "Guide to Gerontology", science popularization press, 1993.

Li Jing et al., "Research on Gerontology Education in China", "Aging Science Research", 2015, No.10.

Fan Suqin: "Seniors Education community construction practice and thinking", "Petroleum Politics Research" 2013 the first period.

Ye Zhonghai: "Research on the Development of Community Education in China in the Early 21st Century", Ocean University of China Press, 2006.

Wang Ying: "Research on Chinese Elderly Community Education", Nankai University Doctoral Dissertation, 2010.

"How to Break the Seniors Education", "Guangming Daily", November 16, 2016.

Beijing Municipal Bureau of Statistics, Beijing Survey Corps, National Bureau of Statistics: Beijing Statistical Yearbook (2016), 2016.

Hao Meiying: "The Concept of Community Education in Northern Europe, the United States, Japan and Singapore", "Adult Education", 2010, No.12.

Osmani Zhang: "Foreign community education model and its enlightenment to our country", "Tianjin Radio University" 2010, No.3.

Fan Lihua et al: "Aged Education Model of Elder Education Model and Development Trend", "Education Exploration" 2013, No.3.

# Beijing Strengthens the Construction of National Culture Center with the Aim of Becoming World Famous Cultural City

## Li Jiansheng[1]

## Abstract

2016 is the year that Beijing initiates its new five-year plan for the construction of the national cultural center. In reference to relevant indexes nationwide in 2016, Beijing ranks first in terms of cultural industry index, cultural consumption composite index, and knowledge city competitiveness index, and comes a close second to Hong Kong as to cultural city competitiveness index. As a national cultural center, Beijing demonstrates a strong competitiveness in cultural development, playing a leading and exemplary role. This report focuses on Beijing's efforts in building up national cultural center as a crucial step in its pursuit of becoming a world famous cultural city. It summarizes Beijing's latest moves to protect and carry forward its historical and cultural heritage, to promote public cultural service, to develop innovative cultural industry, and to extend cultural exchanges and communication, and analyzes advantages and shortcomings in terms of comprehensive and cultural competitiveness via comparison with other cities of China, putting forward with suggestions and countermeasures accordingly.

Keywords: capital city, national cultural center, world famous cultural city, new development pattern

1. Blueprint new development pattern of national cultural center and make a good start at the opening year

2016 is the opening year of Beijing's new five-year plan for building into a national cultural center. Being such a center is a function of Beijing as a capital city, which is given priority to among other functions indicated in the development strategies. It is one of the key pathways to realize "five-in-one" development (specifically in terms of economy, politics, culture, society, and ecological civilization) of Beijing, to build the

---

[1] Li Jiansheng, Director of Research Institute of Culture, Beijing Academy of Social Sciences, Research areas include culture and literary and artistic theory.

capital into the center of politics, of cultural exchanges, of international communications, and of technical innovation, and to promote the construction of a globally advanced, harmonious, and habitable city. In June, 2016, Beijing municipal government launched the *Beijing's Plan to Strengthen the Construction of National Cultural Center during the 13th Five-Year Plan Period* (hereinafter referred to as the *Construction Plan*), sketching the new blueprint for the development of the national cultural center. The *Construction Plan* brings forward with the ambitious goals by 2020, which are to build Beijing into a capital of advanced culture with socialist characteristics, to make a balanced progress in both materials and ideology, in both traditional and modern culture, and in both cultural heritage and innovation, to foster tolerant, amiable social environment with humanistic concern and cultural charm, and to boost the cause of world famous cultural city and world cultural heritage landmark.

The construction of national cultural center was listed in the municipal key special program, being the first of its kind. It verifies the high relevance of the construction plan to Beijing's development strategies and the essential function as a national cultural center. In 2014 when President Xi Jinping inspected Beijing, he put forward with a new strategic plan and new requirements regarding the city's development. To implement the President's messages from his speeches in many occasions, Beijing municipal government issued the *Construction Plan*, making efforts to fortify its top design and accelerate construction process in the background of new phase and situations of city growth. As the *Suggestions on Making the 13th Five-Year Plan for Economic and Social Development of Beijing* mentions, culture is the soul and soft power of a city, because of which Beijing shall strive to become a national cultural center by nurturing a strong cultural awareness and confidence, boosting cultural prosperity, playing a leading role in advanced socialist culture, inheriting and promoting historical and cultural heritage, fastening cultural reform and innovation, and upgrading city civilization.

The *Construction Plan* set up goals of upgrading Beijing as a world famous cultural city and world cultural heritage landmark, being based on the city's superior cultural resources, cultural innovation power, and development targets, and presenting a vision of globe-oriented city. The goals are of strategic significance which gives layout and directions for Beijing's cultural construction during its 13th Five-Year Plan period from the perspective of a high-end, in-depth and extended concept of culture. The *General Development Plan of Beijing* submitted and commented by the State Council of China in 2005 expresses Beijing's resolution to become "a highly tolerant and diversified world famous cultural city with a combination of traditional and modern culture". As a step further, the special program for building up national cultural center is broader strategic vision and a greater development goal. Just as Beijing's 13th Five-Year Plan indicates, Beijing is supposed to grow into a city that harbors both traditional and modern culture, seeks balance between material and spiritual progress, highlights historical heritage as well as in-vogue innovation, and showcases humanistic characteristics, cultural charm and humanistic concerns. These expectations point out the directions towards which Beijing's city culture should develop and the images and spiritual atmosphere Beijing should present, as well as give the approach through which Beijing can realize its goal of world famous cultural city and world cultural heritage landmark.

To realize the aims above, Beijing should intensify the work in building a national cultural center, which is also the goal and mission of cultural construction of Beijing during the 13th Five-Year period. The *Construction Plan* determines the guiding theory, general objectives, and primary principles of the construction of national cultural center, and ascertains the development pattern of the center during 13th Five-Year Period. The goal of becoming a national cultural center has been further ascertained in the *Construction Plan*; the integration of national cultural center and politic center, and international communication center and technological innovation center highlighted; and the national cultural center as a city function, namely gathering together the best of human life, driving the development of neighboring areas, leading innovation, showcasing and communication, and providing services and logistics, given priority. The *Construction Plan* stresses on the leading and exemplary role Beijing shall play in steering social values and promoting cultural development. To be specific, Beijing shall take the lead in building up socialist core values as well as demonstrate the image of the nation and of the capital in aspects of ideological and theoretical research, cultural and artistic creation, and journalism and mass communication, so as to fortify its high standing of ideology, values, and ethics.

In most cases, how city culture functions has a close relation to its layout and the two inter-infiltrate to a large extent. The service upgrading of public culture, the development of cultural creative industries, the presentation of city image and charm, and the aggregation and influence functions of culture rely on the cultural space in a city. Thus the layout issue is crucial to city cultural construction. The program for building up a national cultural center during the 13th Five-Year Plan period is characterized as the intensification of the relevance among cultural themes, forms, functions and space layout. Aiming at building a world-class cultural center and based on the space framework of new modernized capital circle and Beijing-centered world-class agglomeration, the *Construction Plan* put forth a new development layout for the national cultural center with a strategic vision to strengthen and boost the construction of the center. In terms of space, the national cultural center has its core function area cover each district of Beijing. In terms of functions, Beijing is the major carrier of the cultural center nationwide. In terms of role, Beijing is the nest of national cultural innovation and development. Moreover, the *Construction Plan* suggests that cultural resources and advantages of different districts of Beijing should be integrated and efforts should be given to realize balanced development of culture in the capital core function area while optimizing the core functions of Beijing and paying attention to city sub-centers. The function as a national cultural center is enlarged to the area including Beijing, Tianjin, and Hebei Province, acting as the main extended area of the function and a strong support to Beijing to play the exemplary role of cultural development. As a result, the joint cultural development among regions, cities, resources, and industries comes into being, so does the omni-directional, wide-ranging, and multi-level cultural exchanges and cooperation among Beijing, Tianjin, and Hebei Province. The influence area of the national cultural center targets at constructing the center in a broader space and cultural possibilities and into a center that leads the cultural development of the whole country, represents China's soft power in the global community, and intensifies China's cultural influence internationally. Therefore, the function layout of the center, be it space design, concept connotation, orientation, or roles, should be more clear and accurate and be lifted up to a higher strategic level so that it can help push forward the construction of the center and help the center play a better role.

The *Construction Plan* puts emphasis on the determination and implementation of tasks. Beijing municipal government put forward with ten missions, each with clear targets, covering each areas of national cultural center construction. In aspect of ideological and theoretical construction, the plan requires that Beijing should become a national highland of ideology, taking the lead, upholding socialist theories with Chinese characteristics, having confidence in the theories, pursuing theoretical innovation, promoting the theories and social sciences, building up an influential theory brand and a high-level and high-standard new think tank to service the capital and the country, lifting academic creativity, and boosting the prosperous development of philosophy and social sciences in Beijing. In aspect of nurturing core values, Beijing should act as the pioneer to foster socialist core values in many ways such as value promotion and practice in various kinds of activities, integrating the values in and through the whole process of economic and social development, hosting events that involve the bulk of local residents for advocating public civilization, boosting the institutionalization of integrity, and normalizing volunteering works, and creating an atmosphere oriented to the core values. The plan also highlights the era of internet featured by fast and broad transmission, therefore emphasizing on the guiding role of the internet in public opinion and the combination of traditional and emerging media. It suggests Beijing should make the best use of its informational and technological advantages to fasten the construction of digitalized media, raise new-type media companies, and boost easy, healthy and positive internet cultural construction, so as to build up a new modern transmission system.

Beijing is a world famous city characterized by its long and profound history, harboring abundant traditional cultures of the whole China. The *Construction Plan* says that Beijing is forging ahead with its goal of becoming a "world cultural heritage landmark", of which the protection of historical city and the inheritance of the city's culture is a domain requirement and embodiment. Therefore, the fifth main task by the plan is to strengthen the protection towards the historical and cultural sites in Beijing, pass down the excellent traditional Chinese culture, explore to the best the connotations of culture and history of the city, showcase Beijing's historical context, develop the culture while protecting and inheriting, and display the features and charms of the city to the full. Culture requires innovation. As the capital and national cultural center of China, Beijing should develop new culture production mechanism, foster favorable cultural ecology, and demonstrate the high-quality cultural products with Beijing's characteristics which can live up to its role as a capital. The seventh task by the *Construction Plan* is to accelerate the construction of a service system for modern public culture in Beijing through ways of standardization and equalization, integration of public cultural resources, improvement of comprehensive service efficiency of culture, and innovation of operational mechanism of management service, offering better-quality, more-efficient, supply-to-demand, and multi-layer pubic cultural service and meeting the spiritual needs of the people. The cultural creative industries in Beijing have always been taking the lead nationwide, playing a key role in boosting the cultural and economic development of the city. To disperse the non-capital functions of Beijing in order, the plan suggests that Beijing should stimulate the creativity and enthusiasm to innovate of cultural creative industries, continuously optimize industrial development structure, gather together all kinds of innovative elements, spur the market's vitality, enrich cultural connotations, improve the space layout of cultural industries with highlights and a variety of features, develop markets and a market system for cultural products and elements, make the best use of advantageous resources  of culture and scientific innovation, boost the in-depth integration of culture and science & technology, explore more approaches to develop cultural creative industries by applying "Internet Plus" and "Culture Plus", push forward the new-type operation of cultural industries of Beijing, and fasten the process of building a "Creative Beijing". Nowadays, the international transmission and exchanges of culture has become a key criterion to evaluate the influential power and competitiveness of culture. Under this circumstance, the plan requests that Beijing should lay more emphasis on international cultural communication, external trade of culture, and major events for cultural brand making in order to uplift the level of international cultural exchanges of Beijing. At the same time Beijing is attracting talented people from across the nation, its cultural development relies on them. During the 13th Five-Year Plan period, according to the *Construction Plan*, Beijing shall make efforts to cultivate and attract more high-end talents for cultural development with international standards and global visions, pay more attention to nurture cultural leaders and experts, give talents' development the first priority, formulate overall plan for talents' development, inspire creative entrepreneurship of the talents, and build the capital into a galaxy of talents.

The year 2016 is not only the starting point of the 13th Five-Year Plan, but as well the year when Beijing makes endeavor to grow into the national cultural center.

According to the Beijing municipal government report for 2016, Beijing's culture should always go in line with the direction of advanced cultures, acting as a culture leader nationwide, a pioneer to pursue cultural development and prosperity, and a light tower in the voyage of socialist advanced culture. Beijing should also pay continuous attention to the protection and inheritance of culture, setting up an overall plan to preserve key areas such as the Great Wall and "three hills and five gardens", forging ahead with world heritage application for sites lying on the central axis of Beijing, with the construction of charming corridor along "the axis and the line", with the building of exhibition area of Qianmen history and culture, and with the recovery of the Temple of Heaven, and exploring, showcasing and inheriting intangible cultural heritage. At the same time, Beijing should reform on cultural system, create new development mechanism, spur cultural productivity, and boost the blossom of cultural creative industries and integration of relevant ones. In February, 2016, Beijing municipal government proposed one hundred and eighty seven key work plans in the report on its work, nine of which was related to the construction of socialist advanced culture, namely promotion of ideological and political theory and construction of city public civilization, public culture service and creative work of literature and fine art, protection of key cultural regions, world heritage application for Beijing's axis line and building the charming corridor, exploration and inheritance of capital culture, protection of intangible cultural heritage and innovation of old famous brands, reform on cultural system and integrated development with media, guiding catalogue for cultural creative industries and building pilot bases, and new development patterns of cultural industries and integration with relevant industries. These key works are for not only Beijing's annual cultural construction program specifically in the year of 2016, but as well the construction of national cultural center in the beginning year of the 13th Five-Year Plan.

To strengthen the construction of the national cultural center is what Beijing, as a national cultural center city, is supposed to do, as well as what Beijing, as the capital city of China, should function. It is a major strategic measure to fortify Beijing's city strategic positioning, and intensify the functions of the capital. The program for building up national cultural center during the 13th Five-Year Plan period launched by Beijing municipal government puts forward with objectives, tasks and measures, centering around Beijing's core functions such as making examples to the nation, posing influence and driving neighboring areas, demonstration and exchanges and providing services. Moreover, the ambitions to build "world famous cultural city" and "world cultural heritage landmark" will lift the construction of the national cultural center to a higher level.

## 2. Current situations and trends of Beijing's cultural development in 2016

In 2016, Beijing's cultural construction focuses on the maintenance of its function and the consolidation of its role as the national cultural center, and makes a good start of the 13th Five-Year Plan. To be specific, Beijing improved the protection of historical and cultural sites, offered better services in terms of public culture, intensified the advantages of cultural creative industries, and expanded the range of cultural communication and cultural trades. In general, the cultural construction of Beijing in 2016 showed a positive trend of development.

### 2.1 Protection of historical and cultural sites and cultural inheritance

Beijing issued relevant policies to protect and pass down historical and cultural heritage in 2016 to improve the preservation, inheritance, and construction mechanisms of material and intangible cultures, recover historical and cultural streets and blocks, continue historical context of the city, and pass on cultural heritage.

#### 2.1.1 Release protection policies and improve cultural protection mechanism

In May, 2016, Beijing Party Committee passed the *Proposal on Deepening Comprehensive Reform to Improve City Planning, Construction and Management by Beijing CPC Committee and Beijing Municipal Government*, (hereafter referred to as the *Proposal*), which suggests Beijing should make more efforts to protect the ancient city areas to live up to the fame of historical and cultural city, recover original looks of the Forbidden City, the Temple of Heave, the Bell and Drum Towers as well as the ancient rivers and lakes including south Yuhe River and moat in the moon bay region along Qianmen Street, vacate and return, repair and make proper use of cultural relics and courtyards under preservation, and create featured landscape along "the axis and the line". In order to improve protection mechanism, the *Proposal* requests that Beijing should establish an all-rounded protection mechanism, strictly circle out historical and cultural blocks and the range of protection, set up and follow closely standards for protection technologies of traditional style and features, explore new ways to protect and make proper use of ancient city areas which involve and benefit and are under the charge of multi parties, and put up an intellectual protection platform. In June, 2016, Beijing officially released the *Construction Plan*, pointing out the key missions of protection and inheritance of history and culture. Specifically speaking, upholding the principle of "protection as priority, salvage comes first, proper usage and strict management", Beijing should make better performance in protecting historical and cultural relics, lay equal stress on creative transformation and innovative development, promote and pass on excellent Chinese traditional culture, discover and apply resources related to culture of the capital, the royal city, the Beijing local features, and the canal, present to the full Beijing's historical context, upgrade mechanisms for cultural relics protection, capital investment, and innovative inheritance, pay equal attention to protection, inheritance and innovation when protecting the city, showcase the charms of this ancient city, and make Beijing a "golden business card" in terms of ancient city with profound history and culture. In July, 2016, the *13ᵗʰ Five-Year Program on Economic and Social Development of Beijing* was issued, stipulating the objectives, mechanisms, measures, and financial support for shaping the image of ancient capital city with abundant culture, requesting that Beijing should advance the process of intellectualized city protection, fasten the electronic archiving of cultural relics and historical blocks via the latest digitalized and intellectualized technologies, perfect the electronic map for grid management of historical buildings, and enhance efficiency of protection and management. In December, 2016, Beijing released the *Management and Control Guidelines for Preservation of South Luogu Lane (pilot)*, which is the first of its kind, indicating a detailed and accurate data regarding the dimension of the lane, architectures and structure, forms, size, height, and so on. Besides, Xicheng District and Dongcheng District, as two regions with the most intense distribution of historical and cultural relics and resources, have made efforts to protect and pass on their treasures. Xicheng District government drew up *Scheme for Historical and Cultural City Preservation during the 13ᵗʰ Five-Year Plan Period in Xicheng District* and *Action Plan for Preservation of Immovable Relics during the 13ᵗʰ Five-Year Plan Period in Xicheng District*. At the same time, Dongcheng District issued "three action plans", putting forward with the index system for repair of ancient blocks for the first time to strengthen its protection works, optimize the recreation of non-preservation zone, and boost infrastructure construction.

2.1.2 Renovate historical and cultural blocks and recover culture and features of ancient capital

The main content and tasks for city construction of Beijing and inheritance and development of its culture are to protect and use historical and cultural resources, continue its historical context, and reproduce its enchantment. In 2016, based on the overall protection of the city, Beijing paid continuous attention to the recovery of old blocks and streets, gave priority to the protection and usage of "the axis and the line", the "three hills and five gardens", and the Great Wall, stressed on the protection of historical and cultural blocks, siheyuan (courtyards), hutongs (alleys), ancient cultural relics, traditional villages, and industrial heritages, so as to reshape the style and features of the ancient capital. When it comes to the protection of historical and cultural blocks, Beijing launched a project to repair the North Fahai Temple in the Western Hill cultural belt, advanced the project to protect the twenty-eight scenes relics in Fragrance Hill, regained original historical context of hutongs and traditional industries, reproduced the old scenes in Gulou Dajie Street, established and opened up to the public the whole historical and cultural scenes on footbridges in south Beijing as a hallmark of capital city, generally finished the south Yuhe River project and renewed the old waterway followed the completion of the north part, repaired the Changpuhe River which was an important river in the royal city and built the Changpuhe Park, and initiated the reconstruction project of main avenue in South Luogu Lane with a stress on the lane environment improvement. So far, there are 3840 immovable cultural relics under registration in Beijing, among which 126 are national-level key relics, 216 are at municipal level, and nearly 800 at district-level, and 56 are publicly announced places buried with cultural relics underground, 188 buildings in 71 places are listed in the catalogue of excellent modern architectures under protection in Beijing. Besides, 43 places are historical and cultural protection zone of Beijing, 3 historical and cultural blocks in China, 1 place historical and cultural town in China, and 5 historical and cultural villages in China. The historical and cultural relics in Beijing are where old Beijing and real Beijing lie on, as well as the city's historical context that contracts pleasantly with its modern civilization.

2.1.3 Perfect protection mechanism for intangible cultural heritage and inherit cultural legacy

In 2016, Beijing tried to find ways to integrate the protection of intangible cultural heritage with modern cultural industries, invested more on the protection of intangible cultural heritage, and made good results in protecting skills and inheritors of intangible cultural heritage and in carrying out relevant promotion and education. At the same time, Beijing founded a base for intangible cultural heritage industries, making protection works fit into the development pace of cultural industries. *Proposals on Supporting the Inheritance and Development of Chinese Operas by Beijing Municipal Government* was released in the same year to push forward the innovative inheritance and future development of traditional Chinese opera culture. The *Regulation on the Conservation of Intangible Cultural Heritage of Beijing* (hereafter referred to as the *Regulation*) was listed in national legislative plan to complement the *Intangible Heritage Law*, determining the legal status of intangible heritage protection units, rights of inheritors, and duties of relevant government sections. It will be a local regulation that plays a crucial role in conserving and inheriting intangible cultural heritage. In April, 2016, Beijing officially launched the "Industrial Base for Intangible Cultural Heritage Inheritors of China", setting up a national and professional model base that integrates production, study and research. The base will function as China's protection base for intangible cultural heritage, Beijing's demonstration base of key cultural industries, national 4A cultural scenic spot, and patriotism education base for youth, protecting, displaying and passing down the intangible cultural heritage. At the same time, in order to enhance the publicity of intangible cultural heritage and make the residents more exposed to intangible and traditional culture, the Capital Museum joined hands with Beijing-Tianjin-Hebei Collectors Association to co-host a demonstration month for intangible collections. The first O2O Online and off-line interaction experience of intangible cultural heritage was initiated to encourage protection and displaying of the heritage. "Intangible Cultural Heritage Series" have been published in four batches successively including 48 books such as *The Kites* and *Single-String Characteristic Music*. Investment on the protection of intangible cultural heritage has been increased as well. By the end of the "12th Five Year Plan", Beijing has invested 126 million yuan, of which 29.27 million yuan was for supporting representative programs and 9.12 million yuan for representative inheritors. So far, ten pieces of program has been selected into "masterpieces of human intangible cultural heritage" by UNESCO, 126 pieces are state-level representative programs of intangible cultural heritage, 273 pieces are municipal-level ones, and there are 85 representative inheritors of state-level intangible programs and 267 of municipal-level ones. It is not hard to notice that Beijing is giving its full swing in order to the protection and inheritance work of intangible cultural heritage and it is making important progresses.

## 2.2 Enhance construction and service efficiency of public culture

In 2016, Beijing insisted to focus on the people, improved policy system of public culture, perfected service operation mechanism of public culture, pushed forward the construction of the demonstration area of public culture service system, improved relevant facilities, ensured citizen-friendly cultural services, strengthen team building of public culture, spurred cultural and artistic innovation, and promoted brand building of great pieces of culture. Generally speaking, the construction of public culture was enhanced and the service efficiency of public culture boosted.

### 2.2.1 Improve public culture policy system and service operation mechanism

As the *Construction Plan* released in 2016 pointed out, Beijing should improve services of public culture and supply and service abilities of public culture products, support the standardization and equalization of public culture services, implement "1+3" public culture policy, integrate public cultural resources, improve culture service quality, boost comprehensive efficiency of culture services, create new and enrich old mechanism of cultural management and services, mobilize social power, and explore new modes of public culture service. Upholding the development concept of "innovation, coordination, greenness, openness and sharing", Beijing should provide with a support combo of "mechanism, resources, usage, and money" so as to make key breakthroughs in four aspects of macro-policies, facility standards, service specifications, and building capability, to fasten the shaping of modern service system for public culture, to protect citizens' rights of culture, to serve the people's livelihood in terms of culture, and to share cultural achievements. It is estimated that full coverage of public culture service facilities can be generally realized by 2020. According to the *Social Governance Plan of Beijing during "13th Five-Year Plan"* issued in the same year, the coverage of public culture facilities in Beijing will be enhanced to 99% during the 13th Five-Year Plan period. To implement the "1+3" public culture policy system, Beijing published *Tasks and Division of Labor of the Construction of Public Culture Service System in Beijing during the 13th Five-Year*

*Plan Period*, setting up the working objectives for the next five years and the coordination mechanism of joint conference of 16 new district-level public culture service systems, formulating the overall plans for grassroots public culture cultivation. In line with policies from the State Council, Beijing came up with *Guiding Catalogue for Beijing Government Buying Public Culture Services from Social Forces*, which requires innovative service mechanism, as well as a "top down and demand-to-supply" mode of service emphasizing on interaction and menu type to meet the diversified demands from citizens in a more effective and efficient fashion.

2.2.2 Steadily promote the construction of demonstration areas and improve public cultural facilities

The purpose of building a national demonstration area for public cultural services is to promote outstanding contradictions and important issues facing the construction of the public cultural service system throughout the country and to innovate and explore long-term safeguard mechanisms for establishing public cultural service systems so as to formulate public cultural services for the country The relevant policies provide practical experience and scientific basis. Beijing has actively promoted the construction of a demonstration area for public cultural services since the 12th Five-Year Plan period and has made great efforts to create a demonstration area (project) for the national public cultural service system. Following the first batch of "National Public Culture Service area demonstration zone ", Dongcheng District was selected as the second batch of" National Public Cultural Service Demonstration Zone "in 2016. Meanwhile, Daxing District, Haidian District and Yanqing District have successfully passed the inspection of the first and second batch of demonstration projects and Haidian District has selected the third batch of national demonstration area, Shijingshan District and Fangshan District has the third batch of demonstration projects. Drawing on the successful experiences created by the demonstration area of national public cultural services, Beijing fully mobilizes the enthusiasm of Party committees and governments at all levels and plays an exemplary role in bringing about an overall improvement in the standard of public cultural services in Beijing and launches the establishment of a demonstration area for Beijing's public cultural service system . In 2016, Shijingshan, Fengtai District, Fangshan District, Daxing District and Tongzhou District were awarded the first batch of qualifications. In 2017, Beijing will speed up the construction of infrastructure facilities, continuously improve the public cultural service facilities, smoothly carry out the construction of key cultural infrastructure at the municipal level, and accelerate the construction of major cultural facilities such as the Beijing Cultural Center and the Kunqu International Cultural and Art Center in the north. To determine the site selection and construction scale of major cultural facilities such as the Beijing International Cultural and Art Exchange Center; speed up the construction of public cultural facilities at the grass-roots level, and establish a number of cultural and sports facilities at the grass-roots level such as the cultural and recreational centers of key urban centers as well as key cultural centers in key towns People use. By the end of November 2016, the city has a total of 44 cultural centers and libraries, 147 street integrated cultural centers, 182 township cultural centers, 2,919 community comprehensive cultural centers, and 3,666 comprehensive cultural centers in administrative villages. At present, Beijing has initially taken the construction of public cultural service facilities as the core, service-oriented grassroots as the focus, and efficiency enhancement as its purpose to comprehensively promote the construction mode of upgrading and developing the four-level public cultural service system.

2.2.3 Deepen cultural services to benefit the people and strengthen the contingent of public cultural professionals

Adhere to the people as the center's purpose, and actively promote the project of benefiting the people and the development of cultural activities Huimin, enhance the docking of supply and demand of public cultural services, promote public book delivery services, public cultural activities, public cultural performances delivery, innovative service, enrich the diverse citizens Sexual cultural life. In 2016, Beijing Municipality implemented the integration of grassroots book resources, formulated the Administrative Measures for the Integration and Implementation of Grassroots Library Services Resources in Beijing, and the Measures for Selecting and Selecting Bibliographies of Grassroots Libraries in Beijing. The construction of the public library distribution system further improved, at the grassroots level, the service efficiency of the grassroots units was further enhanced, promotion of universal reading was conducted, and brand culture activities such as the "Book Exchange Dajiu", "the first photo forum" and the "citizen reading plan" were carried out continuously. The co-construction and sharing of digital resources were enhanced and the digital management level has improved. At present, there are altogether 4295 sites for sharing cultural information resources in Beijing and 300 digital cultural communities. In the meantime, Beijing has launched a series of cultural activities for citizens, promoted the performance of public welfare services and took the form of extensive publicity, interactive participation and fare subsidies to mobilize the enthusiasm of citizens in participating in cultural activities and enhance their satisfaction with cultural services. For example, in 2016, 58 farms launched Huimin low-priced tickets for 2,400 performances and subsidized low-priced tickets totaling 229056, with a subsidy amount of 26.02 million yuan, an increase of 18.3% over the previous year and benefiting more than 500,000 audience members. For example, as of December 2016, the "Capital Citizens Concert Hall" has gone deep to 16 districts of the city, performing 25 games and 20,000 audiences. It covers grass-roots units such as military units, rural areas, enterprises, institutions, schools, communities and welfare institutions. In 2017, Beijing Municipality will step up its efforts to establish grassroots public cultural service personnel, with a total of 10,379 grassroots cultural groups in townships and community villages. Among them, there are 7,883 grassroots cultural organizers, 9204 cultural and art teams, and 3 cultural volunteers. 270,000, 311 cultural volunteer groups, with as many as 280,000 participants. Beijing continued to carry out the "Training Project of Thousands of Grass-roots Cultural Organizers", and trained about 1,000 cultural organizers every year in the past three years so as to enhance the cultural level and work ability of service personnel.

2.2.4 Prosper cultural and artistic creation, and create capital culture boutique

*The Plan* proposed that Beijing, as a national cultural center, should climb the peak of literature and art. It should actively guide the planning of literary and artistic creation and prosperity, stage art, foster awareness of cultural quality and strengthen literary and artistic creation And guide the theme of major historical themes to guide the creation of literature and art, the introduction of a number of performance of the real theme, reflecting the traditional culture and culture of Beijing Jing outstanding works, of which drama "Mother" and the drama "Beijing Fayuan Temple" selected in 2017 "country Stage art boutique creation project "10 key supporting repertoire," national stage art key creative repertoire. " To support the creation of creative art, construction and operation of the Beijing Repertory Rehearsal Center and the Beijing theater operation service platform, by the end of November 2016, the rehearsal center received a total of 181 literary and art groups, of which more than 98% of private organizations accounted for more than 210 rehearsals, successfully performed 192 plays. The platform has operated 136 sets of screenings for selected operations, 260 performances in 22 theatrical performances in Beijing, 12 theatrical operas and 13 provinces and cities, attracting over 100,000 audiences. Beijing literary and art circles actively created and introduced stage art products, and rehearsed excellent operas such as the "Long March" and "Visitors on the Iceberg" in the opera. Among them, "Guests on the Iceberg" won the gold medal in the Fifth National Minority Arts Festival; Beijing People's Art Theater, Northern Kunqu Theater, China Theater and other critics to create and launch a number of ideological content, excellent art form of outstanding works by the audience's wide acclaim. In 2016, Beijing actively carried out brand-name performances and made great efforts to create and hold influential brand activities such as "Chun Miao Action", "Beijing Story" and "Beijing-Tianjin-Jiarong Repertory Show" to provide citizens with rich and colorful quality excellent cultural products and spiritual food. At the end of November 2016, 14 Beijing municipal arts and cultural centers (including the National Center for the Performing Arts) launched 23 new projects and 18 rehearsal shows, showing the capital's literary creation and culture for the first year of the 13th Five-Year Plan Practice a good situation.

2.3 Describe the blueprint of cultural and creative city to stimulate cultural and creative vitality

In 2016, during the "13th Five-Year Plan" period, the development and layout of cultural and creative industries in the period of "13th Five-Year Plan" will be announced. Five years of development of cultural and creative industries will be launched. Policies for the development of innovative cultural and creative industries will be released. Construction of industrial functional zones and major projects will be speeded up. Construction of cultural market, promotes cultural and financial services, and guides the growth of cultural consumption.


2.3.1 Introduce cultural and creative industries planning; improve the development of creative industries policy

"Beijing plans to strengthen the construction of the National Cultural Center during the 13th Five-Year Plan". It proposes that by optimizing the development structure of cultural and creative industries, improving the spatial distribution of cultural and creative industries, continuously improving the cultural market system, expanding the main body of various cultural markets and accelerating the promotion of cultural and technological Integration and continuous promotion of cultural format innovation in order to stimulate Beijing's creative industries to create innovative vitality and vigorously enhance the scale, quality and quality of Beijing's cultural and creative industries and to promote a better and faster development of the cultural and creative industries in the capital. In July 2016, the "Plan for the Development of Cultural and Creative Industries in Beijing during the Thirteenth Five-year Plan" was officially released. It was proposed that by 2020, the added value of Beijing's cultural and creative industries will account for 15% of the city's GDP and the pillar position of the cultural industry will be even greater Consolidate, improve the system of cultural industries, rationalize the structure and layout, more competitive in the market, drive more innovation, and demonstrate cultural influence, effectively support the innovation and development of the capital's economy and become the "sophisticated" economic structure As an important engine to build Beijing into a city of Chinese culture and creativity with international influence in cultural innovation, cultural transactions, cultural experiences and cultural operations and create the most energetic cultural and creative city. "Construction Plan" also pointed out that Beijing's "13th Five-Year" period should focus on the development of cultural and creative industries in seven areas: First, optimize the layout of cultural and creative industries; Second, strictly implement the industrial guidance directory; Third, to strengthen municipal Cultural and creative industries park construction; Fourth, to promote the "Internet +" new cultural and creative development; Fifth, deepen the reform of cultural system; sixth is to improve the cultural market system; seventh is to enhance the driving force of cultural consumption, so that Beijing has become an industrial structure optimization and upgrading , A well-diversified industry and products, rich products and services, a healthy development of market players, a substantial increase in innovation capability, a sound market system, and a substantial increase in the export of products and services in China's cultural and creative industries with international influence. In 2016, Beijing also issued relevant opinions and measures to promote the development of cultural and creative industries. The Opinions on Implementing "Internet +" Initiatives promulgated in January 2016 put forward that efforts should be made to promote the integration of the Internet with the construction of cultural industries and to build a digital cultural industry cluster centered on digital products and networked communications, and to enhance Beijing's Cultural and creative industries strength. February 2016, the "Detailed Implementing Rules for Subsidies for Beijing's Cultural and Creative Industries Development Special Funding Project (for Trial Implementation)" was promulgated. The "Detailed Rules" refer to the key projects of cultural industries, development plans, As well as the measurement of subsidies. In June 2016, in response to the current fierce confusion in the cultural industry market, Beijing released the first provincial directory of guiding the development of cultural industries - the Catalog for the Guiding of Cultural and Creative Industries Development in Beijing (2016 Edition), putting the various forms of cultural and creative industries There are three categories of encouragement, restriction and prohibition. Encourage high-end cultural industries with high integration of culture and technology and creative ideas, limit the low-end cultural wholesale and retail industry, prohibit labor-intensive and easily lead to environmental pollution Cultural manufacturing format, to straighten out the direction of the development of cultural industries, optimize the cultural industry structure, improve industrial efficiency to provide normative guidance.

From January to November 2016, the cultural and creative industries and corporate units above the designated size in Beijing have achieved revenue of 1,191.76 billion yuan, an increase of 8.3% over the same period of last year. Among the nine sub-sectors of production, sales and other auxiliary services in the fields of culture and the arts, press and publication and distribution, radio and television films, software and information technology, advertising and exhibitions, artwork production and sales, and design, Design services, software and information technology services increased rapidly by 13.4% and 12. 9% respectively over the same period of previous year while growth in the production and sales of stationery equipment and other support bottoms was -1.2%. As a whole, the cultural and creative industries The number of employees was 117,600, representing a decrease of 0.7% as compared with the same period of last year. All except for the software and information technology service personnel, an increase of 1.9%, all were negative growth (Table 1).

Table 1 Cultural and Creative Industries above Designated Size in Beijing from January to November 2016

| Items | Total Revenue (billion yuan) Jan-Nov, 2016 | Year-on-year Growth (%) | Average number of employees Jan-Nov, 2016 | Year-on-year Growth (%) |
|---|---|---|---|---|
| Total | 1191.76 | 8.3 | 117,6000 | -0.7 |
| Culture and art service | 23.82 | 2.3 | 5,4000 | -0.1 |
| Press and publication service | 62.66 | 1.3 | 7,6000 | -3 |
| Broadcast, movies and TV service | 72.68 | 6.5 | 5,1000 | -3.1 |
| Software and IT service | 475.51 | 12.9 | 63,6000 | 1.9 |
| Ads and exhibition service | 150.36 | 11.1 | 6,6000 | -2.8 |
| Production and sale service of art works | 106.60 | 6.0 | 1,8000 | -4 |
| Design service | 26.85 | 13.4 | 7,4000 | -4.4 |
| Culture and entertainment service | 91.83 | 3.7 | 8,5000 | -1.1 |
| Production, sale and auxiliary service of equipment of stationery commodity | 181.45 | -1.2 | 11,6000 | -7.8 |

Note: The above data in all fields according to the 2011 national economic sector classification (GB / T4754 _2011) standard summary.

Source: Beijing Bureau of Statistics.

2.3.2 Accelerate the construction of industrial functional areas and major projects and strengthen the construction of cultural markets

In 2016, Beijing further accelerated the construction of functional areas of cultural and creative industries, actively implemented major projects in cultural and creative industries, and completed the development planning of 17 cultural and creative functional areas in the "13th Five-year Plan" period. Based on their advantages and characteristics, Beijing further clarified the differences the functional orientation, the dominant industry content, the development path and the development goal. To study and establish a statistical evaluation index of cultural industries functional areas and to guide the optimization of functional areas in an effective and scientific manner, promoting the construction of major projects in the cultural and creative industries and fostering the growth of the cultural and creative industries are important measures for the development of the cultural and creative industries in 2016. 90 projects have entered this year's major cultural and creative industries project library with a total investment of 26 billion yuan. Plan the construction of Songzhuang art town, promote the gathering of elements of functional areas, and support and encourage cultural innovation and entrepreneurship. In May, the Beijing Yizhuang Cultural and Creative Industry Alliance were established. Relying on the resources of Yizhuang Economic Development Zone, a cluster of cultural innovation industries was formed to continue building cultural and creative think tanks, cultural and creative talents, cultural and creative talents, cultural and creative exchanges, cultural and creative exchanges Park six cultural and creative platform to promote cultural and creative industries and science and technology, finance and other industries integration development. In September, the Beijing-Tianjin-Hebei Cultural Industry Park (Enterprise) Alliance was established and became the first non-profit collaborative development organization in Beijing-Tianjin-Hebei region to establish a sound industrial ecology with the aim of promoting the coordinated development of the three cultural industries and the cooperation win. In October, the first phase of "Tianning No.1 Cultural Industry Park" was completed. The park's facilities are more complete and the functions are more complete. In 2016, Beijing Municipality will step up its cultural market construction and strongly support the holding of such brand exhibitions as "Art Beijing", "Performing Arts Beijing" and "Animation Beijing", and actively promote cultural project transactions. 94% of the exhibitors in "Art Beijing" realized the deal, "Performing Arts Beijing" launched more than 2,000 repertoires, and participated in more than 1,000 trading units. The sales of "Anime Beijing" games and various derivatives were on the spot Up to 30 million yuan. As of the end of November, the city completed a total of 140890 cultural relics auditing work in 437 auctions, with a turnover of 20.41 billion yuan. At present, there are 179 cultural relics auction houses and 72 cultural relics shops in Beijing. The management of cultural markets is more regulated and the cultural markets are more orderly and prosperous.

2.3.3 Promote cultural and financial services to facilitate the growth of cultural consumption

In 2016, the situation in the field of Beijing's culture is mainly manifested in the following aspects: promoting the operation of the fund-raising of cultural and financial investment, standardizing the management of special funds for the development of the cultural and creative industries and innovating the means of cultural and financial subsidies in the field of finance; deepening the provision of cultural and financial services in the area of cultural finance The continuous development of finance lease business of cultural assets, the initiation of cultural PPP mode and the promotion of investment merger and acquisition in cultural field. Actively promote the Beijing cultural and financial innovation services, a total of 500 million yuan to arrange special funds to support cultural and creative industries 327 projects, bringing about as much as 7.5 billion social investment. Promote the establishment of a national cultural and financial cooperation pilot area, and further improve the service system of Beijing's cultural investment and financing. Good environment for cultural and financial development and continuous improvement of investment and financing services for the cultural industry provide the conditions for the integration of culture and finance. As of November 2016, 209 listed cultural enterprises nationwide, including 57 in Beijing, accounting for 27%. A total of 393.293 billion yuan (305 events in total) were financed by listed cultural enterprises nationwide, with a total investment of 6717.67 billion yuan (1842 events in total). Among them, listed cultural enterprises in Beijing achieved a financing of up to 135.865 billion yuan (97 incidents), accounting for 34.55% of the national total; an investment of 240.19 billion yuan (657 incidents) in total, accounting for 35% 74%. There were 112 cultural and creative enterprises listed in the Beijing area and 33.913 billion yuan were used by cultural and creative enterprises in the capital market. The number of listed and listed companies and financing amounts of cultural and creative enterprises are all in the leading position in China. The siphon effect of cultural and financial capital in Beijing obvious in order to promote the integration of culture and finance, Beijing Municipality's Capital Office has taken the lead in starting the linkage system of "replenishment loans" in the cultural and creative industries in China. Beijing Culture & Technology Leasing Co., Ltd. was selected as one of the first batch of pilot financial institutions. It plans to provide over one billion yuan of financial support to more than 100 cultural and creative enterprises every year. Based on this, Beijing's cultural and financial services will become richer, which will be conducive to promoting the development of the capital's cultural finance and capital markets.

In 2016, Beijing guided and nurtured the cultural consumer market and actively promoted the economic growth of cultural consumption. Since 2013, Beijing has held four cultural consumption quarters. In 2016, the Huimin Cultural Consumer Season, featuring the theme of "Huihui Huihui Life," has initiated innovative ways of stimulating consumption, innovated consumer payment methods and launched the consumer brand list. While raising consumer awareness Participation and enthusiasm at the same time, highlighting and shaping cultural consumer brands. The municipal government distributed a total of 10 million yuan of Beijing Huimin cultural consumer electronic coupons to citizens of all districts in the city and launched the "Beijing Culture Consumers Brand List" for the first time and solicited the "Top Ten Cultural and Creative Products" and "Top Ten Cultural Tourism Routes" for the community. Ten Culture and Tourism Landmarks "," Top Ten Cultural and Sports Events "and" Top Ten Cultural Exhibition Projects ", a total of 50 top five representative brands representing the cultural consumption trend of Beijing in 2016 were selected, forming a number of valuable and influential brands , A word of mouth, can promote the cultural hot brands. The total amount of cultural and consumer activities there are more than 10,000 games, the cumulative consumption of 77.66 million passengers, the cumulative amount of 16.08 billion yuan, an increase of 60% and 43% respectively, the actual transaction contracts signed 17,000, completed the transaction amount of 34.4 billion Yuan (see Table 2).

Table 2 Beijing Wellfare Consumption Season (2013-2016)

| Year | Consumers (million person times) | Consumption sum (billion yuan) | Duration (month) |
| --- | --- | --- | --- |
| 2013 | 2.654 | 5.23 | 1.5 |
| 2014 | 3.7725 | 10.18 | 2.0 |
| 2015 | 4.8574 | 11.21 | 3.0 |
| 2016 | 7.7762 | 16.08 | 3.0 |

As can be seen from Table 2, by guiding the hot spots of cultural consumption, shaping the cultural consumption brand, enriching the cultural consumption activities and expanding the cultural consumption space and groups, since 2013, the consumption and consumption of Beijing Cultural Consumption Season has shown a continuous growth trend, creating a good atmosphere for cultural consumption and effectively activating the consumer market. While boosting the capital's cultural and consumer economic growth, it has also met the needs of the capital's citizens The diversity of cultural needs.

## 2.4 Actively promote "going global" of culture and enhance the influence of cultural exchanges and communication

In 2016, Beijing accelerated the development of foreign cultural trade, enhanced the cultural exchange and communication with other countries, enhanced the influence of cultural transmission in the capital, actively carried out the brand culture of "going global", made full use of Beijing's international exchange platform and stimulated the vitality of cultural development.

### 2.4.1 Accelerate the development of foreign cultural trade and enhance the influence of cultural transmission

As a national cultural center and an international exchange center, Beijing has rich cultural resources, cultural products and strong cultural innovation capabilities. Cultural exchange and dissemination is an important part of enhancing and enhancing the cultural influence of the capital. In March 2016, Beijing Municipality promulgated the Opinions on Accelerating the Development of Foreign Cultural Trade. This is the first special opinion deployment on accelerating the development of foreign cultural and trade. The Opinions on Implementation put forward a proposal to speed up the development of foreign cultural and trade Tasks: Accelerate the infrastructure construction of foreign cultural trade, promote the establishment of a national trading platform for cultural and art ports and the establishment of a national gem trading platform, actively develop international copyright trade, and establish a registration center for copyright works with a significant influence across the country. The Copyright Comprehensive Transaction Market and copyright capital platform for the development of cross-border cultural e-commerce, building an international cultural trade cloud data center, cross-border e-commerce business cloud service center; support cultural enterprises to actively carry out foreign cultural trade business, encourage and support various forms of Cultural enterprises shall engage in foreign cultural and trade businesses in accordance with laws and regulations, expand cultural export channels and conduct various forms of cultural and trade cooperation. They shall make full use of platforms such as Beijing Fair and Beijing International Cultural Fair to play the role of an international cultural exhibition platform and encourage enterprises to increase the number of cultural exchanges R & D investment products and services, and actively promote the integration of culture and technology. Beijing Cultural Enterprise is dedicated to building an international cultural enterprise. From 2015 to 2016, the list of the key enterprises of national cultural exports includes 70 in Beijing, accounting for 19.9% of the national total. Among the key national cultural exports in 2015-2016 Beijing accounted for 37, accounting for 26.6% of the total, both ranked first in the country. In recent years, Beijing has given full play to the advantages of foreign cultural and trade and continuously accelerated the development of cultural trade. Since 2006, Beijing's cultural trade volume increased from 1.265 billion U.S. dollars to 3.08 billion U.S. dollars in 2015, with an average annual growth rate of 10.2% In particular, the export of animation games, the export of book copyrighted materials and the export of movies, Beijing has always been at the forefront of the country. The country has to be the key enterprise for cultural exports and the number of projects ranked first in the country.

Cultural trade is an important carrier of cultural "going global" and also an important way to provide the influence of urban culture. As can be seen from Table 3, the import and export trade of cultural products in Beijing has changed substantially in the five years from 2012 to 2016, with a sharp increase in the import trade in 2013. After the decline in 2014 and 2015, the import of cultural products increased again in Beijing , An increase of 7. 45%. In terms of exports, exports of cultural products in Beijing from 2012 to 2016 showed an increasing trend for five consecutive years, with the largest YOY increase in 2016, an increase of 27. 91%. The total value of the commodities imported and exported by cultural trade in Beijing both increased. It is noteworthy that there has been a deficit in the import and export of cultural products in Beijing and that the trade deficit in 2016 has tended to expand, reaching 844 million U.S. dollars.

Table 3 Comparison of Import and Export Trade of Beijing's cultural products (2012-2016)

| Import and Export Year | Import (thousand dollars) | Year-on-year Increase (%) | Export (thousand dollars) | Year-on-year Increase (%) |
|---|---|---|---|---|
| 2012 | — | — | 142846.66 | 10.65 |
| 2013 | 570929.04 | 42.4532 | 143875.04 | 0.69 |
| 2014 | 448173.149 | -21.5369 | 156964.704 | 11.66 |
| 2015 | 431550.532 | -3.7581 | 177829.445 | 13.28 |
| 2016 | 1465940.05 | 7.4535 | 581500.60 | 27.91 |

2.4.2 Strengthen the exchange of foreign cultural exchanges, and cultivate the "cultural go global" brand activities.

As an international exchange center, Beijing's cultural exchange has insisted on serving the capital for the overall national diplomacy. In 2016, in support of the leaders of the Central Government and other activities, Beijing held the "Beautiful Terracotta Warrior" Beijing Lantern Exhibition in Czechoslovakia, Brazil and Portugal respectively, Olympic House "Dangshan Water" Guqin show and "Beijing Night" concert and other cultural activities with Chinese characteristics; set up in Greece, the capital of Athens, "Qi Baishi Art Center for International Studies • Greek Center"; strengthen cultural cooperation between China and foreign countries, Beijing Actively participate in and participate in the country's "Belt and Road" strategy and enhance cultural exchanges with countries related to the "Belt and Road". This year, it will host the "China-CEEC Forum of Art Cooperation," the Qatar Chinese Contemporary Art Exhibition, the first participation in the "Israel" Arts festivals, etc. Beijing actively organizes cultural activities and theatrical performances in major international exchanges to showcase the charm of Beijing culture and enhance its cultural influence in the exchange of international cultural exchanges. Beijing has actively nurtured the "going global" brand activities of Chinese culture. For example, the "Happy Spring Festival" featuring Chinese culture has been held in Helsinki, Finland and Tallinn, Estonia; the "Beijing Night" cultural event has been held in Croatia, Albania and Bosnia and Herzegovina; Organized innovative "Monkey Monkey Spring Festival" activities, the formation of sharing the Chinese culture, highlighting the value of content, enhance understanding and recognition of the brand of international cultural activities.

2.4.3 Make full use of Beijing's international exchange platform to stimulate cultural development

In 2016, Beijing Municipality will make full use of the platform of Beijing Fair and Beijing International Cultural Fair to actively play the role of an international cultural exhibition platform. From October 27 to 30, the 11th ICIF, which lasted 4 days, was held in Beijing. Under the guidance of the five development concepts of "innovation, coordination, greenness, openness and sharing", this ICIF aims to "stimulate cultural vitality and lead the industry Innovation "as its theme, which will focus on displaying the new appearance, new trends and new achievements of China's cultural and creative industries as the pillar industries in national economy development, embodying the new trend of deepening the integration and development and transformation and upgrading of China's cultural and creative industries. According to incomplete statistics, during the expo, Signed an agreement with a total amount of 95.83 billion yuan on the trading of cultural and creative industries products, artwork transactions and cooperation between banks and enterprises. "Culture + Science and Technology" has distinctive features of cultural innovation at ICIF. Among them, more than one-third has been signed in cultural and technology projects, while design and creative classes have shown strong vitality and good momentum. It is noteworthy that the coordinated development projects of Beijing-Tianjin-Hebei industry attract attention with outstanding results, with a total contract amount of 16.5 billion yuan. The project of cultural and trade projects achieved remarkable results, with the contracted amount accounting for 27%. According to the information of the 4th Beijing Stock Exchange in 2016, the number of overseas participants totaled 171,000, up from the previous one 12%, of which 15% of enterprises participated in the four consecutive Beijing Fair. The fourth Beijing Jiao Tong signed 331 projects, an increase of 40% over the previous session, of which 121 were contracted projects with an intention of signing contracts amounting to US $ 101.08 billion, an increase of 24% over the previous session, of which the contractual amount of international intentions reached 19.88 billion USD, accounting for about 20% of the total amount of the contract of intention. A total of 175 projects signed by cultural enterprises in Beijing reached a total value of USD694.80 billion with a year-on-year increase of 62.1%.[1]

3. A Comparative Analysis of Beijing's Urban Competitiveness and Cultural Power in

---

[1] "The fourth Beijing International Trade Fair closing intention to sign the amount of" triple jump "the first ultra-billions of dollars", http: // www. China * coitl cn / guoqing / 2016 -06 / 01 / content_ 38581516. htm.

2016 among China's Cities

Beijing has clearly defined the strategic positioning of the capital city development and upheld and strengthened the core functions of the national political center, the national cultural center, the international exchange center and the scientific and technological innovation center. This is Beijing's strategic mission and goal as a capital city. To speed up the construction of the national cultural center, Beijing will not only assume its important task as a city of national cultural center, but also play an exemplary role in the cultural construction of the whole country. Cultural development and cultural prosperity are important hallmarks of the national cultural center as well as an important part of the comprehensive competitiveness of cities. Therefore, the cultural construction and development of the capital city need to be analyzed in the competitiveness of domestic cities and the development coordinates of the national urban culture in order to examine the competitiveness and strength of Beijing as a national cultural center in the national cities.

3.1 Comparative analysis of Beijing and other domestic cities in comprehensive competitiveness, innovation and creativity, and comprehensive development

In 2016, Beijing remained at the forefront of the competitiveness of the country in terms of its competitiveness in the city, maintaining its fourth overall competitiveness in 2015; Beijing ranked the second in the ranking of innovation cities in the nation from No. 4 to No. 2; in Creative City Rankings Beijing ranked No. 1 in Beijing. The ranking of this indicator in Beijing jumped from No. 2 in 2014 and 2015 to No. 1 in 2016, indicating that Beijing has a strong competitive edge in creative cities. Beijing ranked the top of the city in terms of comprehensive development indicators. That Beijing has a strong comprehensive competitiveness of urban development. Beijing, as a national cultural center, with its cultural resources and innovative advantages, has become an important factor in the city's overall competitiveness.

Urban comprehensive strength is a comprehensive evaluation of urban competitiveness, covering four major economic, social, resource and cultural resource systems, which generally reflect the ability of a city to compete in regional and international resource allocation. This competitive ability is determined by the comprehensive economic competitiveness of cities, industrial competitiveness, financial and financial competitiveness, commercial and trade competitiveness, infrastructure competitiveness, social system competitiveness, environment / resource / location competitiveness, competitiveness of human capital education, Scientific and technological competitiveness and cultural competitiveness of the image of 1 0 first-level indicators, 50 second-level indicators, 216 third-level indicators. Table 4 is ranked 1 from "Ranking of Urban Competitiveness in China 2016" released by China Institute of Urban Competitiveness. According to the data, Beijing ranks 4th in the overall competitiveness of cities in China, second behind Shanghai, Hong Kong and Shenzhen, Ranking the second among the four municipalities directly under the Central Government in the PRC in 2016. Beijing ranked the same in terms of comprehensive competitiveness of cities in 2016 as in 2015. However, it is noteworthy that the overall urban competitiveness index of Shanghai and Hong Kong has risen compared with that in 2015, While Beijing and Shenzhen experienced a decline. In 2016, Beijing scored 9204. 24, and in 2015 it scored 11099. 48. Data analysis shows that Beijing has relatively strong overall competitiveness in the national urban system and maintained its original competitiveness. However, there is still a long way to go when compared with Shanghai and Hong Kong.

Table 4 Ranking of Beijing in China's Urban Competitiveness, Urban Innovation and Urban Development in 2016

| Type | Ranking list 1 | | Ranking list 2 | | Ranking list 3 | | Ranking list 4 |
|------|----------------|--|----------------|--|----------------|--|----------------|
| | Comprehensive competitiveness | | Innovation competitiveness | | Creativity competitiveness | | Comprehensive development indicators |
| Rank | City | Score | City | Score | City | Score | City |
| 1 | Shanghai | 14325.65 | Shenzhen | 820 | Beijing | 90.9 | Beijing |
| 2 | HK | 13843.13 | Beijing | 806 | Shanghai | 90.46 | Shanghai |
| 3 | Shenzhen | 11754.82 | Shanghai | 544 | Shenzhen | 83.66 | Shenzhen |
| 4 | Beijing | 9204.24 | Suzhou | 542 | Guangzhou | 80.39 | Guangzhou |
| 5 | Guangzhou | 8482.51 | Hangzhou | 534 | Hangzhou | 79.00 | Tianjin |
| 6 | Chongqing | 8315.19 | Xi'an | 476 | Suzhou | 75.14 | Suzhou |
| 7 | Tianjin | 7652.94 | Guangzhou | 468 | Tianjin | 73.85 | Hangzhou |

| 8 | Suzhou | 7066.53 | Zhuhai | 468 | Nanjing | 72.34 | Chongqing |
| 9 | Hangzhou | 6900.4 | Wuxi | 450 | Qingdao | 71.3 | Nanjing |
| 10 | Nanjing | 5897.48 | Ningbo | 430 | Wuhan | 70.99 | Chengdu |

Source: China Urban Competitiveness Ranking 2016 published by China Society for Urban Competitiveness; China Urban Innovation Index jointly released by Guangdong Academy of Social Sciences and Nanfang Daily; Shenzhen University School of Management, Shenzhen University Cultural Industry Institute of National Cultural Innovation Research Center of Shenzhen University jointly completed the "2016 China City Creativity Index (CCCE016)" list; Development and Planning Division of the National Development and Reform Commission, Urban Research Institute of Yunhe released "China's urban development indicators (2016)" .

Innovation is the inner driving force of urban development and also the sustained vitality of urban development. Table 2 shows the rankings of China's urban innovation index. According to the GN evaluation index system independently established by China Urban Competitiveness Research Institute, innovation in science and technology and cultural innovation are taken as The basis of urban innovation evaluation, a comprehensive study and evaluation of the city's ability of independent innovation and the role of the city in transforming the mode of economic growth, to measure the competitiveness of cities. The evaluation index system takes the urban innovation awareness, the gathering status of innovative resources and the creativity of innovation achievements as the important standards. The index rankings consist of 5 first-level indicators, 28 second-level indicators and 123 third-level indicators including economic innovation, political innovation, scientific and technological innovation, cultural innovation and eco-environmental innovation index. The ranking of the index shows that Beijing ranks second in the city and ranks first in the four municipalities after Shanghai and is stronger than Shanghai. Compared with 2015, Beijing Innovative City ranked fourth from No. 2 to No. 2. This shows that in 2016 Beijing's urban innovation index increased significantly and its innovation capability continued to increase. In terms of building an innovative city, Shenzhen and Beijing are far ahead of other cities. It is noteworthy that Beijing and Shenzhen have their own strengths and weaknesses. Shenzhen's urban innovation model is mainly embodied in "enterprise innovation." The advantage lies in innovation in the integration of production and research and technological transformation; While

Beijing has obvious advantages in R & D capability, but it is weaker than Shenzhen in terms of application of technology for smooth R & D of enterprises. This shows that Beijing, as a national science and technology innovation center, has abundant scientific and technological resources and innovative resources, but it still needs to vigorously step up the transformation and application of science and technology.

In recent years, Beijing has vigorously strengthened the construction of a "creative capital". Table 4 shows the rankings of China's urban innovation index jointly issued by Shenzhen University School of Management and Shenzhen Institute of Cultural Industries. The index selects 50 large and medium-sized cities in China for evaluation. The evaluation model covers four modules: 11 factors, 25 indicators and 25 elements, including factor driving force, demand driving force, development support force and industrial influence. Beijing topped the list, ranking second from 2016 and 2015 to No. 1 in 2016, demonstrating that Beijing continues to maintain strong urban competitiveness in the nation's creative city construction. It is noteworthy that, although Beijing ranks the No.1 social index and the 2nd largest economic index, its environmental index ranked 23rd. The good news is that Beijing, as the political center, cultural center and historical and cultural city in the country, has its own world cultural heritage, national cultural relics protection units, intangible cultural heritage, a large number of important cultural facilities and cultural industries. In the creative city It has played an important role in building and unveiling the quality of citizens' cultural life and has become an important factor in Beijing's ranking in the creative city.

Table 4 ranked 4 city comprehensive development indicators rank selected from the National Development and Reform Commission Development and Planning Division and the Urban Research Institute of Yunhe in November 2016 released the "China's comprehensive urban development indicators 2016." This indicator covers three dimensions of society, economy and environment. Three secondary indicators are set up. Each secondary indicator includes three third-level indicators. There are another 133 sub-indicators under 27 third-level indicators, forming 3 x 3 x 3 pyramid structure; data collection Take full advantage of various types of government statistics at all levels, the Internet big data and satellite remote sensing data. The top 10 cities in the data are Beijing, Shanghai, Shenzhen, Guangzhou, Tianjin, Suzhou, Hangzhou, Chongqing, Nanjing and Chengdu. As can be seen in the rankings of cities, Beijing,

Shanghai and Shenzhen always interact with each other The competition between Beijing and Shanghai in particular is particularly evident in the cities, with Beijing outperforming Shanghai in terms of social dimensions and cultural traditions and exchanges, while Shanghai outperforms Beijing in economic and environmental terms.

Based on the data and ranking analysis in Table 4, in 2016, Beijing is still at the forefront of the competitiveness of cities in China and ranks 4th in 2015 in the ranking of comprehensive competitiveness. However, the index of comprehensive competitiveness of Shanghai and Hong Kong cities increased greatly while that of Beijing and Shenzhen declined slightly, indicating that Beijing needs to further enhance the comprehensive competitiveness of the city. Compared with 2015, Beijing ranked No. 2 in Innovation City from No. 2 to No. 2, which shows that Beijing's Innovation Index has risen sharply and its innovation capability has been continuously enhanced. Although Beijing has obvious advantages in scientific and technological research and development capability, it needs to be strengthened in terms of enterprise R & D level and technology transformation and application. Beijing ranked No.1 in the 2016 National Creative City Ranking, jumping from No. 2 in 2014 and 2015 to No. 1 in 2016, showing that Beijing has great advantages in terms of its competitiveness in creative cities. Beijing, as a national culture The advantages of cultural resources in the center play an important role in this. Beijing has obvious advantages in cultural resources and scientific and technological innovation resources, and great achievements can be made in cultural development and scientific and technological innovation. However, Beijing ranks the 23rd in the environmental indicators.

3.2 A Comparative Analysis of Innovation, Industry and Culture between Beijing and Other Cities in China in the Development of "Internet Plus".

In the context of a network power, the proposition of "Internet +" and the necessity of promoting the inevitability and practice of the times with full practice. "Internet +" changes the thinking mode of mankind and changes people's thinking mode in the new information technology revolution. The Internet information technology and Internet platform will effectively promote the cross-border integration of the Internet and different fields, integrate deeply, and realize the mode of production and supply

Ways and consumption patterns to promote the economic and social innovation and development. Currently, Beijing has more than 430,000 registered websites, focusing on 90% of key websites and 80% of Internet users in China. It is a veritable "China Internet Capital." Internet information technology has played an important role in the construction of smart cities and the cultural development of the capital.

Smart city is the use of information technology and communication technology to sense, analyze and integrate the key information of a city running core system to intelligently respond to the various needs of people's livelihood, public safety, urban services, environmental protection, etc. Urban construction plays an extremely important role in solving urban development problems and promoting urban sustainable development. In 2016, the concept of "Internet +" permeated all aspects and levels of capital cities and cultural development. Table 5 Rank 1 Data were selected from "2016 China Smart City Development Level Assessment Report" jointly released by the Information Research Center of Chinese Academy of Social Sciences in November 2016 and the Guimai Interconnection Smart City Research Center. According to the three key elements of "Resource Flow, Application System and Core Objectives" of PSF Model-Smart City Construction and Operation, the "Report" consists of 6 major and 1 level indicators (Wisdom Infrastructure, Wisdom Governance, Wisdom Economy and Wisdom, Livelihood and Wisdom Population and security system) and 17 categories of secondary indicators and additions and subtractions, a nationwide sampling of 201 cities to conduct a comprehensive assessment. The index shows that Beijing ranks fourth overall in smart city construction. After Shenzhen, Shanghai and Hangzhou, although the scores of these four cities are not significantly different from each other, Beijing as a national science and technology innovation center remains to be determined Further strengthen the scientific and technological innovation and the application of information technology and accelerate the construction of a smart city.

Table 5 Beijing's Index Rankings in the Smart city, Internet +, and related fields

|  | Ranking list 1 | Ranking list 2 | Ranking list 3 | Ranking list 4 | Ranking list 5 |
|---|---|---|---|---|---|
| Type | Wisdom City Index | Internet+ City Index | Internet+Industry Index | Internet+Innovation Creativity Index | Internet+Cultu re Ranks in terms of |

195

| Rank | City | Score | City | Score | City | Score | City | Score | City (entertainment) |
|---|---|---|---|---|---|---|---|---|---|
| 1 | Shenzhen | 80.57 | Beijing | 10.191 | Beijing | 11.9748 | Beijing | 17.1480 | Beijing |
| 2 | Shanghai | 80.13 | Shenzhen | 6.809 | Shenzhen | 9.0064 | Shenzhen | 12.0843 | Shenzhen |
| 3 | Hangzhou | 79.06 | Guangzhou | 5.980 | Shanghai | 6.5133 | Shanghai | 8.1260 | Shanghai |
| 4 | Beijing | 78.68 | Shanghai | 5.280 | Guangzhou | 5.5597 | Guangzhou | 6.2958 | Guangzhou |
| 5 | Wuxi | 76.71 | Hangzhou | 2.156 | Hangzhou | 2.5622 | Chongqing | 3.9491 | Hangzhou |
| 6 | Guangzhou | 72.59 | Chengdu | 1.966 | Chengdu | 2.2693 | Hangzhou | 3.7821 | Chengdu |
| 7 | Ningbo | 67.86 | Chongqing | 1.880 | Wuhan | 1.8215 | Chengdu | 2.8845 | Xi'an |
| 8 | Foshan | 66.26 | Wuhan | 1.452 | Changsha | 1.3615 | Xiamen | 2.0548 | Wuhan |
| 9 | Xiamen | 64.08 | Changsha | 1.267 | Nanjing | 1.3269 | Tianjin | 2.0077 | Changsha |
| 10 | Suzhou | 63.12 | Fuzhou | 1.255 | Xi'an | 1.3184 | Nanjing | 1.9285 | Nanjing |

Source: China Smart City Research Center jointly issued by China Academy of Social Sciences and Guimai Interconnect Smart City Research Center; China Internet + Index released by Tencent China 2016 Internet + Summit.

The concept of "Internet +" and the development of the "Internet +" model show that in the era of Internet information technology, the Internet is beyond the purely technical category and has penetrated into all aspects of economic, social, cultural and human life more and more extensively and profoundly, Change the concept of human innovation and change and human production and life. With the advent of new technologies such as mobile Internet, big data, cloud computing and Internet of Things, urban development, industrial forms, innovation and entrepreneurship, and cultural consumption, leisure and entertainment are closely linked with the Internet and become an important index and symbol of urban development. Table 5 Index Ranking of Arrangement 2, Arrangement 3, Arrangement 4 and Arrangement 5 From China Internet + Index released by Tencent Research Institute of China Internet + Summit in November 2016. As can be seen from the rankings 2 to 5, Beijing ranks

No.1 in the country in terms of Internet + City Index, Internet + Industry Index, Internet + Innovation Index, Internet + Cultural Entertainment Index, and is far ahead of other cities in the country. "Today we live in a world that accelerates the hyper-inter-connected world, a global metropolis, filled with systems of interactive communication and communication that inspire profound and complex cultural transformation and re-alignment. The cultural studies of sexual, mass media, Internet-affected worlds must take serious account of the most common aspect of communication - connectivity. " ① [1]In the era of "Internet +", the development with Internet information technology as the core will inevitably drive the development of cultural production, cultural transmission and cultural consumption while promoting social production and lifestyle changes.

In January 2016, the Beijing Municipal Government issued Opinions on Implementing "Internet +" Initiatives. It proposed that in 2018, the level of integration and development between the Internet in the capital and all areas in the economy and society should be significantly raised, and that economic upgrading and efficiency enhancement should be basically formed And the ubiquitous security of the network as well as the intensive and efficient development of the Internet, and create an important source of new technologies, new models, new formats and new services for the country's Internet. In the field of "Internet +" culture, Beijing focuses on the development of digital content industry. With the core of network communication, personalized service and digital products, Beijing will build a national digital content culture industry cluster and create a group of international competitiveness and world influence Chinese Internet Culture Enterprise. At present, the number of IPv4 addresses in Beijing accounts for 25.45% of the total number of IPv4 addresses in the country and continues to rank No.1 in the country. The total number of national websites is 3.2 million, of which nearly 440,000 are in Beijing, accounting for 13.7% of the total number of national websites. In 2016, the number of websites in Beijing increased by 10% over the end of 2012. In 2016, Beijing ranks No.1 in the Internet + City Index, Internet + Industry Index, Internet + Innovation Index and Internet + Cultural Entertainment Index, ranking first in the country for its network cultural production, cultural communication and cultural consumption , Cultural and leisure entertainment laid a solid foundation, and reflects the strong competitiveness.

---

[1] James Rolle: "A Global Approach to Media, Communication and Culture", translated by Dong Hongchuan, Commercial Press, 2015, p.15.

3.3 Comparative Analysis of Beijing's Urban Cultural Industry, Knowledge City and Cultural Urban Competitiveness with Other Cities in China

In 2016, Beijing's cultural industries, cultural consumption, knowledge city competitiveness and cultural city competitiveness still maintained its leading position in the national urban system. The cultural industry index ranked No. 1, the cultural and consumer general index ranked No. 1, and the competitiveness of knowledge cities Ranking No.1 in terms of competitiveness and ranking behind the competitiveness index of cultural cities in Hong Kong. The analysis shows that Beijing, as a national cultural center city, has shown its strong competitiveness in cultural development and has played an exemplary role.

Cultural industries play an important role and role in the development of urban culture and economic growth. Cultural and creative industries have always occupied the position of pillar industries in the cultural and economic growth of Beijing. The knowledge resources and advantages of a city support the innovation and production of urban culture, Plays an important role in knowledge economy. In the era when cultural consumption becomes a kind of lifestyle for people, cultural consumption plays the dual role of social benefits and economic benefits. The cultural development of all aspects of a city constitutes the cultural competitiveness of the city , And become an extremely important part of the comprehensive competitiveness of the city. "Economics and culture have always been two of the most fundamental drivers of human behavior and even though (or especially) for those who already have amassed a great deal of resources, the desire to control material resources is clearly irresistibly attractive, governed Many economic behaviors we have seen. "[1] Table 6 Ranking of the index of the cultural industries comes from the" Provincial Cultural Consumption Development Index (2016) "released by the Institute of Cultural Industries of Renmin University in 2016. The index for the index of cultural industries shows that there are three major elements of productivity, influence and driving force. The index shows that among the top five cities in China's cultural industries index ranking are Beijing, Shanghai, Jiangsu, Zhejiang and Guangdong, Beijing ranked first in the national provinces. Compared with 2015, Beijing's cultural industry index rose from No. 2 to No. 1, with a marked increase in the index.

---

[1] Sylvester: "Economics and Culture", translated by Wang Zhibiao, Renmin University of China Press, 2011, p. 178.

Table 6 Ranking of China's Provinces and Municipalities in Terms of Cultural Industries, Cultural Consumption, Knowledge Cities, and Cultural City Competitiveness

| | Ranking list 1 | | Ranking list 2 | Ranking list 3 | Ranking list 4 |
|---|---|---|---|---|---|
| Type | Cultural Industry Index | | Cultural Consumption Comprehensive Index | Knowledge City Competitiveness | Cultural City Competitiveness |
| Rank | Province and Cities | Score | Province and Cities | City | City |
| 1 | Beijing | 84.72 | Beijing | Beijing | Hong Kong |
| 2 | Shanghai | 80.60 | Shanghai | Shenzhen | Beijing |
| 3 | Jiangsu | 80.12 | Tianjin | Shanghai | Shanghai |
| 4 | Zhejiang | 79.72 | Zhejiang | Nanjing | Macao |
| 5 | Guangdong | 79.23 | Guangdong | Guangzhou | Suzhou |
| 6 | Shandong | 74.98 | Liaoning | Tianjin | Chongqing |
| 7 | Sichuan | 74.47 | Jiangsu | Hangzhou | Guangzhou |
| 8 | Tianjin | 74.40 | Shandong | Suzhou | Hangzhou |
| 9 | Jiangxi | 74.03 | Sichuan | Wuhan | Wuhan |
| 10 | Liaoning | 73.73 | Neimongol | Dalian | Chengdu |

Source: Cultural Industry Research Index released by the Institute of Cultural Industries, Renmin University of China in 2016; Blue Book on Public Service, 2015, Chinese Academy of Social Sciences; Relevant indices released by China Institute of Urban Competitiveness in 2015. China Urban Competitiveness Report 2016 - New Engine: Multicentre Group Network Urban System "issued by Institute of Financial Strategy Research, Chinese Academy of Social Sciences, China Social Sciences Press and Center for City and Competitiveness, Chinese Academy of Social Sciences.

Table 6 Ranking of cultural consumption Consolidation Index rankings are also from the "Cultural and Consumption Index of China Provinces and Cities" (2016) released by the Institute of Cultural Industries Research of Renmin University of China in 2016. The top 5 provinces and municipalities are Beijing, Shanghai, Tianjin, Zhejiang, Guangdong and Beijing ranked No. 1, demonstrating that Beijing, as a national cultural center, has strong cultural spending power and economic growth power of cultural consumption. Table 6 The rankings of Ranking 3 and Rank 4 are from China Urban Competitiveness Report 2016 released by the Institute of Financial Strategy Research of the Chinese Academy of Social Sciences and the Center for Urbanization and Competitiveness of the Chinese Academy of Social Sciences in 2016. In terms of the competitiveness of knowledge-based cities, Beijing Ranking the first in China. Among the top five, Shenzhen, Shanghai, Nanjing, Guangzhou and Beijing ranked the first among the top five cities in terms of their competitiveness in knowledge cities. In the competitiveness of cultural cities After Beijing ranks in Hong Kong, it shows that Beijing, as a national cultural center, has room for improvement in the competitiveness of cultural cities.

In terms of public cultural services, Shanghai Normal University Urban Culture Research Center released the "Report on the Development of China's Public Cultural Services" in October 2016, focusing on 6 first-level indicators such as "public cultural input" and "public cultural institutions", and " The proportion of financial expenditure "and other 58 second-level indicators, from various aspects to assess the provinces, autonomous regions and municipalities of public cultural services investment status, scale and quality of public cultural services. According to the report, the top 5 provinces in the overall index of public cultural services are Guangdong, Zhejiang, Jiangsu, Shandong and Henan, respectively, while none of the four first-tier cities in China are included. The top 5 service provinces are Shanghai, Zhejiang, Beijing, Tibet and Tianjin, respectively, and Beijing is weaker than Shanghai in the index of domestic public cultural services (per capita).

4. Problems and Suggestions
To strengthen the building of a national cultural center is a major strategic move to implement the strategic positioning of the capital city, uphold and strengthen the core functions of the capital city, accelerate the construction of a world-class, harmonious and livable capital, prosper and develop the capital culture, and play a leading role in demonstrating Beijing's leadership. In 2016, the cultural construction of Beijing Municipality focused on the theme of the construction of the National Cultural Center and actively carried out all aspects of Beijing's cultural construction and development. It made important contributions to the protection of historical and cultural cities, the construction of a public cultural service system, the development of cultural and creative industries, and the expansion and spread of culture Score. The analysis of this report shows that in 2016, Beijing was at the forefront of the competitiveness of cities in the country and maintained its 4th overall competitiveness; innovation city ranked

second in competitiveness; and Creative City ranked No.1 in competitiveness in cities Beijing ranks No.1 in comprehensive development index rankings. Among all the indicators of urban competitiveness, Beijing, as a cultural center of the National Cultural Center, has become an important factor in its comprehensive superiority in competitiveness. Beijing as "China's capital city" with a website number of about 440,000, accounts for 13.7% of the total number of websites nationwide. The 2016 national internet + relevant index shows that in the Chinese cities, the Internet + City Index, Internet + Industry Index, Internet + Index of Innovative Creation and Internet + Index of Cultural Entertainment Index ranked No.1 in the country, laying a solid foundation for its development in network cultural production, cultural communication, cultural consumption, cultural and recreational entertainment, and demonstrated a strong Competitiveness. In 2016, Beijing's cultural industry, cultural consumption, knowledgeable city competitiveness and cultural city competitiveness still maintained its leading position in the national urban system. The ranking of cultural industry index rose from No. 2 in 2015 to No. 1 in the Cultural Consumption Index Ranked No. 1 in the rankings and No. 1 in the competitiveness of knowledge cities. It is worth noting that Beijing is slightly behind the rankings of the competitiveness index of cultural cities in Hong Kong, weaker than Shanghai in the per capita composite index of public cultural services, Competence inferior to Shenzhen.

4.1 Implement the national cultural center construction plan for the Thirteenth Five-Year Plan and strengthen process management and mission assessment
"Beijing Plan to Strengthen the Construction of the National Cultural Center During the 13th Five-Year Plan" Put forward a comprehensive plan for the construction of the National Cultural Center in the capital during the 13th Five-Year Plan, clarify the overall planning and objectives and tasks for all aspects of Beijing's cultural construction and development, It will help to promote the construction of the National Cultural Center and put forward the top ten tasks of strengthening the construction of the National Cultural Center. These tasks not only highlight the key cultural construction of the capital in the coming five years, but also cover all aspects of cultural development. First of all, it highlights the direction and orientation of Beijing's cultural development as a capital, the leading role of ideological and theoretical building and core values, and a good public civilization and social customs.

Second, it attaches great importance to the construction of a modern communication system in the Internet age. It is not only related to the well-developed information technology of Beijing as "China's capital city", but also to current and future cultural innovations and dissemination. Third, cultural heritage, cultural and artistic innovations, public cultural services and cultural and creative industries, and international cultures Communication level improvement and cultural talent team building all have definite goals and tasks in the above "construction plan", and each task has a clear construction project and project content. In the process of implementation of "construction plan", the key issue lies in the active and concrete implementation. The first is to clearly plan the responsibilities of the implementation subject and mobilize the enthusiasm and creativity of the main body of the cultural objectives and tasks. The second is to step up the supervision and administration of the project implementation; Third, to enhance the follow-up and performance evaluation of the target and tasks; fourthly, implement the innovation of cultural construction tasks and cultural construction projects and form a scientific and effective institutional mechanism that provides a sound mechanism and policy environment for sound and rapid development of the capital culture.

4.2 In-depth analysis of Beijing's historical and cultural city protection constraints to strengthen the protection and heritage of cultural city

The preservation of Beijing's historical and cultural cities is carried out under the general environment of the present and future development of the capital. It is imperative to coordinate the interests of all parties and properly handle the relationship between the protection of historical and cultural heritage and the economic and social development. At present, the contradiction between protection and development still exists. The old Beijing urban area is not optimistic about the protection situation and the protection situation of cultural relics is rather grim. The phenomenon of illegal construction and dismantling still exists. The legal concept of cultural relic protection needs to be further strengthened, and the laws and regulations on the protection of cultural relics need to be further improved. There is not enough exploitation and utilization of cultural resources, and traditional culture has done a great job of "living up". The means and methods of conservation and utilization need to be updated and should be combined with modern technologies. The transformation and utilization of traditional cultural resources are not enough, and historical and cultural scenic spots need to be upgraded. Therefore, Beijing needs to do the following related work: (1) Strengthen the scientific research on the protection and cultural heritage of historic cities, innovate and change the protection mentality, properly handle the relationship between protection and development; (2) continue to improve the rule of law and improve the protection of cultural relics , Strengthen the administrative law enforcement system of cultural relics, clarify the responsibilities of competent departments, standardize law enforcement procedures, establish inspection mechanism of cultural relics protection, evaluate the effect of law enforcement of cultural relics protection and strengthen the legal consciousness of public cultural relics protection. It is the common responsibility of the whole society to protect cultural relics according to law, Actively create a social atmosphere and cultural atmosphere for the protection of cultural relics in accordance with the law;(3) We will intensify efforts in digging up traditional resources and strive to raise the level of protection for historical and cultural issues. We should make full use of the "Internet +" big data and the results and operation of modern technologies to meet the needs of urban development and the times, enhance the transformation and utilization of historical and cultural resources and create cities Cultural capital, highlighting the charm of the ancient capital in the modern city;(4) Each enterprise or entity that implements the productive protection of intangible cultural heritage shall formulate and implement pertinent and operable rules and regulations on the brands, trademarks and intellectual property owned by the state according to the relevant laws and regulations of the State, and establish a scientific and effective The legal protection barrier, and in practice through the statute, guidance, supervision, inspection and other means to make the legal protection of intangible cultural heritage implemented.

4.3 Innovate Capital Construction of Public Cultural Services and Improve the Efficiency of Public Cultural Services

The unbalanced distribution of infrastructure for public cultural services has long been an obstacle to the development of Beijing's public cultural services. Although Beijing has made great achievements in public cultural service since the 12th Five-Year Plan period, many problems have not been fundamentally solved and it needs to be fully implemented in the "13th Five-Year Plan" period. At present, the main problems are as follows: the distribution of cultural services facilities is still uneven. For example, a large number of high-quality public cultural service resources are concentrated in the six districts of the city while the infrastructure construction of grassroots cultural services in the suburbs lags behind. The coverage rate of Beijing's public cultural services looks like High, but there are still blind spots, blank spots, such as a number of emerging science and technology parks, cultural industry parks lack of supporting public cultural services; community cultural activities center service performance is not high, for many reasons, many suburban government grass-roots culture department full-time staff is very Lack of professional management personnel in comprehensive public cultural facilities is lacking; the cultural identity of street communities needs to be improved; Beijing's newly increased urban population, large floating population and active real estate transactions, together with changes in residential environment caused by urban renewal and relocation , Resulting in the community is not easy to form a stable cultural ecology, residents lack a sense of identity and identity; public service in the suburbs lack of social forces to participate in the city six districts of basic public cultural facilities in the community to participate in the better, and the other ten suburbs of public culture Works hard to get equal opportunities. Based on the requirements of urban planning and public cultural policy system, according to the service population and service range, we should perfect the comprehensive cultural center of the street in the whole city Network to promote the construction of cultural activities center according to the actual demand of public cultural services, and to increase the supply of public cultural services by taking advantage of the transformation of old cities, non-capital functions and demolition of wholesale markets; (2) While strengthening the cultural functions of the downtown area, we should make full use of the suburban space resources to build new public cultural facilities and build a "fill-in" functional area to drive the development of public culture in the suburbs. (3) To play a big data role to improve the effective supply of public culture To realize the transformation from the traditional "sending culture" to "menu-style" public cultural services, fully grasping the actual cultural needs of citizens and the cultural needs of residents in the region, strengthening the integration and utilization of public cultural resources and data, implementing more effective demand docking, data analysis, Service efficiency tracking, the use of information technology to push the information and content of public cultural services to better meet the cultural needs of citizens and improve service performance; (4) to create a multi-participatory community culture of self-government to tap the region's cultural resources and cultural characteristics, Attention should be paid to nurturing the backbone culture team in the neighborhood community, improving residents 'enthusiasm, initiative, creativity and participation, and enhancing residents' community identity and cultural identity.(5) Encourage social forces to participate in public cultural services in the suburbs, further encourage social forces and social capital participation, and integrate cultural tourism, ecotourism and sports recreation, formulate policies to encourage social forces to participate in public cultural services and encourage support for suburbs and public culture Public cultural services in areas with weak services

Improve government procurement of public cultural services measures, the establishment of government procurement policy system, strengthen the macro-system design, expand the scope of purchase of public cultural services, promote the purchase of Fu and the masses demand docking, and promote multi-information communication and resource sharing, Strict public cultural services supervision and evaluation.

4.4 Stimulate the vitality of traditional cultural industries and deepen the integration of creative industries

In recent years, Beijing's cultural and creative industries have always been in the leading position in the country, but they still face problems. Shenzhen and other cities in the strong competition, but also face their own development challenges. In terms of activating the traditional cultural industries, giving play to the advantages of the cultural industries and deepening the integration and development of creative industries, Beijing still needs to enhance institutional and institutional innovation and give full play to its advantages in cultural and scientific resources. (1) further stimulate the vitality of traditional cultural industries, speed up the integration among industries and enhance their development; enhance the innovative level of original works of arts and culture, actively activate and utilize existing cultural facilities and industrial resources, enhance resources integration and promote cross-industry (2) continue to give play to the advantages of cultural industries and promote the growth of cultural and creative industries; accelerate the structural adjustment of convention and exhibition industry and lead the transformation of convention and exhibition industry through innovation Upgrade and constantly optimize the art display and trading platform to promote the fine art, specialization and branding development of the art market; gradually push the mass market of tourism, leisure and entertainment to the high-end development and promote the deep integration of tourism and culture; 3) Actively explore the "culture +" model and further promote the integration of cultural and creative industries; continue to promote the integration of culture and technology, culture and finance, vigorously develop the digital creative industries and continuously strengthen the design service and strategic emerging industries Consumer goods workers (4) improving the cultural and financial policies of finance and sound the capital investment and financing service system in the capital; (4) improving the cultural and financial policies of the capital, Accelerate the establishment of national cultural and financial cooperation pilot area, explore the construction of cultural complement, credit, and investment linkage mechanism, in view of the lack of expertise in the operation of the financial investment fund to strengthen the professional construction, in view of the cultural PPP model problems, and vigorously promote the cultural creativity (5) actively cultivate cultural consumer market and promote cultural and economic growth; and Beijing's cultural consumption ranks the top of the nation However, there is still a low proportion of cultural consumption in China. In response to such problems as lack of cultural facilities and facilities, inadequate facilities, incomplete functions, high prices and lack of supportive policies, Beijing needs to further enhance the cultural consumption in the capital and continue to optimize the capital culture Consumption environment, vigorously Yu capital of culture consumer brands, and actively promote the culture of consumer legislation, to meet the people's demand for high-quality rich culture on the basis of a strong impetus to economic growth in cultural consumption.

4.5 Strengthen the construction of three-dimensional cultural communication system and enhance the cultural influence of the capital

In recent years, great progress has been made in Beijing's urban cultural communication and a good image of urban culture. However, Beijing, as an international metropolis, faces the challenge from the domestic and international cultural media markets. In recent years, the "metropolitan disease" in the capital city of Beijing has become prominent. Concern over such issues as the environment and transportation in Beijing by international media has weakened its attention to the social and cultural development of Beijing. The symbolic system of capital city culture has not reflected the pluralism and overall, in the capital city cultural external communication, the leading role and service function of government communication need to be strengthened. The capital city culture lacks adequate top-level design and strategy co-ordination, yet breaks the fragmentation. Beijing's media and cultural enterprises with strong international influence have brought along the development of cultural trade and markedly improved the scale and quality of overseas communications. However, the export strength of these enterprises needs to be further strengthened. In response to these questions, the author puts forward the following countermeasures and suggestions: (1) To further clarify the goal of Beijing's cultural image transmission and dissemination as a capital city, and to study, analyze and establish the overall train of thought and strategy of urban cultural image creation and dissemination in the urban coordinates at home and abroad (2) Give play to the government's leading force in shaping the city's cultural image and its external communication, clarify the overall framework of the city's cultural image, and make full use of its advantages and breakthrough weaknesses to form the content, tasks and targets of the city's cultural image transmission; Theme design, spatial planning, image system and communication strategy; (3) Beijing's cultural image of the city needs to maintain its continuous competitiveness in external communications, win cultural recognition, have a high audience awareness and acceptance, and achieve an effective urban image (4) speed up the optimization of the media and cultural industry structure, create an international media conglomerate, actively expand the overseas communications market, and guide the remodeling of market order in order to develop and enhance the influence of Beijing's urban cultural communication; (5) Center advantage, with the national politics Pay attention to the overall situation and actively implement the "Belt and Road Initiative" strategy. We will continue to promote the excellent Chinese culture and Beijing's characteristic culture to "go global" and disseminate cultural products and cultural activities with Chinese style and Beijing characteristics to enhance the city's influence in Beijing. (6) In the Internet era, the Internet has become a broad and quick channel and platform for disseminating information on urban economy, society, politics and culture. It has also become an important force in marketing cities and shaping the city's image. It is necessary to give full play to Beijing's message as "China's capital city" Technology advantages, to create an international platform for the capital culture network communication, vigorously promote Beijing culture, disseminate outstanding Chinese culture, improve Beijing's cultural and Chinese culture network internationalization ability and level, and enhance the international influence of network culture communication.

# Beijing Tourism Report under the Framework of "Global Tourism"[1]

## Jing Yanfeng, Lu Yuexiang, Liu Min, Han Xiaoheng[2]

Abstract

This report analyzes policy supply of Beijing's tourism development since the beginning of the "13th Five-Year Plan" and summarizes the status and characteristics of Beijing's tourism market in 2016. It forecasts the development trend and proposes suggestions for development.

Keywords: Global Tourism, Beijing-Tianjin-Hebei Integration, Tourism Development

2016 is the first year of the "13th Five-Year Plan" and also the "Year of Beijing Tourism Service Quality Improvement." At the beginning of this year, the National Tourism Administration put forward the concept of "global tourism" and became the new direction of Beijing's tourism development. In 2016, Beijing's tourism industry centered around "implementing the strategic positioning of the capital city, optimizing and upgrading core functions, and promoting the coordinated development of Beijing, Tianjin and Hebei" under the circumstances of the difficult international economic recovery and the structural adjustment of the new normalcy of the domestic economy, in order to expand tourism consumption As the main line, to promote the upgrading of tourism consumption structure; to improve the consumer environment and standardize the market order as the content, increase the comprehensive management of tourism; to improve the quality of tourism services as the focus, to promote tourism from the number of scale to quality and efficiency changes. As an important functional industry in the capital, tourism has drawn more and more attention to its contribution to the economic and social development in Beijing.

1. Policy Changes for Tourism Development

1.1 policy-oriented reforms at the national and industry levels

1.1.1 Guidance to tourism development by the "13th Five-Year" plans of various

---

[1]This report is the result of a research project entitled "Research on Beijing's Competitiveness of Tourist Services Trade" (15JGA032), a key project of Beijing Social Science Fund

[2] Jing Yanfeng, Ph.D., Associate Professor, School of Tourism, Beijing Union University, with a research focus on tourism economy; Lu Yuexiang, Ph.D., doctoral tutor, School of Economics and Business Administration, Beijing Normal University; Liu Min, Ph.D., Associate Professor of the Tourism College of Beijing Union University; Han Xiaoheng, Green Blue Alliance Marketing Consultants Co., Ltd., Account Manager.

levels

From a national perspective, the mission of tourism development and formulation has undergone significant changes. The "13th Five-Year Plan" proposal adopted by the Fifth Plenary Session of the 18th CPC Central Committee clearly put forward "Vigorously Developing Tourism." At least 15 of the "Outline for the 13th Five-Year Plan for National Economic and Social Development" directly referred to the development of the tourism industry. Among them, attention has been paid to such aspects as promoting consumption, improving quality and enhancing efficiency, industrial integration and tourism poverty alleviation. By the end of 2016, the State Council printed and distributed the "13th Five-Year Plan for the Development of Tourism Industry". The "Plan" was listed as the "National Key Special Plan for the Thirteenth Five-Year Plan" and was promulgated by the tourism department for the first time and released by the State Council. Significant changes have taken place in the impact and importance of tourism. The orientation of tourism is no longer confined to the "strategic pillar industries and the modern service industry satisfied by the people" in the "12th Five-Year Plan" period. It proposes that "cultivating tourism into an important driving force for economic restructuring and upgrading, and ecological civilization will lead the industry and win an important force in offensive and strenuous war "[1]. Visible country's ardent expectations of the tourism industry, the tourism industry has a long way to go.

1.1.2 Release of national documents to strengthen the comprehensive supervision of the tourism market

February 4, 2016 Notice of the General Office of the State Council on Strengthening the Comprehensive Supervision of the Tourism Market (Guo Ban Fa [2016] No. 5) was released. This not only reflects the characteristics and importance of tourism as a comprehensive industry, but also the basic requirement for the development of "global tourism." Tourism market chaos, regulatory difficulties, has been the impact of tourism quality of service, restricting the tourism consumption of chronic diseases. Industrial complex tourism, radiation driven all elements of the whole society requires the healthy participation and joint support. In particular, the development of "global tourism" in the future means that tourism activities will fully penetrate into all aspects of social life. Regulating the tourism market requires not only cross-sectoral and

---

[1]"Notice of the State Council on Printing and Distributing the Development Plan for Tourism in the 13th Five-year Plan Period. Retrieved from http://www.google.com/video/video/content/15299.htm.

transregional supervision, but also expansion from industry regulation to regulation of social affairs. Only the production system, consumption, tourist rights have been fully protected, tourism and consumption can release a stronger.

1.1.3 Release of documents to govern uncivilized behavior in tourism industry

On May 26, 2016, "National Tourism Administration on Interim Measures for the Management of Uncivilized Travel Records" was issued. The establishment of tourism integrity system, enhance civilized travel awareness, standardize the operation of tourism practitioners provide legal basis.

1.1.4 Release of documents by National Development and Reform Commission and the National Tourism Administration to implement major tourism and leisure projects

In December 2016, the National Development and Reform Commission and the National Tourism Administration jointly issued the Notice on Implementing Major Tourism and Leisure Projects. The future will focus on guiding enterprises to carry out project construction in eight areas, including guiding enterprises to carry out the construction of tourism public service support projects, key scenic spots construction projects, poverty alleviation projects for tourism, red tourism development projects and "three changes and one integration" projects for rural poor households, Tourism industry training projects, tourism innovation projects, green tourism guide construction. From these documents, we can read the determination of the country in developing "global tourism" and the direction of strengthening the construction of various large-scale resources and supporting projects.

In addition, the "Outline of National Innovation-Driven Development Strategy", the "Opinions of the State Council on Deepening the Reform of Investment and Financing System", the "Notice on Carrying Out the Cultivation Work of Characteristic Small Towns" and the "General Office of the State Council, Further Expanding Education and Training on Health, Education, Culture, Sports Culture and Pension Opinions on Consumption, "" Opinions of 11 Ministries of Education on Promoting Research Travel of Primary and Secondary Students "and other documents have been promulgated one after another, forming a comprehensive boost to tourism development from different aspects. It can be seen from the strength and frequency of policy support that the government's determination to develop tourism and the dependence and urgency of developing "global tourism" on the institutional environment.

1.2 Supply-side reform on Beijing tourism policy

From the perspective of the city of Beijing, the tourism industry ushered in a golden period of development during the "13th Five-Year Plan" period. The government will implement measures to promote the escalation of consumption, construct the tourism pattern of Beijing-Tianjin-Hebei region and industrial integration. It will pay more attention to the quality and efficiency of tourism development, strengthen the supply-side reform and make up for the shortcomings of public services. Focusing on the strategic positioning of the capital city, it will embody the level of informationization and management in its development.

1.2.1 Beijing Issues Opinions on Implementation of Tourism Reform and Development

In early 2016, the Beijing municipal government document (GZF [2016] No. 9) pointed out that the focus of tourism development in Beijing's future core areas is on order, quality and safety. Suburban tourism emphasizes the pace of development, tourism structure and quality and efficiency, Philosophy, deepen the reform, release the potential and optimize the environment to enhance Beijing's tourism competitiveness, attractiveness, driving force and international influence.

1.2.2 Release of the "Outline of Tourism Development in Beijing Suburbs (2015-2020)"

By the end of 2015, "Outline of Tourism Development in Beijing Suburbs (2015-2020)" pointed out that by the end of the "13th Five-Year Plan" period, Beijing will create 800 new high-end travel formats in the suburbs of Beijing with a reception area of more than 120 million people in the suburbs, Tourism revenue more than 70 billion yuan. Construct a batch of complexes and construct about 20 special economic zones with ditch area[1].

1.2.3 Release of "2016 Annual Travel Service Quality Improvement Action Plan"

The theme of 2016 is "Year of Promotion of Tourism Service Quality". Through a

---

[1]"Beijing Municipal Tourism Commission recently promulgated Outline for the Development of Beijing's Suburb Tourism 2020", China Tourism Information Website, http://news.city.com/Allnews/29177.html.

one-year Beijing tourism service quality improvement activity, it will be more effective in comprehensive management, more standardized market environment, more optimized tourism environment, more perfect public service and more safety management In place, the standard construction more systematic, more comprehensive quality of personnel objectives, improve Beijing tourism satisfaction and city reputation.

### 1.2.4 Consideration of "Beijing Tourism Ordinance (draft for review)"

Beijing Tourism Ordinance (draft for review draft) publicly solicits comments that urban and rural residents can use legitimate residential and other conditions to develop tourism products. Travel agencies operating day trips must be filed.

### 1.2.5 "Opinions of Beijing Municipal People's Government on Speeding up the Development of Ice-Snow Sports (2016-2022)"

Beijing has promulgated documents and supporting plans for the development of the ice movement (referred to as the "1 + 7" document), which has meant that concrete measures to help the winter Olympics and vigorously develop the ice and snow sports industry have started.[1]

Regardless of the frequency and level of supply of policies or the breadth of the participants, the tourism industry, especially Beijing's tourism industry, received unprecedented policy support in 2016. Based on these policies, we can see that: First of all, both the state and Beijing fully understand the development status of tourism, and all sectors and sectors agree on the development thinking of "global tourism" and gradually unite strategic planning, layout and joint promotion actions Second, the support and guidance for "supply-side reform" has been intensified. New tourism consumption hot spots, new tourism formats and tourism innovation enterprises have been nurtured as key supporting targets. Tourism development is more excellent government.

## 2. Tourism market development of Beijing in 2016

### 2.1 Inbound and outbound tourism markets

In 2016, Beijing tourism developed in a contrarian manner, realizing total tourism

---

[1]"Opinions of Beijing Municipal People's Government on Speeding up the Development of Ice and Snow Sports (2016-2022)", Capital Window, http://zhengwu.beijing.gov.cn/gh/dt/t1433074.htm.

revenue of 502.1 billion yuan, an increase of 90% over the same period of previous year. The annual tourism shopping and catering consumption accounted for the total retail sales of social consumer goods 24. 10, the proportion of tourism investment in the total social investment in fixed assets was 9. 40, the tourism market is growing momentum.

2.1.1 Outbound tourism market growth rate return to rational

In 2016, the outbound tourism market in Beijing continued to grow. Although the number of outbound tourists hit another record high, the growth rate has returned to a rational one and tourism in Hong Kong, Maucao and Maui continued to cool down. According to the official website of Beijing Municipal Tourism Commission, in the first three quarters of 2016, the total number of outbound tourists was 4380521, an increase of only 6.5% over the same period of previous year.

The top 5 countries visited by Beijing's outbound travel destinations were Thailand (805,530, up 10%), Japan (730,129, up 10.5%), South Korea (722,325, up 4.18%), France (279,661 person-times, up -10.6%), Switzerland (23,1669 person-times, -8% increase). The rankings have not changed from the previous year.

The number of outbound tourists grew fastest year-on-year to Vietnam (112,190 passengers, growth 129.90%), Egypt (36078, 111%), Philippines (36747, 91%), Portugal (22 089, 63.90), Spain (40919, growth 61.90%), there have been different from the previous outbound tourism hot spots. The destinations of negative growth compared with the previous year were Cambodia (32,996 person-times, -47.30), Taiwan (126,370 person-months, -450 points), Austria (34,250 person-months, -29.30), Hong Kong 97,830 visitors, up -17.50).

To sum up, some changes have taken place in the outbound tourism market in Beijing: one is the growth rate; the other is the increase in the proportion of free exercise; the third is the continuous deepening of the influence of "Internet +"; the other is the decline in the proportion of shopping in the consumption structure than the rise.

2.1.2 Inbound tourism market remained stable

Under the overall trend of international economic downturn and domestic economic restructuring, Beijing has taken some measures to promote its entry into the tourism market, such as continuing to push forward the policy of departure tax refund for overseas tourists, developing customized tailored tourism products and increasing overseas sales. Relatively stable.

According to the statistics from Beijing Tourism Commission, from January to October 2016, Beijing received a total of 3,511,601 overnight tourists, down 0.60% year-on-year. Among them, there were 29,998.25 million foreigners received, a decrease of 0.5.

From the intercontinental source market, from January to October 1046607 tourists came to Beijing in Asia (excluding Hong Kong, Maucao, Taiwan), an increase of -5.40, 903661 tourists in Europe, an increase of -0.50, reception of 817857 passengers, a year-on-year increase 4.30, receiving 152.529 million tourists from Oceania, an increase of 12.40, receiving 74,443 tourists from Africa, an increase of 0.60. Oceania and American tourists increased significantly.

From the main source of tourists, the top 10 countries and regions entering the country are: the United States (603719 person-times, an increase of 1.60), South Korea (326039 person-months, up -50), Hong Kong, China (292 927 person-times, an increase of 0.80 ), Japan (207273 person-times, up -3.90), Taiwan (207109 person-times, -1.60%), Germany (177984 person-times, -1.90%), Britain (157672 person- times, 7.70 increase), Canada , An increase of 17.60% over the same period of last year), Australia (126,893 person-times, an increase of 110%), France (113 135% person-names, an increase of -12.10). Inbound tourists from Japan and South Korea declined in size due to the bilateral relations. The number of inbound tourists from the United States increased steadily, but the top five rankings remained unchanged.

The five countries with the fastest growth in arrivals are + New Zealand (38.30), Spain (25.40), Canada (17.60), Pakistan (17.40) and Australia (110). The slowest growth rates were: North Korea (-48.60), Vietnam (-38.40), Macau (-28.90) and Mongolia (-23.70)[1]. Among them, the increase of immigration in Canada and Australia has a greater impact on the whole.

---

[1]"From January to October 2016, our city welcomes tourists from other places", the official website of Beijing Municipal Tourism Development Committee, http: // ww. BjtA gov. Cn / xxgk / tjxx / rjlyzqk / 387465. htm

2.1.3 Domestic tourism in holidays presents new features

Holiday travel in Beijing presents the following new features in 2016.

First of all, tourist spending has shown a significant increase over the past. During the traditional festivals, the growth rate of total tourism receipts is generally higher than the growth rate of the number of tourists received, to a certain extent, shows good economic benefits. During certain holidays, with a decrease in the number of tourists, the revenue still maintained a clear growth. This shows that the potential for tourism consumption in Beijing is being released.

Second, the rural folk tourism market saw a spurt of growth during the holidays. For example, on the 7th day of the National Day, Beijing received a total of 165,000 folk-custom tourists and realized a tourism income of 6,103,000 yuan, both up three times as much. Some new hot tourism market, such as the ancient North Water Town, Daxing Wildlife Park. The success of bidding for the Winter Olympics has brought the prosperity of the winter ice tourism market. During the Spring Festival holidays, the city's ski resort received 80,000 tourists, an increase of 8.60% over the same period of last year. Snow Mountain Surfing, sled park, snow CS and other projects, attracting a large number of tourists, ranked No. 1 Nanshan Ski Resort 18,000 tourists, an increase of 1.80; Huai North International Ski Resort received 10,000 passengers, an increase of 93%[1].

Finally, the quality of travel services has improved significantly. In the "Year of Promotion of Tourism Service Quality", due to the current-limit measures and the improvement of service quality, the comfort of the tourism environment has been enhanced and the tourism market has maintained a good order with the complaint rate remarkably reduced. For example, on National Day holiday, the number of complaints received by tourists dropped by 310% from a year earlier.

2.1.4 Beijing Beijing, Tianjin and Hebei tourist consumption behavior analysis

In 2016, the author conducted a small-scale sample survey on Beijing's tourism consumption behavior among Beijing citizens. The survey sent a total of 70

---

[1]"Spring Festival Holiday Tourism in 2016," the official website of Beijing Tourism Development Committee, http://www.bj+ta. Gov.cn/xwzx/xwyl/381448. Htm

questionnaires, of which 45 were issued for the network, 25 for the reality. The basic situation of respondents in Table 1.

Table 1 Population Sample

| Items | | Proportion |
|---|---|---|
| gender | Male | 38.57 |
| | Female | 61.43 |
| age | Under 16 | 0 |
| | 16-20 | 27.14 |
| | 23-30 | 15.71 |
| | 31-45 | 27.14 |
| | 46-55 | 17.15 |
| | Above 55 | 12.86 |
| occupation | Students | 27.14 |
| | Government workers | 2.86 |
| | Institution workers | 21.42 |
| | Non-public enterprise staff | 7.15 |
| | Military men | 1.42 |
| | Self-employed persons | 11.43 |
| | Private enterprise staff | 10.00 |
| | others | 18.58 |

As far as travel time is concerned, the survey shows that Beijing citizens take 31% of the trips during the weekend, 25% of them travel in three days and 15% of the trips during the 11th and Spring Festival holidays and 28% of the tourists in other times. Short-term travel is more concentrated.

Traveling style, by age group (16 ~ 45 years old, 45 years of age) control found that: the most common rail travel (16,445 years old accounted for 30. 6%, 45 years old accounted for 61.9%), other Among the modes of travel, young people prefer traveling by car (32. 6%), while middle-aged and elderly people prefer traveling by coach (28. 6%).

As for the number of trips (see Figure 1), 93.30 respondents had more than one trip to Beijing, Tianjin and Hebei each year, 17.8% of respondents averaged 3 ~ 4 times a year, and 13.3% of respondents averaged 5 times and above each year.

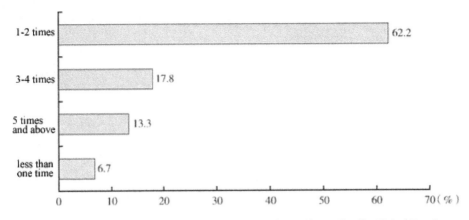

Figure 1 Travel Frequencies of Beijing Citizens in Beijing-Tianjin-Hebei Region

The number of people who spend 100 to 200 yuan per day on tourism accounts for 490, the number of people who spend 50 to 99 yuan accounts for 330 and the number of people who have more than 200 yuan accounts for 180 (see Figure 2). The main source of travel funds, 530 people from the wage, 330 people from family support, and their consumption ability is relatively stable (see Figure 3).

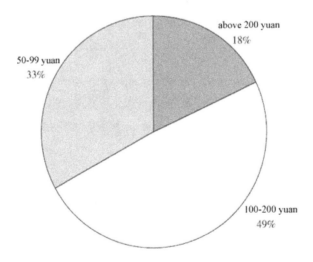

Figure 2 Average Daily Expenditure of Beijing Citizen during Trips to Beijing, Tianjin, and Hebei Province

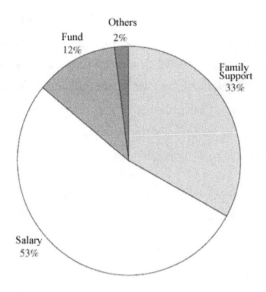

Figure 3 Sources of Travel Funds in Beijing-Tianjin-Hebei Region of Beijing Citizens

In terms of consumption structure (see Figure 4), the higher proportion of consumption includes accommodation, catering, transportation and tickets, accounting for 46.60, 24.440, 13.330 and 11.110 respectively, with a small proportion of other consumption. In Beijing, Tianjin and Hebei tourism development to increase cultural and other entertainment consumption, to transition from low-end tourism to high-end tourism, and promote the development of tourism.

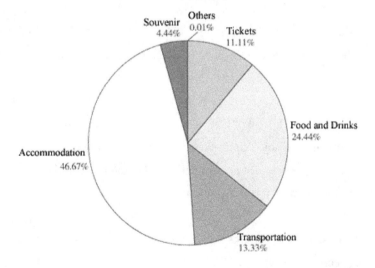

Figure 4 Consumption Structure of Travel in Beijing-Tianjin-Hebei Region of Beijing Citizens

In terms of information sources (see Figure 5), the highest percentage of information received from the Internet was 33.3%, followed by friends, accounting for 30.5%. Beijing-Tianjin-Hebei tourism related departments in attracting tourists should pay attention to both online publicity, but also attach importance to tourists in the local tourism, as far as possible by telephone or online return, improve service quality, and with major travel agencies, television stations and newspapers Strengthen cooperation and increase visual impact so as to attract tourists.

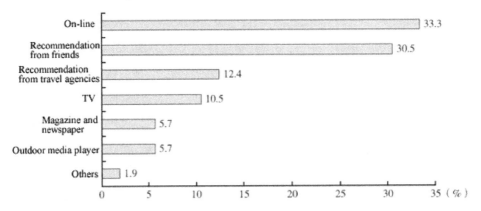

Figure 5 Access Channels to Travel Information in Beijing-Tianjin-Hebei Region of Beijing Citizens

In terms of consumer preferences, the highest proportion is the seaside beach, about 26%, the theme park accounted for 16.8%, 16% historical sites, landscaped gardens accounted for 12.2%, mountains and rivers accounted for 11.5%, exploration and entertainment accounted for 9.9%, ethnic Style accounted for 7.6%, indicating that tourists from heavy travel before the heavy weight into heavy enjoyment.

In terms of booking methods, the population aged 16-45 is the elite with the highest ratio of 95. 6%, while the lowest of Ctrip is 32%. This is because the main demand for Beijing residents in Beijing-Tianjin-Hebei tourism is booking hotels and other Booking service less, eLong has always been in the hotel reservation level, Ctrip is mainly a full range of travel products booking.

In terms of consumption patterns, cash consumption accounted for the highest proportion of people over the age of 45 (76%), savings card consumption accounted for 52%, third-party consumption accounted for 40%, accounting for the lowest proportion of credit card spending (credit card, 36%). The lowest proportion of cash consumers (37.8%), the highest is the credit card spending (savings card 75.6%), while the third-party consumer and credit card consumer group was flat (57.8%). Visible in the elderly population to cash, savings card spending, young people like to credit card spending and consumption through the third party trading platform. Therefore, in the ever-increasing popularity of mobile phone networks, third-party transactions should be increased in the tourism development of Beijing-Tianjin-Hebei.

## 2.2 Landmark events in Beijing tourism in 2016

### 2.2.1 The First World Tourism Development Conference

From May 18 to May 2016, the first World Tourism Development Conference was held in Beijing. The main topics are tourism for development, tourism for poverty alleviation and tourism for peace. Heads of tourism departments from more than 100 countries and regions, heads of the UN World Tourism Organization and more than 10 international organizations attended the meeting.

### 2.2.2 "Trip to Beijing Suburbans" brand unveiled

"Touring the suburbs of Beijing" will become an important platform for Beijing Tourism Commission to publicize and promote the tourism in the suburbs of Beijing. Through the "Traveling Outskirts of Beijing" brand, it will promote the tourism transformation from sightseeing to leisure in the suburbs of Beijing and promote the brand-name, large-scale and distinctive development of tourism in the suburbs of Beijing. Beijing will become a tourism resource, a boutique route and a tourism product promotion channel.

### 2.2.3 Beijing International Youth Tourism Festival

Beijing International Youth Tourism Season, with the theme of "YOUNG Outstanding Beijing, Sharing the World", provides a platform for young students and tourists to exchange and interact with each other, launching youth "painting" Beijing, youth "making" Beijing and youth "traveling" Beijing's three major Theme activities, but also produced a number of outstanding works, excellent photography and translation of the results of Beijing gift products.

### 2.2.4 The First Plenary Session of Beijing Municipal Committee for the Development of Ice and Snow Sports

In recent years, the rapid development of snow and ice movement in Beijing, especially the successful bid for the 2022 Beijing Olympic Winter Games, has greatly stimulated the public's enthusiasm for participating in the ice and snow sports. The popularity and the development of the snow industry go into a strong impetus. Approved by the Beijing Municipal Government, the relevant agencies have established a joint ice and snow sports development system to facilitate the overall development of the city's ice and snow sports. December 15, 2016, Beijing held the first plenary session of the joint meeting on ice and snow sports. Joint meeting by the city's 40 departments and units, in ice sports co-ordination, public services, activities and other organizations to work together to vigorously develop the Beijing ice market.

3. 2016 Beijing tourism development characteristics

3.1 The tourism in the suburbs of the whole country travel to branding

From the perspective of global tourism, the development of tourism in the suburbs of Beijing embarks on a fast lane of transformation and upgrading and quality improvement and efficiency enhancement. With Changping District, Pinggu District, Yanqing District included in the first batch of "global tourism demonstration zone", the construction of tourism and leisure system in Beijing suburbs began to fully promote.

Beijing suburbs tourism is to promote tourism supply-side reform focus. At present, Beijing has promoted the implementation of the "50-trillion-trillion-yuan project" (the transformation of a traditional village with a development proposal, a map leaflet, a mobile consultation station, an ecological toilet, a free Wi-Fi station, Five "project; the overall development of the" ten new formats "of international postcards, recreational farms, picking hedgerows, ethnic customs centers, village hotels, health bar, ecological fisherman, landscapes, wineries, car camp; Create 100 tourism and leisure villages and towns with special features; promote the construction of 3000km leisure trails; organize the training of 10,000 folk-custom households in suburbs of Beijing; and provide 3 billion yuan of financial support by using the financing guarantee service system for suburban tourism in Beijing to create a special tourism town and village Rural tourism brand, expand Beijing tourism development space)[1], improve the supply of leisure products structure. The development of tourism and

---

[1]"2016 Beijing Tourism Work Conference", China Travel Information Network, http: // news. Cthy. / Allnews / 30563. html

leisure in the suburbs of Beijing is not only an important link in realizing global tourism, but also an important support for the adjustment of economic structure and upgrading of industries in rural areas. It is also an effective measure to reduce poverty and increase farmers' income. In 2016, the three key tasks for tourism in the suburbs of Beijing are to strengthen the construction of tourism and leisure trails, traditional villages and rural tourism. Tourism in the suburbs of Beijing has become a trial field for "double creation" operations. With the review of the quality of new formats, the construction of self-driving motor home camps, the promotion of funds for the development of tourism and leisure investment in Beijing suburbs, the standard management of distinctive formats, Training, and Beijing suburban tourism financing guarantee system, the establishment of the suburbs tourism insurance system, the tourism in Beijing will continue to launch boutique projects.

3.2 Deepen the Structural Reform of Tourism Supply Side

3.2.1 Expand the effective supply of tourism products

Beijing tourism product brand and reputation increase. In 2016, Beijing Gifts first entered the high-tech product catalog encouraged by Beijing Municipality (2016 Edition). Through such events as holding the Tourism Commodities Competition, the Beijing International Tourism Commodities Fair, the establishment of a special support fund for tourism products, the revision and improvement of the "Beijing Gifts" operation standard and the establishment of the "Beijing Gifts" tourism and cultural experience shopping district, the operation has attracted more social capital to invest in tourism products R & D and production. At present, the superior resources of science and technology such as high-tech, cultural and creative, traditional culture, old-fashioned and characteristic agriculture continue to be collected and transformed. The capital tourist commodities have formed a good development trend of "brand excellence, high quality and variety" Reform, service environment optimization, improvement of consumption level has played a positive role in promoting. In the first half of 2016, the city's tourist shopping spending reached 65.74 billion yuan, an increase of 13.3% over the same period of previous year, accounting for 13.2% of the total retail sales of consumer goods[1]. At the same time, the consumption environment has been improved through measures such as duty-free shops and departure tax rebates, releasing new space for consumption.

---

[1]"'Beijing Gift' boosts the development of tourism products, "" People's Daily - Overseas Version ", http://m paper.oplem> m.> / Rmrbhwb / html / 2016-11 / 17 / content_ 1724730. htm

Research tourism products to the world. At present, Beijing has launched 11 quality tourist routes for students, covering topics such as world heritage, festival festivals, fine arts and cultural events, sports events, science education and traditional Chinese medicine. Some scientific and technological tourism enterprises (such as Scientific International Travel, Century Matilda, etc.) research tourism products (such as Songshan Insect Science Camp, military summer camps, capital camps, etc.) has become a brand.

Chinese culture experience and medical tourism continue to enrich and regulate. At present, there are 13 Chinese medicine culture experience tours and 31 international medical tourism service packages with Chinese medicine characteristics and treatment advantages to meet the needs of different tourists and patients. In 2016, China National Tourism Administration announced the first batch of 10 cities of "China's Research Tourism Destination" as well as the first batch of 20 "National Research Tourism Demonstration Base" list. Among them, Beijing Haidian District, Beijing Lugouqiao Chinese People's Anti-Japanese War Memorial Hall was selected.

The number of award-winning travel and specifications continue to be the highest in the country. According to the ICCA statistics, among the ranking of the number of city international conferences held in 2015, Beijing hosted 95 international conferences and ranked first in the country (55 in Shanghai and second in the rankings) and fifth in the cities in the Asia Pacific region (following Singapore , Seoul, Hong Kong, Bangkok), ranking 19th in the world. In the future, Beijing will mainly support the development of convention and exhibition industry in the fields of science and technology information, cultural creativity, education and training, emerging industries, high-end consumption and medical health care, and increase policy support to play a more active role in the function building of Beijing International Exchange Center.

Sports and leisure tourism has become the new growth pole of tourism consumption. 2022 The successful bid for the Beijing Olympic Winter Games has stimulated new hot spots in winter tourism. With the promotion of infrastructure construction and personnel training, Winter Games will add new consumption levels to winter tourism in Beijing. At the same time, caravan camping tourism in the ascendant, Beijing RV Camping Travel Association was established. At the same time, sports tourism and leisure product innovation, project management and security also put forward new requirements.

Tourism resident performance to the specialization, quality and brand guidance and development. Some key projects such as the historical musical "Forbidden City,""Dancing Horse,""Distant Dinosaur," and the China Acrobatic Troupe's tourism resident performance projects are under preparation or have been launched. Relevant supportive policies and docking with the market of tourism enterprises are also In the gradual promotion of tourism in Beijing to expand consumer hot spots have a positive meaning.

3.2.2 Tap the potential of tourism supply

In accordance with the "Guiding Opinions on Encouraging Enterprises, Institutions and Governmental Organs in Beijing to Set Up Tourism Open Days" promulgated by the Beijing Municipal Government, Beijing actively promotes the tourism of social resources and the diversification of tourist resources, and organizes 134 enterprises, institutions and government departments The establishment of the Tourism Open Day requires the tourism open units to strengthen the renovation and renovation of infrastructure such as tourist signs, tour routes, toilets and parking lots, organize distinctive tourism theme activities, enhance service quality and service awareness, and provide citizens and tourists with safe, Convenient and comfortable travel environment. Tiananmen Square Administrative Committee is the first batch of open tourism units. In addition, Beijing will also promote 20 cultural collection units, celebrities and other cultural heritage tourism units open to tourists, the introduction of more than 10 sports tourism demonstration products, and constantly promote supply-side reform, and fully tap the capital's cultural relics, ecological environment, folk culture, Science and technology exhibition, the Olympic heritage and other resource advantages, and further enrich the tourism products.

3.2.3 Innovative institutional mechanisms to stimulate new vitality of tourism enterprises

Tourism enterprises are the main body of the market. Tourism companies have the ability to innovate; the tourism market is constantly enriching the premise. In 2016, some large-scale tourism enterprises carried out brand expansion and adjustment through various means of resource integration and integration. Small and medium-sized enterprises (SMEs) have also been developed through innovative and specialized means. In addition, the establishment of a base for making passenger business and building a base for making passenger business have also promoted the start-up and employment of tourism and created a good market atmosphere.

## 3.3 Optimize the tourism development environment

The 2016 Government Work Report states: "To implement the system of paid leave, standardize the tourism market order and meet the rising age of mass tourism." In 2016, Beijing Municipality comprehensively upgraded tourism service levels in terms of administration, hardware facilities, service standards and user-friendly experience.

### 3.3.1 Rehabilitate tourism consumption environment

With the introduction of "Beijing Tourism Ordinance" as an opportunity to improve tourism laws and regulations system. Tourism facilities, tourist toilets, recreational trails, parking lots and emergency rescue areas have been built as the key points of construction. Tourism functions such as tourist traffic, scenic spots, self-driving camps, tourist information centers and tourist hubs have been continuously improved, and smart tourist cities have been built speed up.

In 2016, Beijing's departure tax rebate sales exceeded 100 million yuan. As of November 9, 2016, there were 503 tax refund stores examined and filed, with 3464 tax refund receipts and tax rebates of RMB 8.38 million, and the application rate surpassed 64%[1]. By optimizing the environment, inbound tourists' satisfaction and international competitiveness have been effectively enhanced.

### 3.3.2 Regulate the tourism market order

To govern the order of the tourism market is the basic requirement to enhance the quality of tourist services and maintain the reputation of Beijing tourism. In 2016, the General Office of the State Council promulgated the Circular on Strengthening the Comprehensive Supervision of the Tourism Market, putting tourism market

---

[1]"Beijing 2016 overseas tourists shopping departure tax rebate sales" billion ", People's Network, http: // bj. PeopTcn / n2 / 2016/1109 / c233080 -29282315.

governance under the special focus of the municipal government; the Measures for the Administration of Tourism Safety since 2016 December 1, the year shall come into force. In the "Year of Promotion of Tourism Service Quality", the Beijing tourism market focused on the issues of "illegal day trips" and "unreasonable low prices." Baidu search engine launched the "Beijing travel safety tips", Beijing tourism network information service channel opened trial operation, clean-up network fake tourism information special rectification work orderly, and the use of travel team electronic itinerary system, guide 1C management system and other information supervision Means to play credit system functions, increase the loss of trust in tourism companies and tourists uncivilized behavior exposure. At the same time promote the standardization of production safety in the industry, increase the safety supervision of travel agencies, folklore households, social hotels, to ensure the healthy development of tourism industry.

3.4 The regional cooperation in the sharing economy has achieved fruitful results

Since the central government first proposed "developing a shared economy" in 2015, it has been deepening its tourism development based on resource sharing.

Beijing-Tianjin-Hebei tourism supply-side structural reform, as the main line, deepens collaborative innovation. In 2016, the "Beijing-Tianjin-Hebei Tourism Cooperative Development Plan of Action (2016 ~ 2018)" was adopted and an alliance of rural tourism industries in Beijing, Tianjin and Hebei was established to jointly develop rural leisure and holiday products. Set up a rural tourism financial service platform to carry out intelligence tourism activities in Beijing, Tianjin and Hebei rural tourism so as to achieve precise poverty alleviation. Beijing-Tianjin-Hebei Tourism Distribution Center through train industry associations, Beijing-Tianjin-Hebei Zijia RV camp tourism cooperation intention reached. Following the Beijing-Tianjin-Hebei Red Tour, Beijing, Tianjin and Hebei famous village tour, Beijing-Tianjin-Hebei RV tour, Beijing-Tianjin-Hebei ride tour, the Spring Festival folk shopping tours, ice and hot spring tours and other tourist routes continue to launch. Car cruise activities will be three places of red tourism resources to travel caravans travel with a combination of new formats. In particular, the popular tourist activities in Beijing, Tianjin, and Hebei Province, which are conducted in the style of "tourism + science popularization", embody the cooperation model of "tourism" industry integration across different departments, regions and types. Not only the resources for science popularization have been revitalized by "tourism" But also enriched the tourism products of special characteristics of Beijing, Tianjin and Ji. These activities fully embody the spiritual core of sharing economy and provide a more open and free choice for both supply and demand parties and achieve a win-win situation between economic and social interests. Formed Beijing-Tianjin-Hebei tourism development layout has played a significant role in promoting.

In addition, tourism cooperation in "9 + 10" region continued to deepen, and counterpart support work also showed the sharing of achievements. Has opened in Beijing to Hotan, Wulanchabu, Nanyang, Shiyan, Chifeng and other places more travel trips.

3.5 More emphasis on the quality of travel services

2016 is the year of "quality of tourist service promotion." To improve the quality of tourism services and rectify the tourist market order is the focus of 2016. To this end, Beijing Municipal Tourism Commission released "Beijing 2016 Tourism Quality of Service Year Action Plan."

From the perspective of specific actions, the tourism public service has carried out multilingual tourism translation service platform, early warning information release, travel team management system and the attempt of using electronic itinerary, in improving travel public service facilities such as toilets and toilets, strengthening tourism service system and The establishment of tourism volunteer service stations and service teams and many other innovations; through the development and promotion of "promotion of rural tourism characteristics of the format and assessment of Part 10: Winery""tourist town characteristics and service requirements""National Green Tourism Demonstration Base "" National health tourism demonstration base "and other local standards and industry standards, the national service industry standardization pilot to improve the construction of tourism quality standards; through the A-level scenic spot review, A-class travel agencies to re-evaluate the work of standardized management mechanism; through the promotion The reform of the tour guide management system will provide training to practitioners and enhance their service enthusiasm and service skills. The service industry in Beijing will expand and open a comprehensive pilot program to support joint venture foreign-funded travel agencies in developing their business overseas and enhancing their ability to serve tourists.

In 2016, Beijing won the CTF China Travel 2015 "Best Domestic Travel City Award". According to the National Tourism Administration of China Tourist Satisfaction Survey, Beijing's first quarter 2016 satisfaction index (77.78) is higher than the national average (75.02).

## 4. Beijing tourism development trends and suggestions

### 4.1 Global tourism: from "walking and watching" into "another place to live"

Global tourism emphasizes full-field vision. The experience of traveling is not only focused on a few scenic spots and several routes, but the way of traveling is changed from "watching over" to "overcoming experience." Visitors hope to integrate themselves into the local social and cultural life, fully and slowly experience the local people's feelings, folk customs, folk customs, tastes different from everyday life, another fresh state. This poses new requirements for public service facilities and public information services. Urban construction must first ensure livable, especially for "outsiders" feel livable, access is simple and convenient. Study the overall facility design, promotional design, service design, information supply, is the destination of travel.

### 4.2 Tourism +: from integration to sharing

The past understanding of tourism, is just an industry, a pillar industry, a strategic pillar industries related to national economy and the people's livelihood. Global tourism means that tourism is becoming a platform for the integration of economy, culture and science and technology in the entire society. All resources in society are shared by the development of tourism. Regions, industries, departments and markets gradually converge due to tourism. Tourists are more diversified and segmented. Special products and customized tourism products are more abundant. Travel-driven consumption potential to be fully released.

### 4.3 Needs pf experience quality: from basic elements to cultural connotation

Global tourism pays more attention to the quality of deep experience, and people will choose fresh, comfortable and different experiences after focusing on scenic spots and cursory sightseeing tours. Quality of experience has become the sole criterion for people to vote with their feet. Global travel experience is a full range of experience. How to create a unique, refreshing or refreshing experience, the protection of the unique culture of the local and depth mining is an important part. The infiltration of culture will be a source of deep experience.

4.4 Tourism Civilization: a test to all-round social development

In 2016, the "Interim Measures for the Administration of Records of Uncivilized Travels under the National Tourism Administration" was revised and released. Beijing Municipality took the lead in promulgating the "Detailed Rules for Management of Uncivilized Tourism Records", incorporating the requirements of civilized tourism and the specific contents of the Measures into the travel contracts, travel notes, service guides, safety tips, excursions, etc. Documents or announcements, "travel uncivilized behavior records" will be included in the integrity system, while strengthening the reminder, education and training. With the joint conference mechanism of "Promoting the Quality of Tourism Civilization for Capital Citizens", Beijing also launched the special topic of "Great Civilization Tourism in 2016", the Youth Student Travel Volunteer Yuanmingyuan Advocacy Civilized Tourism, the "Civilization Tourism Philanthropy for China", the "Green Tourism "Theme activities, selected 20 civilized tourism public service ambassador," the most beautiful one meter landscape "civilized tourism theme promotional activities to jointly create a capital of the civilized tourism order and atmosphere.

However, as of the end of 2016, there are still many tourist uncivilized incidents coming from the community. This shows that not only the positive guidance and negative warnings, the establishment of social environment, the formation of civilized accomplishments, and the inclusion of civilized education in the education system are needed for the realization of civilized tourism Is the direction that the entire country and people need long-term efforts in the future. Tourism civilization is not only a specific manifestation of behavior, but also the result of the internalization of civilized human qualities. Civilized tourism is a microcosm of the all-round social development and progress.

# Historical and Cultural City Protection of Beijing in 2016

Yan Chen[1]

## Abstract

In order to carry out the requirements of Beijing's urban planning for the protection of historical and cultural cities during the "13th Five-Year Plan" period, the historical and cultural relics in Beijing are being protected in a continuous manner. With the appearance of the old city, the protection and utilization of cultural belts and the development of cultural relics However, the contradictions between protection and development still exist, the legal system of cultural relics protection has not been established yet, and the problems of low level of heritage development and utilization are in urgent need of solution. This report outlines the basic and major tasks for the protection of historical and cultural cities in Beijing in 2016, points out the main problems at this stage and proposes relevant countermeasures in a targeted manner.

Keywords: historical and cultural city protection, basic orientation, key task

With the protection of historical and cultural cities in Beijing progressing year by year, the protection of famous cities has entered the normalization stage and the protection work has been continuously consolidated and upgraded. In 2016, in accordance with the "Beijing Plan for Building a National Cultural Center during the 13th Five-Year Plan" and the "Opinions on Deepening the Reform and Enhancing the Management of Urban Planning and Construction in an All-Round Way," Beijing continued to deepen the protection of historical and cultural cities to reproduce history Style and strive to further improve the protection of the old city, the Great Wall, the canal, Xishan significant effect of protection of the three cultural zones; comply with the requirements of national cultural relics, Beijing Municipal Bureau of cultural relics solidly promote the protection of cultural relics, the degree of legal protection of cultural relics has been improved; promote Cultural heritage into the modern life, cultural heritage protection and utilization of continuous innovation. However, we must also see achievements made at the same time. There are still some problems in the protection of famous cities such as the coordination between protection and

---

[1]Yan Chen, Asistant Researcher, Research Institute of Culture, Beijing Academy of Social Sciences

development, the improvement of the legal system of cultural relics protection and the improvement of the level of protection and utilization of heritage. We need to seriously analyze and study in practice and solve the problems that restrict the protection of famous cities. The bottleneck of work, and actively respond to the new problems Beijing's historical and cultural cities are facing, and further promote the city's protection to a new level.

1. The basic protection of Beijing's historical and cultural cities

In 2016, the routine protection work of historical and cultural cities in Beijing continued. The protection of historical and cultural cities, the protection of cultural belts (historical and cultural protected areas) and the protection of cultural relics protection units have been gradually deepened. The top-level design has become clearer and the protection mechanism has been continuously improved, The mode of protection is keeping pace with the times, the space pattern of the famous city is increasingly clear, the traditional and cultural features are highlighted, and the protection work of historical and cultural cities in Beijing is promoted overall and in an orderly manner and new achievements are continuously obtained.

1.1 City protection is integrated into urban planning and development

Guided by the new urban planning, the positioning of the historical and cultural city clearly incorporates Beijing's urban functions and becomes an important aspect that demonstrates the city's characteristics and qualities. Beijing reappears with its ancient capital style to create the "gold name card" of the city. The historical and cultural blocks, historical and cultural scenic spots and the "one axis" landscape in the old city gradually return to life. In June 2016, the "Plan for Strengthening the Construction of the National Cultural Center in Beijing" for the "Thirteenth Five-Year" Plan was drawn up in June 2016 to draw a blueprint for the construction of the Beijing National Cultural Center and to move toward the world famous cultural city with the world's cultural relics as its grand goal and history The protection of cultural city has become an important part of the construction of Beijing National Cultural Center. It needs to be strengthened from the aspects of improving the protection level of the famous city, strengthening the inheritance of traditional culture, excavating and displaying the historical context, highlighting the stigma of historical and cultural city in the process of protection, inheritance and development , The protection of Chinese civilization "gold card."

1.2 The protection of Cultural Belt (Historical and Cultural Preservation Area) proceeded steadily

According to the "Beijing Plan for Strengthening the Construction of National Cultural Center during the 13th Five-Year Plan", the Great Wall Cultural Belt in the north, the canal culture belt in the east, and the Western Xishan Cultural Belt construction are the major tasks for the overall protection of Beijing's historic and cultural heritage. The Great Wall culture belt, canal culture belt, Xishan culture belt protection and utilization of new into.

In 2016, at the 10th anniversary of the implementation of the "Great Wall Protection Ordinance," the State Administration of Cultural Heritage officially released the "Great Wall of China Conservation Report" to the public. From the Great Wall Resources Investigation and Research, the protection and management, maintenance practice and philosophy, culture and the times value, protection Goals and actions were summarized in five aspects, with the significance of bearing in mind. As an important area for the distribution of resources in the Great Wall, Beijing Great Wall Cultural Belt protection is based on repairs. On the existing basis, Mutianyu, Arrow buckles and the Great Wall of South China have been further protected and renovated. Perfect protection and utilization, Huairou District of Mutianyu Great Wall draws a 24 square kilometers of protected areas, the protection of the Great Wall surrounding the scope of the expansion from 300 meters to 1000 meters, cleared the illegal contracted shops, will also build a complete set of tourist facilities Tourist service As the famous "Great Wall of the Wild," the Jiankou Great Wall, due to the disrepair coupled with the large number of tourists climbing, has caused many collapsing and destruction of the side walls and the enemy building, resulting in a great potential for structural safety hazards. In October 2016, the Great Wall of Jiankou started the repair work. With the prerequisite of repairing the old and minimizing the intervention, the two sections of Falconry inverted and the ladder were mainly repaired and strengthened, and the side walls, enemy platforms and the enemy building along the line were also repaired. The same repair Changping Nanchang Great Wall City section.

With respect to the protection of the canal cultural belt, following the success of the trans-regional joint inscription, Tongzhou, Xianghe and Wuqing sections of the Beijing-Hangzhou Grand Canal will be formally navigable during the 13th Five-Year Plan and the cultural relics protection along the canal and The restoration of the landscape will continue to be strengthened. The joint efforts of the three places will help to further develop the deep historical and cultural background and the natural hydrological charm of the Grand Canal. The protection and utilization of Tongzhou section of the Grand Canal is also an important aspect of the protection of famous cities in the construction of Beijing's urban sub-center. In the context of the success of the Grand Canal inscriptions, the annual Tongzhou Cultural Festival Canal held a canal culture digging, dissemination of Tongzhou cultural image, building an important center of the sub-carrier, the Cultural Festival in 2016 as the "Cultural New Tongzhou Charm Deputy Center" as the theme, combines the ancient charm of the canal and the contemporary style with the fusion of art and folklore. It presents various forms of art performances (including canal trumpets, chorus, symphony and storytelling, crosstalk, bass drums), photography, mini-films, exhibitions, The combination of art and history has effectively promoted the protection and inheritance of the canal and enhanced the attractiveness and influence of the canal culture.

In 2016, the Xishan Cultural Belt started the renovation and protection of the North Fahai Temple, promoted the Xiangshan 28 Cultural Relics Protection Project and restored some historical and cultural scenic spots. In recent years, historical and cultural scenic spots of Sanshan-Wuyuan Realize the integration of cultural heritage from point to surface, and gradually restore the surrounding environment and ecology, as well as the related history and culture research work On the basis of protection and utilization in the field, the cultural connotation excavation of three mountains and five parks continued to deepen. In order to promote the charm of the scenic area and expand the influence of the cultural symbols of the three mountains and five parks, the Sanshan-Wuyuan Dialogue around literary and artistic creation and cultural diffusion was held in early 2016. The dialogue gathered experts and scholars from universities and theaters and radio writers and artists How to promote dialogue and exchange of thematic literature and art creation will help to further enhance the visibility and cultural influence of the three mountains and five parks. The theme of the Symposium on the Value and Function of Historical and Cultural Heritage of Three Mountains and Five Parks held in October focused on heritage conservation and industrialization. Specifically, the theme of heritage value, industrialization and landscape restoration was explored to promote the history of the three mountains and five parks Cultural construction work. In addition, the western suburbs of modern tram under construction play a series of gardens such as Fragrant Hills, the Summer Palace and the Kunyu River and the water diversion canal of South-to-North Water Diversion Project. In 2017, the opening of the whole railway will greatly facilitate citizens and tourists to visit and sightseeing.

1.3 Cultural relics protection carried out in full swing

2016 national cultural relics climax. From the policy level to protect and make good use of cultural relics resources, promote Chinese excellent traditional culture. In March, the State Council printed and issued the Guiding Opinions on Further Strengthening Cultural Relics. In April, the National Cultural Relics Work Conference was convened to comprehensively deploy the cultural relics in the new period. From strengthening cultural relics protection, actively exploiting and utilizing, strictly enforcing the law, and improving security, Made a clear provision; to explore the combination of traditional culture and innovation, so that the traditional culture and creative products to develop multi-directional force; in May, "on the promotion of cultural and cultural heritage of cultural and creative products, a number of opinions" was formally introduced; December, "The launch of the Internet + Chinese Civilization" Three-Year Plan of Action "will inject a strong impetus into the development of the creative industries in the cultural and arts industries from the institutional level and will promote the relics to truly" live together. "

Protection practice level, cultural relics highlights: Beijing removable cultural relics find out the family, with the first national cultural relics census work, as of April 2016, Beijing City, declared movable artifacts 6383254 / sets, accounting for 18. 930; of which 439,388 pieces of precious cultural relics / sets, accounting for 22.760 of the country, ranking the forefront of the country; the Forbidden City cultural and creative products to the rich Imperial Palace line of offline products and the popular culture of the Forbidden City APP, continue to lead the creative industry in the cultural industry; During the exhibition, academic conferences and lectures were held many times to become a major event in the museum exhibition. The documentary of "CCTV Documentary""I Repaired Cultural Relics in the Forbidden City" surprisingly became popular Network, documentary will be the original unknown National Palace Museum repair artifacts routine work presented in the public field of vision, tells the delicate, warmth, his right, simple craftsmen heartily harvest a lot of young people like.

In 2016, with the work and deployment of the Municipal Bureau of Cultural Relics, the routine work of protecting cultural relics has been progressing steadily. Taking Beijing's central axis as a turning point, the central axis of the ancient buildings vacate and repair continued to carry out, Bell and Drum Tower, Shichahai, Dazhalan surrounding environment has been significantly improved as a major breakthrough in the axis of the inscription, after the return of the National Palace Museum Gao Hyun-tien main body structure repair completed by the end of the Shou-Huang Temple repair has also been started; Fu Wang Fu Fu rear fencing with the South Nansha wall reinforcement project, the Great Wall Yuanmingyuan Temple protection display project, the Great Wall Juyong Guan South Urn strengthening treatment project Get pushed forward Cultural relics display and cultural heritage, combined with traditional festivals, the ancient bell Museum Dazhongsi held "Wenzhong-the moon" elegant Mid-Autumn Festival activities; Chihuahua Beijing concert team to participate in " Music appreciation evening party ", Allelupa rhyme across time and space and modern audience meet; Beijing Wen Bo Exchange Hall held" look at ancient buildings, listen to ancient music, doing tie-dye "activities to promote the material and intangible cultural heritage advocacy and heritage. In addition, the Capital Museum, the Confucius Temple and State Administration Museum, the Museum of Ancient Architecture and so on also carried out various exhibitions, lectures and exchanges in various forms with their own contents. Traditional culture is gaining popularity and the work of cultural relics has achieved substantial results.

2. Annual priorities
2.1 Vigorously protect the style of the old city, the implementation of district refinement management
Into the "13th Five-Year" period, Beijing in the planning of urban environmental construction restores the style of the old city and a new regulation. In December 2016, "Beijing Urban and Rural Environment Construction Plan for the Thirteenth Five-year Plan" was officially released, requiring the core functions of the capital to implement

the overall protection of the old city and inherit the style of the ancient capital. The city of West-East will gradually restore the ancient capital according to the speed of eight regions each year Style, street alley within the region will gradually restore the late Qing and Republican period style.

To protect the style of the old city, Dongcheng District, in-depth explores block and alley protection. First, the combination of urban renewal and overall planning of the city and capital function will lead to the new practice of upgrading and reconstructing the historical and cultural blocks in Dongcheng City, and guiding the retreat of houses, population deconstruction, repair and remediation, renovation of facilities, upgrading of industries, improvement of people's livelihood and regional governance And the overall protection work smoothly. Dongcheng District and SASAC cooperate with each other to carry out interoperability and renovations of historic blocks. For example, First Capital Group will participate in the project of transforming "Static Alleys • New Ecology One East Four or Eight to Historic Environment Blocks Comprehensive Environment Management" in Dongsai District. East Fourth Street on the alley facades, windows and other unified planning and transformation of business openings in the wall to engage in business operations to block plug-ins, illegal shops advertisements, plaques, light boxes and other remediation, and actively create "static alley • new Ecology. " Second, introduce new protection and management measures. The first guideline for the protection and control of the style and appearance of historical and cultural blocks - the introduction of the Guidance on the Protection and Control of the Style and Appearance of Nanluoguxiang Historical and Cultural Street Blocks - regulates the elements, mechanisms and measures for the control of alleyways, the dimensions of the alley, the spatial pattern of courtyards, the external appearance of buildings Color, etc. made a clear provision. This is an important measure for Nanluogu Alley to cope with over-commercialization of the block and restore the original appearance. According to the principle of "first style after operation, first alley after the Main Street, first increase and then decrease", the overall protection is achieved through small-scale incremental updating, Restore the alley ecological purpose. Nanluogu Lane, a former tourist destination, took the initiative to abolish the 3A-class scenic spot and ceased to be constructed according to the scenic spot standards. The adjustment and upgrading will play an effective role of demonstration and promotion and promote the control of other historical and cultural blocks through experience.

As another core area where the old city of Beijing is protected and the ancient capital style reappears, the protection of historic and cultural cities and towns in Xicheng District has been at the forefront of all districts and counties. In 2014, Xicheng District took the lead in opening "four" ("famous city" Industry "" celebrity "" King ") unique protection methods and expand the city's work within the system of systematic protection. To protect the western axis of the hand, Xicheng District in the city to improve the work of protecting the city to dig deeper connotation of protection continue to increase, reflecting the protection of individuals, local protection to the city as a whole, from the regional and phased goals Changes in public cultural services. Around the historical and cultural cities to protect the "four" working system, Xicheng District, continue to promote the protection and utilization of cultural heritage in the region, and actively implement the protection of neighborhoods to explore new ways to protect the city. First, Xicheng District will integrate street planning with alley protection and cultural relics protection to create a humanistic space such as neighborhoods and shedding projects, greening the environment and public reading space. Secondly, it will outline the features of the area and inherit the live culture. The Xicheng District Launching Museum Build a three-year plan of action and strive for the construction of a neighborhood museum in each street that reflects the cultural history of the neighborhood; thirdly, enhance the quality and standard of cultural relics protection; and continue to carry out the work of "endangering, liberating and interpreting" during the "thirteenth five-year plan" Solution "project to comprehensively promote the celebrity residence, hall of the retreat of protection work. Xicheng District plans to invest more than 100 billion yuan to start the work of cultural relics vacated. The retired straight-through public cultural relics include Liuyang Hall, Yixing Hall and Tan Xinpei's Former Residence. During the year, 17 projects have been started and 14 places will be launched in 2017, forming a whole Concentrate on the protection and repair of major historical buildings. This is also the vacancy of Beijing's largest cultural relics started in 2017.

Remodeling the original appearance of history and culture, Beijing Science and Technology Commission will provide technical reference and design guidance for the protection of historical and cultural blocks through the special topic of "Planning,

Designing and Demonstrating Protection and Reform of Historic Cultural Districts". Beijing Science and Technology Commission selected Shichahai, Dashilan and other representative historical and cultural blocks, the preparation of "protection of historical and cultural blocks Design Guidelines", on the architectural style and other guidance and design guidelines made provisions and instructions conducive to improving the historical and cultural blocks Landscape system, reshaping the street environment and spatial pattern, to achieve the comprehensive protection and revitalization of traditional neighborhoods.

2.2 In order to safeguard cultural relics, the legalization of cultural relics has been strengthened

In 2016, the intensity of enforcement of cultural relics in Beijing will increase, and the law enforcement environment for cultural relics will be further optimized. First, under the situation that the safety of cultural relics is affected; the public security organs in Beijing have taken active actions to effectively detect cases of illegal cultural relics. Strengthening departmental cooperation, Beijing in recent years the largest excavation of ancient cultural sites in the case of "May 18 Jin and Yuan Dynasties ancient cultural sites during the digging case" in Yanqing District, cultural relics, public security and local government departments successfully cracked, after 17 days, four perpetrators of all Arrested. There was no complete utensil in the excavation site, but there was a building base. After the trial excavation, the tomb pit had been backfilled, and the cultural relics department will formulate the next protection plan according to the actual situation.

Second, Beijing Customs made significant achievements in combating the smuggling of illegal cultural relics and illegally entering and exiting the country. In December, Beijing Customs handed over more than 10,000 pieces of cultural relics to the city's Cultural Relics Bureau, punishing cultural relics including coins, ceramics, jade and ancient books, The number and type of Beijing Customs are the largest in history, and this is also the performance of the Customs actively playing the role of gatekeeper, enhancing the ability of management and law enforcement, and properly protecting and using the cultural relics involved.

Third, clear the responsibility for law enforcement, and actively implement the law enforcement work to improve the ability of law enforcement, increase penalties, Haidian District, Dongcheng District, Xicheng District in the country's cultural relics administrative law enforcement work to set an example. According to the State Cultural Relics Bureau released the 2016 annual national cultural relics administrative penalties review results, Haidian District, the Executive Committee of Administrative Law enforcement team run "Beijing Lionken Science and Technology Development Co., Ltd. without permission to repair the area-level cultural relics protection unit Miaoyun Temple significantly changed the original case of cultural relics Selected as the National Top 10 Case Files for the Review of Administrative Punishment on Cultural Relics of the People's Republic of China, Project Construction by Beijing Haixin Oriental Cultural Property Management Co., Ltd. under the protection of Lejia Garden, a municipality-level cultural relic protection institution, and Dongcheng District Cultural relics under the auspices of the "Beijing million Ze Star Housing Demolition Engineering Co., Ltd. unauthorized removal of immovable cultural relics Dahe Hutong No. 32 Siheyuan case" was selected as the annual national cultural relics administrative penalties outstanding case file. In addition, the State Administration of Cultural Heritage released the "2014-2015 Ten Guiding Cases on Administrative Enforcement of Cultural Relics", selected the illegal construction projects within the protection scope of Tianning Temple in Xicheng District, and removed the illegal structures through law enforcement. The responsible party was fined 300,000 yuan, in the whole society played a warning role.

Fourthly, in order to improve the overall protection effectiveness and solve the boundary problems of cross-regional law enforcement, Beijing, Tianjin and Hebei have decided the relevant agendas for the cooperation in law enforcement and law enforcement. In March, Beijing Cultural Relics Bureau, Hebei Provincial Cultural Relics Bureau and Tianjin Municipal Cultural Market Administrative Law Enforcement Corps signed the Beijing-Tianjin-Hebei Cultural Relic Cooperation Framework Agreement in Beijing to establish the all-round strategic cooperation relationship between the three places. Through a joint conference system, The three places at the junction of cultural relics protection inspection tour and law enforcement supervision, and three experts and talented people to strengthen the building of teams to create three cultural heritage of law enforcement platform for publicity, to achieve Unicom sharing. In August, Beijing Pinggu District, Tianjin Zhuozhou District and

Xinglong County of Hebei Province signed the "Agreement for the Joint Inspection of the Law Enforcement of the Beijing-Tianjin-Ji Great Wall" and set up a joint inspection team to strengthen cooperation in jointly protecting the ancient Great Wall.

2.3 Inheritance of the ancient capital of history and culture, and new vitality of traditional culture

The traditional culture into the modern civilization, cultural heritage into the modern life, cultural relics protection work into the people, the annual cultural heritage day activities to provide people with the opportunity to experience traditional culture and cultural propaganda and education strong social atmosphere, making people More opportunities to gain access to knowledge of the physical and intangible cultural heritage that surrounds them. On the one hand, it meets people's spiritual and cultural needs and creates a society-wide atmosphere that cherishes the protection of cultural relics. On the other hand, it can also rejuvenate the cultural relics and heritage and adapt to the needs of the times to spread and inherit the historical and cultural heritage. Taking this as a point of concern, the theme of the 2016 Cultural Heritage Day is "Integrating Cultural Heritage into Modern Life", safeguarding cultural heritage and preserving nostalgia. It is through various forms of exhibition display that the general public can perceive the protection of cultural heritage. Experience the richness of cultural heritage. In addition to following the theme exhibitions and non-performing performances, the 2016 Beijing Cultural Heritage Day also adopted a new form of public participation that will allow the public to have the enthusiasm for the protection of cultural relics during field trips on cultural relics. Activities on the morning of June 11 will be held at Yuanmingyuan Park, including the non-performing performance of the Western Taiping Drum and the exhibition of achievements in cultural heritage protection in 2015. Activities such as book debut, poetry recitation, public archeology, "walking + heritage" It opened the curtain and let the audience experience the profound connotation of traditional culture during the participation so that the traditional culture can truly "live" in the public life in the modern society.

Innovative cultural heritage protection model to explore new forms of cultural relics utilization, "Internet +% in the protection of heritage, inheritance of ancient history and culture play an active role. With the Internet platform and the mass media, cultural heritage and modern life, the combination of more and more close to

Forbidden City culture as the core APP, born in the Forbidden City image of the "Meng Department of" handicrafts get the public's attention and favor is a good example.Enhance the cultural heritage of creative transformation ability, Beijing Wen Bo industry protection practice to start a new exploration: for protection The Great Wall Cultural Heritage and Chinese Cultural Relics Protection Fund launched the "Great Wall Protection 2016% Public Offering, Innovatively Adopting" Internet + Public Welfare "to raise public funds to urge people to participate in the Great Wall as much as possible. The public can scan the QR code As a cultural brand project in Beijing, Beijing Huimin Cultural Consumption Season 2016 "Golden Autumn Relics Artwork Auction Month "In," Internet +% became the most active Highlight, online auctioneer use the "easy to take the world" network platform and "palm on the phone" platform to get rid of the geographical limitations, anytime, anywhere to participate in the auction or watch the live scene, it is learned that this auction month online auction sales accounted for the proportion of up to 270. The auction of cultural relics and art goods is closer to the common people's life, expanding the impact of the auction month and expanding the participants to the whole country and even the whole world. On June 13, 2016, the Standing Committee of the Beijing Municipal Government examined and adopted the Opinions on Fully Deepening Reform and Enhancing the Management of Urban Planning and Construction, which clearly stipulated the functions of the capital city and the improvement of urban quality, and put the historic and cultural cities on the top schedule. In the reappearance of the ancient capital style, the overall protection of the old city has become the focus of the "One Axis and One Line" landscape, the historical and cultural scenic spots of "Three Mountains and Five Parks" and the protection and utilization of the Great Wall cultural belt. The historic and cultural blocks, courtyard, alley texture and ancient cultural sites, Traditional villages, industrial heritage, etc. are all included in the scope of protection and utilization. Through building a comprehensive protection pattern and a complete protection mechanism, the capital builds urban features and attractive landscapes. With historical and cultural protection, it promotes the adjustment of urban functions, population demystification and improvement of people's livelihood, and integration of city protection into the overall work of urban planning, construction and development. The importance of historical and cultural protection to Beijing's social and economic development has become increasingly prominent.

In 2016, the highlight of Beijing's historical and cultural city protection lies in the recurrence of the traditional landscape. First, according to the design plan of the Municipal Planning Commission, as one of the pilot projects, the old landscape of Jinghua in Gulou Street will be reconstructed. This area will retain the traditional alley pattern of streets and alleys. For the demolished part of the old urban area, historical information such as street regulation, courtyard layout and building facade will be restored in the form of "darning and complementing" according to the original alley vein and traditional formats. Second, to recreate the iconic landscape of the capital city, the historical and cultural landscape of the flyover of Beijing's Nancheng City has been completed and opened up. The landscape belt is 600 meters in length and fully displays the seven ancient bridges and the four directions on the flyover, stele, There are also public leisure venues and ceramic mural laying underground passage open to the public. Tianqiao traditional landscape and modern cultural facilities (Tianqiao Art Center) adjacent to create a new landscape of traditional style. Third, restore the ancient waterway in the capital. Following the restoration of the north section of Yuhe River, the extension project of Yuhe Nanyan Project has basically been completed and the historical features of water passing through the streets and streets have been restored. The historical relics of "clarifying the floodgate" will be protected and displayed as they are, while the south section of Yuhe River is also expected to be included in the Grand Canal Follow-up sites left. In addition, the original moat location, the front door Moon Bay landscape project also officially debut in October.

3. Constraints of Beijing historical and cultural city protection

Under the situation that the national cultural relics usher in major favorable conditions, the protection of historical and cultural cities in Beijing in 2016 has also made great progress and dazzling achievements in many aspects. The overall protection of the famous cities goes hand in hand with the work of various cultural relics, and the traditional culture goes deeper into the modern Life, get people's attention and activation of the widespread use. At the same time, we must also see the arduousness and long-term nature of the protection work in the famous cities. Once the ancient cultural relics, alleyets, historical features and appearances are completely destroyed, we can not resume the work of cultural relics. We must correctly treat and analyze the history of Beijing. The existing problems and constraints in the protection of cultural cities provide reference for the next step of work.

3.1 The conflict between protection and development still exists

The preservation of Beijing's historical and cultural cities is carried out under the general environment of present and future urban development. It is imperative to coordinate the interests of all parties and properly handle the relationship between historical and cultural protection and economic and social development. In a benign and sustainable context, the propositions for protection and development should be interdependent and mutually reinforcing. Otherwise, there will be an imbalance of interests, sacrificing long-term benefits in pursuit of short-term interests and neglect of cultural values due to unilateral consideration of economic interests , Social benefits, will eventually hinder the city's comprehensive and coordinated development of health. Therefore, regardless of the protection of the whole city or the specific work of cultural relics, we must consider the overall situation and weigh the advantages and disadvantages. We should consider not only the moment but also the future generations and care for the common cultural heritage of the entire society. In addition, protection and development are not mutually exclusive either. Economic and social development need not sacrifice protection at the expense of effective protection and utilization, which will stimulate economic development.

Looking at the present situation, the protection of the old urban areas in Beijing is not optimistic. Many scholars and volunteers have pointed out that the protection of the famous houses such as Dongtizi Hutong, Bulu Hutong, Panjia Hutong and other celebrities such as Kang Youwei and Tan Siton is challenging[1], and illegal construction and demolition occurs to Dajiang Hutong No.29, Dajiang Hutong No.32 and Bingli Xiejie No.15[2]. "Behind these problems, real estate development and economic benefits are still the crux of the problem. Driven by commercial development and economic interests, the sustainable development of the old city has been severely challenged. The development thinking of sacrificing the historical style and cultural connotation of the block in exchange for short-term economic benefits has not been fundamentally reversed. The cultural value of cultural relics has been neglected. The importance of cultural relic protection has been obscured by economic

[1]Yuan Jixi: "Strengthening Beijing's historical and cultural city construction to change the status of protection", http://www.china.ppcc/ 2016 -02 / 01 / content_ 37707998. htm.
[2]Zeng Yi-chih: "There is only one place where six unmovable cultural relics are demolished and demolished in Dongcheng District, Beijing." Http://blog.sina.com.cn/s/blog4ac20ab60102w0gr.html

interests. City protection cannot resist the pace of development, cultural relics protection is high but the actual situation is worrying reasons.

## 3.2 The concept of legal protection of cultural relics is not strong and the illegal cost is too low

The high incidence of cultural relics and illegal cases and people's awareness of the protection of cultural heritage is poor, the concept of legal system is not strong also have relations. Small violations of the law in the museum improper touch of cultural relics, in the historical monuments or even stampede doodle monuments ruins, large without the approval of unauthorized demolitions to transform the protection of the courtyard or within the cultural protection unit, take the consequences of private chaos, the consequences Although light and heavy, they are irreversible damage to precious and fragile artifacts. For a long time, the destruction of cultural relics and monuments has not caused enough attention and attention from people. Undeniably, the current laws and regulations on the protection of cultural relics are not yet perfect. However, people are weak in legal protection and are not well aware of the legal system.

Unlawful punishment of cultural relics punishment is not strict, the law is a small but also illegal violations of the law. In recent years, violations of the Great Wall itself and its historical features (especially the Great Wall) have occurred in a number of cases, but the penalties have been unexpectedly mild.[1] In 2009, the former residence of Lin Hui-Yin, who had a huge social repercussion, was demolished. Only 500,000 yuan , Which at the time was the highest punishment for the dismantling of cultural relics. In 2016, Tianning Temple was illegally built with a fine of 300,000. However, the penalties for the actual situation and the losses caused were still too low to the due disciplinary effect. Faced with the grim situation of cultural relics safety, Beijing still needs to maintain a high-pressured situation in punishing cultural relics and illegally violating the law. It has continued to carry out rectification of illegal activities, intensified its punishments and continuously improved its working mechanism so as to raise the level of legalization of cultural relics.

---

[1] In July 2016, the case of bringing a man to steal the ancient Great Wall caused more concern about the network but was detained for 10 days only for a fine of 500 yuan, http://news!63.>m/16/0723/13/ BSLNHKPA00014JB5.html.

3.3 Inadequate excavation and utilization of historical and cultural resources, and lots of possibilities to "alive" traditional culture

In line with the city's modernization and development, the protection work of historical and cultural cities is also under continuous renewal and development. It is necessary to continuously update work ideas and raise the standard of work. At present, the protection work cannot well adapt to the reality of social development. There are still a lot of articles to do, which are embodied as follows: the ways and means of protection and utilization are relatively old and the combination with modern technology is not very close; the excavation and utilization of traditional cultural resources are inadequate; the historical and cultural scenic spots are repeatedly constructed with a low level and the stereotyped traditional cultural performances , Non-heritage display and cultural goods have greatly reduced people's interest in history and culture, cultural features and profound connotation have not been properly displayed; traditional culture into a limited degree of modern life, the ability to be creative to be improved, the use of cultural relics is still being explored Among the historical and cultural city protection practice, it is only the first step to realize that cultural heritage needs to be protected. However, how to protect and how to improve the efficiency of protection and how to maximize the development of traditional cultural resources need to be deeply pondered at work research.

4. Protection methods, countermeasures and suggestions

4.1 Strengthen scientific research, change the thinking of protection and balance the relationship between protection and development

Historical and cultural protection and economic development are not diametrically opposed to each other. We must abandon the simple binary opposition that protection is not economic. It should be recognized that economic factors are always an indispensable dimension of historical protection. Protection must be backed by a strong economic foundation. However, protection does not necessarily mean sacrificing economic interests. The historical culture of the city has always been a precious asset for its present and future development. Resources, what we need to oppose is just the act of destroying the historical culture with the protection of cultural relics (for example, the construction of antique streets to stimulate tourism development and increase local revenues, the demolition of old cultural relics, the over-exploitation of historic scenic spots, etc.) Organic renewal, reuse and function adjustment and other methods for cultural relics protection and utilization. Of course, in addition to the economic factors, the protection also includes the concern for the aesthetic value and social benefits, as well as the quality of urban life. When the urban development reaches a certain level, the pursuit of cultural values and aesthetics becomes more important to the public interest. The relevant aspects of theoretical exploration and research should be strengthened. Therefore, the protection of historical and cultural cities can not stay in the economic precedent of the past, to protect the traditional ideas for giving way for development must coordinate the relationship between protection and development. The positioning of Beijing's historical and cultural cities is an integral part of Beijing's urban planning and development. This requires that we respect and value historic and cultural heritage in the protection practices and affirm the multiple values of traditional cultural heritage in order to protect and promote development and to protect In fact.

4.2 Improve the rule of law of cultural relics, increase the intensity of cultural relics protection and law enforcement

For a long time, in the process of cultural relics protection and utilization, the law enforcement of cultural relics has not been given due attention, developers without the approval of cultural relics department without permission of the building demolition of building renovation cases occur from time to time, making the cultural heritage suffered a huge loss. Cultural relics protection work in the new period urgently needs to establish a perfect legal system for the protection of cultural relics. Only by strictly handling cases of cultural relics violations, perfecting the system of administrative enforcement of cultural relics and actually increasing the penalties for illegal cases, and actively promoting the popularization of civil law, can we effectively deal with and prevent the occurrence of cultural relics illegal cases. First, improve the legal system of cultural relics protection. At present, the laws and regulations on the protection of cultural relics are not yet perfect, the contents of the relevant laws and regulations are missing, the provisions of the gaps make the illegal take advantage of the protection of cultural relics is facing challenges, which should be clearly stated in the provisions and the development of supporting implementation details. Precious relics are invaluable for serious acts of destruction of cultural relics, must increase penalties to raise the cost of illegal, if necessary, into the sentence. Second, we should step up administration of cultural relics and enforce laws, clarify the responsibilities of competent departments, standardize law enforcement procedures, enforce justice strictly and, when necessary, carry out joint law enforcement with public security organs, industrial and commercial administrative departments, and customs to resolutely crack down on illegal and criminal acts of cultural relics. Third, the establishment of inspection mechanism for cultural relics protection, to strengthen the performance of official duties, strengthen the review and inspectors in the handling of cases, to assess the effectiveness of law enforcement through a return visit, the competent leadership to implement a strict system of accountability. Fourth, strengthen the awareness of legal protection of public cultural relics. The protection of cultural relics in accordance with the law is the common responsibility of the whole society. The government departments should actively publicize the importance of protecting cultural relics in accordance with the law, and achieve the purpose of publicity and education by means of cultural relics protection safety week, public interest lectures, Society creates a cultural atmosphere to protect law and law.

4.3 Increase efforts to develop traditional resources, and strive to enhance the protection of history and culture

In the context of "internet +% and big data prevailing, the achievements of modern technology and mode of operation in the protection of cultural relics and culture Inheritance of promising, need to actively explore the historical and cultural city of digital protection and utilization of the implementation of ways to promote conservation and utilization of science and technology innovation, the traditional culture and creative research and development combined with the development of distinctive products; Second, the traditional culture should continue to dig deeper , Adapt to the needs of the times, and dig deep into the cultural values and cultural connotation is the basis to improve the transformation and utilization of historical and cultural resources and the development of urban cultural capital, tap the connotation to create distinctive urban cultural symbols, create unique urban cultural landscape and promote traditional culture Modern heritage; third is to promote the integration of traditional culture into the modern society, facing the modern, life-oriented, the general public, the traditional culture and the spirit of the times, modern cultural production, fashion consumption, find the right combination of resource conversion points for the traditional culture into new vitality.

# Investigation Report on Productive Protection of Beijing Intangible Cultural Heritage
## ---Taking the four non-heritage conservation demonstration bases in Beijing for example[1]

## Li Rongqi[2]

## Abstract

Productive protection is an important way to protect intangible cultural heritage. Based on the field investigation, this article summarizes the practices, achievements and existing problems of the non-material cultural heritage productivity protection in four non-heritage conservation demonstration bases in Beijing (four old Chinese enterprises) proposed a reasonable, feasible, forward-looking countermeasures and suggestions.

Keywords: intangible cultural heritage, productive protection, inheritance and development

Productive protection is an important way to protect intangible cultural heritage. The so-called productive protection of intangible cultural heritage refers to the rational utilization of the non-material cultural heritage on the premise of protection. At present, four enterprises in Beijing are selected as the demonstration bases for the national intangible cultural heritage productivity protection, namely Beijing Lianliansheng Shoes Co., Ltd., Rongbaozhai, Beijing Enamel Factory Co., Ltd., Beijing Tong Ren Tang (Group) limited liability Company. These four companies are renowned at home and abroad of the old Chinese, they have a long history, deep accumulation, heritage development, fame. The national-level intangible cultural heritage projects they carry have superb skills and rich connotation.

## 1. The effectiveness of the "model base" for productive protection

Four non-material cultural heritage protection demonstration bases, "to promote

---

[1]This article is one of the milestones of the 2013 National Social Science Fund Art Project "The Protection of Intangible Cultural Heritage Science" (Project No. 13BH076).
[2]Li Rongqi, Researcher, Chinese Academy of Arts, Member of Expert Committee of China Yearbook of Intangible Cultural Heritage

national culture as its own responsibility", follow the project's own heritage and development of the specific laws and regulations, rational use of productive protection, to grasp the principle of proper protection of intangible cultural heritage in the representative. The project's protection and inheritance have achieved remarkable results. Their practices and experiences are mainly reflected in the following aspects.

1.1 Attach great importance to establish an effective management and protection mechanism
The responsible units of the four demonstration bases all attach great importance to the protection and inheritance of the intangible cultural heritage projects and establish different modes of operation and management.

Inline or Shoe Co., Ltd. Practice to retain the cause of use, with the system to retain the concept. On the personnel system, the implementation of the sloping policy on personal income has improved the working environment and adopted the incentive measures. At the same time, it has also established a mechanism for employing heirs to stabilize the ranks of successors through the management of teachers and students.

Rong Bao vegetarian adhere to the mechanism to promote protection. Rong Bao Zhai's leading group put forward the "adhere to the corporate culture, sense of responsibility, improve the production organization mode, the project with technology, lessons learned, temper technical standards, with the enterprise labor protection system to improve the protection of qualified personnel to the market concept of marketing means of survival and development" Policy, follow the non-legacy characteristics and development situation, considering its cultural value and market demand, product technology content, to establish an effective operating mechanism.

"Protection first, rescue first, rational use, inheritance and development", which is Beijing's enamel factory adhere to the work guidelines, and constantly establish and improve the protection and inheritance mechanism. Aiming at the age structure aging of Cloisonne production artistes, the lack of follow-up and the failure of personnel delivery, the company formulated a systematic mode of inheritance training and carried out the activity of carrying out the art of accomplishing with the organized, planned and examining activities for each inheritance People have arranged four to five new apprenticeship, adhere to the combination of theory and practice, through pass, help, bring the bearing of skill.

Tong Ren Tang set up the Group Culture and Education Committee, Cultural Heritage Center, Chief Technician Management Office and other related protection work to develop a number of management systems, such as "China Beijing Tong Ren Tang (Group) Co., Ltd. Intangible Cultural Heritage Management Measures""Teachers education (teachers with only) work management approach""chief technician studio management system" and so on. Formulate matching fund policy, the group company is responsible for managing, supervising and guiding the secondary group to carry out the construction of the demonstration base of productive protection.

1.2 Promote Project Inheritance and Development Innovation in Productive Management

All four "demonstration bases" can adhere to the principle of protection, take protection as the driving force, promote development through protection, and coordinate the relationship between protection and development so as to achieve the protection of inheritance and development in production.

Inline or Shoe Co., Ltd. in the inheritance Miaobianbiao shoes production skills at the same time, increase research and development efforts, independent design of new products to meet the contemporary aesthetic needs of all age groups. The company insisted on carrying out design and development work, there will be new products launched quarterly. In May 2015, Inline Shoe Co., Ltd., in cooperation with the fashion designer of Beijing Institute of Clothing Technology, conducted extensive brand communication and brand culture infiltration in the fashion design circle to further enhance the company's popularity in the fashion circle and broke. In the past the old established in the hearts of people conservative traditional stereotypes.

Rong Baozhai set up a special woodblock watermarking production center, mounted repair production center and process square three departments. Woodblock watermarking and restoration As Rongbaozhai ancient and important business projects, in the long-term development, have been a complete and orderly protection of heritage. With the progress of the times and the development of enterprises, Rong

Baozhai constantly innovates and protects the mode of operation and realizes a more scientific and reasonable long-term protection. For example, Rong Bao Zhai has done a great deal of work in protecting woodcut watermarking techniques. Established a constant temperature and humidity workshop in line with the requirements of the wood-based watermarking process, and improved the environment of wood-based watermarking. On the market-oriented development topic, the woodblock watermark of "second authenticity" was used to develop the limited copy artwork "Level market".

Beijing enamel factory focus on promoting "pioneering and innovative, heritage development, created brilliant" spirit of enterprise, continue to increase the intensity of project protection. In recent years, the company has improved the working environment and improved its skill level by building an intelligent temperature controlled cloisonne gas burning blue furnace and an electric furnace, abandoning the traditional burning blue technique based on coal. In 2016, the company deeply cooperated with Dean Chang Sha Na, former dean of the Central Academy of Arts and Design, our famous art and design educator, and numerous students to develop and design dozens of cloisonne works with Dunhuang cultural and artistic elements. These works are novel in design and rich in cultural connotations and are widely recognized by the society. The company focuses on excavating and restoring the works of old artists. Since 2015, the company has excavated, sorted out and restored more than 60 sets of works elaborately designed so that the works designed by many old artists and masters can be reproduced in the early days. These masterpieces Is the company's key preservation and protection of treasures. During the Spring Festival in 2016, the company successfully held the "Re-exhibition of the Historical Works of the Old Beijing-based enamel" and was welcomed by the general public.

Tong Ren Tang, a pharmaceutical company, has always been committed to improving human health and quality of life. It insists on using the principle of justice and trustworthiness to protect and develop Tong Ren Tang's Chinese medicine culture. According to the requirements of GMP in modern production, the company strictly complies with the quality standards, technical procedures and standard operating procedures of GMP to ensure the authenticity, integrity and core skills of the project. Adhere to the traditional Chinese medicine authentic, pseudo, excellent, inferior traditional traits identification methods, that is, the traditional seeing, hand touch, nasal smell, taste of traditional Chinese medicine identification methods, while using modern high-tech equipment for further identification analysis, the implementation of medicinal double check. In the investment Tongrentang Chinese herbal medicine concocted production base, according to local conditions to upgrade the Chinese herbal medicines concocted equipment and equipment, focusing on not abandon the traditional methods of production at the same time into the modern production elements, while retaining the traditional manual skills at the same time continue to enhance the traditional skills Modern performance.

1.3 Inherit the project in many forms to keep the project going

Tolerance Zhuanshiteng is the basic feature of the intangible cultural heritage, inheritance training is the top priority of non-material cultural heritage protection. Only the successors of representative projects can make these projects have the basis of sustainable development in productive protection. These four demonstration bases of productive protection have paid great attention to inheriting works of art and have trained representatives in many ways [heritage project successors and established an effective inheritance mechanism to ensure the successor protection and development of the project.]

After the rigorous selection, Neiliansheng Shoes Co., Ltd. held two apprenticeship ceremonies in 2009 and 2014. One after another, four young workers under the age of 35 became apprentice to He Kaiying, the national successor of the Melaleuca shoes production technique. The establishment of the country with miscellaneous and inheritance led by the "teacher with only" positions and skills training inheritance mechanism.

Rong Bao Zhai adopts three ways to train successors and ensure the effective inheritance of traditional skills: First, to formulate a training plan and establish a system of inheritance and apprentice. By inheritors, senior technicians and other young workers to pass, help, with, and as one of the important content of the assessment. The second is to carry out technical training, skills assessment, to strengthen project personnel training. By organizing staff and workers to participate in "Beijing Occupational Skill Contest", wood-based watermarking, mounting and repair vocational skills test, internal staff skills appraisal and other activities, to strengthen personnel training for the project's heritage and development to provide a strong talent protection. Third, the establishment of heritage studio. Strengthen the protection and support for the successors, and form a successor echelon of talents by enrolling and cultivating more potential apprentices, and ensure that there will be successors to every technical link.

Beijing enamel factory for the production of Cloisonne aged arts age structure aging, lack of successors, personnel delivery facing the status of the file, developed a system of successor training mode, for each representative inheritors arranged four to five new apprentices, the company Four studios have also been established for the four representative heirs. To do a good job of personnel training, the company implemented a full range of training. During the 13th Five-Year Plan period, the company seeks to introduce 10-20 designers and technicians every year. Under the leadership of masters and advanced craftsmen, the company inherits the good craftsmanship of cloisonne.

Tong Ren Tang implementation of the "pyramid talent project." On the basis of the traditional model of mentoring, we have created a way of inheritance of studios integrating research with production, research with science and education. The organization of training and apprenticeship at all levels of heritage work to ensure the continuation of the traditional core technologies. In 2014, the company set up the "Chief Chemist's Laboratory for Sinopharm Medicine in Baoqing". Yu Tak-ku currently with students only 8 people, learning Tong Ren Tang Chinese medicine processing technology and project research Chinese medicine processing skills. In 2015, Science and Technology Group established a special technician studio before its disposal in Daxing. The three experts led and inherited skills, skills and innovations to solve practical problems. Tong Ren Tang also through the establishment of relevant systems, and continuously improve the enterprise experts, stunt heritage division, the key positions of front-line workers benefits, job allowance, focusing on the funding of successors.

1.4 Emphasis on infrastructure, and pay attention to publicity

In 2008, Inline Shoe Co., Ltd. opened an intangible heritage exhibition hall and a workshop in Dashilan Commercial Street. By demonstrating the different layers of cloth shoes at the end of Melaleuca shoes, shoes, tools, materials and historical pictures, text and other physical and information, a comprehensive introduction to the history and culture of this business, the end of cloth shoes production skills protection heritage and a brief history of shoe culture and so on. Since the establishment of the exhibition hall, the exhibition hall has been open to the public all year round. It has become a publicity and exhibition center, a special service center and a sales center for intangible cultural heritage projects and products of this enterprise. It is also the first choice place for the old propaganda activities in the region.

After selecting "Demonstration Base", Rong Baozhai pays more attention to relying on brand advantages to form a new situation in which "non-legacy" projects jointly protect and develop. During the 13th Five-Year Plan period, Rongbaozhai will build Rongshou Zhaiyi Cultural and Creative Park and Rongbao Zaixi Cultural and Creative Park. According to the plan, Rongbaizhai Shunyi Cultural and Creative Park will construct "one hospital and one base and five centers", namely Rongbaozhai Painting Institute, national non-heritage conservation demonstration base, artist creation center, new product research and development center, digital publishing center , Printing center and logistics center. November 23, 2015, Rong Bao Zhai Shunyi Cultural and Creative Park held its groundbreaking ceremony. Rongbao Zaixi Cultural and Creative Industry Park plans to build "one village and two centers", namely Rongbaozhai artist village, new cultural product research center and non-heritage production center. Rongbaozhai specially planned "non-legacy" in both cultural and creative parks to further promote the inheritance and protection of "non-reserved" skills and to develop in multi-dimensions such as content, form and series according to market demand Woodblock watermark new varieties of works of art to promote brand communication and product sales. Foster the integration of the intangible cultural heritage into the contemporary world, integrate with the general public and integrate into the life, and at the same time achieve greater economic benefits, better transfer and develop traditional skills and bring "non-heritage" protection into a new stage of development.

From 2011 to October 2015, Beijing Fagan invested heavily in the construction of the Cloisonne Art Museum. Museum supporting more than 1,000 square meters of art shows, interactive areas and a multimedia conference room.

In 2016, the Company demolished the equipment and facilities in the original canteen and renovated it in-house. HD projectors, large-sized TVs and filigree lines were installed, and the necessary equipment for blue spots were set up. A meeting area, an experience area and a creative area were set up so that The company visits, M business customers, students and the general public can enjoy cloisonne, visit cloisonne art museum at the same time, experience cloisonne production skills, in order to promote enterprise management mode, research and development model, the marketing model of innovation, the formation of new business Business growth point. In 2016, the company revised its official website. In order to put the China cloisonne art museum online, the company developed and set up the 3D China Cloisonniel Museum of Art. From the end of 2015, the company and Beijing Municipal Bureau of Culture and the City Board of Education launched a series of activities called "rejuvenating traditional crafts from dolls", and invited 200 students from more than 20 primary schools in Beijing to go to France and France in installments, Visit Cloisonnac Museum of Art, learn cloisonne making skills and personally involved in the design, filigree, point blue and other major production links, and ultimately completed a creative and imaginative 200 pieces of cloisonné DIY. And held the "Children's Unusual Childhood Cloisonniere Exhibition" at the National Center for the Performing Arts on June 1 Children's Day and Cultural Heritage Day 2016, causing a sensation in the society and generating excellent social effects.

In March 2007, Tong Ren Tang (Group) Co., Ltd., Beijing, China, created the Tong Ren Tang Museum which was renovated in 2014. The museum is a museum of traditional Chinese medicine with a rich collection of cultural relics and unique content. Tong Ren Tang Museum since its opening has attracted the attention of the world attention, an endless stream of visitors. In recent years, the museum has received a total of nearly 40,000 Chinese and foreign visitors, involving more than 50 countries and regions. In 2015, Tong Ren Tang (Group) Co., Ltd. and Dongcheng District Primary School Activity Curriculum Center conducted a theme cooperation project entitled "Enrichment of Primary School Activities Curriculum Projects to Promote Non-heritage Culture of Tong Ren Tang" and settled "Tong Ren Tang Non-Legacy Inheritance Curriculum" in "Non- Cultural transfer base "a primary school activities Dongcheng District Center. In addition, based on the construction of the database of intangible cultural heritage, a non-heritage resource platform for Tong Ren Tang was established. In 2016, a non-heritage database of the Group system was initially established. Based on this, a mechanism for sharing survey information was established. Attach great importance to dissemination and popularization of work and introduce and display Tong Ren Tang's traditional Chinese medicine culture and skills through "Non-Heritage Window", "Medicine Sincere", "Famous Drug Archives" and other columns; digitize the results of "The Whole and Study of Royal Pharmacy Archives Related to Tong Ren Tang" Recorded as a file; completed the "Palace Museum Hospital Tibetan medicine cultural relics and Chinese medicine health culture exhibition" and Tong Ren Tang content screening and other work.

## 2. The main problems in the production protection

Although the four demonstration bases for the productive protection of non-material cultural heritage in Beijing have achieved remarkable results and some worthy promotion experiences in the practice of productive protection, the protection and inheritance of the representative items of the intangible cultural heritage have also entered a period of sustainable development New stage However, the productive protection of intangible cultural heritage is, after all, a new way of protecting the practice that is still under exploration and will inevitably encounter some new situations and new problems. Some of these problems have certain universality and deserve the attention of relevant departments and attach importance to and solve them in the future productive protection of intangible cultural heritage. The main problems encountered in the productive protection of intangible cultural heritage are as follows.

## 2.1 Strong brand awareness but weak protection according to law

Four companies are Beijing faction old; its brand value is high. Due to the accumulation of long-term brand name, won the trust of customers, nurtured a strong market. At the same time, however, it is also faced with infringement of its products by counterfeit and shoddy products and various forms of infringement risks. Without a sense of rights protection and a barrier to legal protection, enterprises will suffer tremendous losses and injuries. For example, Beijing Inline Shoe Co., Ltd. has been repeatedly infringed in recent years and has dealt with the infringement of trademarks and patent rights of Hangzhou Bofu Mao Infringement and FFA together. However, with the rising popularity of in-brand liters, various forms of infringement are still emerging. In order to protect the intellectual property of enterprises and the old brand name interests, Inline Shoe Co., Ltd. has trademark extension registered 18,25,26,37,40 a total of five major categories of goods, but also in the context of the Madrid Agreement inline or 1 Trademark registration overseas. In spite of this, its counterfeit rights still appear to be more passive, as if firefighters found that the point of ignition went to flapping fire and extinguishing the fire in general. Therefore, how to realize the rights protection operation from passive to active and fundamentally solve the problem of protecting according to law is a more common problem that other old-timed enterprises are facing and it is urgent to discuss and strengthen it.

2.2 Insufficient successors require strengthening of effective inheritance

In recent years, all units have paid more attention to the protection of the representative heirs and the training of a new generation of successors, and have succeeded in inheriting the project and the contingent of qualified personnel has continuously grown. However, there is still a shortage of talents, which still lags behind the requirements of project protection and enterprise development. Although the old brand in China has attracted some young people because of its influence and appeal, on the whole it is relatively uncommon for those young people who are able to stop and study traditional skills, especially if they are bigger and stronger, Train more masters of project art heritage, so that each process has a solid technical backbone, excellent personnel. For example, Tong Ren Tang traditional Chinese herbal medicines processed more and more large-scale development, the existing Beijing Daxing base is under construction in Hebei Anguo base and Anhui Bozhou base. However, at present, only one state-level successor (Lu Guangrong, 79), a city-level successor (Zhao Xiaogang, 57) inherits the art of traditional Chinese medicinal materials. Taking into account the project heritage and personnel training of the three major bases in different provinces and cities, it is urgent for Tong Ren Tang to take measures to strengthen the training of successors and the construction of succession teams for this project.

2.3 Explore the cultural connotation of representative projects of intangible cultural heritage and promote theoretical studies

Four demonstration bases all attach importance to the promotion, dissemination, protection and development of the projects of intangible cultural heritage. However, some "model bases" have carried out in-depth excavation and research on the intangible cultural heritage projects that carry out productive protection in their enterprises insufficient. For example, in the questionnaire, questions were asked about "whether the main theoretical research results of this unit have been published or not, and so on. There were two units that did not provide any answer.

## 2.4 Insufficient funds and high taxes

In addition to the fact that Tong Ren Tang has made itself bigger and stronger, the other four units belong to the relatively small units. As a result, the funding and tax issues are more prominent. Although all levels of government have given certain financial support to the representatives of intangible cultural heritage items and representative inheritors, due to the particularity of the project itself, a large amount of financial support is still needed in order to obtain better protection, inheritance and development. For example, Rong Bao Zhai will be published with the combination of wood-based watermarking, undoubtedly quite distinctive and collectible value of an innovative mode of protection. However, when applying for the publication of funds, they encountered embarrassment. Relevant management departments think this is different from the traditional publication, and it is difficult to obtain financial support or inclination. However, the publishing cost of wooden version watermarking books is far greater than that of ordinary books. So in the end it may make the project hard to implement. If enterprises raise funds by themselves, they will have to bear greater economic pressure. In addition, the current tax rate, that is, the annual income of more than 500,000 yuan, will have to pay 17% of the tax, which adhere to the traditional handicraft enterprises overwhelmed. For example, in-liter liter Footwear Co., Ltd. in recent years, the average annual tax of 15 million yuan; Rong Bao Zhai and Beijing enamel plant there are the same high tax rates, the issue of pressure.

## 3. Countermeasures and Suggestions

The above problems and difficulties that arise in the productive protection of intangible cultural heritage are bound to arise during the development and construction of the "demonstration base." However, if the problem is solved promptly, it will be able to push forward the productive protection of the intangible cultural heritage to a new stage of development. In view of the problems combed in the survey,

I think we should attach importance to and strengthen the following aspects of the work.

## 3.1 Further enhance the awareness of legal protection and strive to protect the intangible cultural heritage in accordance with the law

From the national level, strengthen the construction of special laws and regulations, based on the "Intangible Cultural Heritage Law", on the basis of full investigation and research, regulations such as the traditional Chinese medicine protection of knowledge and the protection of traditional handicrafts should be promulgated and formulated as intangible cultural heritage Provide professional legal protection. Enterprises and units that implement the productive protection of intangible cultural heritage shall formulate and implement pertinent and operable rules and regulations in accordance with the relevant state laws and regulations and establish scientific and effective laws on their respective brands, trademarks and intellectual property rights Protect the barrier, and in practice through the statute, guidance, supervision, inspection and other means to make the legal protection of intangible cultural heritage implemented.

## 3.2 Emphasize on the building of qualified personnel and establish a scientific and rational inheritance system

The Fifth Plenary Session of the 18th CPC Central Committee put forward the requirements of "building an excellent inheritance system of traditional Chinese culture, strengthening cultural heritage protection and rejuvenating traditional crafts," which embodies the party's emphasis on the protection and inheritance of the intangible cultural heritage. The construction of the inheritance system needs to continue to explore and adopt a variety of effective ways of inheritance: (1) The system of apprenticeship requires a system of supporting, supporting, supporting and funding the master studios; (2) Inheritance and construction of the unit's transfer centers, museums, make full use of these infrastructure to carry out mass heritage; (3) production-style heritage, through job skills training, production line workers can become technical experts to ensure that all processes Technical backbone; (4) educational heritage, selection of outstanding young employees within the enterprise through vocational education, academic education and other systems to learn ways to comprehensively enhance the overall quality, skill level. Only through a variety of means of inheritance, can we cultivate different levels of talent, and establish a reasonable successor echelon. When delegating the skills, the representative heirs should pay attention to teaching the apprentice the historical evolution of the traditional skills, the cultural connotations contained therein, and instructing the new generation of descendants with their own words and decency, and sincerely enjoy and persevere Study their own traditional crafts. Retain the craft premise is to retain talent, when a business talent, heritage and its inheritance of intangible cultural heritage projects must be able to pass torch, sustainable development.

3.3 Properly handle the relationship between heritage preservation and innovation and development, and integrate the intangible cultural heritage into people's lives

Living rheology is the essential characteristic of intangible cultural heritage. The purpose of protecting inheritance is to enable it to develop sustainably in the contemporary era. However, development must inevitably innovate on the basis of inheritance. Innovation can stimulate the vitality of the project and maintain its vitality. All four units in this survey agree that intangible cultural heritage can innovate and should innovate. However, there is a lack of clear and correct understanding on how to innovate. Therefore, it is necessary for theorists to conduct in-depth study and discussion on this issue and require relevant government departments to give proper guidance. The author believes that to treat the innovation of intangible cultural heritage, we should clarify the two meanings of innovation. One is to innovate the representative item of intangible cultural heritage itself, and put forward a modest innovation, that is, to uphold the principle of authenticity, without changing Based on the core skills and core values of the project, we can integrate new cultural elements, make use of new carriers, or integrate scientific and rational technologies with modern technologies. The second is to use the traditional cultural elements of the project of intangible cultural heritage to create and create derivatives that are acceptable to contemporary people. Such as the use of Li Jin pattern-like elements and cultural symbols designed to create modern life items; the use of brocade element design to create a variety of accessories, accessories, and so on. Such development and innovation should be promoted and supported. These cultural and creative products can better integrate the excellent traditional culture of all ethnic groups in China into people's lives and bring economic benefits to enterprises engaged in the productive protection of intangible cultural heritage projects, so that Its better to survive and develop.

3.4 Pay attention to solve the problem of lack of liquidity and excessive taxation

This issue is a common problem faced by SMEs currently engaged in the productive protection of intangible cultural heritage projects. To solve this problem requires the joint efforts of relevant departments and an enterprise at all levels of government themselves in two aspects. The government should give some assistance to the government, for example, subsidize or subsidize a certain amount of loans (Beijing Municipal Government has already implemented this measure); preferential tax policies should be promulgated on the basis of investigation and research; if tax exemption cannot be temporarily imposed, can be rewarded to the enterprise as part of the incentives to reduce the economic pressure on enterprises. Enterprises should plan their own development. Enterprises engaged in the production of traditional handicrafts should not blindly seek to expand their scale and expand their enterprises. Instead, they should pursue fine development, develop stronger and make realistic development goals. In addition, on the basis of doing a good job of project protection and inheritance, we seek scientific and sustainable development. Through down-to-earth efforts, we will continue to enhance the social and economic benefits of enterprises so that they will remain invincible in the competition.

# Quantity to Quality Transformation of Beijing's Public Service

"Beijing Public Service Innovation and Development Research" group[1],

1. Overall comments: Beijing's public service has entered the ranks of the world's cities, and public demand for public service is getting higher and higher

2016 is an important time point for comprehensively implementing the spirit of the 6th Plenary Session of the 18th CPC Central Committee and launching the "13th Five-Year Plan". Driven by the key construction of city sub-centers and the implementation of the coordinated development strategy of Beijing, Tianjin and Hebei, Beijing's public services have reached a new level with the scale and mass already entering the ranks of the world's cities. However, the quality of public services needs to be improved and public services Quality requirements are getting higher and higher, Beijing public service from the number of expansion into quality improvement stage.

1.1 Beijing public service ranks among the world's cities

In science and technology, from January to September 2016, 12,388 state-owned high-tech enterprises were recognized in Beijing, accounting for nearly 16% of the national total, achieving total revenue of 1,219.2 billion yuan, an increase of 7.3% over the same period of last year. The city's technology contract turnover of 239.110 billion yuan, an increase of 11%. Among them, the flow to other provinces and municipalities and exports accounted for 74%. Technology services added value of 168.28 billion yuan, an increase of 10. 9%. The number of new three board listed companies reached 1185, among the 170 selected innovation layers, ranking first in the country and the national science and technology innovation center is in a stable position. In basic education, the rate of recent enrollment in compulsory education has been increasing year by year. In 2016, the ratio of primary school and junior high school admission to nearby schools reached 94.5% and 90.68% respectively. In public culture, in the first half of 2016, the city carried out 16,564 large-scale and distinctive

[1] The members of group include Shi Changkui, Pang Shihui, Bi Juan, Wu Xiangyang, Yan Shengwen and Li Zhibin. Shi Changkui, Reseacher, Director of Research Institute of Management, Beijing Academy of Social Sciences. Research areas include public management and charity; Pang Shihui, Associate Researcher, Beijing Academy of Social Sciences, research areas: public finance and public policy; Bi Juan , Associate Researcher, Beijing Academy of Social Sciences, research areas: public administration, technical and economics; Wu Xiangyang, Associate Reseacher, Beijing Academy of Social Sciences, the main research area is economics; Yan Shengwen, Associate Researcher, Research Institute of Management, Beijing Academy of Social Sciences. Research areas include social security, human resources management; Li Zhibin, Assistant Research at the Research Institute of Management, Beijing Academy of Social Sciences. Main research areas include public management, infrastructure.

mass cultural activities with a total participation of 17.52 million people. From January to August 2016, the corporate unit of cultural and creative industries above designated size in the city of Beijing achieved revenue of 826.27 billion yuan, an increase of 8.9% over the same period of last year and employing 1.175 million people. In terms of social security, the implementation of accurate poverty alleviation, improvement of the relief system, raising the minimum wage, unemployment insurance, the treatment of workers injured and their families, social security standards steadily improved. Since January 2016, the urban and rural minimum living standards have been adjusted from the per capita monthly family budget of 710 yuan to 800 yuan. The standard for urban and rural low-income families has been adjusted from 930 yuan per month for a family to 1,050 yuan. Since September 1, 2016, the minimum wage in Beijing has been adjusted to not lower than 10.86 yuan per hour and not lower than 1890 yuan per month. In terms of infrastructure, the proportion of green trips in the central city reached 71% and the total orbital mileage reached 574 kilometers. The construction of urban sub-centers was fully rolled out, the new airport project accelerated and the relocation work within the red line was fully completed. Dahongmen, zoo, God willingness to ease the withdrawal of significant withdrawal of the wholesale market, completed the construction area of 7.03 million square meters. In public safety, from April to August 2016, the police cracked over 25,000 criminal cases of various kinds and detained more than 12,000 people in criminal detentions, up by 44.4% and 23.4% respectively on a month-on-month basis. The city's 110 criminal and police order dropped by 13.6% and 18.3% respectively over the same period of the previous year. Social order continued to improve, with 1735 batches of drugs supervised and sampled, with a pass rate of 99.83%. In environmental protection, as of the end of November 2016, the average concentration of fine particulate matter (PM2.5) in Beijing air was 67 μg / m3, down 9.5% from the same period of last year. The average concentrations of other major pollutants, sulfur dioxide, nitrogen dioxide and particulate matter (PM10) were 10, 45 and 86 μg / m3, down 23.1%, 6.3% and 10.4% respectively over the previous year. Air quality standards 185 days, an increase of 10 days.[1] Up to the end of November 2016, more than 8,400 steam tons of coal-fired boilers clean energy was transformed. In 2016, the Company continued to phase out 380,000 old motor vehicles, increased the number plate of new energy vehicles by 30,000 and increased the total number of new energy

[1]Beijing EPA website, http: // www. Bjepb. Gov.cn/.

sources to 60,000, and launched the special campaign "Year of Air Pollution Enforcement" with the emphasis on " Increase the emission of coal, "" net four gas "(coal-burning waste gas, volatile organic waste gas, industrial waste gas and motor vehicle exhaust)," reduce the dust "(construction dust, road dust, dust caused by burning) Strength. From January to November of 2016, the city's environmental supervision departments punished 1254 air pollution violations, 184 water and water environmental violations, 851 construction-related offenses, 255 solid waste offenses and 61 other types of offenses Starting from a fine of 100 million yuan, effectively cracking down on environmental violations.

1.2 Beijing 16 public service levels were "U" shaped arrangement

From the comprehensive scores of public services in various districts in Beijing, it can be seen that the top six districts are Xicheng District (0.7034), Dongcheng District (0.6912), Yanqing District (0.6672), Mentougou District (0.6169), Chaoyang District ) And Huairou District (0.6000). The top five are Pinggu (0.5967), Miyun (0.5828), Haidian (0.5605), Shijingshan (0.5537) and Changping (0.5335) respectively. In the last five are Fengtai District (0.5175), Shunyi District (0.5072), Fangshan District (0.4969), Tongzhou District (0.4897) and Daxing District (0.4896). Although the evaluation system in 2016 added two indicators reflecting the level of effort in environmental protection, it did not change the arrangement of the nearly "U" shape as a whole. Although the ranking of environmental protection in Tongzhou District increased significantly, the rank of comprehensive evaluation increased by only one place.

Under the impetus of speeding up the construction of Beijing's city sub-center, Tongzhou District has indeed made a lot of efforts in public service construction. In most of the major supply of public service resources, Tongzhou District has a certain degree of improvement. In terms of basic education services, the ratio of teachers and students in secondary education increased from 12.64 in 2014 to 13.82 in 2003, an increase of 9.34%; the number of children in the park increased by 11.40%; the number of teachers and students in kindergartens increased from 8. 46 in 2014 to 8.74, An increase of 3.31%. In respect of social security services, the number of beds for people adopting adoptees increased by 7.08% and the number of community service organizations by 10,000 persons increased by 10.29%. In the area of medical and health services, the number of visits per capita increased by 5.70%, that of doctors per 1,000 increased by 9.05%, that of nurses per thousand increased by 7.45% and that of beds per thousand increased by 9.43%. In respect of cultural and sports services, the per capita collection of books increased by 9.14% and the total circulation of libraries increased by 10.61%. In terms of environmental protection, annual average SO2 concentration dropped 30.21%, annual NO2 concentration decreased 7.93%, PM10 annual average concentration decreased 10.66% and PM2.5 annual average concentration decreased 12.74% GDP power consumption dropped by 4 25%. In spite of this, many public service resources in Tongzhou District are still at a relatively low level in absolute terms in the absolute amount. There are 32.79 beds for adoption units per 10,000 people, ranking 10th in the city, 4.85 community service agencies per 10,000 people, and ranking 11th in the city. Per capita diagnosis and treatment of 3.44 passengers, ranking 14$^{th}$ in the city. 2.44 per 1,000 physicians, 2.45 per 1,000 nurses and 1.94 per 1,000 hospital beds, all at the end of the city. PM2.5 annual average concentration of 92.5 micrograms / cubic meter, only lower than Fangshan District and Daxing District. It can be seen from this that although the public service resources in Tongzhou District have made a certain degree of progress, there is still a long way to go before they are located in Beijing's sub-centers.

1.3 The public is increasingly demanding on the quality of public services

Although the public service in Beijing has reached a new stage and its scale and mass have entered the ranks of the world's cities, the quality of public services is not satisfactory. Therefore, improving the quality of urban public services is the focus of the next step. In terms of basic education, we still need to further promote the balanced and balanced development of basic education in the capital, solve the problem of inadequate supply of qualified resources and allocation of unreasonable resources, and improve the modern education governance system. In the area of public culture, a series of issues such as uncoordinated regional development, unbalanced urban-rural development, inadequate content-building, asymmetric supply and demand, low service composite index and weak delicacy management need to be solved. In terms of social security, from the perspective of enhancing the people's well-being and promoting people's all-round development, we should push forward the reform of the pension insurance system for government agencies and public institutions, increase the overall medical and health care insurance coverage in urban and rural areas, innovate the medical and healthcare system, raise social security standards and expand the society Welfare coverage. In terms of infrastructure, we should focus on addressing the structural deficiencies in the supply of public facilities and the unsustainable disease that can not guarantee the smooth operation of the city, enlightening the construction of smart city infrastructure, building a big data system of cities and upgrading the fields of water, electricity, gas, heat and public transport Intelligent service standards. In the field of public safety, special rectifications should be carried out in eight aspects of public order, fire safety, food and drug safety, and the establishment of a sound and normal grassroots joint law enforcement and remediation mechanism, with a focus on law enforcement. In urban environmental governance, we must focus on urban garbage and air pollution, intensify joint law enforcement and punishment efforts, and achieve constant blue sky and constant green water flow, constantly meeting the public's ever-increasing demands for public service quality.

2. Science and education have been developing steadily, and the structural reforms on the supply side still need improving

2.1 The development of innovation-driven development has been effective, comprehensive and innovative reform has entered a crucial period

In 2016, under the guidance of innovation-driven development strategy and comprehensive innovation and reform experiments, Beijing continued to build a nationwide center for scientific and technological innovation in depth and ordered all science and technology work in Beijing to be organized around these strategic tasks.

2.1.1 Steady growth in all indicators of science and technology development

From January to September 2016, Beijing's 12,388 state-owned high-tech enterprises were accredited, accounting for nearly 16% of the national total, achieving total revenue of 1,219.2 billion yuan, an increase of 7.3% over the same period of last year. Turnover of the city's technology contracts reached 239.1 billion yuan (66% of the full-year target), an increase of 11% over the same period of last year. Among them, the flow to other provinces and municipalities and exports accounted for 74%. The added value of science and technology service industry reached 168.28 billion yuan, up 10.9% over the same period of last year. The number of new three board listed companies reached 1185, 170 candidates for innovation, ranking first in the country.

In the first half of this year, nearly 40,000 science and technology enterprises were newly added, nearly 400,000 in total.

2.1.2 There are highlights in deepening innovation and reform in an all-round way

With the Ministry of Science and Technology, National Development and Reform Commission jointly study and formulate "Beijing to strengthen national science and technology innovation center construction overall plan", the State Council has issued. On September 22, 2016, the Beijing Municipal Government officially released the "Plan for Strengthening the Construction of National Science and Technology Innovation Centers during the Thirteenth Five-year Plan". At the same time, the study and formulation of the "Beijing-Tianjin-Hebei system to promote comprehensive innovation reform pilot program""Beijing to further improve the financial research projects and funding management of a number of policy measures,""Beijing to promote the transfer of scientific and technological achievements transfer action plan."

2.1.3 Technological innovation system continues to develop

First, the construction of science and technology innovation centers has taken a solid step and produced a batch of major international high-level innovations. Successfully developed the world's first carbon annotate integrated circuit calculator, the world's first 5G large-scale antenna equipment, and strengthen the first-class research institutions, universities and personnel team building. Second, technological innovation fosters new momentum for economic and social development, and R & D builds the first commercial breeding cloud service platform (Golden Seed Cloud Platform) in China to promote the application of technologies in the field of high-end equipment manufacturing. From January to September 2016, it added 45,000 pure electric vehicles and started the "Graphene Technology Innovation Plan (2016 ~ 2025)". Third, the radiation led role to continue to strengthen. To study and formulate the "Implementation Plan of Beijing Municipality on Implementing the Guiding Opinions on Innovation-driven Development of Beijing-Tianjin-Hebei" and to promote the establishment of the Beijing-Tianjin-Hebei Collaborative Innovation Alliance for Technology Transfer from January to September 2016, the amount of technology contracts output by Beijing to Tianjin-Ji reached 7.41 billion yuan, an increase of 52.7% over the same period of last year. More than 30% of Beijing's

Chong Chong space radiation output to Beijing, the establishment of more than 150 branches. Fourth, innovation and business booming. Optimize the market environment that encourages innovation, set up 24 emerging industry venture capital funds with a total scale of 64.1 billion yuan. To support the creation of high-end space for development, a total of 141 institutions awarded the "Beijing Chong creating space," the title.

However, there are still some breakthroughs in the process of comprehensive innovation and reform that need to be overcome. For instance, it is difficult for the reform measures at the municipal level to be implemented by the units affiliated with the Central Government. Urgent efforts should be made to push forward the reform to the depth by the Central Government and the Central Government. There is an urgent need to further improve the co-ordination and coordination mechanism and form a joint force for reform.

2.2 The comprehensive reform of basic education has made great progress, and the development of high quality and balanced development still needs to be further promoted. Beijing regards education as an important livelihood project and popular project, gives priority to education, actively responds to the people's expectation of education, and has made great progress in the reform and development of basic education.

2.2.1 Various types of education at all levels maintained a healthy development trend
By 2015, the early childhood education service network for 0-6-year-olds in Beijing will continue to expand. The gross enrollment rate will reach 95% in the first three years of school. The gross enrollment rate in compulsory education will remain at 100%. The gross enrollment rate in senior secondary education will reach 99%. Higher The gross enrollment rate of education (the proportion of people aged 18-22 who have received higher education) has reached 60%. The entrance examination rate for college entrance examination has remained at over 80% for many years in a row.

2.2.2 Compulsory education enters a phase of high quality and balanced development
In April 2015, 16 districts in the city passed the assessment of basic balanced counties (districts) through the development of national compulsory education at one go, which

marks Beijing's compulsory education taking the stage of high-quality balanced development. On April 23, 2015, the "Proposal of Beijing Municipal People's Government of Beijing Municipal CPC Committee on Promoting the Balanced Development of Compulsory Education" was issued on April 23, 2015 (Jing Fa [2015] No. 5). In the past year or so, Beijing has taken a series of vigorous measures to expand both its high-quality resources and balanced allocation of resources simultaneously. The gap in basic education areas, urban and rural areas and between schools has further narrowed. First, deepen the reform of enrollment examination system. For the first time in 2016, we started a small registration as soon as possible to register a student and set up a general public junior high school entrance inquiry system for quality high schools. We will expand the scope of our counterparts' helicopters over a nine-year period so that some children in primary schools will be able to take up high-quality junior high schools after graduation. In the meantime, the further improvement of the allocation of high-quality high school places to junior high schools in the region was lean towards rural areas and general schools. The quota allocation ratio increased from 30% in 2014 to 49% in 2016. In 2016, the rate of recent schooling in compulsory education in Beijing increased year by year. In 2016, the ratio of primary school and junior high school admission to nearby schools reached 94.5% and 90.68% respectively. Second, innovation and resource supply model. Integrate existing resources and establish a resource sharing system that spans school boundaries, regional boundaries and system boundaries, and support the expansion of quality education resources in all districts. Since 2016, an annual special fund of 44 million yuan has been set up to support and guide all districts of the city to expand the coverage of quality resources in various forms, such as school district system and nine-year system.

2.2.3 Breakthrough Development of Education System Reform

In 2016, the Municipal Board of Education formulated the "Beijing Guiding Opinion on Further Promoting the Exchange of Principals and Teachers for School-based Compulsory Education" and other documents to promote the balanced allocation of teachers in the region by educational administration departments. On June 28, 2016, Beijing issued a number of opinions on supporting the development of rural schools (Beijing Jiao Ren [2016] No. 17), supporting the construction of rural teachers and the development of rural schools. We will improve the system of school governance, study and formulate the Implementation Plan for Running a School by Law in Beijing (2016-2020), Opinions on the Implementation of Law Enforcing Schools by Law and the Guidance Opinions on the Construction of Constitution of Primary and Secondary Schools, and promote the constitutional development of primary and secondary schools. Strengthen funding protection, increase market-level co-ordination guidance. In 2015, the total amount of compulsory education reached 41.9 billion yuan, and the average per student education expenditure and the average public utility expenses gradually increased, ranking the top in the country. For new education funding, the proportion of compulsory education funds allocated by the municipalities in the rural areas has reached 70%, and an additional 60% of the education surcharges have been leveled off to financially weak areas and rural areas.

At present, there are still a series of problems in the development of basic education in Beijing. For example, the insufficient supply and allocation of quality resources in compulsory education still need to be improved; the professionalization of teachers' ranks needs to be improved; and the modern education governance system needs to be improved. Therefore, we still need to reform and innovate to further promote the balanced and balanced development of basic education in Beijing.

2.3 The construction of Beijing's public cultural service demonstration zone has achieved remarkable results, and the potential of public cultural services needs to be further stimulated

2016 marks the first year of the "13th Five-Year Plan", with the capital's cultural reform and development steadily advancing. The construction of the demonstration area of public cultural services in the capital was markedly effective and the cultural life of the masses was further enriched. The excavation and inheritance of the ancient capital culture and Beijing culture continued and the cultural and creative industries continued to grow at a high rate.

2.3.1 Construction of public cultural service demonstration area progressed steadily

In the first half of 2016, the "Plan for Establishing the Capital Public Cultural Service Demonstration Area" was revised and the establishment of the demonstration area of capital public cultural services was organized. Drafting and formulating the overall plan for cultural activities of the capital citizens series from 2016 to 2020 "and making arrangements for the activities during the" 13th Five-Year Plan "period.

Driven by the formation of four cultural activities linkage mechanism to create municipal, district level, township level, community-level cultural characteristics of brand activities. At the same time, it will carry forward the theme and carry out the practical activities of the theme of "deepening life and rooting in people". For example, the Beijing Symphony Orchestra set up a base for Yanqing Dazha. Carry out public welfare Huimin performance activities, extensive and in-depth "Spark Performance Project in rural areas""Weekend performance program""Weekend big stage" and other public welfare activities enrich the grass-roots masses of spiritual and cultural life. In the first half of 2016, over 150 state-owned and private performing arts groups in the city have completed more than 4,800 performances at the grassroots level, attracting nearly 180 audiences.

2.3.2 The mass cultural life has been enriched

The program consists of six major sections: singing Beijing, dancing Beijing, Yi Yun Beijing, Beijing Opera Beijing, Beijing reading and Beijing. Formulate the "Three Venues and Demonstrations of Stars, Jing-Hua-Beijing-Tianjin-Hebei Mass Fine Art Programs" and arrange the performances of outstanding people in the three places. The district organized a series of mass cultural activities around the holidays such as New Year's Day, Spring Festival, Ching Ming, May Day International Labor Day and June 1 Children's Day to create a harmonious and strong capital cultural atmosphere. According to preliminary statistics, in the first half of 2016, the city carried out 16,564 large-scale and distinctive mass cultural activities with a total participation of 17.52 million people.

2.3.3 The cultural heritage of the capital has been valued

To increase support for traditional Chinese opera and traditional arts and crafts, pass on traditional culture through data collation and publication, and introduce traditional culture to promote urban construction and development. Since early 2016, the Municipal Culture Bureau has organized 200 students from 20 primary schools into the cloisonne production arts project protection unit to learn the cloisonne traditional craft process and to design and manufacture cloisonne works. At the same time, we will continue to excavate and safeguard the intangible cultural heritage and encourage constant innovation and development of old brands. Through the collection and collation of materials, oral interviews and the shooting of video materials, we conducted a number of salvos on the succession of many national-level successors such as K Yusheng and Thunder Rain Sexual record.

2.3.4 Cultural and creative industries continued to grow

In 2015, the added value of cultural and creative industries in Beijing reached 307.23 billion yuan, an increase of 8.7% over the previous year and accounting for 13.4% of the GDP of the region, ranking the first in the country. From January to August 2016, the corporate unit of cultural and creative industries above designated size in the city of Beijing achieved an revenue of 826.27 billion yuan, an increase of 8.9% over the same period of last year. The number of employees reached 117.5 million.

However, it should not be overlooked that the development of Beijing's public cultural service system is characterized by uncoordinated regional development, unbalanced urban-rural development, rich content construction, asymmetric supply and demand, low comprehensive service index and the need to strengthen fine management And other issues, these are also the future Beijing's public cultural development needs to be considered an important issue.

3. Targeted alleviation of poverty increased social security benefits

2016 is the first year of advancing the "four comprehensive" strategic layout and the decisive stage in realizing the building of an overall well-to-do society. It is also a crucial period for promoting the maturity and finalization of the system of human resources and social security. Since the beginning of this year, Beijing has fully implemented the important speech of General Secretary Xi Jinping's series and the important directives on Beijing's work. From the perspective of enhancing the people's well-being and promoting the all-round development of people, Beijing implemented the state's top-level design and promoted pension insurance for government departments and public institutions System reform, urban and rural residents' medical insurance co-ordination, medical and health. At the same time, deepen the reform of the medical and health system, deepen the reform of the public hospital pay system, improve the social assistance policy and implement accurate poverty alleviation, promote the linkage of the minimum wage and unemployment insurance benefits, protect the rights and interests of low-income groups, and standardize the management and service. Specific performance: the implementation of precise poverty alleviation, improve the relief system, raise the minimum wage, unemployment insurance, the treatment of workers and their families, social security standards steadily improved, unified urban and rural subsistence allowances standards and expand the coverage of social welfare. The main policies and regulations of Beijing Municipality on social security in 2016 are shown in Table 1.

Table 1 Major Policies and Regulations in Terms of Social Security issued in Beijing in 2016

| Time of Release | Documents |
| --- | --- |
| Jan 29, 2016 | Notice on Adjusting the Policy on Industrial Injury Insurance Rates in Beijing |
| Mar 17, 2016 | Notice on Adjusting Beijing Social Assistance Standards |
| Apr 15, 2016 | Notice on Increasing Banks that withhold the Basic Endowment Insurance for Urban and Rural Residents |
| Jun 1, 2016 | Notice on Adjusting the Relevant Policies on Maternity Insurance for Workers in Beijing |
| Aug 5, 2016 | Circular on Reducing the Proportion of Social Insurance Subsidy Invoked by Employers in Beijing |
| Aug 10, 2016 | Notice on Adjusting the Minimum Wage in Beijing in 2016 |
| Aug 11, 2016 | Notice of Beijing on Adjusting the Periodic Wages in Workers' Injury Insurance Provided for Kinsmen of Injured or Deceased Workers in 2016 |
| Aug 11, 2016 | Notice on Adjusting the Basic Pension for Entrepreneurial Retirees in Beijing in 2016 |
| Aug 15, 2016 | Notice on Adjusting the Standard for Issuing Unemployment Insurance Benefits |
| Aug 19, 2016 | Opinions on Improving the Agreement Management of Fixed Medical Institutions in Basic Medical Insurance in Beijing |
| Oct 26, 2016 | Beijing Trial Measures on Floating Rate Management of Work Injury Insurance |
| Nov 25, 2016 | Opinions on Implementing Precise Aid in the "Thirteen Five-Year Plan" Period |

3.1 The minimum wage steady increase, and the precise implementation details to be determined

In 2016, in order to continue deepening the reform of the income distribution system, speeding up the establishment of a reasonable income growth mechanism and earnestly ensuring the basic livelihood of low-income workers, Beijing Municipality issued the Notice on Adjusting the 2016 Minimum Wage Standard in Beijing on

August 10, Provides / September 1, the minimum wage adjusted to no less than 10. 86 yuan per hour, not less than 1890 yuan per month. The minimum wage of part-time workers increased to 21 yuan / hour; the minimum wage of part-time workers was increased to 49.9 yuan / hour. The above standards include employers and workers themselves should pay the pension, medical care, unemployment insurance premiums. At the same time, Beijing Municipality steadily raised social assistance standards and formulated adjustment programs for urban-rural subsistence allowances and urban-rural low-income families. Since January 2016, the urban and rural minimum living standards have been adjusted from the per capita monthly family budget of 710 yuan to 800 yuan. The urban and rural low-income families have been adjusted to 1050 yuan per month from the average of 930 yuan per month. On November 25, 2016, the "Opinions on Implementing Precise Aid in the Thirteenth Five-year Plan" was promulgated, with a focus on proactive discovery, strict management and precise rescue as the focus of work. The precise aid policy system and the establishment of a precise and accurate management system were clearly established , Including strengthening the basic living security, the implementation of medical aid project, the implementation of the education assistance program, increase employment assistance, improve housing and heating assistance policy, strengthen the temporary assistance function, integration of charity resources and the implementation of professional social work services and other relief system content. In order to ensure that the accurate rescue policy lies in place, relevant implementation rules need to be further formulated.

3.2 Improve the maternity insurance delay affixed and Medicare fixed-point agreement of the medical agency management.

The maternity insurance policy has been further improved by increasing the female reproductive leave and maternity benefits. According to the newly revised "Beijing Population and Family Planning Regulations" to increase the birth bonus 30 days, the abolition of 30 days of late childcare provisions of the Municipality to participate in maternity insurance officers in accordance with the provisions of the birth, increase the maternity benefits allowance for 30 days, Cancellation of childbirth allowance for 30 days of late childcare leave. Payments for maternity leave and maternity leave entitlements provided by the state shall be paid by the maternity insurance fund according to the payment standard of maternity benefits.

In order to implement the "Decision of the State Council on Canceling 62 Centrally Designated Localities for the Implementation of Administrative Examination and Approval Matters" (Guo Fa [2015] No. 57) issued by the State Council, "Guidance of the Ministry of Human Resources and Social Security on Perfecting the Agreement Management of the Fixed Medical Institutions for Basic Medical Insurance Opinions "(People's Social Department issued 〔2015〕 98) to further regulate the city's basic medical insurance designated medical institutions and designated retail pharmacy management, Beijing canceled the implementation of the social insurance administrative department of" basic medical insurance designated medical institutions qualification review " And "basic medical insurance designated retail pharmacies eligibility review" two qualifications. However, basic medical insurance agencies and medical institutions and retail pharmacies under the guidance of how to effectively carry out agreement management, but also need to be further improved.

3.3 Joint adjustment of social security benefits, and floating duty management of work injury insurance have become more difficult.

In addition to the minimum wage, social insurance benefits have also been linked up. On August 11, 2016, the "Notice on Adjusting the Basic Pension for Entrepreneurial Retirees in Beijing Municipality" was released in 2016. In order to reduce the post-retirement income gap, the basic pension was adjusted for the difference on the basis of the original treatment and paid according to the payment Years of implementation of the pension incentive adjustment policy. On August 15, 2016, Beijing Municipality issued the Notice on Adjusting the Standard for Issuing Unemployment Insurance Benefits. Since September 2016, when the accumulated payment time has reached 1 year and less than 5 years, the monthly unemployment insurance payment standard is 1,212 yuan. Farmers contract workers one-time living allowance standard adjusted from 958 yuan to 1048 yuan.

At the same time, in order to improve the efficiency of using work-related injury insurance funds, Beijing Municipality promulgated the "Notice on Adjusting Work-related Injury Workers and Workers' Deaths in Beijing in 2016 on Work-Injury Prevention and Ensuring the Safety, Health, Safety and Legitimate Rights and Interests of Workers and Staff members Notice on Periodic Treatment of Insurance, and the adjustment of the disability allowances for workers with a grade 1 to 4 increase by RMB 350 to RMB 410 per person per month respectively according to the level of disability. On October 8, the Trial Measures for Floating Rates Management of Work-related Injury Insurance in Beijing were issued. The work-related injury insurance agency pays the expense growth rate according to the work-related injury insurance fund of the employer and the standardization of production safety of enterprises, and the enterprise produces a production safety responsibility accident Situation, approved in the next payment year (July to June next year) should be floating level of occupational injury insurance, a corresponding increase in the handling of insurance agencies and employers more difficult.

4. The capacity of urban operation support has risen and the level of infrastructure intelligence needs to be improved

2016 marks the first year of the "13th Five-Year Plan". Beijing further optimizes the layout of urban public facilities, attracts social capital by means of PPP in the fields of infrastructure and public utilities, accelerates urban public transport, and provides drainage, heat supply, Gas supply and other public utilities construction speed.

4.1 The overall capacity of urban management has been further strengthened

Beijing City in the field of urban management reform initiatives. July 28 and 29, 2016, the Beijing Municipal Commission of Urban Management and Beijing Municipal Planning and Land Resources Commission have been two major institutions set up. Beijing Municipal Administration Commission will conduct unified management on the related functions and compilation of daily operation management of coal-oil and gas and other resources, recovery and management of renewable resources, and environmental sanitation management of urban green belts originally managed by other government departments in Beijing. Beijing has also set up a high-level platform for deliberation on this basis. The Capital Urban Environment Construction and Management Committee and the mayor are personally in command and form a powerful working platform that integrates major decisions, co-ordination and coordination and supervision and assessment. Beijing "Geotechnical Committee" is composed of two functional departments of planning and national territory. It is a "unified system of two rules" for the overall land use planning and overall city planning, and lays the foundation for the system in terms of rigid constraints on construction.

4.2 The city's operational support capability has been further enhanced

In the first three quarters of 2016, infrastructure investment in Beijing completed 154.42 billion yuan, an increase of 14.6% over the same period of last year. Utilization of reclaimed water in Beijing's water sector amounted to 950 million cubic meters in 2015, accounting for 1/4 of the total water consumption of the city, with rainwater. The utilization capacity of comprehensive utilization of the project reached 63.66 million cubic meters, and the capital water source security capability has been comprehensively improved. The gas supply capacity has been steadily improved. The construction of the natural gas transmission and distribution system and the urban transmission and distribution system has been strengthened. The urban transmission and distribution system has been initially formed, covering the entire central urban area and all new towns except Yanqing. The average annual growth of natural gas consumption will reach 10%. By the end of 2015, the volume will reach 14.3 billion cubic meters. The central urban area will basically realize the heating without coalification. City heating area increased from 603 million square meters to 705.4 million square meters. The proportion of heating and clean energy has risen sharply from 65% to 83%. The four thermal power centers have been put into operation and the urban heating network has been further improved. Organize the renovation of old heating pipe network 1800 km, the completion of heat measurement and transformation area 90 million square meters, to achieve measurement and charging area of 170 million square meters; the city's unit area heating energy consumption decreased by 15%. Underground pipeline blanking renovation project to active promote and transform the old power pipe network 51.7km.

4.3 The infrastructure challenges for urban development have been given priority

In 2016, Beijing Municipality will promote the implementation of "Beijing's overall plan to ease traffic congestion (2015-2020)", implement traffic congestion reconstruction projects and promote the construction of park-and-ride parking facilities. Priority will be given to public transport to speed up construction To promote the city's orderly operation of the convenient, efficient and green integrated transport system; to promote the central city population and industry ease, encourage new urbanization and new rural construction, strongly support the development of weak areas, all aspects of cracked urban development problems.

## 4.4 Construction of Beijing Sub-center is in full swing

In 2016, Beijing concentrated its efforts on the construction of the Beijing Sub-center and proposed completion of all kinds of planning work for urban sub-centers by the end of the year. By the end of 2017, it will complete construction of municipal-level administrative offices, sub-centers of forest and water environment in 2020, and transport, education and medical, Health and other related infrastructure to meet the scheduled goals and other eight tasks. Beijing City Sub-center construction pilot pilot sponge city construction, clearly to build three networks, four zones, more water, more wetland water environment pattern. In traffic, Beijing city center to achieve rail transit within 500 meters can be transferred.

## 4.5 PPP boosted the construction of public facilities

Beijing will promote PPP cooperation in the construction of the Olympic Winter Games, the new airport and urban sub-centers. At the same time, Beijing will explore establishing a PPP promotion fund to enrich and improve Beijing's financing model. In 2016, Beijing also attracted social capital in urban public facilities and used PPP to boost the construction of urban public facilities. At the same time, it introduced financial support policies to attract social capital participation.

Although Beijing made great achievements in infrastructure in 2016, the inadequate structural supply of public facilities can not meet the needs of citizens. The chronic diseases that can not fully guarantee the smooth operation of the city still exist. There are still not enough infrastructures for smart cities to be built. Urban big data have not yet been used in depth and there is an urgent need to upgrade the level of intelligent services in the areas of water, gas, heat and public transport, water scarcity, air pollution, municipal underground pipelines and overhead lines And other issues remain prominent. Beijing's infrastructure area has a long way to go in building "four centers" and satisfying the "four services."

## 5. The public security situation is generally favorable and the number of cybercrime cases and accidents is still relatively large

### 5.1 Social order continued to improve, and public security at urban and rural junctions remained prominent

Beijing "Spring-Summer 2016 Ping an Action" gratifying achievements. From April to the end of August 2016, the police uncovered more than 250,000 criminal cases of various kinds and criminal detention of more than 12,000 people, up by 44.4% and 23.4% respectively on a month-on-month basis. The city's 110 criminal and police order dropped by 13.6% and 18.3% respectively over the same period of the previous year, and social order continued to improve. During the operation, relying on such mechanisms as the "big data" police service, all police battalions and departments continuously strengthened resource sharing and synthetic operations and cracked over 1,900 criminal cases of "eight types of crimes" with a detection rate of 74.3% for the year 2000 Since the highest level over the same period[1], effectively purifying the city's public security environment, people's sense of security, satisfaction has been raised.

Urban and rural areas to increase the comprehensive management of joint efforts. Social security in the urban-rural junction area has always been the most prominent short-board in urban construction and management, seriously restricting the process of capitalist modernization. In 2016, the Municipal Party Committee and the Municipal Government established the general headquarters of the comprehensive renovation work in the key areas of the junction of urban and rural areas in the city and made overall plans to promote the comprehensive improvement work in these areas with intensified rectification. In view of the outstanding problems and serious hidden dangers in key areas such as social security in urban and rural areas, special arrangements were made for the eight aspects of public order, fire safety and food and drug safety, and the establishment of a sound and normal grass-roots joint enforcement and remediation mechanism. Strength to carry out law enforcement, with remarkable results.

5.2 Internet scams report ranks first in the country, and people expressed concern about network security.

Judging from the crime of fraud in China's telecommunications networks, the number of crimes in recent years has risen at an average annual rate of 20% and 30%, especially damaging to people's livelihood. In 2014, Beijing established the nation's first anti-fraud coalition and set up a hunting network platform, which is the first

---

[1]Beijing announced the "Spring-Summer 2016 Ping An Action" transcript ", the Chinese police network, http://home.cpd.com.cn/thread-298706-1-1.html.

application platform for online fraud reporting and advanced claims settlement in China. The platform in 2015 received a total of 24,886 cases of online fraud reported, of which the top ten cities reported the highest among Beijing, Beijing ranks first. In 2015, 806 cases of Beijing Telecom network fraud were deceived by an amount of 5,857,000 yuan with a per capita loss of 7,266 yuan.[1] In 2016, Beijing stepped up its efforts to crack down on new types of crimes committed in the telecommunications network, resolutely punished criminal acts such as telecommunications fraud and network investment fraud, and actively participated in the crackdown and punishments in key criminal areas and key areas, and promoted telecommunications, finance and other fields The source of regulation. Beijing made heavy blows so as to improve the integrated detection mechanism so as to improve the combat effectiveness and deepen the police-communications linkage mechanism to form an effective guard to push forward the linkage mechanism between the police and the police to crack down on the stolen goods. Initially, a series of measures have been taken to "fight both prevention and defense, department cooperation, internal and external cooperation, Source decapitation "with the Beijing characteristics of the fight against telecom network fraud crime system, multi-police linkage, innovation and integration of detection mechanisms to achieve large-scale combat, effectively curbed the high incidence of telecommunications network fraud cases, to achieve a" case of attack, combat Rise, detract from rising ". In the first half of 2016, Beijing cracked a total of 6,248 cases, seized 1435 suspects, destroyed 101 criminal gangs, and stopped the loss of 1.01 billion yuan through professional interception, arrest and arrest to stop the freezing of funds involved in the case of the whole country. In the amount of 2.3 billion yuan, the number of cases of fraud committed abroad has dropped by 50% from the same period of last year. The total amount of losses has also dropped by 60% over 2015. Police and police linkage, innovative fraud telephone notification block mechanism to achieve the source of prevention, take direct call to discourage measures to intercept transfer 8677, directly to avoid loss of 86.54 million yuan. From the telecommunications network fraud criminal communications chain started to strengthen cooperation with the communications management departments and operating companies to establish a set of working mechanism, the first time found that the first time notification, blocking the first block, blocking all kinds of fraudulent communications Tools, to achieve effective prevention.

---

[1] Capital Window, http: // www. beijing. gov. cn /, Beijing Daily , 20 September 2016.

5.3 The food and drug markets were stable and orderly, and the food and drug safety supervision was fruitful

According to the Beijing Pharmaceutical Quality and Safety Notice, "2016 Beijing Municipality, Uniform Monitoring Plan for Food and Drug Safety", the third quarter of 2016 carried out supervision and sampling on the production, operation and use of pharmaceuticals and pharmaceutical packaging materials in the city and completed the drug sampling 1735 Batch, with a pass rate of 99.83%.

Fully implement the "Beijing Food and Drug Safety Three-Year Action Plan (2016-2018)" and gradually improve the local laws, regulations and standards system, effectively guarantee the supply of food and drug safety and mobilize all social forces actively create a safe city for food and medicine and accelerate the construction of health Beijing. Grass-roots infrastructure more solid to ensure that the major events of the food and drug safety and security. Actively promote the integration of food and drug supervision in Beijing, Tianjin and promote the establishment of national food safety city.

5.4 The overall epidemic report is stable, and the control of key epidemic situations needs to be strengthened

According to the monthly report of Beijing epidemic situation, the epidemic report of the whole city in 2016 was generally stable. The seasonal characteristics of the infectious disease report were obvious, and no major epidemic occurred. Beijing calendar year influenza surveillance data show that with the arrival of autumn and winter, the city is about to enter the seasonal influenza epidemic, the current number of influenza-like cases and influenza virus positive rate increased. In 2016, the preferential vaccination campaign for primary and secondary school students and the elderly in the city started on October 15, which provided free vaccination for primary and secondary school students and the elderly in the city for the first 10 years by the Beijing municipal government. By the end of 2015, more than 10 million people had been vaccinated Enjoy the government care. From the relevant monitoring and survey data, this work has achieved good social effects.

In 1985, Beijing reported the first case of AIDS in the country. As of October 31,

2016, a total of 21,886 cases of HIV-infected people and patients have been reported. Among them, 4954 cases of household registration in the city accounted for 22.6%; 16,237 cases of household registrations in other provinces and cities accounted for 74.2%; 695 cases of expatriates accounted for 3.2%. From January to October 2016, the city reported 3135 cases of HIV-infected patients and patients, down 1.45% from 3181 cases in the same period of last year. Currently, there are 15,668 active HIV infected patients and patients in the city, mainly distributed in 3 districts of Chaoyang, Haidian and Fengtai, accounting for 58.1% of the total reported number of the city. The AIDS epidemic in the city showed the following characteristics: First, the reported figures tended to be stable; the epidemic situation had slowed down since 2013, the overall outbreak was at a low epidemic level; second, the high proportion of floating population; thirdly, the sexual behavior became the spread of AIDS The number of infected persons and patients reported in recent years increased from 87.1% in 2011 to 96.9% at the end of October 2016. Fourthly, the number of surviving people continues to rise and now lives in Beijing Of infected persons and patients increased from 6442 cases in 2011 to 15,668 cases at the end of October 2016, showing a continuous upward trend with a marked decrease in case fatality rate. Fifth, the spread of injecting drug abuse continued to be kept at a low level. From 2013 to 2015, Of the past more than 2000 cases of heroin addicts, no case of a new infection, high-risk groups of new infections have been controlled; Sixteen 15-24-year-olds increased more than the overall increase in outbreaks, January-October 2016 report 15 In the 24-year-old group, 647 cases were infected and patients, an increase of 23 cases (3.69%) over the same period of last year (624 cases), of which 88 cases were reported among young students aged 15-24 years.

5.5 Larger total number of safety accidents means that the task of rectifying security risks is still arduous

In 2016, the overall situation of public security in the city remained stable and improved. However, the total number of accidents was still large. Taking the fire accident as an example, the situation was rather grim. In the first half of the year, a total of 2,619 fire accidents occurred in the city, killing 37 people and injuring 15 others. The direct economic loss was 28.937 million yuan, especially in the urban-rural junction and in rural areas. There are still a large number of potential safety hazards in some industries, leading security awareness is not strong, and there are still many aspects of security weaknesses. Part of the primary responsibility for the safety of the unit still to be implemented, safety hazard rectification progress is slow, such as "1.124" Sunhe Township, Chaoyang District, fire accidents, practitioners did not pay attention to local police station personnel found hidden problems rectification is not timely, resulting in 8 Death, great social impact. In the first half of 2016, 16 gas pipeline accidents that caused construction damage have occurred, which have had a huge impact on the safe operation of the city and the order of citizens' normal life. Remediation of potential safety hazards in oil and gas transmission pipelines and urban gas pipelines.

6. Significant achievements have been made in air pollution control and a long way to go in ecological civilization construction

In recent years, Beijing has earnestly implemented the policy-making and deployment concerning the construction of ecological civilization, the coordinated development of Beijing, Tianjin and Hebei and environmental protection, and vigorously controlled pollution reduction with the goal of building a world-class, harmonious and livable city with remarkable results. In the just past "12th Five-Year" period, the drop in pollutants in Beijing greatly exceeded the target tasks as shown in Table 2.

Table 2 Reduction of Major Pollutants in Beijing during the "12th-Five-Year Plan" period

Unit: %

| Major Pollutants | Yearly Reduction Proportion | | | | | Accumulated Reduction Proportion | "12th-Five-Year" Goal | Goal Completion Rate |
|---|---|---|---|---|---|---|---|---|
| | 2011 | 2012 | 2013 | 2014 | 2015 | | | |
| PM2.5 | 4.08 | 5.39 | (89.5) 10.37 | (85.9) 4.00 | (80.6) 6.20 | — | — | — |
| Sulfur Dioxide | 6.22 | 4.12 | 7.25 | 9.35 | 9.80 | 31.81 | 13.40 | 237 |
| Nitrogen Oxides | 4.75 | 5.75 | 6.29 | 9.24 | 8.83 | 30.39 | 12.30 | 247 |
| Chemical Oxygen Demand | 3.53 | 3.46 | 4.30 | 5.40 | 4.33 | 19.34 | 8.70 | 222 |
| Ammonia Nitrogen | 2.98 | 3.95 | 3.80 | 3.82 | 12.98 | 24.96 | 10.10 | 247 |

Note: Official statistics on PM2.5 data began in 2013 and there are no targets set for the 12th Five-Year Plan. The data in brackets is the annual average in micrograms per cubic meter.

Source: Website of Beijing Development and Reform Commission, http: // www. bjpc.gov.cn/.

2016 marks the first year of the "13th Five-Year Plan". Beijing will continue to step up its efforts in environmental pollution control and give top priority to the air quality. Special attention will be given to key areas, industries and time zones so as to enhance supervision and inspection and law enforcement. Problem-oriented, fill the short board, and achieved good results. As of the end of November 2016, the average concentration of fine particulate matter (PM2.5) in Beijing air was 67 μg / m3, down 9.5% from the same period of last year. The average concentrations of other major pollutants, sulfur dioxide, nitrogen dioxide and particulate matter (PM10) were 10, 45 and 86 μg / m3, down 23.1% 6.3% and 10.4% respectively over the previous year. Air quality standards 185 days, an increase of 10 days. [1]

In the "13th Five-Year Plan" in Beijing, it is clearly pointed out that an overall improvement in the quality of ecological environment should be achieved at this stage. In 2016, we will continue to make great efforts to control air pollution and continue to implement the Beijing Clean Air Action Plan 2013-2017. We will continue to implement the Clean Air Action Plan for Beijing 2013-2017, which will include reducing coal consumption, controlling gasoline vehicles to encourage new energy vehicles, controlling dust emissions, Law enforcement and other measures taken. The focus of the work is to control the sale and use of bulk coal in the rural areas in winter, to control high-emission vehicles and to control the junction of urban and rural areas, and to continue the "Year of Air Pollution Enforcement" campaign to promote pollution prevention and control with extraordinary measures and efforts.

6.1 Increase the reduction of coal

2016 is the city's coal-fired boilers, clean energy transformation of the largest and most vigorous year. As of the end of November, coal-fired boiler clean energy reform more than 8400 steam tons, 2.8 times the task at the beginning of the year. Following the completion of the renovation of the six districts of Jiuliu, the project will continue to be promoted to invalid districts and counties in 2016 and Tongzhou District will take the lead in realizing the basic coal-fired boiler reconstruction. In recent years,

---

[1]Beijing EPB website, http: // www.bjepb.gov.cn /.

according to the Municipal Environmental Protection Bureau statistics, the city's sulfur dioxide in the air has entered a steady decline in the channel, with the average non-heating city level in the South equivalent. Vigorously promote alternative coal cleaning energy. In rural areas 463 villages scattered coal to clean energy; completed Chaoyang, Haidian, Fengtai, Shijingshan City residents scattered clean coal alternative 75,000. It is estimated that by the end of 2016, the total amount of coal in the city will be reduced to less than 10 million tons, and the target of five years' total coal consumption control will be realized one year ahead of schedule.

6.2 Improve policies regarding car control and fuel efficiency

In 2016, Beijing continued to strictly control the total number of motor vehicles. In 2016, the number of passenger cars in the city's Yaohao was reduced to 90,000, a 40% decrease from 150,000 in the previous year. At the same time, it will continue to encourage the development of new energy vehicles. In 2016, the number of NEV license plates will increase by 30,000, bringing the total number of new energy indicators to 60,000. In 2016, a total of 2,700 buses were renewed, of which 2,390 were electric-driven vehicles and 310 were ultra-low-emission Euro VI diesel vehicles. In 2016, it continued to phase out 380,000 old motor vehicles. Promulgated the sixth phase of automotive gasoline and diesel standards, the introduction of restrictions on national I, II emission standards of light petrol vehicles within the Fifth Ring Road (excluding) the provisions of the road and developed a scrapped I, II light gasoline vehicles Related preferential policies.

6.3 Strengthen pollution control measures

Continue to clear the polluting enterprises that do not meet the functional orientation of the capital and have already implemented zero-forcing items. In 2016, Beijing adjusted its exit from the 335 general manufacturing and polluting industries such as printing and furniture, while the number of industrial workers decreased by 64,000. Quit out 1200 tasks within five years ahead of schedule. The nation has spearheaded the retrofit of low-NOx combustion of gas-fired boilers. Currently, it has started to launch 13,000 tons of steam, of which 4,700 tons of steam has been completed and more than 50% of the total emissions of nitrogen oxides have been discharged by a single boiler. The emission reduction of volatile organic compounds in key industries1 has been completed. 370,000 tons, organizing the implementation of more than 100 environmental technology projects. Beijing has continuously perfected standards construction, and the discharge limits of pollutants in boilers, oil refining and petrochemicals, printing, wood furniture manufacturing and crematoria have all reached the international advanced level. Meanwhile, the coordinated development strategy of Beijing, Tianjin and Ji also played a supportive role in pollution control and emission reduction in Beijing. In the first half of 2016, the three places signed a total of 60 industrial cooperation projects and built a number of industrial parks.

6.4 Enhance public satisfaction

From January to August 2016, Beijing Municipality handled a total of 27,000 complaints about petitions and complaints related to environmental issues, down by 16.5% over the same period of last year. Among them, involving the air pollution in the same period a year earlier to reduce the 5727, a decrease of 23.8%. This shows from the side that the public are gradually raising their satisfaction with the environment in Beijing and fully affirming the government's efforts in improving the quality of the environment and reducing air pollution.

6.5 Increase the intensity of joint law enforcement

We carried out the special campaign "Year of Air Pollution Enforcement" with the focus on "managing scattered coal,""net four gas" (coal-fired exhaust gas, volatile organic waste gas, industrial exhaust gas and motor vehicle exhaust), "lowering three dusts" Road dust, due to burning dust), increase environmental penalties for illegal inspection. From January to November 2016, the city's environmental supervision departments imposed a total of 1254 air pollution violations, 184 environmental violations, 851 construction-related offenses, 255 solid waste offenses and 61 other types of offenses Starting from a fine of 100 million yuan, effectively cracking down on environmental violations. Regional joint prevention and control gradually improved and launched the "triple" (geographical, time, personnel), "quadruple" (with elevated source, heavy pollution emergency, coal burning, mobile source as the key content) Beijing-Tianjin-Hebei linkage law enforcement, Achieve some results.

Although some achievements have been made in environmental protection, we must also clearly recognize that the pollution in the capital is complex, urgent and compressive. The air pollution, water pollution and land pollution are still grim. The air quality is away from the national standards. There is still a long way to go. In particular, the level of development of Beijing-Tianjin-Hebei region and its surrounding areas still shows differences in understanding of the environment and in checking and enforcing the law. It will take time to improve the overall environment. The ecological environment is the biggest concern of the present masses. At the time of "the 13th Five-Year Plan", the five development concepts proposed by our country are right at the right moment. In particular, the concept of green development has pointed out the direction for the capital to control pollution and improve the environment. Looking forward, the "13th Five-Year Plan" proposed by Beijing proposed that before 2020, the annual average concentration of PM2.5 will be 15% lower than that of 2015; by the end of 2017, the black-stinking water of the river in urban built-up areas will be basically eliminated emission. We look forward to an early completion of a road of civilized development featuring productive development, well-off life and good ecology in Beijing. The green hills and blue sky are often the new normal in the capital environment.

# Comprehensive Evaluation of Public Service Performance of Sixteen Districts in Beijing

"Beijing Sixteen Districts Public Service Performance Comprehensive Evaluation Study Group"[1]

## Abstract

Through the public service performance evaluation index system, this study makes a comprehensive comparison and ranking of public service performance in all districts of Beijing. Evaluation results show that although the Tongzhou District located in the "city sub-center" has made a certain degree of efforts, its supply of public service resources is still at a relatively low level in the whole city.

Keywords: public service, evaluation index system, comprehensive evaluation

## 1. Comprehensive Evaluation Index System for Public Service Performance

Through the comprehensive evaluation of the performance of public services in Beijing over the past four years, we have gradually formed an evaluation system that includes six dimensions: basic education, social security, medical care, culture and sports, environmental protection and public safety. Each dimension contains 4 ~ 8 evaluation indicators. In 2016, we still use the previous evaluation system. However, in order to reflect the efforts of each district, we add two evaluation indicators reflecting the degree of efforts in the environmental protection dimension: the decrease rate of PM2.5 and the energy consumption rate of GDP per 10,000 yuan. In the meantime, in order to maintain the conciseness of evaluation indexes, we excluded a "greening rate" of the forest with little change and significant regional characteristics, and a strong correlation index with "the electricity consumption of 10,000 yuan of GDP" GDP energy consumption." The adjusted evaluation index system is shown in Table 1.

Table 1 Public Service Performance Evaluation Indicator System of Beijing

| Target Layer | Standard Layer | Indicator Layer |
|---|---|---|
| Public | Basic | Number of fully employed teachers for every 100 students in primary |

---

[1] The members of group are Shi Changkui, Luo Zhi. Shi Changkui, Reseacher, Director of Research Institute of Management, Beijing Academy of Social Sciences. Research areas include public management and charity; Luo Zhi, Ph.D., Associate Researcher Beijing Academy of Social Sciences. Research areas includes public management, public policy, management innovation.

| Service Performanc e Evaluation Indicator System of Beijing X | Education X1 | schoolsX11<br>Number of fully employed teachers for every 100 students in secondar schoolsX12<br>Number of children in kindergarten every ten thousand people X13<br>Number of fully employed teachers for every 100 kindergarten childre X14 |
|---|---|---|
| | Social Security X2 | Number of beds in adoption institutes for every ten thousand people X21<br>Number of community service institutes for every ten thousand peopl X22<br>Coverage of general endowment insurance (%)X23<br>Coverage of general health care insurance (%) X24<br>Coverage of employment insurance (%) X25<br>Number of people living on minimum living allowance every te thousand people X26<br>Number of people under special care and pensions every ten thousan people X27<br>Number of people under social aids every ten thousand people X28 |
| | Health Care X3 | Average person times under treatment X31<br>Average person times for physical check X32<br>Doctors for every thousand people X33<br>Registered nurses for every thousand people X34<br>Number of beds in hospital for every thousand people X35<br>Professional staff in community health care service institutes for ever thousand people X36<br>Average person times under treatment in community health care servic institutes X37 |
| | Culture and Sports X4 | Per-capita collection of public libraries X41<br>Total number of people in public libraries (10 thousand person times X42<br>Number of gyms for every ten thousand people X43<br>Person times to visit museums X44 |
| | Environment Protection X5 | Yearly average concentration of sulfur dioxide (Mg/m3) X51<br>Yearly average concentration of nitrogen dioxide (Mg/m3) X52<br>Yearly average concentration of PM 10 (Mg/m3) X53<br>Yearly average concentration of PM2.5 (Mg/m3) X54<br>Reduction rate of PM2.5 (%) X55<br>Electricity used every ten thousand yuan GDP(KWh) X56<br>Reduction rate of energy consumption every ten thousand yuan GDP(% X57 |
| | Public Safety X6 | Number of criminal cases solved every ten thousand people X61<br>Death toll in fire accidents every ten thousand people X62<br>Direct economic loss in fire accidents every ten thousand people X63<br>Death toll in traffic accidents every ten thousand people X64<br>Direct economic loss in traffic accidents every ten thousand people X65 |

| | | Death toll in production safety accidents every ten thousand people X66 |
|---|---|---|

2. The source and processing of comprehensive evaluation of public service performance

The main basis for the comprehensive evaluation of public service performance in all districts in Beijing is the progress statistics released by the Beijing Municipal Bureau of Statistics in 2016 which measure the public service levels of all districts in Beijing in 2015. Because of the differences in type and dimensionality of the original statistics, these raw data need to be normalized or dimensionless before they can be used. In accordance with the usual approach, the original data is still processed in two different ways: normal and reverse.

2.1 Preliminary data and processing of basic education service index

In 2015, the basic education service levels in various districts of Beijing are shown in Table 2, and the specific index rankings can refer to the results of the non-dimensional treatment shown in Figure 1. From the number of full-time teachers in every 100 primary schools, the levels in various districts are basically the same as those in the previous year. Tongzhou District, Shunyi District and Changping District are slightly better than the previous year. In addition to ecological conservation areas due to the positioning of the top factor in the region, Dongcheng District and Xicheng District obvious advantages, Haidian District in the "number" is still in the final. Ordinary secondary schools each hundred students have full-time teachers to enhance the overall level of the obvious. Among them, Chaoyang District, ranked close to 20 people in the first level. Afterwards, Changping District, Huairou District and Pinggu District still remained. Haidian District, although improved, but in the "number" is still in the final. The number of children per 10,000 in the park increased significantly, Fangshan District, Huairou District and Miyun District are still ranked first in the city. Changping District and Xicheng District, kindergarten resources obviously insufficient, at the end of the city. The number of full-time teachers in each of the 100 children in the park did not change much. The number in Xicheng District rose to double-digit number, ranking the top two in the city with Dongcheng District. Chaoyang District and Changping District came close to double digits. Daxing District The number of full-time teachers in kindergartens in Shunyi District was significantly lower.

Table 2 Preliminary Level of Indicators in Basic Education Service in Districts of Beijing in 2015

| Indicators / District | Number of fully employed teachers for every 100 students in primary schools X11 | Number of fully employed teachers for every 100 students in secondary schools X12 | Number of children in kindergarten every ten thousand people X13 | Number of fully employed teachers for every 100 kindergarten children X14 |
|---|---|---|---|---|
| Dongcheng | 7.15 | 12.47 | 159.82 | 10.18 |
| Xicheng | 6.77 | 13.61 | 131.95 | 10.60 |
| Chaoyang | 5.11 | 19.77 | 168.19 | 9.85 |
| Fengtai | 6.10 | 14.63 | 179.54 | 8.44 |
| Shijingshan | 5.69 | 15.57 | 227.81 | 8.11 |
| Haidian | 4.69 | 10.70 | 163.62 | 8.14 |
| Fangshan | 6.14 | 12.79 | 289.48 | 9.07 |
| Tongzhou | 5.84 | 13.82 | 209.12 | 8.74 |
| Shunyi | 6.11 | 13.32 | 223.03 | 6.42 |
| Changping | 5.85 | 17.10 | 131.71 | 9.72 |
| Daxing | 5.93 | 15.48 | 181.63 | 6.15 |
| Mentougou | 7.50 | 13.11 | 192.95 | 8.88 |
| Huairou | 6.36 | 15.64 | 247.99 | 7.99 |
| Pinggu | 8.53 | 15.45 | 215.08 | 7.24 |
| Miyun | 6.88 | 12.10 | 236.24 | 8.80 |
| Yanqing | 8.80 | 15.09 | 224.30 | 8.89 |

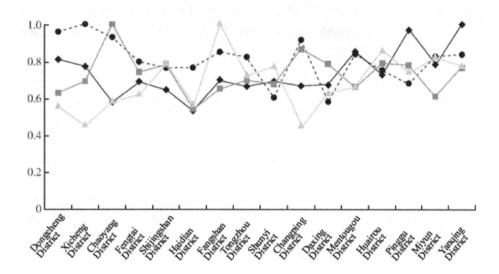

- Number of fully employed teachers for every 100 students in primary schoolsX11
- Number of fully employed teachers for every 100 students in secondary schoolsX12
- Number of children in kindergarten every ten thousand people X13
- Number of fully employed teachers for every 100 kindergarten children X14

Figure 1 Dimensionless Level of Basic Education Service Indicators in Each District
of Beijing in 2015

2.2 The original data and processing of social security service indicators

In 2015, the levels of social security services in various districts of Beijing are shown in Table 3, and the rankings of specific indicators can refer to the results of the non-dimensional treatment shown in Figure 2. The number of beds per adoptee has no change compared with that of the previous year. The ecological conservation area has obvious advantages due to its function orientation. There are nearly 200 Yanqing districts, more than 100 Pinggu districts and nearly 100 in Huairou district and Miyun district. The number of community service organizations per 10,000 people increased significantly. The number of Huairou District and Mentougou District increased from less than 10 in the previous year to more than 20 and nearly 20 in 2015 respectively. Although Dongcheng District and Xicheng District are absolutely not high, Last year, the area more than doubled. Other districts also saw some improvements. The proportions of the three types of insurance in all districts of the city did not change much compared with that of the previous year, and the separation of working place and residence caused the participation proportion of Dongcheng District and Xicheng District to exceed 100%, while some urban development new areas and ecological conservation areas were insufficient 40%. There are significant differences in the

293

minimum subsistence allowance for urban and rural residents per 10,000 population in each district, with ecological conservation areas and urban core functional areas generally above 100 or even 200, urban functional areas and urban development areas generally below 50, Only Shijingshan District, more than 100 people. However, the overall distribution of minimum subsistence allowance for urban and rural residents per 10,000 populations is different, both of which are relatively high in urban development new areas and ecological conservation areas In urban function core area and urban function area.

Table 3 Preliminary Level of Public Security Service Indicators in Each District of Beijing in 2015

| Indicators District | Number of beds in adoption institutes for every ten thousand people X21 | Number of communi ty service institutes for every ten thousand people X22 | Coverag e of general endowm ent insurance (%) X23 | Coverage of general health care insurance (%) X24 | Coverage of employm ent insurance (%) X25 | Number of people living on minimum living allowance every ten thousand people X26 | Number of people under special care and pensions every ten thousand people X27 | Number of people under social aids every ten thousand people X28 |
|---|---|---|---|---|---|---|---|---|
| Dongcheng | 10.27 | 5.07 | 152 | 177 | 119 | 143.59 | 10.18 | 143.59 |
| Xicheng | 15.20 | 5.53 | 148 | 164 | 111 | 143.01 | 11.49 | 143.01 |
| Chaoyang | 32.41 | 2.75 | 76 | 80 | 59 | 33.50 | 8.62 | 33.56 |
| Fengtai | 23.62 | 2.91 | 38 | 42 | 26 | 42.63 | 11.39 | 42.75 |
| Shijingshan | 47.59 | 5.52 | 64 | 68 | 40 | 123.74 | 10.71 | 123.74 |
| Haidian | 25.03 | 2.69 | 67 | 76 | 57 | 14.96 | 10.89 | 15.11 |
| Fangshan | 64.45 | 9.73 | 34 | 36 | 25 | 81.85 | 46.28 | 87.42 |
| Tongzhou | 32.79 | 4.85 | 33 | 35 | 24 | 49.99 | 29.08 | 51.34 |
| Shunyi | 30.67 | 10.93 | 56 | 55 | 44 | 43.66 | 46.28 | 45.42 |
| Changping | 70.80 | 3.06 | 22 | 24 | 17 | 14.08 | 13.83 | 14.62 |
| Daxing | 37.73 | 4.32 | 32 | 32 | 24 | 19.65 | 21.63 | 20.79 |
| Mentougou | 63.44 | 18.34 | 69 | 69 | 47 | 260.49 | 23.34 | 270.97 |
| Huairou | 83.33 | 22.08 | 53 | 54 | 44 | 123.49 | 63.75 | 151.80 |
| Pinggu | 116.90 | 8.65 | 45 | 48 | 34 | 194.63 | 66.31 | 200.83 |
| Miyun | 96.14 | 14.11 | 39 | 43 | 30 | 255.66 | 66.24 | 269.90 |
| Yanqing | 184.87 | 15.70 | 28 | 35 | 21 | 151.21 | 76.27 | 175.29 |

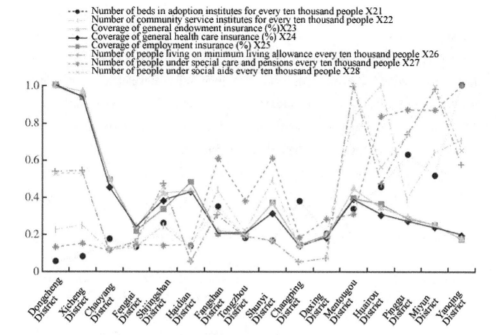

Figure 2 Dimensionless Levels of Public Security Service Indicators in Each District of Beijing in 2015

2.3 Original data and processing of medical service indicators

In 2015, the levels of health care services in various districts of Beijing are shown in Table 4, and the rankings of specific indicators can refer to the results of the non-dimensional treatment shown in Figure 3. In terms of per capita consultation and treatment, most of the districts have been upgraded. However, Dongcheng District and Xicheng District are still the highlands of the city's medical and health services. They bear the medical and health services of all districts in the city and even the whole country. The number of visits per capita is more than 20, The districts are more than three times, even more than seven times. From the per capita health examination trips, the advantages of Dongcheng District and Xicheng District are still obvious. Tongzhou District, Changping District and Daxing District are the three districts with a minimum of 0 persons, with the least in the city. From the perspective of medical and health resources, the number of licensed doctors per 1,000 people in each district, the number of registered nurses per 1,000 population and the number of hospital beds per 1,000 people all have varying degrees of improvement. However, there are still a large number of medical and health care facilities in Dongcheng District and Xicheng District Resources, with the absolute superiority of two digits or nearly double digits came in the top two in the city, which is also the main reason that the per capita health checkup rate and per capita health checkup rate are significantly higher than those in other districts. From the community health resources, ecological conservation development zone has certain advantages; the new urban development came in the last. Overall, it can be seen more clearly from the dimensionless results in Figure 3 that health care services have a higher, lower middle distribution. In other words, in the area of health care services, the core urban functions and ecological conservation areas are better, and the city function development areas and urban development new areas are relatively poor.

Table 4 Preliminary Level of Health Care Service Indicators in Each District of Beijing in 2015

| Indicators / District | Average person times under treatment X31 | Average person times for physical check X32 | Doctors for every thousand people X33 | Registered nurses for every thousand people X34 | Number of beds in hospital for every thousand people X35 | Professional staff in community health care service institutes for every thousand people X36 | Average person times under treatment in community health care service institutes X37 |
|---|---|---|---|---|---|---|---|
| Dongcheng | 22.96 | 0.39 | 10.82 | 11.38 | 12.03 | 1.28 | 2.53 |
| Xicheng | 21.71 | 0.27 | 9.24 | 11.82 | 11.98 | 1.35 | 2.45 |
| Chaoyang | 6.82 | 0.17 | 4.51 | 4.80 | 4.90 | 1.12 | 2.44 |
| Fengtai | 4.43 | 0.11 | 2.80 | 3.30 | 4.06 | 1.02 | 2.53 |
| Shijingshan | 6.31 | 0.26 | 4.37 | 5.14 | 7.02 | 1.31 | 3.10 |
| Haidian | 4.99 | 0.15 | 2.91 | 3.43 | 2.83 | 0.93 | 2.30 |
| Fangshan | 6.36 | 0.12 | 3.36 | 3.60 | 5.36 | 1.29 | 1.92 |
| Tongzhou | 3.44 | 0.08 | 2.44 | 2.45 | 1.94 | 1.28 | 1.65 |
| Shunyi | 4.30 | 0.18 | 3.13 | 2.75 | 2.52 | 1.48 | 2.09 |
| Changping | 3.03 | 0.09 | 2.45 | 3.02 | 5.00 | 0.73 | 1.24 |
| Daxing | 3.35 | 0.08 | 2.57 | 2.76 | 3.87 | 1.51 | 1.97 |
| Mentougou | 6.68 | 0.26 | 3.80 | 4.68 | 7.83 | 1.80 | 1.66 |
| Huairou | 5.31 | 0.24 | 3.61 | 2.94 | 3.79 | 1.78 | 2.28 |
| Pinggu | 5.57 | 0.13 | 3.62 | 3.50 | 4.02 | 2.15 | 2.86 |
| Miyun | 4.97 | 0.16 | 3.30 | 2.51 | 2.76 | 1.94 | 3.83 |
| Yanqing | 3.97 | 0.22 | 3.00 | 2.81 | 2.41 | 2.21 | 3.31 |

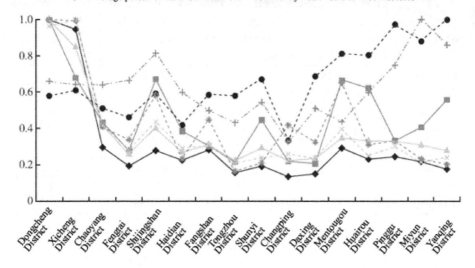

Average person times under treatment X31
Average person times for physical check X32
Doctors for every thousand people X33
Registered nurses for every thousand people X34
Number of beds in hospital for every thousand people X35
Professional staff in community health care service institutes for every thousand people X36
Average person times under treatment in community health care service institutes X37

Figure 3 Dimensionless Levels of Health Care Service Indicators in Each District of
Beijing in 2015

2.4 Original data and processing of cultural and sports services indicators

In 2015, the cultural and sports service levels of various districts in Beijing are shown in Table 5, and the specific index rankings can refer to the result of non-dimensional treatment shown in Figure 4. In terms of the total number of public libraries per capita, Haidian District still ranks first in the list. The new urban development areas overall are not as good as the other districts. Although the ecological conservation areas are generally high, this is mainly due to the fact that there are fewer permanent residents. From the total circulation of public libraries, Chaoyang District reached 5.9 million in 2015, 43.9% more than the 4.1 million in Haidian District. Although the average amount of books per capita in Mentougou District is not low, the circulating population is only 10,000, which is the last in the city . Due to the fact that many people in the outer suburbs are small in number, the number of stadiums owned by 10,000 people has obvious advantages. Most districts have reached double digits. The number of visitors to Changping District's museum increased significantly over the previous year, taking the absolute advantage of 62 million person-times in the city's No. 1 and second and third in Dongcheng District and Xicheng District, less than 1/3 and 1/4 respectively.

Table 5 Preliminary Level of Culture and Sports Service Indicators in Each District of Beijing in 2015

| Indicators / District | Per-capita collection of public libraries X41 | Total number of people in public libraries (10 thousand person times) X42 | Number of gyms for every ten thousand people X43 | Person times to visit museums X44 |
|---|---|---|---|---|
| Dongcheng | 1.5359 | 76 | 7.7127 | 1902 |
| Xicheng | 1.4099 | 158 | 8.1510 | 1527 |
| Chaoyang | 2.5917 | 590 | 6.5740 | 106 |
| Fengtai | 0.4131 | 41 | 5.4862 | 51 |
| Shijingshan | 1.6564 | 57 | 3.2669 | 27 |
| Haidian | 9.7834 | 410 | 6.4943 | 652 |
| Fangshan | 1.0612 | 26 | 14.7706 | 306 |
| Tongzhou | 0.4427 | 73 | 6.8940 | 10 |
| Shunyi | 0.8627 | 35 | 22.4020 | 400 |
| Changping | 0.3311 | 41 | 10.9170 | 6200 |
| Daxing | 0.6082 | 46 | 9.2766 | 0 |
| Mentougou | 2.8247 | 1 | 15.0649 | 45 |
| Huairou | 1.7708 | 48 | 19.7135 | 4 |
| Pinggu | 2.0095 | 21 | 18.7707 | 10 |
| Miyun | 1.4405 | 12 | 16.0752 | 11 |
| Yanqing | 1.5605 | 17 | 21.4968 | 751 |

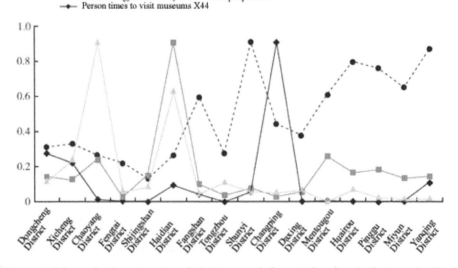

Figure 4 Dimensionless Levels of Culture and Sports Service Indicators in Each District of Beijing in 2015

2.5 Original data and processing of environmental protection service indicators

In 2015, the environmental protection service levels in various districts of Beijing are shown in Table 6, and the specific index rankings can refer to the results of the non-dimensional treatment shown in FIG. 5. Because of the historical and functional differences in positioning and other factors, so only concerned about the current actual level may underestimate the various areas of environmental protection in the work. In order to reflect the efforts of various districts in environmental protection services, the evaluation indicators in 2016 increased the PM2.5 reduction rate and the energy consumption reduction rate of GDP by 10 yuan per unit to two indicators that reflect the improvement. From the annual average concentration of sulfur dioxide values, the decline significantly in all districts, the city's average from 21. 52 micrograms / cubic meter in the previous year to 13. 81 micrograms / cubic meter in 2015, a decline of up to 35.83%, only Tongzhou District Above 20 micrograms / cubic meter . The annual average concentrations of nitrogen dioxide in various districts also dropped to varying degrees, decreasing from 52. 89 micrograms / cubic meter in the previous year to 46. 49 micrograms / cubic meter in 2015, a decrease of 12.10%. The annual average concentration of PM10 in various districts decreased slightly, but the decrease was not significant. The average value of the whole city dropped from 115. 78 micrograms / cubic meter in the previous year to 102. 39 micrograms / cubic meter in 2015, a decrease of 11. 57%. According to the average annual concentration of PM2.5, all districts have dropped below 100 micrograms / cubic meter, but there is still a long way to go from the national standards of average annual concentration of 35 micrograms / cubic meter. From the drop rate of PM2.5, Yanqing District saw the largest decline, reaching 18.67%, followed by Tongzhou District, Haidian District and Changping District, respectively, with declines of 10% or more and the lowest decrease of 1.98% in Dongcheng District. Because of the different functions and functions of different districts, the difference in electricity consumption per 10,000 yuan of GDP is large. The functional core area and functional extension area are relatively low, and the urban development new areas and ecological conservation areas are relatively high. In all districts, with the exception of Fangshan District and Daxing District, the others are under 1,000 kWh. From the yuan GDP energy consumption rate of decline, Shijingshan District, the highest decline of 16.06%, followed by Changping District, Tongzhou District and Huairou District, the decline of more than 10%, Dongcheng District and Xicheng District due to The starting point is higher, so the decline is relatively low.

Table 6 Preliminary Level of Environment Protection Indicators in Each District of Beijing in 2015

| Indicators / District | Yearly average concentration of sulfur dioxide (Mg/m3) X51 | Yearly average concentration of nitrogen dioxide (Mg/m3) X52 | Yearly average concentration of PM10 (Mg/m3) X53 | Yearly average concentration of PM2.5 (Mg/m3) X54 | Reduction rate of PM2.5 (%) X55 | Electricity used every ten thousand yuan GDP(KWh) X56 | Reduction rate of energy consumption every ten thousand yuan GDP(%) X57 |
|---|---|---|---|---|---|---|---|
| | 13.8 | 51.2 | 103.4 | 84.3 | 1.98 | 227.11 | 2.82 |
| Xicheng | 14.5 | 54 | 105.8 | 83 | 5.68 | 168.50 | 3.91 |
| Chaoyang | 15.5 | 59.4 | 106.4 | 83.4 | 5.23 | 345.15 | 6.45 |
| Fengtai | 14.3 | 51.5 | 115.6 | 86.7 | 8.74 | 636.50 | 3.43 |
| Shijingshan | 13.5 | 50.3 | 113 | 83.5 | 6.18 | 389.49 | 16.06 |
| Haidian | 15.2 | 56.1 | 102.9 | 80 | 11.11 | 273.28 | 5.08 |
| Fangshan | 15.6 | 56 | 112.2 | 96.2 | 4.75 | 1015.60 | 7.08 |
| Tongzhou | 20.1 | 55.7 | 122.4 | 92.5 | 12.74 | 872.60 | 10.67 |
| Shunyi | 11 | 43.3 | 93.9 | 81.4 | 3.10 | 416.50 | 3.67 |
| Changping | 12.1 | 42.7 | 93.3 | 70.6 | 10.63 | 895.34 | 10.68 |
| Daxing | 18.3 | 55.1 | 119.2 | 96.4 | 7.31 | 1006.58 | 6.36 |
| Mentougou | 11 | 41.2 | 97.3 | 77 | 8.33 | 645.98 | 6.18 |
| Huairou | 9.2 | 29.1 | 84.6 | 70.1 | 7.76 | 711.06 | 10.51 |
| Pinggu | 13.3 | 33.2 | 100.3 | 78.8 | 5.06 | 673.33 | 5.78 |
| Miyun | 11.9 | 34.3 | 87.6 | 67.8 | 7.12 | 678.15 | 6.9 |
| Yanqing | 11.7 | 30.8 | 80.3 | 61 | 18.67 | 730.50 | 2.01 |

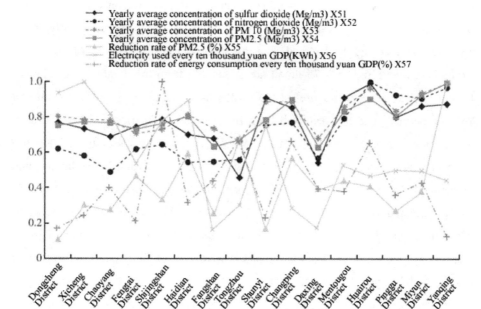

Figure 5 Dimensionless Levels of Environment Protection Indicators in Each District
of Beijing in 2015

## 2.6 Original data and processing of public service indicators

In 2015, the levels of public safety services in various districts of Beijing are shown in Table 7, and the rankings of specific indicators can refer to the results of the non-dimensional treatment shown in FIG. 6. Except for the number of criminal cases solved per 10,000 people, all the indicators of the public security dimension are indicators of adverseness, that is, the lower the value, the higher the score. The number of criminal cases per 10,000 criminal cases is rather special. If it is assumed that the criminal rates of criminal cases of 10,000 people in different districts are roughly the same, then the higher number of criminal cases indicates that the detection rate is higher, that is, it is generally safer. On the contrary, if it is assumed that the detection rates in all districts are roughly the same, and then the higher number of criminal cases indicates that the number of criminal cases per 10,000 people is higher, that is, the overall situation is even more unsafe. In consideration of the fact that the number of cases solved by 10,000 people in each district is concentrated at 50 levels, we tend to adopt the previous assumption that the number of criminal cases per 10,000 people is a normal indicator, indicating that the higher the number, the more secure it is. Judging from the number of criminal cases per

10,000 criminal cases, the districts did not change much from the previous year, while Dongcheng District, Xicheng District and Fangshan District increased slightly, while the other districts slightly declined. The lowest Miyun District was less than 27 and the highest west More than 75 urban areas. Judging from the number of deaths per 10,000 fires, there were no fire-related deaths in Mentougou, Huairou, Miyun and Yanqing districts, and the death toll from fire in Huairou District was the highest in Shijingshan for three years. In terms of the direct economic losses per 10,000 fire accidents, the economic losses in all districts except Tongzhou District and Mentougou District are all over 10,000 yuan, and Pinggu District is the highest in 2015, exceeding 110,000 yuan. Due to the special road network structure, the death toll of traffic accidents per 10,000 people in Dongcheng District and Xicheng District was relatively low at 1.15. The other districts were generally higher, of which Shunyi District and Yanqing District had the highest number of deaths, each exceeding 1 person, that is, More than one in ten thousand people died of traffic accidents. From the direct economic loss per 10,000 traffic accidents, Miyun District exceeded 40,000 yuan for two consecutive years, the highest in the city. Dongcheng District remained the city's lowest in 2015, with only 19,116 yuan in 2015. Among the death toll of safety accidents per 10,000 people, although the Huairou District was significantly lower than the previous year, it was still the highest in the city with 0.0781 people killed due to safety accidents per 10,000 people, with other districts basically below 0. 05 Except Mentougou), the lowest Changping District, no production safety accidental deaths.

Table 7 Preliminary Level of Public Safety Service Indicators in Each District of Beijing in 2015

| Indicators  District | Number of criminal cases solved every ten thousand people X61 | Death toll in fire accidents every ten thousand people X62 | Direct economic loss in fire accidents every ten thousand people X63 | Death toll in traffic accidents every ten thousand people X64 | Direct economic loss in traffic accidents every ten thousand people X65 | Death toll in production safety accidents every ten thousand people X66 |
|---|---|---|---|---|---|---|
| Dongcheng | 49.8674 | 0.0442 | 32378.24 | 0.1326 | 1911.60 | 0.0110 |
| Xicheng | 75.7858 | 0.0077 | 38424.16 | 0.1002 | 4892.14 | 0.0231 |
| Chaoyang | 65.2415 | 0.0202 | 18481.19 | 0.3641 | 4208.34 | 0.0253 |

302

| Fengtai | 55.2367 | 0.0129 | 25609.09 | 0.2711 | 6313.68 | 0.0086 |
|---|---|---|---|---|---|---|
| Shijingshan | 36.3957 | 0.0767 | 17172.70 | 0.1687 | 5952.45 | 0.0460 |
| Haidian | 62.2171 | 0.0135 | 42754.54 | 0.2112 | 7905.52 | 0.0244 |
| Fangshan | 45.6310 | 0.0191 | 16636.34 | 0.9369 | 7875.72 | 0.0287 |
| Tongzhou | 39.9347 | 0.0218 | 9993.55 | 0.6894 | 20679.97 | 0.0218 |
| Shunyi | 56.1961 | 0.0490 | 48328.49 | 1.0686 | 25616.67 | 0.0098 |
| Changping | 27.2491 | 0.0408 | 12605.94 | 0.5349 | 8176.77 | 0.0000 |
| Daxing | 36.4341 | 0.0192 | 19938.26 | 0.3201 | 12921.90 | 0.0128 |
| Mentougou | 47.2403 | 0.0000 | 7688.54 | 0.4221 | 14295.45 | 0.0649 |
| Huairou | 39.1927 | 0.0000 | 54116.98 | 0.7292 | 10377.60 | 0.0781 |
| Pinggu | 41.2766 | 0.0236 | 113714.14 | 0.5910 | 9113.48 | 0.0236 |
| Miyun | 26.5136 | 0.0000 | 26934.47 | 0.8142 | 40323.59 | 0.0209 |
| Yanqing | 30.5732 | 0.0000 | 19809.43 | 1.0191 | 7614.65 | 0.0318 |

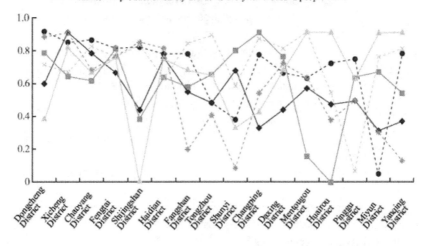

Graph 6 Dimensionless Levels of Public Safety Service Indicators in Each District of Beijing in 2015

3. The weights of comprehensive public service performance evaluation indicators

Compared with 2015, the indicator system in 2016 changed little, only adding two indexes reflecting the level of effort in the environmental protection guidelines.

Therefore, in addition to the dimensions of environmental protection, the index weights in other dimensions and the standards No need to adjust the weight of layers. Based on the analytic hierarchy process (AHP), the index weights of environmental protection dimensions were readjusted by summarizing the scores and discussions of more than 20 experts on environmental protection indicators. As the adjustment of the two indicators is more important, so the weight of environmental protection indicators varies greatly. Although the weights of the annual average concentrations of the four major pollutants have decreased, the weight of the PM2.5 descent rate is second only to that of the PM2.5 average annual concentration, so the total weight of PM2.5 is actually higher. The adjusted indicator weights are shown in Table 8.

Table 8 Weights of Public Service Performance Evaluation Indicators in Each District of Beijing

| Target Layer | Standard Layer | Indicator Layer | Weight |
|---|---|---|---|
| Public Service Performance Evaluation Indicator System of Beijing X | Basic Education X1 | Number of fully employed teachers for every 100 students in primary schoolsX11 | 0.3937 |
| | | Number of fully employed teachers for every 100 students in secondary schoolsX12 | 0.3937 |
| | | Number of children in kindergarten every ten thousand people X13 | 0.0752 |
| | | Number of fully employed teachers for every 100 kindergarten children X14 | 0.1374 |
| | Social Security X2 | Number of beds in adoption institutes for every ten thousand people X21 | 0.1163 |
| | | Number of community service institutes for every ten thousand people X22 | 0.0927 |
| | | Coverage of general endowment insurance (%)X23 | 0.2767 |
| | | Coverage of general health care insurance (%) X24 | 0.2767 |
| | | Coverage of employment insurance (%) X25 | 0.1536 |
| | | Number of people living on minimum living allowance every ten thousand people X26 | 0.0280 |
| | | Number of people under special care and pensions every ten thousand people X27 | 0.0280 |
| | | Number of people under social aids every ten thousand people X28 | 0.0280 |
| | Health Care X3 | Average person times under treatment X31 | 0.0498 |
| | | Average person times for physical check X32 | 0.0311 |
| | | Doctors for every thousand people X33 | 0.2540 |
| | | Registered nurses for every thousand people X34 | 0.1172 |
| | | Number of beds in hospital for every thousand people X35 | 0.1725 |
| | | Professional staff in community health care service institutes for every thousand people X36 | 0.2692 |
| | | Average person times under treatment in community health care service institutes X37 | 0.1061 |
| | Culture | Per-capita collection of public libraries X41 | 0.4204 |

| | | | | | | | | |
|---|---|---|---|---|---|---|---|---|
| and Sports X4 | Total number of people in public libraries (10 thousand person times) X42 | | | | | | | 0.4204 |
| | Number of gyms for every ten thousand people X43 | | | | | | | 0.1156 |
| | Person times to visit museums X44 | | | | | | | 0.0437 |
| Environment Protecti on X5 | Yearly average concentration of sulfur dioxide (Mg/m3) X51 | | | | | | | 0.0768 |
| | Yearly average concentration of nitrogen dioxide (Mg/m3) X52 | | | | | | | 0.0768 |
| | Yearly average concentration of PM 10 (Mg/m3) X53 | | | | | | | 0.1838 |
| | Yearly average concentration of PM2.5 (Mg/m3) X54 | | | | | | | 0.3349 |
| | Reduction rate of PM2.5 (%) X55 | | | | | | | 0.2433 |
| | Electricity used every ten thousand yuan GDP(KWh) X56 | | | | | | | 0.0421 |
| | Reduction rate of energy consumption every ten thousand yuan GDP(%) X57 | | | | | | | 0.0424 |
| Public Safety X6 | Number of criminal cases solved every ten thousand people X61 | | | | | | | 0.0349 |
| | Death toll in fire accidents every ten thousand people X62 | | | | | | | 0.2507 |
| | Direct economic loss in fire accidents every ten thousand people X63 | | | | | | | 0.1193 |
| | Death toll in traffic accidents every ten thousand people X64 | | | | | | | 0.2344 |
| | Direct economic loss in traffic accidents every ten thousand people X65 | | | | | | | 0.1149 |
| | Death toll in production safety accidents every ten thousand people X66 | | | | | | | 0.2459 |

## 4. Score and evaluation of public service performance

According to the weight of experts' scoring adjustment and standardized non-dimensional data, the comprehensive evaluation value of public service in various districts of Beijing is calculated by arithmetic weighted average. The calculation results are shown in Table 9. The scores and rankings of the six basic standards of education, social security, health care, culture and sports, environmental protection and public safety, as well as the scores and rankings of the comprehensive evaluation are shown in Figure 7 to Figure 13.

Table 9 Comprehensive Evaluation on Public Service Performance of Each District of Beijing in 2015

| Indicators / District | Basic Educatio n X1 | Social Securit y X2 | Healt h Care X3 | Cultur e and Sports X4 | Environme nt Protection X5 | Publi c Safet y X6 | Comprehensiv e Evaluation | Overal l Rank |
|---|---|---|---|---|---|---|---|---|
| Dongcheng | 0.7417 | 0.7688 | 0.845 9 | 0.173 4 | 0.5834 | 0.775 9 | 0.6912 | 2 |
| Xicheng | 0.7457 | 0.7376 | 0.806 4 | 0.226 0 | 0.6316 | 0.861 4 | 0.7034 | 1 |
| Chaoyang | 0.7939 | 0.3826 | 0.456 2 | 0.566 4 | 0.6119 | 0.773 8 | 0.6048 | 5 |
| Fengtai | 0.7202 | 0.2083 | 0.369 | 0.075 | 0.6271 | 0.852 | 0.5174 | 1012 |

305

| | | | 1 | 6 | | 5 | | |
|---|---|---|---|---|---|---|---|---|
| Shijingshan | 0.7290 | 0.3576 | 0.5336 | 0.1288 | 0.6570 | 0.5499 | 0.5537 | 10 |
| Haidian | 0.5710 | 0.3497 | 0.3422 | 0.7507 | 0.7104 | 0.7947 | 0.5606 | 9 |
| Fangshan | 0.7224 | 0.2655 | 0.4244 | 0.1425 | 0.2305 | 0.6235 | 0.4969 | 14 |
| Tongzhou | 0.7042 | 0.2086 | 0.3248 | 0.1067 | 0.6306 | 0.6587 | 0.4897 | 15 |
| Shunyi | 0.6800 | 0.3371 | 0.3975 | 0.1804 | 0.6376 | 0.4774 | 0.5072 | 13 |
| Changping | 0.7625 | 0.1162 | 0.2963 | 0.1435 | 0.7695 | 0.7261 | 0.5335 | 11 |
| Daxing | 0.7003 | 0.1918 | 0.3957 | 0.1068 | 0.5419 | 0.7864 | 0.4896 | 16 |
| Mentougou | 0.7620 | 0.4748 | 0.5478 | 0.2001 | 0.7159 | 0.6767 | 0.6169 | 4 |
| Huairou | 0.7640 | 0.4645 | 0.4786 | 0.2121 | 0.7827 | 0.5265 | 0.6000 | 6 |
| Pinggu | 0.8391 | 0.3764 | 0.5392 | 0.1982 | 0.6618 | 0.5931 | 0.5967 | 7 |
| Miyun | 0.7243 | 0.3754 | 0.5082 | 0.1535 | 0.7527 | 0.6254 | 0.5828 | 8 |
| Yanqing | 0.8675 | 0.3775 | 0.5194 | 0.1954 | 0.9279 | 0.6485 | 0.6672 | 3 |

The comprehensive scores and ranking of the basic education service levels in various districts of Beijing are shown in Figure 7. As can be seen from the score, all districts in Beijing have little difference in basic education dimensions, and there is not much difference between functional areas. From the ranking situation, Yanqing District score although declined over the previous year, but still ranked first with weak advantages. Chaoyang District, the same as last year, continues to maintain the third position. Because quality factors are difficult to measure quantitatively, the evaluation focuses more on quantitative differences. Therefore, Haidian District is still a district with less educational resources such as students per student. Admittedly, the quality of educational resources in Haidian District is high, but high-quality educational resources also attract more students, resulting in relatively few living resources per student, which is the last in this evaluation. At the same time, it should be noted that although the evaluation index does not reflect the quality level, the evaluation results from a quantitative point of view at least indicate that the education resources in these districts have different levels of congestion.

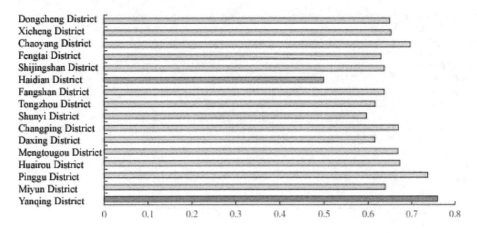

Graph 7 Comprehensive Evaluations on Basic Education Service of Each District of Beijing in 2015

The overall scores and rankings of social security services in all districts of Beijing are shown in Figure 8. Compared with the previous year, the ranking of comprehensive evaluation of social security services has not changed much. Due to the separation of work and residence, Dongcheng District and Xicheng District still have obvious advantages over the other districts, which are located in the top two cities respectively. Except for Dongcheng District and Xicheng District, the differences among other districts are relatively small. As a whole, the urban development new area is less than the ecological conservation area and urban function expansion area, of which Changping District is still the last one.

The overall scores and rankings of health service levels in various districts of Beijing are shown in Figure 9. The comprehensive evaluation of medical and health services is not only exactly the same rankings as in the previous year, but also the scores of all districts are basically the same as the previous year, indicating that the absolute level and relative level of medical and health services in various districts have not changed much. Due to the concentration of a large number of high-quality medical and health resources, Dongcheng District and Xicheng District are still ranked in the top two with great advantages. Ecological conservation area due to the relative advantages of community medical and health resources ranks in Dongcheng District and Xicheng

District. Urban development of new medical and health resources are still inadequate, and bear more pressure on the population ease, it is still ranked last in the city.

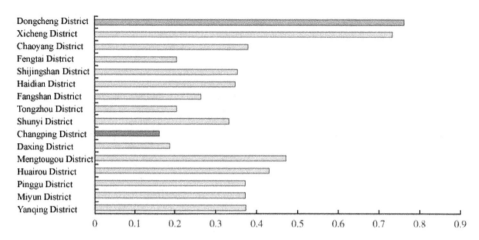

Graph 8 Comprehensive Evaluations on Social Security Service of Each District of Beijing in 2015

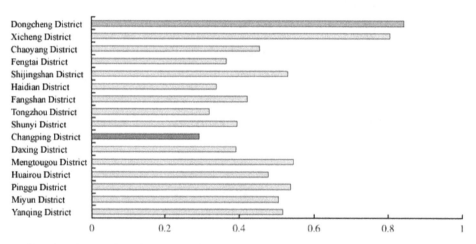

Graph 9 Comprehensive Evaluations on Health Care Service of Each District of Beijing in 2015

The overall scores and rankings of cultural and sports services in various districts of Beijing are shown in Figure 10. Haidian District and Chaoyang District are the cultural resources concentrated in Beijing. Both have been ranked in the top two in the city with absolute superiority. The rest of the districts are hard pressed to find their own way. In addition to Haidian District and Chaoyang District, the other districts are not different. And, compared with the previous year, scores and rankings have not changed much. Fengtai District, less cultural and sports resources, its score is still the lowest, the same as last year came in the last.

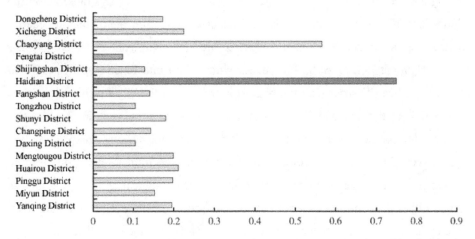

Graph 10 Comprehensive Evaluations on Culture and Sports Service of Each District of Beijing in 2015

The overall scores and rankings of environmental protection service levels in various districts of Beijing are shown in Figure 11. In recent years, Beijing has done a lot of work in environmental protection, especially in the area of atmospheric management. Although there is still a long way to go from national standards, after several years of governance, the air quality in Beijing from January to October has already been significantly improved. This should be something that everyone can understand. 83%. In 2015, annual average concentration of sulfur dioxide once again dropped significantly, the city's level further decreased from 21. 52 micrograms/cubic meter to 13.81 micrograms/cubic meter, a decline of 35.83%. PM2.5 year average concentration values have also declined to some extent, the city's average level from 87.56 micrograms / cubic meter down to 80.79 micrograms/cubic meter, a decrease of 73.3%. After introducing two indicators that reflect the efforts of environmental protection services, the scores and rankings of environmental protection in each district have been greatly changed. First, although the highest score or Yanqing District, but its relative to other districts to further expand the advantages. Second, Tongzhou District rose to 11th from the last place in the previous year, and the drop rate of PM2.5 has greatly helped its rankings rise. Third, although the overall ranking of new urban development areas is still at the end, the obvious arrangement of "highs of two heads and lows of the middle" is not obvious. This shows that while the air quality in the urban development zone is still poor, the improvement is relatively high. The overall scores and rankings of public security service levels in various districts of Beijing are shown in Figure 12. As can be seen from the scores and ranking, on the whole, in addition to slightly lower ecological conservation areas, public security service evaluation scores of other districts are not significantly related to their functional orientation, and the differences within the same functional area are also obvious. Xicheng District with the highest score among the city function core areas ranked first in the city and Fengtai District with the highest score among the city function development areas ranked second in the city and Daxing District with the highest score in the urban development new area ranked third, Mentougou with the highest score in conservation areas came in eighth. Ecological conservation area is mainly affected by the fire situation, the overall score, urban development and urban development area is mainly due to traffic accidents affecting the overall score.

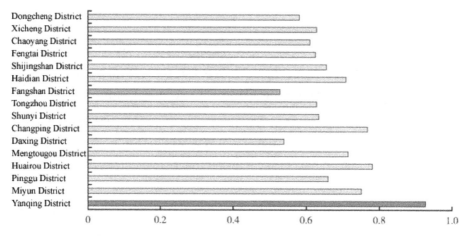

Graph 11 Comprehensive Evaluations on Environment Protection Service of Each District of Beijing in 2015

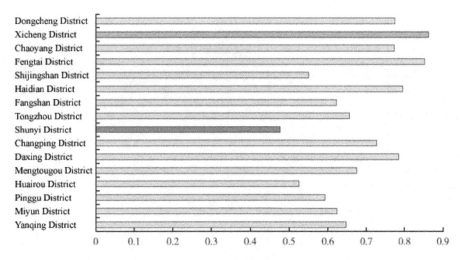

Graph 12 Comprehensive Evaluations on Public Safety Service of Each District of
Beijing in 2015

Figure 13 shows the overall scores and rankings of public services in various districts
of Beijing. The top six cities are Xicheng District (0.7034), Dongcheng District
(0.6912), Yanqing District (0.6672), Mentougou District (0.6169), Chaoyang District
(0.6048) and Huairou District (0.6000). Among the top six in the overall score, the top
two are still the core of the city function, but the rankings swap a bit. There is a city
function development area, state conservation development zone has 3, Chaoyang
District, a higher than the previous year. The top five are Pinggu (0.5967), Miyun
(0.5828), Haidian (0.5605), Shijingshan (0.5537) and Changping (0.5335)
respectively. In the last five were Fengtai District (0.5175), Shunyi District (0.5072),
Fangshan District (0.4969), Tongzhou District (0.4897) and Daxing District (0.4896).
Although the evaluation system in 2016 added two indicators reflecting the level of
effort in environmental protection, it did not change the arrangement of the nearly "U"
shape as a whole. Although the ranking of environmental protection in Tongzhou
District increased significantly, the ranking of comprehensive evaluation increased by
only one place.

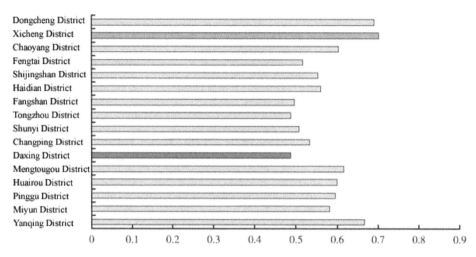

Graph 13 Comprehensive Evaluations on Public Service Performance of Each District of Beijing in 2015

5. Greater efforts have been made to construct Beijing's urban sub-centers of public service

In 2015, under the impetus of accelerating the construction of Beijing's city sub-centers, Tongzhou District has indeed made a lot of efforts in public service construction. In most of the major supply of public service resources, Tongzhou District has a certain degree of improvement. In terms of basic education services, the ratio of teachers and students in secondary education increased by 9.34%, that of children in the park increased by 11.40% per 10,000 population, and that of the kindergarten teachers increased by 3.31%. In terms of social security services, the number of beds for people-to-people adoptions increased by 7.08% and the number of community service organizations by 10,000 persons increased by 10.29%. In the area of medical and health services, the number of visits per capita increased by 5.70%, that of physicians per 1000 people increased by 9.55%, that of nurses per thousand increased by 7.45%, and that of beds per 1,000 people increased by 9.43%. In respect of cultural and sports services, the per capita collection of books increased by 9.14% and the total circulation of libraries increased by 10.61%. For environmental protection, annual average SO2 concentration decreased by 30.21%, annual average NO2 concentration decreased by 7.93%, PM10 annual average concentration decreased by 10.66% and PM2.5 annual average concentration decreased by 12.74 %. Electricity consumption per ten thousand GDP dropped by 4.25%.

In spite of this, many public service resources in Tongzhou District are still at a relatively low level in absolute terms in absolute terms. The number of beds for adoption units per 10,000 persons was 32.79, which was only higher than Shunyi District in the urban development new areas and ecological conservation areas, ranking 10th in the city. There are 4.85 community service organizations per 10,000 people, which are only higher than Changping District and Daxing District in the urban development new areas and ecological conservation areas, ranking 11th in the city. Per capita diagnosis and treatment 3.44 people, less than 1/6 of Dongcheng District and Xicheng District, 39% lower than the average level of the city's function expansion area, which is the 14th in the city. 2.44 per thousand doctors, less than 1/4 Dongcheng District, in the last place in the city. There are 2.45 nurses per thousand people, less than one quarter of Dongcheng District and Xicheng District, and the last one in the city. 1.94 beds per 1,000 people, less than 1/6 of Dongcheng District and also the last of the city, the only area below 2 in the city. The annual average concentration of sulfur dioxide is 20.1 µg / m3, making it the only district in the city that is above 20 µg / m3. The annual average concentration of nitrogen dioxide 55. 7 micrograms / cubic meter, only lower than Chaoyang District, Haidian District and Fangshan District. The average annual PM10 concentration was 122.4 µg / m3, making it the only one in the city that is above 120 µg / m3. PM2.5 average annual concentration of 92.5 mg / m3, only lower than Fangshan District and Daxing District. 10,000 yuan GDP power consumption 872. 60 kwh, the city is more than 2 times the average level of functional development area, in the city 13th.

Thus, although Tongzhou District has made some progress in terms of public service resources in 2015, it still remains at a low level in the whole city in terms of the stock level, and there is still a long way to go from the location of Beijing's city sub-center. Tongzhou District has not only a large gap with functional core areas and functional extension areas, but also is less than some ecological conservation areas in some aspects and even ranks behind in the new urban development areas. In the future, Tongzhou will also assume more responsibilities in alleviating Beijing's "non-capitalist function" and population demystification. Its efforts in providing public service resources will also need to be maintained and strengthened over the long term.

References:

Beijing Municipal Bureau of Statistics. Beijing Regional Statistical Yearbook, 2016.

Beijing Municipal Bureau of Statistics, Beijing National Bureau of Investigation Corps. Beijing Statistical Yearbook (2016), China Statistics Press, 2016.

Shi Changkui, Beijing Public Service Development Report (2013 ~ 2014), Comprehensive Evaluation of Public Service Performance in 16 districts and counties in Beijing, Social Sciences Academic Press, 2014.

Shi Changkui, Beijing Public Service Development Report (2014 ~ 2015), Comprehensive Evaluation of Public Service Performance in 16 districts and counties in Beijing, Social Science Academic Press, 2015.

Shi Changkui, Beijing Public Service Development Report (2015 ~ 2016), Comprehensive Evaluation of Public Service Performance in 16 districts and counties in Beijing, Social Science Academic Press, 2016.

# Problems and Countermeasures in the Construction of Beijing Government Service Centers

**Shi Changkui[1]**

## Abstract

The government service center shoulders the mission of deepening the reform in an all-round way. It is the "exhibition field" with the largest image of the government, the "experimental field" of the reform of the government administration system, the "performance field" of the service-oriented government with people as the center, Under the new situation, it is a "demonstration field" for combating corruption and building a clean government. Beijing government affairs center initially formed a four-level linkage mechanism and innovated many grass-roots government service modes. However, there are still problems such as inadequate co-ordination, lack of implementation of "two centralizations and two positions", lack of staff management means, and lagging system network platform construction , The solution is to achieve "five unification and create": unified name identification, establish a new image of the government; unify institutional responsibilities and enhance the legitimacy and enhance the level of modernization; unify the standards of government services, open and optimize the work process; unified supervision and incentive mechanism, We will intensify the management of government services, unify the government service information system, promote the "Internet+ government service", and unite with and innovate the government service areas and concepts.

Keywords: government service center, sense of gain, standardization construction, combination of discharge and management

1. The significance of building a government service center

Since February 2015, during the many meetings of the Central Commission for the Reorganization of the Central Committee, General Secretary Xi repeatedly emphasized that "letting the masses have more sense of gain in reform" and that "they should bring more sense of gain to the people through the reform""Give the people a

---

[1]Shi Changkui, Reseacher, Director of Research Institute of Management, Beijing Academy of Social Sciences. Research areas include public management and charity.

sense of gain" as an important criterion for testing the effectiveness of the reform. [1] On April 14, 2016, the State Council issued "Implementation Plan for Pilot Implementation of Information Huimin Project to Promote Internet + Government Services" with the goal of realizing "No. 1 Window".[2] "One application" is to give full play to the role of ID card code. "One Window Acceptance" refers to the integrated construction of integrated government services window, build integrated online and offline government service system. "One net" is to achieve "anytime, anywhere political services at your fingertips." The construction of a government affairs center is to move in the direction of "convenience, comfort and speediness" so as to increase the "sense of gain" of the broad masses of the people.

The government affairs center is the place where the masses of the people have the most direct contacts with the government, represents the new image of the government and shoulders the mission of deepening the overall reform.

First, the government service center is the "exhibition site" with the largest image of the government. There are many places to show the image of the government, but the government center is the largest government image display place, from the appearance to the interior, from the quality of personnel to service attitude, from process optimization to efficiency, from comfort to convenience, from information to Intelligent, should be first class: first-class facilities, first-class staff, first-class efficiency, first-class service. Government service center is the government's front office, must move toward convenience and efficiency.

Second, the government service center is the "experimental field" for the reform of the administrative system of the government. The establishment, reform, centralization and decentralization of administrative examination and approval authority are reflected in the administrative affairs centers at all levels, and the reform measures such as the shift of administrative center of gravity and the subsidence of examination and approval functions must all be conducted in the administrative service center.

---

[1] "Xi Jinping's speech delivered at the Tenth Meeting of the Leading Group for Overall Deepening Reform of the Central Governmenton February 27, 2015" People's Daily, February 28, 2015.
[2] General Office of the State Council. Implementation Plan for Carrying out Social Benefiting Pilot Project of Information Service and "Internet + Administrative Services", April 14, 2016

Third, the government service center is a service-oriented government people-centered "performance field." In this place, work efficiency and ability to work is the first one, the people's interests above everything else.

Fourthly, the government affairs service center is a "gathering ground" for contradictions between cadres and the masses under the new normal. Especially at the grass-roots level, this contradiction is more concentrated. Contradictions are better centralized and contradictions are concentrated here. As long as feasible solutions are come out, these social contradictions can be solved, social conflicts can be resolved, and social stability can be maintained.

Fifth, the government service center is a "demonstration field" for fighting corruption and building a clean government under the new situation. Focus on the office, mutual supervision and mutual promotion, more conducive to the new situation under the work of fighting corruption and promoting clean government, Miyun's "shop before the factory" approach is a good example, so that the office workers and approvers do not meet, the implementation of physical isolation, to avoid the "rent-seeking" behavior.

From the mission of the Administrative Service Center, the construction of the administrative service center has a broader space for development. Both the central government and the local government should pay attention to the development and reform of the administrative centers at all levels.

2. Features of Beijing Municipal Government Service Center

From May to July 2016, the Beijing Municipal Administration Office of Government Affairs and the Beijing Academy of Social Sciences jointly set up a research group to conduct a comprehensive investigation and study on all 16 administrative districts in Beijing and Yizhuang at all levels of government affairs centers. The government agencies, personnel, Stationed matters, sorting out and level management conducted a comprehensive survey, and sort out and summarize the characteristics and highlights of Beijing Municipal Government Center. The basic situation is shown in Table 1.

Table 1 District-level Administrative Centers of Beijing

| Districts | Institute Name | Institute Attribute | Current number of administrative posts | Current number of institutional posts | Stationed agencies | Stationed items |
|---|---|---|---|---|---|---|
| Dongcheng | Administrative Service Center | Administrative agency | 15/14 | 14/13 | 17 | 236 |
| Xicheng | Comprehensive Administrative Service Center | Administrative agency | 19/19 | 22/20 | 32 | 418 |
| Chaoyang | Administrative Service Center | Base of district-level government | 10/10 | 0/0 | 13 | 96 |
| Haidian | Administrative Service Center | Administrative agency | 18/18 | 50/28 | 26 | 548 |
| Fengtai | Administrative Service Center | Base of district-level government | 12/2 | 0/0 | 11 | 111 |
| Shijingshan | Administrative Service Center | Department-level administrative agency | 8/8 | 4/4 | 22 | 240 |
| Mentougou | Administrative Service Center | Wholly-government-sponsored institution | 0/0 | 4/2 | 16 | 315 |
| Fangshan | Comprehensive Administrative Service Center | Wholly-government-sponsored institution | 5/3 | 41/35 | 24 | 442 |
| Tongzhou | Administrative Service Center | Administrative agency | 15/13 | 0/0 | 15 | 210 |
| Shunyi | Investment Service Center | Wholly-government-sponsored institution | 0/0 | 13/10 | 21 | 123 |
| Daxing | Comprehensive Administrative Service Center | Permanent offices of District Commission of Administrative License and Service Coordination and Management | 10/10 | 9/7 | 28 | 283 |
| Changping | Comprehensive Administrative | Administrative agency | 15/13 | 17/15 | 29 | 337 |

| | Service Center | | | | | |
|---|---|---|---|---|---|---|
| Pinggu | Comprehensive Administrative Service Center | Administrative agency | 4/4 | 10/10 | 27 | 576 |
| Huairou | Office of Administrative License, Management and Coordination | Administrative agency | 16/14 | 10/9 | 31 | 419 |
| Miyun | Comprehensive Administrative Service Center | Administrative agency | 15/12 | 2/2 | 28 | 516 |
| Yanqing | Administrative Service Center | Administrative agency | 8/8 | 15/12 | 26 | 224 |
| Yizhuang | Administrative Service Center | Escrow by Investment Promotion Bureau of Management Commission (Investment Promotion Center) | 1/1 | 2/2 | 26 | 205 |

## 2.1 Guarantee the operation of district-level administrative center in line with rules and regulations

16 districts under investigation and Yizhuang Development Zone, all established district-level government service or administrative service center, and an independent department or by the escrow department (Fangshan, Yizhuang escrow department escrow, Fengtai escort department by the hair , Director of Mentougou Center by the Secretary for the promotion of PPC) management. All districts can, according to the actual situation, centralize and approve some of the windows and examination and approval items in the area and uniformly stationed them in the administrative center and set forth a relatively complete regulatory and management system. Various districts generally adopt various methods such as performance appraisal, appraisal, public appraisal and other ways to strengthen the management of the stationed departments and stationed personnel. Some districts also enhanced their sense of belonging and identity by establishing relations among party organizations, treating window work as a grass-roots experience, implementing promotion recommendation

mechanisms and separately giving performance awards.

2.2 Expand district-level administrative center network in a three linkage fashion

Due to different starting conditions and their different situations, progress has been made in the construction of the third-level government affairs centers in all districts. However, a general service center for street level (conveniences) has not yet been established, providing a corresponding Physical platform. Among them, Miyun, Daxing, Haidian and other districts have basically formed the level-level linkage with the District Government Affairs Center as the focal point and the various street (township) convenience service centers as focal points, and the extended service stations for all communities (villages) , The overall coordination, network coverage of the "three linkage" government affairs center.

2.3 Promote the standardization of government affairs system through sorting out items and issues

In each district's work practice, the basic approval service items such as social security, civil affairs, family planning, CDPF, livelihood insurance, etc., are sunk to the streets and convenience service centers or service stations at the community level for handling or handling matters; In the face of social legal entities, the matters concerning examination and approval involving cross-departmental and multi-linkages are more reserved at district-level administrative centers, providing a working train of thought for building a system around the issues. The cities of Xicheng, Dongcheng, Chaoyang and Shijingshan closely followed the issues and services and carried out standardization and formed standardization system documents of their own characteristics, which were used to guide the construction of the political affairs center and the innovation of government affairs in this area.

2.4 Improve the lobby environment to ensure a nice experience of the mass

In accordance with their actual conditions, all districts continuously optimize the environment and facilities of their government service halls, provide convenient facilities and take various convenient measures to improve the efficiency of enterprises and people and improve the working environment of enterprises and people. For example, the government service hall generally develops the humanized hall guidance system; optimizes the layout of the seat waiting area and the fill-in area;

unifies printing one-time convenient notice or service guide; sets fax machines, printers, cell phone gas stations, convenient Service packages, self-service payment machines and other convenience facilities and equipment; set up 24-hour self-service area; through the construction of online lobby and the implementation of online booking service and other means to provide services. In short, all districts are doing their best to optimize the environment and facilities of the government service hall and provide a convenient and comfortable working environment for the masses.

2.5 Create "Internet + Government Services" patter with the help of information technology

In the process of implementing the State Council's "Proposal on Promoting Internet + Government Services" and "Carrying Out Information Wiminong Pilot Project", all districts in Beijing actively utilized technologies such as the Internet to enhance the quality of government services and innovated a number of "Internet X government service" approaches, such as Dongcheng District adhere to the information construction as a means to promote the "whole process of administrative examination and approval of electronic procuratorial system" as the starting point, and actively create a diversified service model and established a "two micro-line" (government affairs WeChat, government microblogging, online real-time Online) "point-to-point" politician-citizen interactive service model. Xicheng District, the development and construction of "Xicheng District government service data resource management system" to form a unified standard of administrative services, resources import and export, administrative services dynamic management mechanism. Haidian District set up an interactive online platform that includes the functions of government affairs, lobby service, service guideline, investment consultation, network inquiry and progress inquiry, and realizes the organic combination of tangible and intangible services in the lobby.

2.6 Stimulate innovation in grassroots government service by reducing and diverting central government's power and authority

All districts can try their best to innovate the government service according to their own conditions. Dongcheng District try to establish a "government service station" in three incubator-based enterprises to provide approval and counseling, guidance and business agency services to enterprises in the area. Xicheng District to service demand-oriented, matters as the core, service Raiders and Encyclopedia as a carrier, pushing more than 20 government service products, services to the masses. Chaoyang District to explore "a table to accept a simultaneous informed of a parallel approval," the working mechanism to optimize the approval process of investment projects pilot work to promote the city's approval of fixed assets investment system implementation. Haidian District, actively promote the four phase of the region investment projects in parallel examination and approval of the pilot, building a "whole process of external four things, one thing a window finish; the four modules, the module within a window of receipt, multi-departmental parallel approval" Modular mode of operation. Tongzhou District, try to explore the business sector through the government branch network for the tax department to provide search files, transfer files and other services, and as a breakthrough to promote cross-sectoral resource sharing. Fengtai District, the city set up the first District Internal Revenue Service and the Inland Revenue Department "joint tax registration service center" to achieve tax, local tax registration of "two cards one""is subject to do." Shijingshan District and Yizhuang Development Zone by taking government center stationed in the park, integration and coordination of taxation, housing registration and other departments stationed in the center and other measures to strengthen the resident enterprises and service masses, to maximize the convenience of the masses, to solve the "service to the masses Last mile "problem. Changping District, the establishment of "town-level integrated administrative service center management approach" to form matters for the whole process of supervision, remote monitoring window service, the hall run the field inspection of the regulatory system, and regular notification, analysis of business data. Shunyi District set up a project reporting agent, district center unified management and training, improve efficiency, to facilitate business and the masses. Huairou District has set up a four-level coordination mechanism for "center secretary, section chief, deputy director and director" of the center. In accordance with the principle of "solving simple problems, resolving complex problems, negotiating complex problems, asking for difficult questions separately, and reporting concentratedly principle problems", the department broke the department Boundaries, improve service efficiency. Pinggu District for the working day at noon and Saturdays have day-to-day needs of the masses to provide agency services to provide QQ consulting group, appointment service, on-site service, online guidance services and a series of convenience services. Miyun District in the streets (township) Administration Center to implement the "shop before the factory" workflow, formed an "approval, implementation, supervision," the relative separation and mutual restraint of the working mechanism. Mentougou District and Yanqing District actively promote the government affairs center site selection site, and strive to serve the masses of enterprises provide a more excellent working environment.

3. Problems in the government service center of Beijing

Through the survey, we found that there are five major problems in the construction of Beijing government affairs center.

First, there is not enough co-ordination in building a government affairs center. Due to the problems of the establishment of the administrative institutions and the inadequate responsibility of the administrative institutions, some districts do not adequately manage the construction of the administrative center. In particular, there is a lack of an effective and unified guideline for the construction of convenience centers and community service stations in Xt streets, Department "long" management ubiquitous.

Second, "two concentration, two in place," the implementation is not in place. Although districts work hard to promote departments and examine and approve matters stationed in the centralized administrative centers, there is still a long way to go from the principle of "progress to be required". Some departments that should and can be allowed to proceed are still accepting work on external issues and lacking effective supervision and management. Even if there are departments stationed at all levels of the center, due to inadequate authorization, the service window still remains in the low-level stage of "reception room" and "information desk." It is difficult to exert the centralized examination and approval advantages. The efficiency of examination and approval and the effect of service are hard to be fundamentally Enhance.

Thirdly, the construction of government affairs center is characterized by its spontaneity and regional characteristics. Due to the lack of co-ordination norms at the city level, the districts are more independent and differentiated in promoting the standardization of the center, with different standards in different districts, inconsistent content forms and in-depth degrees of unification. This will make it possible to standardize the construction and implementation of government services in the future Faced with more complicated situation.

Fourth, the lack of effective management tools for government services staff. In many areas, there were problems such as inadequate staffing, low-level personnel treatment at the grassroots level, inadequate personnel evaluation and training, and unsystematic training for personnel exchanges, which undermined the management of the departments and personnel stationed at all levels and undermined the work of government affairs Stable team and service personnel quality, service quality improvement.

Fifth, the construction of a unified information system network platform lags behind. All districts have done a lot of useful attempts in strengthening the construction of government affairs information services and have achieved good results. However, as a whole, the phenomena of "chimneys everywhere" and "islands of information" in the administrative centers at various levels are still widespread. The problems of non-uniform information construction, non-standardization and non-sharing of information are still severe, and the "open circuit" of information becomes a solution "Serve the last kilometer of the masses," an important obstacle to the issue.

The reasons for the above problems, not only lack of ideological understanding, but also institutional constraints, can be attributed to five aspects: First, the ideological understanding of the demand side of the degree of attention is not enough; second is the institutional environment, the lack of Laws and regulations; Third, in the coordination efforts, the supply side of the top of the design is not enough; Fourth, in the administrative system, cannot match the demand side of the request; Fifth, in e-government, their own affairs hindered the construction of government affairs center. In a word, it is caused by many reasons, such as lack of understanding of the ideology, inadequate top-level design and mismatch of the administrative system.

4. Suggestions on the Construction of Beijing Municipal Government Service Center
The basic principle for the construction of Beijing Municipal Government Service Center is to unify and coordinate with the administration and discharge. The goal is to build the government affairs center into a national first-class government resources gathering platform, an information integration platform, a platform for business

coordination, a gathering platform for people's wisdom and public opinion, Exchange platform, government effectiveness monitoring platform, the government image display platform, to create a Beijing Municipal Government with the characteristics of government services, "gold brand""gold card."

4.1 use a unified name logo, establish a new government image

Among the various aspects of building a government service center, the name and logo are the most basic elements and are the most direct first impressions of the government and enterprises by the government and the masses. Due to the late establishment of municipal government service centers, there is no specific regulation and management measures for the construction of municipal government service centers in various districts. Therefore, there are many kinds of names and logos at the district, street and village level. This not only caused confusion to the enterprises and the masses, but also brought a lot of trouble to the unified management at the municipal level. In order for enterprises and the masses to have a consistent understanding of CSC, they should have a uniform name and logo.

In terms of the name, according to the current actual situation in Beijing, it is suggested that the names of the administrative service centers at all levels be as follows: the district-level administrative service centers shall be unified as the "XXX District Administrative Service Centers"; the unified administrative functions of the district-level administrative service centers shall be XXX Street (Township) government affairs service center (hall) ". Each community (village) should rely on the community service station (convenient service station, charge d'affaires, etc.) with the sign of" XXX community (village) government service station ". After consent of governments at all levels, the professional hall set up separately by the government affairs department shall be the sub-center of the same-level government affairs service center with the unified registration of "XXX Center of Beijing Municipal Government (or XXX District) Administrative Service Center".

On the logo, on the one hand should design a unified Logo, on the other hand should also design a uniform image of clothing and window, even if the city cannot be unified in the short term, should also try to zoning unity.

4.2 Unify institutional responsibilities, enhance legitimacy and upgrade modernization

To provide first-class government services to enterprises and the masses cannot be separated from a set of management and service agencies with clear responsibilities, lawfulness and stability.

First, there must be a legal and stable institutional setup. Beijing Municipal Government Service Management Office is responsible for the administration of municipal government services. All districts shall set up administrative service management offices and shall be responsible for the administrative agencies that administer the administrative services of their respective administrative regions. Each township (street) should establish or clarify its own level of government service management agencies. Village (community) should rely on convenient service points, community service stations and other government services. To ensure the legitimacy and stability of government services, the municipal and district government service departments should be uniformly incorporated into the administrative establishment, and relevant management and operation funds and personnel office expenses should be included in the budget of this level.

Second, clear the main functions of government offices at all levels. At all levels, government service agencies at all levels organize the implementation of this level and guide the work of subordinate government services. They are responsible for guiding and promoting the construction of the government affairs center and innovations in service methods. They are responsible for the construction, operation, supervision and management of their own government service centers. They also guide, coordinate and supervise the professional halls And construction, operation and management of subordinate government service centers' to coordinate the construction of "Internet X government service". Government departments at all levels and their subordinate agencies (hereinafter referred to as government departments) are specifically responsible for combing the affairs of government affairs in their respective departments, compiling guidance for service work, docking service systems, opening up data resources, optimizing service processes and innovating service modes.

4.3 Unified government services related standards, and open and optimize the work process

The main carrier of government service is the specific service items. The whole process of government service is the process of handling matters. To optimize working procedures and improve the quality of government services requires a unified government service standard.

On the one hand, the municipal government service office shall be responsible for organizing the municipal government departments and the district government service offices to sort out and compile the list of government affairs services issues, and make public the publicity, real-time updates and dynamic management after being confirmed by the reform department of the municipal administrative examination and approval system. Administrative affairs matters shall be handled by the government affairs service center in accordance with the principle of "an imperative for entry into the country". Administrative matters of the dual management and vertical management departments can be handled by the Administrative Services Center. Government affairs service centers handled by Viennese people shall not be accepted by other administrative departments at any other places. The government departments at the same level shall temporarily decide not to go to the administrative affairs service centers and shall be subject to the unified management and information sharing of administrative services of the local government.

On the other hand, government service agencies should standardize the operation of government service centers and improve various working systems so as to establish a "one-window reception, one-stop handling, one platform sharing and one network operation" operating mechanism. Municipal and district government service offices should promote the standardization of government affairs services, study and formulate relevant standards, and implement specialized, standardized and refined management. Promote the centralized examination and approval, with the conditions of the government departments should promote examination and approval authority to the Department of Examination and Approval Branch (Section) room concentration, approval office (Section) room to the Center for Administrative Services focus.

On the basis of continuous improvement of various mechanisms, municipal and district government service agencies should gradually refer to the relevant national standards of the standardization of government service centers and gradually explore, study and formulate the construction standards, operational standards, service standards and standards of this level of government service centers, Information standards, performance appraisal standards and logistics support standards such as standard system to achieve the standardization of government service centers and refined management. The district government service management agencies should also be responsible for co-ordinating and guiding the standardization of government services in the streets (townships) and communities (villages) in the district.

4.4 Unify the supervision and incentive mechanism and intensify the administration of government affairs

First-class government service requires a first-class government service team. A first-class workforce, in addition to the need for system-level protection, also needs a set of scientific, effective and unified supervision and incentive mechanisms.

In staff matching, all levels of government should be in accordance with the principle of "streamlining, unification, efficiency" for the government service agencies equipped with functions and workload matching staffing. As a local administrative organ, the municipal and district government service administration agencies should be equipped with adequate administrative establishment and business establishment. Township (street) government service center, village (community) government service station can be provided through government services such as staffing. Administrative departments should be selected to meet the requirements of qualifications stationed personnel stationed in the service center, and carry out the necessary business training.

In terms of staff motivation, government service personnel may refer to urban management and the police for certain special allowances, and continuous working hours of one year and over should be regarded as grassroots work experiences. Administrative service management agencies should establish a comprehensive evaluation mechanism for the presence of government service centers and reward incentives at the grass-roots level. According to their work needs, they should organize and implement special training for personnel and strengthen the training of government service personnel. At the same time, we should promote the spirit of government service, promote the building of a government service culture, enhance the exchange and study among government officials, enhance the sense of belonging of government service personnel and enhance their professionalism and ability.

In supervision and administration, the administrative agencies for government affairs should strengthen the supervision and inspection of handling of administrative affairs matters, service behaviors, service efficiency and service style, improve and perfect the electronic supervision system and realize the dynamic supervision of the whole process of government affairs services. Establish an evaluation mechanism for government affairs work in public participation, set up an interactive platform for both government and people, and take the initiative to respond to social concerns. Strict accountability, the supervision and inspection found violations of rules and regulations should be promptly corrected, rectification; alleged violations of discipline by the relevant departments according to the law.

4.5 unified government service information system, promote the "Internet + government service"

Therefore, to improve the efficiency and quality of government services, on the one hand, the online government services should be continuously optimized; on the other hand, the information system should be unified as soon as possible to break the monopoly of information between departments and eliminate "Information Island" to achieve data sharing.

The municipal government service office shall perfect the unified administrative examination and approval management platform of the city and the online supervision platform of investment projects. All the municipal governments and municipal government departments should take the initiative to make use of docking with related platforms, open up data resources, Village (community) extension. Promote the city's government services interoperability, business collaboration and information sharing, make full use of social credit, population, legal persons, space geography and other basic information resources to eliminate data barriers to promote online and offline integration of government services, integration of business systems, co-ordinate services Resources, unified service standards, to achieve seamless convergence, a network management, to achieve "Internet X government services" full coverage.

4.6 Combination of discharge, innovation and government service areas and concepts

The five "unification" do not mean completely unified management of the city's government services. Instead, they should give grass-roots units the freedom to develop their own initiative and innovate their service areas and concepts within such a unified standardization framework. Encourage government service agencies at all levels and government service departments to try first, actively innovate the government service model, optimize the service process and expand the service content.

First, optimize the service process. Administrative service administrative agencies and government departments should work in accordance with the needs of the masses prepared and open work guidelines, to provide product, modular, scene-oriented and convenient services. Implementation of home-made, appointment for processing, self-service, commissioned agents, city offices and other services. We will promote the online handling of government affairs affairs matters and all the government affairs matters closely related to the business services and residents' life of enterprises shall implement the online consultation, online declaration, online acceptance and online feedback so as to achieve the goal of "". Promote the sharing of materials for office work network and work information network verification, and promote the application of electronic certificates, electronic official documents and electronic signatures in government affairs services. Explore the introduction of social forces, the use of third-party platform to carry out booking queries, license delivery, online payment and other services, to maximize the facilitation of government services.

The second is to expand the service content. Relying on the entity service platform of the government service center and the online service platform, we will explore ways to promote public service such as water, electricity, intellectual property protection, legal and information consultation, education and training, policy issuance and public service announcements. With the conditions, the central unit for service administration, the units in charge of the administration of troops in Beijing and the agencies in other cities, the government information disclosure, the government service hotline, the public opinions collection and the comprehensive supervision shall be taken into consideration with the construction of the government affairs center and concertedly promoted.

References:

People's Daily, February 28, 2015.

General Office of the State Council. Implementation Plan for Carrying out Social Benefiting Pilot Project of Information Service and"Internet + Administrative Services", April 14, 2016.

Beijing Bureau of Statistics, Beijing Survey Corps, National Bureau of Statistics, Beijing Statistical Yearbook (2016), China Statistics Press, 2016.

Cai Guohua, "Analysis on three centralized administrative examination and approval system", China's Administration, 2012,No.12.

Shi Changkui and Luo Zhi, "Beijing Public Service Performance Evaluation in 16 Districts and Counties", Beijing Public Service Development Report (2015 - 2016), Social Science Association Press, 2016.

This book is the result of a co-publication agreement between Social Sciences Academic Press (China) and Paths International Ltd.

------------------------------------------------------------

**Analysis of the Development of Beijing in China**
**Author: Beijing Academy of Social Sciences**
**ISBN: 978-1-84464-516-9**
**EBook ISBN: 978-184464-517-6**

**Copyright © 2018 by Paths International Ltd and by Social Sciences Academic Press, China**

All rights reserved. No part of this publication may be reproduced, translated, stored in a retrieval system, or transmitted in any form or by any means, electronic, mechanical, photocopying or otherwise, without the prior permission of the publisher.

The copyright to this title is owned by Social Sciences Academic Press (China). This book is made available internationally through an exclusive arrangement with Paths International Ltd of the United Kingdom and is only permitted for sale outside China.

**Paths International Ltd**
**www.pathsinternational.com**

**Published in the United Kingdom**

CPSIA information can be obtained
at www.ICGtesting.com
Printed in the USA
LVHW100238130419
614016LV00008B/49/P

9 781844 645169